Modernism in Irish Women's Contemporary Writing

Modernism in Irish Women's Contemporary Writing

The Stubborn Mode

PAIGE REYNOLDS

OXFORD
UNIVERSITY PRESS

Great Clarendon Street, Oxford, OX2 6DP,
United Kingdom

Oxford University Press is a department of the University of Oxford.
It furthers the University's objective of excellence in research, scholarship,
and education by publishing worldwide. Oxford is a registered trade mark of
Oxford University Press in the UK and in certain other countries

© Paige Reynolds 2024

The moral rights of the author have been asserted

All rights reserved. No part of this publication may be reproduced, stored in
a retrieval system, or transmitted, in any form or by any means, without the
prior permission in writing of Oxford University Press, or as expressly permitted
by law, by licence or under terms agreed with the appropriate reprographics
rights organization. Enquiries concerning reproduction outside the scope of the
above should be sent to the Rights Department, Oxford University Press, at the
address above

You must not circulate this work in any other form
and you must impose this same condition on any acquirer

Published in the United States of America by Oxford University Press
198 Madison Avenue, New York, NY 10016, United States of America

British Library Cataloguing in Publication Data

Data available

Library of Congress Control Number: 2023943454

ISBN 9780198881056

DOI: 10.1093/9780191990540.001.0001

Pod

Links to third party websites are provided by Oxford in good faith and
for information only. Oxford disclaims any responsibility for the materials
contained in any third party website referenced in this work.

Acknowledgments

In 2007, at the Dublin conference where I presented my earliest work on Irish women writers and "modernist afterlives," a prominent academic explained to me that there were no Irish women modernist writers, ever. Since then, I have watched with glee as scholars have proven this claim wrong and as the stature of Irish women writers from all periods has risen in the public eye. Nonetheless, *Modernism in Irish Women's Contemporary Writing* encountered roadblocks on its path to publication, so my first thanks go to Oxford University Press for recognizing, immediately and without reservation, the value of this project centered on Irish women's writing. Jack McNichol and Henry Clarke were impressive editors, Ellie Collins a helpful advocate, the anonymous readers fair-minded in their feedback, and Roopa Vineetha Nelson a thorough project manager.

This book can be attributed in no small part to the support and good humor of cherished colleagues. Margaret Kelleher, whose acumen so often is directed toward helping others flourish, was throughout an invaluable interlocutor, as were Claire Connolly and David James. From the very start, Emilie Pine refused to let me shelve this project, and Eric Falci pushed me to refine my conceptual categories. At crucial moments, Aeron Hunt asked important questions about realism, Lisa Ruddick about periodicity, Cara Lewis about mode. The intellectual range and indefatigable curiosity of Anne Fogarty and Steve Watt remain a particular inspiration. And Shawn Maurer, whose ability to see the forest for the trees in all things, including too many drafts of this manuscript, has been a gift beyond measure.

Writing this book truly felt like a conversation with friends and the names of many appear in footnotes rather than listed here. Margot Backus, Lucy Collins, Evelyn Conlon, Liz Cullingford, Jed Esty, Susan Harris, Liam Harrison, Marjorie Howes, Clare Hutton, Sarah McKibben, Mark Morrisson, James O'Sullivan, John Plotz, Laura Reed-Morrisson, Stephanie Scott, and Joe Valente have offered particular support. While working on this book, I continued to enjoy shared projects with colleagues in Irish theater studies, among them Beatriz Kopschitz Bastos, David Clare, Marguérite Corporaal, Patrick Lonergan, Lance Pettitt, Michael Pierse, Shaun Richards, Tony Roche, Mary Trotter, and Ruud van den Beuken. I also wish to thank the many contributors to publications I've edited over the years; you have taught me much, and I treasure our work together.

A great deal has changed as this project has been adapted to accommodate new writing and evolving conceptual frameworks. Throughout, aspects of my

vi ACKNOWLEDGMENTS

arguments have been presented in invited lectures for events that were spear-headed by valued colleagues, hosted by generous institutions and organizations, and attended by smart and helpful interlocutors. Relevant lectures included those for the Irish Studies Seminar, Institute of English Studies, University of London; the Keough-Naughton Institute for Irish Studies, University of Notre Dame; the Marianna O'Gallagher Lecture in Irish Studies, Canadian Association for Irish Studies; the Modernist Speakers Series, Penn State University; the Modernism Seminar, University College Cork; a plenary for the American Conference for Irish Studies, University College Dublin; the W. B. Yeats Lecture, SUNY University at Buffalo; Marginal Irish Modernisms (AHRC Symposium), St Mary's University, London; the Institute of European Studies, University of California Berkeley; a plenary for the International Association for the Study of Irish Literature, Radboud University, Netherlands; the Irish Studies Seminar, Newberry Library, Chicago; and Jornada do Núcleo de Estudos Irlandeses, USCF Florianópolis, Brazil. Across my career, I have enjoyed the camaraderie and support of those affiliated with the Boston College Irish Studies Program, and I am especially grateful to Mike Cronin and the staff of Boston College Ireland for hosting the "Modernist Afterlives in Irish Literature and Culture" symposium during my tenure as the 2013 Neenan Fellow. I also shared many hours of productive discussion with speakers and par-ticipants as co-director, with the late John Paul Riquelme and Sam Alexander, of the Modernism Seminar at Harvard's Mahindra Humanities Center.

Librarians and archivists are always among my favorite people. For this project, special appreciation goes to Eileen Cravedi (Dinand Library, College of the Holy Cross), Eugene Roche (Special Collections, University College Dublin), Ken Bergin (Special Collections and Archives, Glucksman Library, University of Limerick), and Jason Nargis (Charles Deering McCormick Library of Spe-cial Collections and University Archives, Northwestern University Libraries). A portion of my argument about *Milkman* appeared in *Alluvium*'s 2021 special issue "Twenty-First-Century Irish Women Writers" edited by Orlaith Darling and Dearbhaile Houston. Mary Morrissy brought the artist Una Watters, whose pitch-perfect painting graces the book cover, to my attention. I am grateful to Faber and Faber Ltd. for permission to reproduce a section of "Morning at the Window" by T. S. Eliot. Doireann Ní Ghríofa kindly granted permission for the book's epi-graph; the awe-inspiring Lisa Coen and Sarah Davis-Goff of Tramp Press helped to facilitate that permission.

At Holy Cross, thanks to my colleagues Morris Collins, Kyle Frisina, Deb Gettelman, Madigan Haley, Jonathan Mulrooney, Sarah Stanbury, and Melissa Schoenberger for their insights. The McFarland Center for Religion, Ethics, and Culture, and its director Tom Landy, generously hosted events related to this project. The Edward Callahan Irish Studies Support Fund, ably abetted by Peter Merrigan and Phil Gibson, has supported important opportunities, not least the chance to introduce Holy Cross students personally to Irish contemporary writers and their craft. A Williams Career Development Grant, the Arthur J. O'Leary Faculty Recognition Award, and Charles and Rosanna Batchelor (Ford) Foundation Grants provided financial support. Thanks are due as well to the J. D. Power Center for Liberal Arts in the World, which sponsored Bella Bokan, Clara Gibson, Colleen Mulhern, and Nicole Nover as undergraduate research associates, and to the Weiss Summer Research Program, which supported the undergraduate research of Abby Kehoe and Sean O'Rourke.

Completing a second monograph in mid-career while the caregiver for young and old is no joke, so this nod goes to those who have managed it, as well as to those who are trying. Overdue thanks to Anne Inge and Irene McDonald, the teachers who introduced me to close reading, and Eric Stracener, who first insisted I read *Dubliners*. Gratitude for those friends and colleagues not listed above who have shared nourishing pleasures across the challenging past few years: Phillip Petrie, Paul and Olan O'Donovan, Ulf Messner, Maurice Devlin and the late Kieran Cooney, Maeve Lewis, Nick Daly, Moynagh Sullivan, Colin Murphy, Simon O'Connor, Adam Hanna, Alex Davis, Lee Jenkins, Kate Costello-Sullivan, Eimear McBride, Alinne Fernandes, the Bastos de Lima family, Margaret Keller and Brendan Mathews, Jamil Mustafa, Paul Peppis, Kelly and Angela Miller, Gia Elsevier, the Dabrowski family, Sheri and Steve Dumas, Glynn Haines, Katie Murray, Beth and Jared Weissman.

Finally, and predictably, I dedicate this book to Mario and Asher, loving instructors in the many and various gratifications of persistence and resistance.

Contents

Introduction: Looking	1
1. Refashioning Modernism (Elizabeth Bowen, Maeve Kelly, Evelyn Conlon, June Caldwell)	29
2. Praying (Kate O'Brien, Mary Lavin, Emma Donoghue, Eimear McBride)	59
3. Daydreaming (Edna O'Brien, Anne Enright, Deirdre Madden)	94
4. Logging Off (Éilís Ní Dhuibhne, Claire-Louise Bennett, Louise O'Neill)	134
5. Reading (Sally Rooney, Anna Burns)	165
Coda: Recalibrating (Mike McCormack)	194
References	204
Index	221

This is a female text, written in the twenty-first century. How late it is. How much has changed. How little.

Doireann Ní Ghríofa, *A Ghost in the Throat* (2020)

Introduction: Looking

Set in contemporary Ireland, Sally Rooney's third novel *Beautiful World, Where Are You* (2021) focuses on the friendship shared by two young women, university friends now on the cusp of thirty. We watch as the novelist Alice begins a relationship with Felix, a warehouse worker whom she met through the online dating app Tinder, and as Eileen, an editorial assistant for a Dublin literary magazine, becomes romantically involved with her childhood crush, the left-wing activist Simon. By and large, Rooney hews to literary realism, providing an accessible account of the characters' activities and thoughts through chapters that alternate between a third-person omniscient narrative and a series of emails exchanged by Alice and Eileen. However, alongside these user-friendly depictions of daily life in the present, runs a surprising strand of modernism, both formal and allusive, as when Alice experiences a "loose and dissociative" feeling that prompts her to think of Rilke's poetry or professes her love "for Charles Swann, or for Isabel Archer," or when Eileen copy-edits a document citing Auden and reads *The Golden Bowl*.[1] It also emerges in resonant forms, themes, and narrative devices: the taut prose of the opening chapters suggests the style of Hemingway, an impressionistic account of a dinner party evokes the experiments of Woolf, the polyvocal catalog of social ills throughout conjures Eliot's *The Waste Land* (1922).

One of the novel's most overt allusions to modernism comes late in the novel, when Felix sings "The Lass of Aughrim" at a birthday party. In Joyce's short story "The Dead," written in 1907 and published in 1914, the character Gretta Conroy listens silently as Bartell D'Arcy sings this same traditional ballad at a Christmas party. Observing her from afar, her husband Gabriel imagines himself a painter rendering her in a portrait he titles "Distant Music." This scene suggests Gabriel's unrealized aesthetic ambitions, but it also exposes his limited understanding of his wife's interior life, a point driven home when he subsequently learns that this song reminded Gretta of the tragic death of her first love. A solicitous if self-absorbed husband, Gabriel finds himself wounded by this previously undisclosed aspect of his wife's personal history, and baffled by the unexpected exposure of her private thoughts and feelings. At first glance, the resuscitation of this illustrious moment in *Beautiful World, Where Are You* suggests that, roughly a century later, everything has changed. In this scene, Alice, a highly successful writer, observes Felix

---

[1] Sally Rooney, *Beautiful World, Where Are You* (New York: Farrar, Straus and Giroux, 2021), 20, 195. Future references parenthetical.

Modernism in Irish Women's Contemporary Writing. Paige Reynolds, Oxford University Press. © Paige Reynolds (2024).
DOI: 10.1093/9780191990540.003.0001

2 INTRODUCTION

from a distance and occupies a position of cultural and economic authority once held almost exclusively by men. Moreover, this Ireland seems one where individuals appear to hold few secrets and to suffer little shame. Early in the novel, Alice openly shares with Felix that she was hospitalized for a nervous breakdown, and when she stumbles across graphic pornography on Felix's smartphone, she accepts his disclosures of a problematic sexual history largely without upset or judgment. Theirs is a world seemingly both more transparent and tolerant than that of their Joycean precursors.

This shout-out to "The Dead" alerts savvy readers to certain dramatic social and cultural transformations that have transpired since the advent of high modernism. Yet the allusion also invites them to see that aspects of human experience are little altered, despite the intervening century or so. Rooney's characters in many ways remain as limited as those who people Joyce's short story. As Felix sings "The Lass of Aughrim," Alice, whose "eyes filled with tears as she watched him" (318), is unable to identify what sparked this emotion, while Felix says only that the song is "a sad one anyway, whatever it's about" (320). Felix's performance suggests, in Rooney's iteration and the literary history it evokes, that the contours of individual consciousness remain stubbornly elusive, not only to outsiders but even to the characters themselves. This point is confirmed by Eileen's position, both literally and imaginatively, on the periphery of this scene. Feeling isolated and mired in her own heightened self-consciousness, she watches the interactions among Alice, Felix, and Simon from a distance. In this moment, the narrative zooms out from the domestic interior to the indifferent exterior world, from self to nature: "And out the windows the sky was still dimming, darkening, the vast earth turning slowly on its axis" (319).

The shift in attention here, marked by an omniscient narrator, chimes with the startling epiphany that concludes Joyce's story, which moves from Gabriel's personal cogitations to "the snow falling faintly through the universe and faintly falling, like the descent of their last end, upon all the living and the dead."[2] But Rooney's loaded diction also points to the work of another Irish modernist who grappled with the distressing revelations elicited by his contemporary conditions. The "turning" and "dimming" in this line evoke the dire pessimism of "The Second Coming" (1920), a poem written by Yeats as he worried over the possibility of a Second World War and suffered through the Anglo-Irish War, yet another violent political struggle fought on Irish soil. Perhaps even more pertinently, Yeats wrote "The Second Coming"—an auspicious title given the larger arguments of this study—amid the 1918 flu pandemic, just as Rooney wrote her novel and set its conclusion during the Covid-19 pandemic. A refashioned Irish modernism here underscores the unavoidable fact that Rooney's sharp and self-sufficient young

---

[2] James Joyce, "The Dead," *Dubliners: Viking Critical Edition*, eds. Robert Scholes and A. Walton Litz (New York: Penguin, 1969), 175–224, 224.

characters who navigate particular, twenty-first-century circumstances nonetheless must contend, like all generations before them, with the shadow of mortality hovering over human experience.

Beautiful World, Where Are You thus employs familiar aspects of the modernist tradition to remind readers that, even in what seems at first glance a vastly different historical moment, certain problems remain intransigent. Conflicts arise, greed motivates, inequality prevails, pandemics erupt, human failure is unavoidable, optimism difficult to maintain—and people die. To convey such elemental lessons, Rooney recapitulates literary historical references and aesthetic practices readily associated with the high modernism of the late nineteenth and early twentieth centuries. She uses here what I label the stubborn mode of modernism. Stubborn modes are tried-and-true literary tactics that trigger a sense of recognition when readers encounter them, a constellation of traits—including style, tone, forms, content, and history—commonly associated with a particular literary movement or school that travels across time. Composed of literary conventions, the stubborn mode of modernism sustains the aesthetic as well as the political impulses associated with the movement's early history.

The term "mode," the French word for fashion, usefully invites us to consider this deliberate refashioning of modernism—to ask why writers like Rooney use it, when they use it, how they use it. Such a legible modernism, of the type one might find trotted out in an open-source encyclopedia entry or an undergraduate lecture on high modernism, gives recognizable shape in *Beautiful World, Where Are You* to nebulous aspects of contemporary experience. It imagines high modernism can correct the past, as well as provide a relevant tool to represent the present. There is a deliberate knowingness baked into this mode, one insisting that the assimilation of its more well-known features does not preclude but rather enables its interventions. The stubborn mode helps to remind readers of the sweep of history, using literary form and content to accentuate certain ongoing cultural problems, as well as to spotlight remedies previously imagined for such familiar problems, whether the outcomes of those interventions have proven to be successful, unsuccessful, or (more likely, as seen across time) a measure of both. Like many Irish women writers, Rooney does not eschew or evade the pre-packaged quality of high modernism to accomplish this end; she neither disavows her complicity in the literary marketplace, nor performs the calculated irony often associated with postmodernism. Instead, she calls to attention the aesthetic and social potential of a commodified and popularized modernism, laying bare the deep work the movement's tenacious surface gestures might provoke in the present day.

Of course, mode can lead to modish, and this might suggest that Rooney's engagement with modernism is a stylish trend, a passing fad. Currently, Irish women's writing is in vogue, sometimes literally in *Vogue*, with Tara McEvoy proclaiming in a 2019 issue of the influential fashion magazine, "Rarely has there been such an intense spotlight on Irish writing—and Irish women's writing, in

4 INTRODUCTION

particular—as there is today."[3] Literary critics have observed that traces of high modernism appear in the work of contemporary writers across the globe, but Anne Enright is among those who have identified a particularly powerful strain of "resurgent modernism" in recent fiction by Irish women writers.[4] Writing in 2015, she cited as examples Eimear McBride's *A Girl Is a Half-formed Thing* (2013) and Claire-Louise Bennett's *Pond* (2015), and that same year also saw the publication of Sara Baume's *Spill Simmer Falter Wither*, Caitriona Lally's *Eggshells*, and Anakana Schofield's *Martin John*. Each offers readers an isolated and alienated central character, a narrative heavily inflected by stream of consciousness, and formal tactics ranging from non-linear plots to broken syntax to unconventional punctuation, among the various other aspects of style, tone, form, and content that collectively telegraph the modernist mode.

An overt engagement with modernism informs not only these recent novels but a surprising array of Irish women's fiction written from the immediate aftermath of the movement's early twentieth-century prime into the present day. The modernist mode appears throughout the work of Kate O'Brien, Elizabeth Bowen, Mary Lavin, Maeve Kelly, Evelyn Conlon, Deirdre Madden, Éilís Ní Dhuibhne, Anna Burns, Emma Donoghue, June Caldwell, and Louise O'Neill, to name only a few. In fits and starts across the past century, these women have rehearsed and refashioned aspects of Euro-American modernism, employing in their fiction features easily recognizable from the movement's forms and themes, its canonical texts and authors. By untangling the profound and intricate relationship of these writers with the modernist mode, we can come to understand better its remarkable aesthetic traction as well as its ongoing political and social efficacy. In the twenty-first century, the familiarity of modernism—its intellectual challenges, its cultural cachet, its historical resonance—has rendered it a particularly meaningful device for underscoring the obduracy of certain social, cultural, and personal problems that women have faced across the past century, even amid the dramatic cultural changes that have altered life in the Republic and Northern Ireland across recent decades.[5] The interpretive challenges the stubborn mode of modernism poses,

---

[3] Tara McEvoy, "How a New Wave of Irish Women Writers Are Making Their Mark," *Vogue*, March 2, 2019, https://www.vogue.co.uk/article/irish-female-writers-sally-rooney-anna-burns-emilie-pine.

[4] Tramp Press (@TrampPress), "Anne Enright: 'since the crash a lot has been disrupted. There's a resurgent modernism in writers like Eimear McBride and @emollientfibs,'" March 8, 2015, 11:23 a.m., Tweet. On modernism in contemporary fiction, see Doug Battersby, *Troubling Late Modernism: Ethics, Feeling, and the Novel Form* (Oxford: Oxford University Press, 2022); Michaela Bronstein, *Out of Context: The Uses of Modernist Fiction* (Oxford: Oxford University Press, 2018); Michael D'Arcy and Mathias Nilges, eds., *The Contemporaneity of Modernism: Literature, Media, Culture* (New York: Routledge, 2016); David James, ed., *The Legacies of Modernism: Historicising Postwar and Contemporary Fiction* (Cambridge: Cambridge University Press, 2012); David James, *Modernist Futures: Innovation and Inheritance in the Contemporary Novel* (Cambridge: Cambridge University Press, 2012); Jesse Matz, *Lasting Impressions: The Legacies of Impressionism in Contemporary Culture* (New York: Columbia University Press, 2017).

[5] In this study, where there is a risk of confusion, I employ "the Republic" to describe the Republic of Ireland, "the North" to describe Northern Ireland, and "Ireland" to describe the island as a whole.

even today, demand that readers work harder to identify and understand intransigent socio-cultural problems still before us, as well as to attend closely to those characters who encounter, assess, and seek with uneven success to solve them.

The Occluded History of Irish Women's Modernism

In *Beautiful World, Where Are You*, the interrogation of looking charted by Rooney through the forms and themes of high modernism invites us to ask a larger literary historical question about what we as readers and critics do and do not see. For a small country, Ireland looms especially large in our understanding of modernism because, since its inception as a critical category, Yeats, Joyce, and Beckett have been among the movement's most influential figures. Yet despite its disproportionate presence in modernist studies, Ireland lacks a "major" female modernist writer like Woolf or Stein. Over the years, Irish women's writing has been dismissed as largely peripheral to the narrative of the modern literary tradition for reasons ranging from overt sexism to misunderstandings about the relationship between realist and experimental writing. Changing critical approaches have helped us to recognize what has been hiding in plain sight. When literary studies in the late twentieth century opened itself up to a wider variety of textual forms, ranging from popular literature to periodicals, and to different practices, such as the salon and political protest, a more meaningful station in the modernist movement was attributed to women. As well, with the advent of the "new modernisms" scholars were encouraged to relinquish certain conceptual divides that had long defined high modernism and to embrace temporal, spatial, and vertical expansions as their modus operandi; we began to unsettle the movement's traditional periodization located in the decades around the turn of the twentieth century, to investigate a wider range of texts and practices from across the globe, and to dismantle further the divide separating high and low cultures.[6]

Particularly pertinent to the study of Irish women artists, scholars began to identify overlaps between international modernism and Irish revivalism, a gesture that invited recognition that these two movements share important characteristics and aims.[7] During the Irish Literary Revival, which ran roughly between 1890 and

---

The descriptor "Ireland" or "Irish" often refers here to a tradition of contemporary women's writing that draws from historical commonalities and signals the enhanced porousness of the border in recent decades. Throughout, the book endeavors to acknowledge the rapidly changing vocabulary employed for not only political and critical concepts but also subject positions.

[6] See Douglas Mao and Rebecca L. Walkowitz, "The New Modernist Studies," *PMLA* 123:3 (2008): 737–48, and Douglas Mao, ed., *The New Modernist Studies* (Cambridge: Cambridge University Press, 2021). For an introduction to, and explicit demonstrations of, this approach in an Irish context, see Paul Fagan, John Greaney, and Tamara Radak, eds., *Irish Modernisms: Gaps, Conjectures, Possibilities* (London: Bloomsbury, 2021).

[7] See Emer Nolan, "Modernism and the Irish Revival," *The Cambridge Companion to Modern Irish Culture*, eds. Joe Cleary and Claire Connolly (Cambridge: Cambridge University Press, 2005),

6   INTRODUCTION

1922, Irish artists worked toward producing, performing, and promoting native art to build and buoy national self-interest—art that, notably, was often drawn from past traditions, recuperated and reworked. The commitment of Irish women to "making it new" during these years manifested chiefly in collectives, performances, and other aesthetically self-conscious practices resonant with those of the historical avant-garde. In general, their early engagement with modernism was pitched less toward individual readers than toward collective audiences of all sizes, appearing in such groundbreaking endeavors as Maud Gonne's radical deployment of public spectacle, Augusta Gregory's creation of an early experimental theater, and literary salons hosted by writers including Katharine Tynan and Blanaid Salkeld. Across these years, Irish women founded innovative periodicals and presses; they organized female-driven collectives to produce experimental drama and dance; they crafted art, design, and architecture inspired by the tenets of international modernism; they promoted international cinema and made their own films; they scripted and declared their polemical views in manifestos; they founded organizations to promote modernist aesthetics.[8]

For women writing fiction, the Revival was a double-edged sword. The Revival provided them with the foundational understanding that literature and the arts can have a widespread effect on everyday experience, which infused their relationship to the high modernist experiment that ran concurrently across Europe and America. Both revivalism and modernism in Ireland can locate their origins in a historical moment when the arts were directed toward large publics, when aesthetic experiments successfully helped to provoke a shared national feeling that

157–172; Paige Reynolds, *Modernism, Drama, and the Audience for Irish Spectacle* (Cambridge: Cambridge University Press, 2007); Rónán McDonald, "The Irish Revival and Modernism," *The Cambridge Companion to Irish Modernism*, ed. Joe Cleary (Cambridge: Cambridge University Press, 2014), 51–62.

[8] For examples, see Lauren Arrington, *Revolutionary Lives: Constance and Casimir Markievicz* (Princeton: Princeton University Press, 2016); Faith Binckes and Kathryn Laing, "A Forgotten Franco-Irish Literary Network: Hannah Lynch, Arvède Barine, and Salon Culture of Fin-de-Siècle Paris," *Études Irlandaises* 36:2 (2011): 157–171; Selena Daly, "Mary Swanzy (1882–1978): A Futurist Painter from Ireland," *International Yearbook of Futurism Studies* 5, ed. Günter Berghaus (Berlin: de Gruyter, 2015): 70–86; Lucy McDiarmid, *The Irish Art of Controversy* (Ithaca: Cornell University Press, 2005); Catherine Morris, *Alice Milligan and the Irish Cultural Revival* (Dublin: Four Courts Press, 2012); Simone Murray, "The Cuala Press: Women, Publishing, and the Conflicted Genealogies of 'Feminist Publishing,'" *Women's Studies International Forum* 27:5 (2004): 489–506; Anthony Roche, "Re-working 'The Workhouse Ward': McDonagh, Beckett, Gregory," *Irish University Review* 34:1 (Spring—Summer 2004): 171–184; Elaine Sisson, "Experimentalism and the Irish Stage: Theatre and German Expressionism in the 1920s," *Ireland, Design, and Visual Culture: Negotiating Modernity, 1922–1992*, eds. Linda King and Elaine Sisson (Cork: Cork University Press, 2011), 39–58. For scholarship on this topic as it appears, see updates from the *Irish Women's Writing Network (1880–1920)*, https://irishwomenswritingnetwork.com/. For similar interventions by Irish women in the near wake of high modernism, see Nicholas Allen, *Modernism, Ireland, and the Civil War* (Cambridge: Cambridge University Press, 2009); Deirdre Brady, *Literary Coteries and the Irish Women Writers' Club (1933–1958)* (Liverpool: Liverpool University Press, 2021); David Clare, "Reflections on Classic Gate Plays by Mary Manning, Christine Longford, and Maura Laverty," *Irish Archives: Journal of the Irish Society for Archives* 25 (2018): 28–34; Anne Mulhall, "'The Well-Known, Old, but Still Unbeaten Track': Women Poets and Irish Periodical Culture in the Mid-Twentieth Century," *Irish University Review* 42:1 (2012): 32–52.

contributed in part to the political outcome of Irish independence, however messy and imbalanced. Consequently, as I will demonstrate, Irish women writers drawing from modernism rarely regard literary experiment as divorced entirely from political and social ambitions. But the architects of the Revival, who emphasized the importance of native myth and history in national literature, also valorized poetry and drama as the genres best suited to representing Irish experience, a predisposition reinforced by subsequent appraisals of the movement.[9] This helped to secure a narrative in which fiction was the lesser genre in modern Irish writing. Such a bias presented a particular problem for historical assessments of Irish women writers, among them Maria Edgeworth, the author of *Castle Rackrent* (1800), the first regional novel in English. In the twentieth century, Joyce's experimental fiction would earn dispensation from this bias, which may help to explain why Irish writers so often invoke his legacy, sometimes using it as a shorthand for modernism more generally. Nevertheless, as late as 1984, Seán Ó Faoláin would claim that "there is no such genre as the Irish Novel."[10] It remains a commonplace of literary history to note the belated arrival of the novel in Irish writing, attributable to factors ranging from an unstable middle class to a reluctance to employ a literary form so powerfully associated with English culture.[11]

This history has helped to contribute to a misunderstanding about Irish women's fiction and modernist experiment. It is true that during the prime of high modernism few Irish women produced novels or short stories that aggressively deployed modernist forms. Nonetheless, during these decades, an impressive group of Irish women wrote hundreds of novels and short stories, among them Jane Barlow, Emily Lawless, Somerville and Ross, Katharine Tynan, Miss L. McManus, M. E. Francis (Mary Elizabeth Blundell), Rosa Mulholland (Lady Gilbert), Charlotte Riddell, L. T. Meade (Elizabeth Smith), Katherine Cecil Thurston, and W. M. Letts. Many were astonishingly prolific: Tynan wrote over one hundred novels and Mulholland more than fifty. Because these women often wrote for foreign audiences on Irish themes, they were concerned with starkly representing the recognizable and unique external characteristics of the country and its people, a seductive topic for readers, especially those in the ever-expanding Irish diaspora. In their pursuit of a broad national and international readership, many of them employed literary modes that were more familiar and thus less

---

[9] Paige Reynolds, "An Ordinary Revival: Yeats and Irish Women Novelists," *The Irish Revival: A Complex Vision*, eds. Marjorie Howes and Joseph Valente (Syracuse: Syracuse University Press, 2023), 126–148.

[10] Seán Ó Faoláin, *Vive Moi!* (London: Sinclair Stevenson, 1993), 300. Cited in Frank Shovlin, "The Struggle for Form: Seán Ó Faoláin's Autobiographies," *The Yearbook of English Studies* 35 (2005): 161–170, 169.

[11] See Terry Eagleton, *Heathcliff and the Great Hunger: Studies in Irish Culture* (London: Verso, 1995), Derek Hand, *A History of the Irish Novel* (Cambridge: Cambridge University Press, 2011), and Heather Ingman, *Irish Women's Fiction: From Edgeworth to Enright* (Dublin: Irish Academic Press, 2013).

8 INTRODUCTION

alienating, and as a result, the subtle variations of modernist experiment in their fiction generally went unnoticed and unaddressed.

In 1938, the English writer Dorothy Richardson, in the preface to her modernist masterpiece *Pilgrimage*, implored her contemporaries "to produce a feminine equivalent of the current masculine realism."[12] We now can see varieties of the "feminine equivalent" in Irish women's fiction thanks in part to the renovation of critical narratives that reflexively positioned realism as the enervated other to modernism.[13] As one example, in Emily Lawless' novel *Grania* (1892), the dark naturalism veers at points toward expressionism, and the dialogue conveys modern notions of female autonomy in a largely dialect-free English that readers were meant to assume, and asked to read as if, it were in Irish—providing an early example of a "born translated" novel.[14] Other early twentieth-century novels acknowledged modernism in their content if not their form. Modernist concerns lurked in certain late Victorian novels, including those of Sarah Grand and Anna Parnell, who invoked the "New Woman" to offer liberating alternatives to the constraints of gendered imperial and national discourses.[15] Taking on other modernist themes, Rosa Mulholland's *Cousin Sara: A Story of Arts and Crafts* (1909) follows Sara's artistic explorations in Europe that were influenced in part by her father's socialism and her copy of Ruskin's *Modern Painters*, while W. M. Letts's novel *The Rough Way* (1912) tracks a male protagonist and the "Modernist opinions that he had gathered in hasty glimpses of work beyond his grasp."[16] Placing women's fiction in the picture of Irish modernism exposes not only the ideological biases that shaped our understandings of realism and modernism at the fin de siècle, but also an ongoing dialectic between these two modes in postcolonial and post-revolutionary Irish fiction.[17]

More flexible understandings of modernist periodicity have helped clear away certain blockages that prevented us from seeing and understanding Irish women's

---

[12] Dorothy Richardson, "Foreword," *Pilgrimage 1* (New York: Popular Library, 1976), 9.

[13] See Simon Joyce, "Impressionism, Naturalism, Symbolism: Trajectories of Anglo-Irish Fiction at the Fin-de-Siècle," *Modernism/modernity* 21:3 (September 2014): 787–803; Alison Harvey, "Irish Aestheticism in Fin-de-Siècle Women's Writing: Art, Realism, and the Nation," *Modernism/modernity* 21:3 (September 2014): 805–826; James H. Murphy, "Fiction, 1845–1900," *A History of Modern Irish Women's Literature*, eds. Heather Ingman and Clíona Ó Gallchoir (Cambridge: Cambridge University Press, 2018), 96–113; Tina O'Toole, "New Woman Writers," *A History of Modern Irish Women's Literature*, 114–130.

[14] Rebecca Walkowitz, *Born Translated: The Contemporary Novel in an Age of World Literature* (New York: Columbia University Press, 2015).

[15] See Tina O'Toole, *The Irish New Woman* (London: Palgrave, 2013) and Whitney Standlee, "Power to Observe": *Irish Women Novelists in Britain, 1890–1916* (Oxford: Peter Lang, 2015).

[16] W. M. Letts, *The Rough Way* (Milwaukee: The Young Churchman Co., 1912), 140. Cited in John Wilson Foster, "The Irish Renaissance, 1890–1940: Prose in English," *The Cambridge History of Irish Literature* (1890–2000), vol. 2, eds. Margaret Kelleher and Philip O'Leary (Cambridge: Cambridge University Press, 2006), 113–180, 117.

[17] See Mark Quigley, "Re-imagining Realism in Post-Independence Irish Writing," *Irish Literature in Transition* (1880–1940), vol. 4, ed. Marjorie Howes (Cambridge: Cambridge University Press, 2020), 265–284.

THE OCCLUDED HISTORY OF IRISH WOMEN'S MODERNISM 9

modernism. These more generally have unveiled how the formal patterns, themes, and practices of a high modernism born in the late nineteenth century have moved across subsequent decades into the present day. A cottage industry of scholarship now considers the place of modernism in contemporary culture, elucidating how its experimental forms have resurfaced in literature, as well as other arts and practices.[18] Such approaches invite a particularly important revision for our assessment of Irish literature and the place of women writers within it.[19] As merely one example, Elizabeth Bowen in this light has become central to our understanding of late modernism, due to her reworking of modernism to consider the legacies of imperialism and the effects of the world wars on her characters.[20] The increased attention awarded to Bowen in scholarship, and in classrooms, confirms that we can reshape canons, incorporating Irish women writers in meaningful ways into our understandings of both modernism and contemporary literature.

Blurring the once clear divides that separated discrete cultural movements, neat generic categories, and orderly developmental timelines has allowed us to see Irish women's modernist experiments and afforded opportunities to imagine a different type of tradition for Irish writing, as well as to make evident how, and to question why, certain critical biases adhere unevenly to particular genres, national traditions, and identity categories. In their account of "Peripheral Realisms," for example, Jed Esty and Colleen Lye argue that the manifestation of realist form in different traditions and at different historical moments provides a valuable tool "for thinking relationally across different kinds of subordinated positions

---

[18] Postmodernism provided an early theoretical framework for understanding experimental writing produced in modernism's seeming aftermath, one that reached its height of influence in the second half of the twentieth century. See Brian McHale and Len Platt, eds., *The Cambridge History of Postmodern Literature* (Cambridge: Cambridge University Press, 2016). In its wake, critics have generated additional demarcated periods and aesthetic categories defined in part by their relationship to the modernism that preceded them—late modernism, limit modernism, intermodernism, metamodernism, retromodernism, and neomodernism among them. See Tyrus Miller, *Late Modernism: Politics, Fiction and the Arts Between the World Wars* (Berkeley: University of California Press, 1999); Kristin Bluemel, ed., *Intermodernism: Literary Culture in Mid-Twentieth Century Britain* (Edinburgh: Edinburgh University Press, 2009); James Smethurst, *The New Red Negro: The Literary Left and African American Poetry, 1930–1946* (New York: Oxford University Press, 1999); Robin van den Akker, Alison Gibbons, and Timotheus Vermeulen, eds., *Metamodernism: Historicity, Affect, and Depth after Postmodernism* (London: Rowman and Littlefield International, Ltd., 2017).

[19] See Martha C. Carpentier, ed., *Joycean Legacies* (London: Palgrave Macmillan, 2015); Joseph McMinn, "Versions of Banville: Versions of Modernism," *Contemporary Irish Fiction: Themes, Tropes, Theories*, eds. Liam Harte and Michael Parker (London: Palgrave Macmillan, 2000), 79–99; Paige Reynolds, ed. *Modernist Afterlives in Irish Literature and Culture* (London: Anthem Press, 2016); Richard Robinson, *John McGahern and Modernism* (London: Bloomsbury, 2016); Stephen Watt, *Beckett and Contemporary Irish Writing* (Cambridge: Cambridge University Press, 2012).

[20] Studies not mentioned elsewhere include Nels Pearson, *Irish Cosmopolitanism: Location and Dislocation in James Joyce, Elizabeth Bowen, and Samuel Beckett* (Gainesville, FL: University Press of Florida, 2015); Claire Seiler, *Midcentury Suspension: Literature and Feeling in the Wake of World War II* (New York: Columbia University Press, 2020); Anna Teekell, *Emergency Writing: Irish Literature, Neutrality, and the Second World War* (Evanston, IL: Northwestern University Press, 2018). See also Tina O'Toole and Anna Teekell, eds., Special issue on Elizabeth Bowen, *Irish University Review* 51:1 (2021).

10 INTRODUCTION

on different scales."[21] They showcase work outside of the Euro-American literary tradition by looking at what happens to realism on the peripheries. But in any consideration of peripheral literary traditions, Ireland offers an unsettling case study. Despite the country's fringe status, the "Irish miracle"—to cite Pascale Casanova's formulation—produced the major modernist writers Yeats, Joyce, and Beckett.[22] Yet, as I argue here, Irish women remained on the periphery of this peripheral miracle because their modernism emerged largely in performance and the visual arts during the movement's zenith, and when it appeared in fiction, it often was muted by realism or published after the modernist moment supposedly had passed.[23]

Finally, the exclusion of Irish women from the modernist canon was not entirely the result of the outside imposition of obdurate gender and genre biases. As this study shows, the marginal status of Irish women writers is often a problem of their own making. Throughout the twentieth century, many Irish women writers expressed skepticism about the public value of experimental literature, fearing that overt experiment in their fiction might somehow obscure its public impact. In a 1967 interview, for example, Mary Lavin asserted that "even the wild experimentalists like Joyce (and the same goes for Beckett) may only extend the frontier of expression very slightly whereas I think he had a great deal more to say than he said or could say while he was so preoccupied with experiment. I would say about myself that I was a very conservative experimentalist."[24] These writers welcomed

---

[21] Jed Esty and Colleen Lye, "Peripheral Realisms Now," *Modern Language Quarterly* 73:3 (September 2012): 269–288, 272.

[22] Pascale Casanova, *The World Republic of Letters*, trans. Malcolm B. DeBevoise (Cambridge: Harvard University Press, 2005).

[23] This helps to explain the lack of attention granted women writers in *The Cambridge Companion to Irish Modernism*, though Joe Cleary acknowledges "a considerable body of Irish visual artists, many of them women, attentive to new developments in European painting, sculpture, and design" in his introduction to that volume, 1–18, 2. Salient analyses of modernism in Irish women's writing include John Brannigan, "Explaining Ourselves: Hannah Berman, Jewish Nationalism and Irish Modernism," *Irish Modernisms*, 15–28; Lucy Collins, "Poetry, 1920–1970," *A History of Modern Irish Women's Literature*, 167–186; Alex Davis, "'Wilds to Alter, Forms to Build': The Writings of Sheila Wingfield," *Irish University Review* 31:2 (2001): 334–352; Elke D'hoker, "A Forgotten Irish Modernist: Ethel Colburn Mayne," *Irish Modernisms*, 29–41; Anne Fogarty, "Women and Modernism," *The Cambridge Companion to Irish Modernism*, 147–160; Gerardine Meaney, *Gender, Ireland, and Cultural Change: Race, Sex, and Nation* (London: Routledge, 2010), 81–120; Tina O'Toole, "George Egerton's Translocational Subjects," *Modernism/modernity* 21:3 (September 2014): 827–842; Donna Potts, "Irish Poetry and the Modernist Canon: A Reappraisal of the Poetry of Katharine Tynan," *Border Crossings: Irish Women Writers and Nationalism*, ed. Kathryn Kirkpatrick (Tuscaloosa: University of Alabama Press, 2000), 79–99; Paige Reynolds, "Prose, Drama, and Poetry, 1891–1920," *A History of Modern Irish Women's Literature*, 131–148; Moynagh Sullivan, "'I Am Not Yet Delivered of the Past': The Poetry of Blanaid Salkeld," *Irish University Review* 33:1 (Spring/Summer 2003): 182–200. Even still, as Deaglán Ó Donghaile and Gerry Smyth observe, the bulk of criticism on Irish modernism attends to "dead white guys" thus "servicing a raft of largely unexamined (gender and racial) privileges." See "Remapping Irish Modernism," *Irish Studies Review* 26:3 (2018): 297–303, 298.

[24] Interview with Mary Lavin, 3 November 1967 ML/5/3 dft. C, p. 31. Courtesy of UCD Special Collections.

modernism's techniques and vocabularies for describing the workings of the psyche, as well as its status as a formal receptacle granting authority and integrity to
the detailed ruminations and experiences of women. But by and large, they were
so committed to the wider social interventions made possible by literature that
many (though not all) of them worried that aggressive experiment might alienate
the very readers whom they hoped to engage and perhaps motivate.[25] The "conservative experimental[ism]" identified by Lavin stems from a desire to appeal to
broad audiences, a commitment that informed their early public and performative
modernism. Yet this deliberate caution has long obscured the nature of their innovations as well as their contributions to a modernist tradition. To remain blind to
such fiction across the twentieth century because it employed accessible forms and
themes, or because it was commercially successful, or because it was out of sync
with familiar literary historical timelines, inevitably results in the erasure of a substantial corpus of women's writing and thwarts any understanding of its influence
on subsequent fiction.

A Contemporary of Their Own

Seen in light of this history, *Beautiful World, Where Are You* can be understood as
part of a tradition of Irish women's writing that conscripts familiar literary modes,
references renowned writers and works, reimagines time-honored themes, and
recapitulates well-known forms. In part, this strategy functions to remind readers
of a past that seems to recede more readily in our contemporary moment. As Eileen
reflects in a missive to Alice, in a digital world rife with political crises "each day
has now become a new and unique informational unit, interrupting and replacing the informational world of the day before" (42). She wonders how this affects
culture and the arts, noting, "I mean, we're used to engaging with cultural works
set 'in the present.' But this sense of the continuous present is no longer a feature
of our lives. The present has become discontinuous. Each day, even each hour
of each day, replaces and makes irrelevant the time before, and the events of our
lives make sense only in relation to a perpetually updating timeline of news content" (42). She then speculates about "whether this will give rise to new forms in
the arts or just mean the end of the arts altogether, at least as we know them" (43).

---

[25] Similar concerns infiltrate critical accounts of contemporary Irish women's writing, with some
championing realism for its accessibility and others advocating experiment, modernist and otherwise,
for its capacity to unsettle and challenge norms. See Aaron Kelly, *Twentieth-Century Irish Literature:
A Reader's Guide to Essential Criticism* (Houndsmill: Palgrave Macmillan, 2008), 105–130. For sample arguments on each side, see Rebecca Pelan, *Two Irelands: Literary Feminisms North and South*
(Syracuse: Syracuse University Press, 2005), and Eve Patten, "Women and Fiction, 1985–1990," *Krino,
1986–1996: An Anthology of Modern Irish Writing*, eds. Gerald Dawe and Jonathan Williams (Dublin:
Gill and Macmillan, 1996), 8–16.

12   INTRODUCTION

And yet this dichotomy is one that Rooney's novel refuses. With its aggressive invocation of a literary mode that reminds us of a longer historical, cultural, and social timeline, Rooney embraces neither relentless innovation nor unavoidable obsolescence. Modernism announces itself in such works of contemporary fiction as a reminder of the questions it asks, the problems it seeks to solve, the issues it has yet to resolve.

The persistent nature of modernism in Irish women's fiction demands that this study cover an expansive stretch of time, one commencing in 1939 and continuing into the present day. In an Irish context, 1939 makes particular sense to signal the end of high modernism: it was the year that Yeats died, the year Joyce's *Finnegans Wake* was published, the year Flann O'Brien's metafictional *At Swim-Two-Birds* appeared. The year 1939 also marked the political retreat of Ireland and the securing of a national imaginary predicated on looking inward and backward. In February 1938, President Éamon de Valera announced that Ireland would remain neutral in the Second World War, a policy he affirmed later that same year. Neutrality was justified as a policy that would shore up the state's nascent sovereignty and protect it from foreign invasion, as well as contain the internal discord that had erupted in the Anglo-Irish War (1919–21) and Civil War (1922–23). More generally, neutrality reflected the quest of de Valera's Fianna Fáil government to extract Ireland from manifestations of modernity such as cosmopolitanism and secularism, and thus from many of the political and social advances for women slowly taking hold in many parts of the world. In concert, these events signal the expiration—or at the very least, a marked diminishment—of the revolutionary qualities, aesthetic and political, associated with high modernism's zenith. This was not simply an issue in the south. After partition, Northern Irish women suffered from long-standing ideological biases and practical constraints that, while having different and distinctive features, were built on a similar foundation of antiquated attitudes about femininity derived from colonial legacies and religious traditions, Catholic as well as Protestant.[26]

Uniquely meaningful in Irish literary history, the year 1939 provides the launching point for this book's claim that particular contexts and conditions (such as entrenched patriarchy, national identity, political conditions, or aesthetic commitments) enable different conceptions of the contemporary for different traditions. In literary studies, the temporal boundaries for the contemporary period vary. Long attached to the close of the Second World War and the purported demise of high modernism, its onset has inched forward with the passing of time. Scholars of Irish writing have defined the contemporary by decades proximate to the present in which they write, or they have attached their accounts to local historical events,

---

[26] For an overview, see Diarmaid Ferriter, *The Transformation of Ireland, 1900–2000* (London: Profile Books, 2004). On morality and female sexuality in Northern Ireland, see Leanne McCormick, *Regulating Sexuality: Women in Twentieth-Century Northern Ireland* (Manchester: Manchester University Press, 2009).

such as the Troubles or the Celtic Tiger, or to global conditions, such as the rise of the environmental movement or the economic crash of 2008.[27] This study demarcates what might seem a suspiciously long period as the "contemporary" for Irish women's writing, but it does so in order to call attention to the startling obduracy of those historical structures—political, social, religious, domestic, educational, technological, economic—that shape the lives of female characters considered in these works, as well as to the fact that the preoccupations of women writers in the aftermath of high modernism have remained, in form as well as content, strikingly consistent in the face of such stubborn problems.

To track the persistence of modernism, we need a long view, even as the persistence of so many problems warps time, situating us in a perpetual "contemporary" in which these dilemmas never seem to go away. A deliberately baggy conception of the contemporary also accommodates the reality that modernist experiment in Irish women's fiction does not fit a tidy evolutionary trajectory. Accounts of Irish modernism that break down its experiments into parcels of decades can be useful to highlight particular interventions. Joe Cleary, for example, has proposed a timeline marked by three different generations of Irish modernism, which runs from Wilde, Shaw, Moore, and Egerton born in the immediate aftermath of the Famine, to a second generation with more complex affiliations to Ireland that includes Yeats, Synge, Joyce, and O'Casey, as well as the visual artists May Guinness and Eileen Gray, to a third and final phase marked by "something leached about Irish modernism" that includes Beckett, Bowen, Máirtín Ó Cadhain, Francis Stuart, and Flann O'Brien.[28] This facilitates, according to Cleary, a historical narrative that asks, "After the early modernist panache of the parvenu and the high modernist mandarin, the late modernist bust?" (48) But as the question mark concedes, this represents only part of the story, especially if you take into account the experiments of Irish women writers. Their fiction exposes a disjunctive trajectory, one in which modernist experiment appears unevenly and often belatedly over more than a century.[29] It might be in tune with the formal innovations of the time, as seen in the late modernism of Kathleen Coyle's novel *A Flock of Birds*

---

[27] For studies tied to historical conditions, see Susan Cahill, *Irish Literature in the Celtic Tiger Years, 1990–2008: Gender, Bodies, Memory* (London: Continuum Books, 2011); Deirdre Flynn and Ciara L. Murphy, eds., *Austerity and Irish Women's Writing and Culture, 1980–2020* (London: Routledge, 2022); Donna Potts, *Contemporary Irish Writing and Environmentalism: The Wearing of the Deep Green* (London: Palgrave, 2018); Caroline Magennis, *Northern Irish Writing after the Troubles: Intimacies, Affects, Pleasures* (London: Bloomsbury, 2021), Paige Reynolds, ed., *The New Irish Studies* (Cambridge: Cambridge University Press, 2020). For examples defined by bracketing decades, see Eric Falci and Paige Reynolds, eds., *Irish Literature in Transition* (1980–2020), vol. 6, *Irish Literature in Transition*, eds. Claire Connolly and Marjorie Howes (Cambridge: Cambridge University Press, 2020); Liam Harte, *Reading the Contemporary Irish Novel, 1987–2007* (Chichester: Wiley-Blackwell, 2014); and George O'Brien, *The Irish Novel: 1960–2010* (Cork: Cork University Press, 2012).
[28] Joe Cleary, "European, American, and Imperial Conjunctures," *The Cambridge Companion to Irish Modernism*, 35–50, 46.
[29] See Jane Elizabeth Dougherty, "Edna O'Brien and the Politics of Belatedness," *The Oxford Handbook of Modern Irish Fiction*, ed. Liam Harte (Oxford: Oxford University Press, 2020), 289–304;

14 INTRODUCTION

from 1930 or the postmodernism of Brigid Brophy's *In Transit: An Heroi-Cyclic Novel* from 1969. Or it might not be, as evidenced by the predominance of women's realist fiction published during the early decades of high modernism or the flurry of women's modernist novels that appeared in the early twenty-first century. A prolonged time span for the contemporary allows us to capture those instances of muted, or heightened, engagement with modernist experiment found in Irish women's fiction, and to understand such recurrence as neither evolutionary nor culminating in some kind of late-stage modernist apotheosis.

This study endeavors in part to demonstrate further the benefits of loosening traditional notions of periodization. An expansive notion of the contemporary not only accommodates the realities of Irish women's engagement with modernism across so many decades, and offers a longer historical arc that allows us better to trace certain stubborn patterns, it also invites us to see the resurgence of modernist experimentation as interventionist. Wendy Knepper and Sharae Deckard likewise understand literary experimentation as "occurring in multiple periods with intensities that wax and wane in conjuncture with socio-economic crises and political moments that demand new varieties of mimesis."[30] Their approach, which ropes instances of aesthetic innovation to the movements of global capitalism, helps us to avoid the parsing out of periods, with their formulated characteristics and representative authors, and urges us not to regard familiar forms as exhausted, historical movements as spent, critical possibilities as expended and therefore foreclosed. The interventionist promise of such experimentation, as I will demonstrate, derives in no small part from the legacy of Irish women's modernism.

To make this analytical move, we have to see such patterns clearly and follow them across time. So rather than expanding high modernism indefinitely in its geographical and temporal registers, as the new modernism has suggested, I employ a definition of high modernism that is discrete, one practically learned by rote, so that we might more readily recognize it as a distinct critical construct defined by its particular historical moment. In doing so, I adhere to the logic of "metamodernism" offered by David James and Urmila Seshagiri, which advocates "a temporally bounded and formally precise understanding of what modernism does and means in any cultural moment" in order to make "aesthetic and historical

---

Edwina Keown, "New Horizons: Irish Aviation, Lemass and Deferred Anglo-Irish Modernism in Elizabeth Bowen's *A World of Love*," *Irish Modernism: Origins, Contexts, Publics*, eds. Edwina Keown and Carol Taaffe (Oxford: Lang, 2010), 217–236; Gerardine Meaney, "A Disruptive Modernist: Kate O'Brien and Irish Women's Writing," *A History of Irish Modernism*, eds. Gregory Castle and Patrick Bixby (Cambridge: Cambridge University Press, 2019), 276–291; Paige Reynolds, "Colleen Modernism: Modernism's Afterlife in Irish Women's Writing," *Éire-Ireland* 44:3–4 (Fall/Winter 2009): 94–117.

[30] Wendy Knepper and Sharae Deckard, "Towards a Radical World Literature: Experimental Writing in a Globalizing World," *ariel: A Review of International English Literature* 47:1–2 (2016): 1–25, 10.

claims about its contemporary reactivation."[31] This study does not endeavor to unsettle the accepted temporal boundaries of high modernism, nor to shoehorn late nineteenth and early twentieth-century fiction by Irish women that is obviously not modernist into that brief cultural instance. Instead, it identifies and considers the peregrinations of early modernist themes and formal tactics across the later twentieth and early twenty-first centuries to showcase the important ways that Irish women writers have self-consciously engaged the modernist tradition as a tradition, as a set of conventions embedded in the past. For example, many of the women writers under study here explicitly write back to a masculinist modernism and its architects. They retool modernism's repertoire to account for what its masculinist logics ignored or elided, seeking to capture and correct the gendered predispositions that characterized the movement's early experiments.

This approach allows us to see past the accepted narratives of modernist literary authority, to regard those long-standing assessments as the artifacts that they are so that we do not continue to replicate their limitations. In addition, I concentrate almost exclusively on a Euro-American modernist tradition and its influence on women writers identified as Irish, whether by birth or residence, writing English-language fiction. Consequently, the critical framework structuring this study is nation-based, which may appear to some as limited and out of tune with the more expansive transnational and global approaches that currently dominate literary studies. Likewise, my reappraisal of a tradition of women's writing may seem old-fashioned and recuperative to others, a dusty vintage pulled from the racks of early feminist scholarship. But this stubborn approach is a deliberate and necessary riposte to a stubborn problem. This basic work still needs to be done since Irish women writers have never been granted the same sustained critical energies and attention as Irish male writers.

That such strict attention remains necessary and important can be made evident, once again, by a turn to Rooney's *Beautiful World, Where Are You*, which orbits around the lives of Alice and Eileen, both Irish women writers. The novel briefly but blatantly simulates Woolf's trademark style, and Eileen publishes an essay on the novels of Natalia Ginzburg, the Italian writer and critic of modernism, while Alice reads online about the experimental French novelist Annie Ernaux. But not a single Irish woman writer is mentioned by name in the book. Such an absence is not, as this study will reveal, because their unspoken interventions and experiments have not had a profound effect on contemporary Irish writing. Upon close examination, Rooney's work—as I demonstrate in a subsequent chapter that considers her second novel, *Normal People*—reveals the impact of this important tradition, one easy enough to recognize once we connect the dots. However, those dots have never before been arranged so that, when connected, we can see a

---

[31] David James and Urmila Seshagiri, "Metamodernism: Narratives of Continuity and Revolution," *PMLA* 129:1 (2014): 87–100, 88.

16 INTRODUCTION

recognizable pattern. Building on previous scholarship, this project sets them out in order to make this specific tradition identifiable on its own terms to readers. I am beating the same drum as others when I announce that the neglect of women's writing is a problem. But in this instance, the Irish case is distinctive because, as this study makes clear, there is enough concrete evidence to assert that if we do not give women half the credit for Irish modernism, we are missing half the story of Irish modernism. This more expansive and complex tradition, and the revisions it necessitates, come to light only if we take into account the stubborn mode.

The Stubborn Mode

In *Beautiful World, Where Are You*, form provides one means of identifying and articulating what might otherwise escape attention or elude expression. In an email to Eileen musing on sexuality, Alice ponders the function of form: "At times I think of human relationships as something soft like sand or water, and by pouring them into particular vessels we give them shape" (100). This observation—which precedes her speculation, "But what would it be like to form a relationship with no preordained shape of any kind?" (100)—chimes with critical assessments that regard form as an ordering structure in the world, something that gives certain shape to the ineffable, the pliable, the inexpressible. Whether embraced or refused, form provides Alice a nomenclature for understanding and representing her relationship with Felix as it unfolds. In these speculations, she might be seen to retrofit one famous tenet of high modernism to her personal experience. In his 1923 essay "*Ulysses*, Order, and Myth," T. S. Eliot famously claimed *Ulysses* as "the most important expression which this present age has found," commending Joyce's use of "mythical modernism" and in particular his invocation of Homer's *Odyssey* as "a way of controlling, of ordering, of giving a shape and a significance to the immense panorama of futility and anarchy which is contemporary history."[32] For Eliot, a long established and easily recognized literary form offers the contemporary writer "a way ... of giving a shape" to the mind-boggling complexities of the present day.

Such an understanding of form's function helps to explain the flamboyant modernism that appears in twenty-first-century Irish women's fiction. These works use modernism as a framework to give recognizable shape to contemporary experience. But to highlight the traction of the concerns represented, their "new" modernism often looks much like the "old" modernism. It responds to the shock of sudden and vast alterations in technologies, politics, and ways of thinking. It

---

[32] T. S. Eliot, "*Ulysses*, Order, and Myth (1923)," *Selected Prose of T. S. Eliot*, ed. Frank Kermode (New York: Harcourt, Brace & Co., 1975), 175–178, 177. For a valuable account of form and modernist history, see Cara Lewis, *Dynamic Form: How Intermediality Made Modernism* (Ithaca, NY: Cornell University Press, 2020).

represents the interiority of its subjects through stream of consciousness, among other apposite experiments. It subverts linear narratives by employing fragmentation or collage. It offers unreliable narrators and resists narrative closure. It shifts among multiple points of view, and these frequently go unindicated. It is aggressively allusive, and it works through rejiggered modernist form and historically germane content to "make it new." It disrupts standard syntax, spelling, and punctuation, and often is deliberately difficult, abstract, and abstruse. It is inspired by a roster composed primarily of renowned writers, including Proust, Yeats, Pound, Joyce, Eliot, Hemingway, Beckett, as well as Mansfield, Stein, and Woolf. It regularly attends to the lives of English speakers in the West, and fits our understanding of a traditional Euro-American rather than global modernism. Even the means of production seem recognizable from modernist history, as much of this fiction has been published first by little magazines like *The Stinging Fly* or small presses like Galley Beggar, Liberties, or Tramp Press.

As this list makes clear, modernist form is only part of the story. These writers overtly employ and refashion various literary techniques associated with high modernism, but they also are in dialogue with other aspects of modernism—its themes and contexts, its architects and canon, its history and criticism. For these writers, modernism is a mode: a pliable and portable set of features readily and broadly identified as "modernist" by readers. The mode, in the words of Fredric Jameson, is "a particular type of literary discourse ... not bound to the conventions of a given age," and as the many scholarly accounts of the "melodramatic mode" have demonstrated, the mode can move among not only historical periods, but also genres, media, national traditions, settings, and audiences.[33] Amid these travels, the mode remains recognizable because it adheres to its original conventions. But it also is adaptive, and may resist or exceed those conventions. In texts that employ a familiar literary mode, as in the works of fiction studied here, the mode, and the history it accrues, generate a kind of interpretive friction for readers familiar with its norms, one that helps to uncover certain cultural fault lines, particularly those historical problems that persist into the present moment.

But if the mode has already been defined by its durability and portability, by its detectable appearance in different moments and venues, why add the descriptor

---

[33] Fredric Jameson, "Magical Narratives: Romance as Genre," *New Literary History* 7:1 (Autumn 1975): 135–163, 142. For influential studies of the "melodramatic mode," see Peter Brooks, *The Melodramatic Imagination: Balzac, Henry James, Melodrama, and the Mode of Excess* (New Haven: Yale University Press, 1976); Christine Gledhill and Linda Williams, eds., *Melodrama Unbound: Across History, Media, and National Cultures* (New York: Columbia University Press, 2018); Elaine Hadley, *Melodramatic Tactics: Theatricalized Dissent in the English Marketplace, 1800–1885* (Stanford: Stanford University Press, 1995); and Linda Williams, *Playing the Race Card: Melodramas of Black and White from Uncle Tom to O. J. Simpson* (Princeton: Princeton University Press, 2001), who argues that "a broader melodramatic mode can more fully grasp the complex networks and recombinations of racial victimization and vilification in American culture" (44). See also Agustin Zarzosa, "Melodrama and the Modes of the World," *Discourse* 32:2 (Spring 2010): 236–255, which likewise announces the social impulse of the melodramatic mode.

18 INTRODUCTION

"stubborn" when thinking about modernism in contemporary fiction by Irish women? To be stubborn, the dictionary tells us, is to refuse to change one's position or attitude, to be likened to a mule or an unreasonable child. It is a strategy of repetition and adamancy, of overstaying your welcome, of demanding to be acknowledged. Often gendered, such behavior undergirds disparaging tropes like the nagging wife, mutton dressed as lamb, the aggressive career woman, and the entitled Karen. Such stubbornness, for many female protagonists in Irish women's writing, has real costs. Think, for instance, of "stubborn" Eily, the teenager who follows her desires, becomes pregnant out of wedlock, and finds herself consigned to an adult fate of madness and drugged obeisance in Edna O'Brien's "A Scandalous Woman" (1974), or of The Mai, an accomplished professional who, despite repeated counsel, cleaves to her faithless husband until her tragic death in Marina Carr's play *The Mai* (1994).[34] But a public and political stubbornness also represents for oft-silenced women a means of advocating and forging necessary if unwelcome change. Such a logic is reflected by the feminist rallying cry "Nevertheless, she persisted," repurposed from a dismissive putdown when Senator Elizabeth Warren in 2017 refused to cede the floor during a debate in the United States Senate. A deliberate recalcitrance imagined as productive public intervention characterizes the position of the speaker in Eavan Boland's poem "Mise Éire" (1987), who insists "I won't go back to it—" and refuses to recapitulate the feminine tropes used to justify and promote the Irish national project, and the efforts of the real-life historian Catherine Corless celebrated in 2021 by Taoiseach Micheál Martin as a "tireless crusader of dignity and truth" for her relentless investigation of the records of the Bon Secours Mother and Baby Home in Tuam.[35]

Irish women writers using the modernist mode are among this cohort. There are plenty of good reasons they should have shed such experimentation as mere imitation, as outmoded (to indulge the obvious play on words). Nonetheless, they demonstrated over and over the particular suitability of the modernist mode to the representation of female experience in contemporary Ireland. Sara Ahmed has explored the consequences of bodies, language, gestures, and affective registers that refuse to accommodate surrounding norms and expectations, among them the "feminist killjoy" who speaks uncomfortable but necessary truths.[36] The stubborn mode provides a literary manifestation of similar defiance, one marked by its anachronistic aesthetics and uneven history. Tailored to contemporary contexts, modernism serves many different purposes for these writers. For example, as this study will show, it complicates notions of female privacy in Ireland. The

[34] Edna O'Brien, "A Scandalous Woman," *The Love Object: Selected Stories* (New York: Little, Brown and Company, 2015), 60–89, 60.

[35] Megan Specia, "Report Gives Glimpse into Horrors of Ireland's Mother and Baby Homes," *New York Times*, January 12, 2021, https://www.nytimes.com/2021/01/12/world/europe/ireland-mother-baby-home-report.html.

[36] Sara Ahmed, *The Promise of Happiness* (Durham, NC: Duke University Press, 2010).

understanding of specular authority announced by Foucault's *Discipline and Punish* (1975) has had a powerful influence on studies of Irish literature and culture, and it holds especial relevance for accounts of Irish womanhood, as these women found themselves represented by church and state as objects requiring constant surveillance. Such a pernicious logic, as histories have revealed, was manifest in literal institutions, including the Magdalene Laundries and Mother and Baby Homes, as well as in more commonplace structures such as the nuclear family.[37] Not without cause, these accounts suggest there is little room for a safe or productive privacy for Irish women even into the present day. The texts under study here acknowledge the actual threats posed by the retreat, elective or forced, of women into private spaces or into the private world of the psyche, but they also identify the valuable aspects of such privacy, using modernist tactics to depict such complexities. That so many of these writers harness the modernist mode even today as a recognizable shorthand for the obliquity of consciousness is no accident. Even as they capture the hidden or neglected aspects of female interiority, modernism's obscurities and opacities impede easy access, easy interpretation—they demand we work hard to witness the veiled contours of individual perception, thinking, and feeling.

The strategies of the stubborn mode reveal themselves not only in content, but also in reception. The current enthusiasm for these authors and books has been enabled partially by recent structural changes supporting female artists more broadly: women have enhanced access to institutions that encourage them to produce, publish, and promote their work; new technologies enable cheaper printing, targeted print runs, and more expansive marketing strategies for lesser-known talents; gender equality initiatives, such as *VIDA: Women in Literary Arts* and *Time's Up*, have pulled the spotlight to women artists internationally. As the most recent chapter in a long history of feminist literary activism, grassroots initiatives in Ireland such as *Waking the Feminists* and *Fired! Irish Women Poets and the Canon* have drawn global attention to the inequities that plague women theater-makers and poets. Marketing and celebrity have a role to play as well. In our media-saturated culture, the widely recognized cultural capital that long adhered to those toting thick copies of *Ulysses* can now be obtained from novels written by Irish women. The warm critical embrace offered to many of these challenging novels published in recent decades confirms that not only the modernist mode, but also modernist prestige travels. For example, Emma Donoghue appeared on the red carpet in 2016, having adapted her novel *Room* (2010) into an Oscar-nominated Hollywood film, and McBride's *A Girl Is a Half-formed Thing* was indirectly

---

[37] For salient examples see Margot Backus, *The Gothic Family Romance: Heterosexuality, Child Sacrifice, and the Anglo-Irish Colonial Order* (Durham, NC: Duke University Press, 1999); Emilie Pine, *The Politics of Irish Memory: Performing Remembrance in Contemporary Irish Culture* (Houndsmill: Palgrave Macmillan, 2011); James Smith, *Ireland's Magdalen Laundries and the Nation's Architecture of Containment* (South Bend, IN: University of Notre Dame Press, 2007).

20 INTRODUCTION

promoted on *The Late Show* with David Letterman, where the American actor Sarah Jessica Parker clutched a copy of the book as if it were a trendy accessory. Perhaps most notoriously, Rooney's best-selling novels have been championed by millennial celebrities including Lena Dunham and Taylor Swift on Instagram and have provided status-conscious readers, in the words of Jessa Crispin, a means to "adroitly signal to everyone around you your great taste and your with-it-ness in regards to cultural developments."[38]

The stubborn mode can be an easier sell in the contemporary moment: like the coffee drinker who seeks out Starbucks in an unfamiliar city, many readers welcome the overt deployment of modernism in contemporary fiction. Such familiarity is not inherently and inevitably a liability. Instead, it suggests that the disruptive potential of these books rests not always in radical formal innovation but instead in the creative adaptation of old forms to convey aspects of female experience that are upsetting and unsettling—and marketable to large audiences curious about the complex interior lives of such characters and able to decipher modernism's codes. Read in such a materialist context, these novels might be interpreted as product, with their refashioning of modernism the literary equivalent of upcycling, the creative reuse of old materials.[39] A contemporary manifestation of the modernist "object trouvé," the stubborn mode seems to resist the planned obsolescence that characterizes the consumer market, its worth stemming from the apparent artistry that transforms an old object into a particularly desirable new one constructed from salvaged forms. Just as the recycled object has become a political statement with a certain social value, so too has a recycled modernism in contemporary writing—in part by similarly refusing the ever-quicker cycles of planned obsolescence. Readily recognizable, the modernist mode nonetheless continues to pose interpretive challenges, ones that like the problems it represents in these books require that readers carefully attend to what stands before them, despite having seen it many times before. The lessons offered, as my readings demonstrate, are often distressing. The stubborn problems depicted by the stubborn mode are often exhaustive (this problem is everywhere), exhausted (we've seen it a million times), and exhausting (and yet it continues).

Close Reading the Stubborn Mode

Altered cultural attitudes and revamped critical approaches have brought to light the long and complex history of Irish women's modernism, which helps to expose

---

[38] Jessa Crispin, "*Normal People* Is Little More Than a Gutless Soap Opera for Millennials," *The Guardian*, May 5, 2020, https://www.theguardian.com/commentisfree/2020/may/05/sally-rooney-normal-people-hulu-bbc-soap-opera.

[39] This notion of "upcyling" is in tune with that proposed in Robin van den Akker and Timotheus Vermeulen, "Periodising the 2000s, or, the Emergence of Metamodernism," *Metamodernism: Historicity, Affect, and Depth after Postmodernism*, 1–19, 10.

the aesthetic and socio-cultural work of the stubborn mode. This perspective allows us not only to identify the various forces that previously obscured this distinctive literary tradition, but also to forge a new genealogy for contemporary writing. But a wide-angle view is not enough: we also need to zoom in on the particular products of this strain of modernism, which often have gone overlooked, in order to understand its aims and achievements. This book will reveal traits specific to Irish women's contemporary fiction that derive directly from a historical modernism generated and sustained by Irish women artists, one marked by its commitment to addressing the altered role of women in a changing society, to testing formal experiments for representing perception, to refashioning modernist influences that are national as well as international, to remedying the movement's various blind spots. The stubborn mode of modernism in contemporary Irish fiction situates the concerns of these women writers within a protracted historical sweep, while also reminding readers—and sometimes the characters themselves—that the concerns articulated in modernist classics from a century prior remain relevant even now. This is of especial importance given that so much fiction by Irish women depicts female characters who fixate on the past, both personal and public, and parse its implications for the present.

With an awareness of its particular contours and characteristics, and the capacity to track and analyze it in tandem with historical contexts, the stubborn mode of modernism heightens our awareness that different social realities prompt and sustain a different relationship to different forms. As Houston Baker demonstrated, writers of the Harlem Renaissance employed in their modernism strategies derived from African American traditions, and as a result, their works were often dismissed as outmoded and provincial. But these refashioned aesthetics, imagined in part as a challenge to systemic racism, were every bit as innovative as those of Anglo-American modernism and continue to influence contemporary writing, music, and art.[40] These lessons about the obduracy of particular modes, especially those that resist dominant critical conceptions, are important to remember as women of color, among them the fiction writers Ifedinma Dimbo, Melatu Uche Okorie, and Kit de Waal, are now diversifying and enriching the canon of Irish writing.[41] Contemporary fiction that employs modernism might risk being dismissed as kitsch, an indication that a writer simply is exploiting the logics of a market that profits on the familiar. But fiction that hazards new experiment can be so alienating that readers walk away from its crucial messages. This is a gamble some writers from marginalized subject positions may not wish to make, including many Irish women writers who for decades struggled for recognition.

---

[40] Houston Baker, *Modernism and the Harlem Renaissance* (Chicago: University of Chicago Press, 1987).

[41] For a reading of form in Okorie's short fiction, see Mary M. McGlynn, *Broken Irelands: Literary Form in Post-Crash Irish Fiction* (Syracuse: Syracuse University Press, 2022), 238–245.

22 INTRODUCTION

This is important: my concentrated focus on a particular genealogy of influ-ence in Irish writing is not to devalue or erase other diverse voices, but instead to demonstrate the ongoing importance of close attention to literary works drawn from one neglected, or previously unidentified, tradition. Of course, those tac-tics of reading might be (and I would argue, should be) transported and adapted to other neglected traditions, writers, texts, and modes. Nonetheless, the books under study here manifest the limitations cited by Rooney's Alice, a contemporary writer who eschews contemporary writing, and who is alert to the inadequacies of literary form, its constraints and prohibitions. She notes, "The problem with the contemporary Euro-American novel is that it relies for its structural integrity on suppressing the lived realities of most human beings on earth" (103). Contempo-rary fiction by Irish women often unfolds amid acutely specific locales and eras such as Limerick during the Irish Revival, Belfast during the Troubles, or Dublin during the Celtic Tiger's boom and bust. These writers draw from an expansive understanding of local experience derived in part from Joyce's celebrated repre-sentation of the Irish quotidian: "For myself, I always write about Dublin, because if I can get to the heart of Dublin I can get to the heart of all the cities of the world. In the particular is contained the universal."[42] Yet the limitations of established lit-erary modes in the face of inequitable representation, a quandary Rooney's novel performs even as her protagonist calls it out, underscore the obduracy of narra-tive strategies as well as that of the broader social problems those strategies fail to combat. For instance, this book does not suppose that simply adding Irish women to the modernist canon can correct gender bias and inequity in the literary field. Instead, the stubborn mode and its affordances, to invoke Caroline Levine's for-mulation of the latent capabilities of forms that are revealed as they move across time and space, can accentuate the aesthetic and the socio-political work that can be done by literature—as well as the work that remains to be done, and even the work that cannot be done.[43]

To see the literary modernism of Irish women, and the broader public inter-ventions that the stubborn mode seeks to make, we must not only attend to the long arc of literary history but also assiduously analyze particular examples of form and content. Close reading is both the dominant methodology and the urgent argument of this book. Sustained, rigorous attention to the fiction of Irish women writers engaged with modernism allows us deliberately to test if modernist

[42] James Joyce, quoted in Richard Ellmann, *James Joyce* (Oxford: Oxford University Press, 1982), 505.
[43] Caroline Levine, *Forms: Whole, Rhythm, Hierarchy, Network* (Princeton: Princeton University Press, 2015). For other influential accounts of form, which similarly consider its social potential and limitations, see Anna Kornbluh, *The Order of Forms: Realism, Formalism, and Social Space* (Chicago: University of Chicago Press, 2019) and Anahid Nersessian, *The Calamity Form: On Poetry and Social Life* (Chicago: University of Chicago Press, 2020). For a study that shifts such concerns to style, see Michael Dango, *Crisis Style: The Aesthetics of Repair* (Palo Alto: Stanford University Press, 2021).

afterlives—and the reading practices that they demand—can move us past the satisfactions of our own virtuosity, our ability to identify modernist allusions and tactics, and expose the social and political implications of using modernism after modernism. The close reading of such works can stoke richer and more realistic understandings of the real-world interventions made possible through literature, in part by demanding that readers come to terms with the difficult and time-consuming intellectual, affective, and practical labor necessary to realize those interventions. Reading the modernist mode in contemporary Irish fiction allows us to extend the imbricated history of modernism and close reading, while also inviting provocative new questions.[44] For example, current conceptions of the "global novel" might threaten once again to erase the contributions of Irish women writers, given that their fiction so often is focused tightly on the experiences of Irish women and set in the Republic or Northern Ireland.[45] Yet to denigrate Irish fiction that piggybacks on familiar (and marketable) aspects of national identity, to denounce it because it focuses on characters who stay home and are plagued by the same old problems, and therefore seem untouched by certain contemporary crises, is to refuse to see how such assessments elevate certain types of writers and subjects, and necessarily preclude others. That Irish women for so long fell victim to critical biases that charged them with parochialism or traditionalism or crass commercialism is troubling; that they seem to be so neatly avoiding those same charges today seems both welcome and odd given their long-standing and ongoing commitment to depicting Irish characters, Irish settings, and Irish contexts for international readers.

By looking closely at "the words on the page," the mantra I press upon my students, we can see how these novels and short stories center on the experiences of Irish women in a century that witnessed first slow then rapid social transformation. In these works, we view the stubborn mode of modernism in motion, reshaped when it collides with different objects and practices, when it encounters different forms both literary and social. In the spirit of the public-facing legacies of Irish women's modernism, I also would make here a case for giving ourselves permission carefully to blur the divide between the labor of scholarship and the classroom, as well as between historicism and presentism. By following the evaluation and interpretation of modernist forms, themes, and history in Irish women's fiction across the twentieth and twenty-first centuries, we learn a great deal not only about Ireland during these decades, but also about the value of literary studies in the present moment. Modernism, as I have argued elsewhere, is of particular

---

[44] For accounts of the critical history of close reading, and its relationship to modernism, that undergird my claims, see David James, "Introduction," *Modernism and Close Reading*, ed. David James (Oxford: Oxford University Press, 2020), 1–18, and Battersby, "Modernist Liabilities," 1–34.

[45] See Adam Kirsch, *The Global Novel: Writing the World in the 21st Century* (Columbia: Columbia University Press, 2016).

24 INTRODUCTION

benefit in the classroom because it is affectively as well as stylistically difficult.[46] It demands that students learn and rehearse how to slowly and intelligently sift through difficult texts—books with oblique allusions and vocabulary, unfamiliar historical or global contexts, challenging formal techniques. These endeavors abet critical thinking and intellectual patience. The contemporary fiction under study here demands that readers, whether students or not, parse still alienating modernist strategies, that they muscle through interpretive challenges. To read these books in light of the moral and ethical standards of the present day is not a shameless quest for "relatability," the term uncomfortably invoked when we imagine how to engage skeptics in the deep study of literature, but a method Irish women writers invite through their use of the stubborn mode of modernism, which encourages us to reinterpret and reevaluate a flawed past so that we might do better in the future.

Modernism and Contemporary Irish Women's Experience

Recent decades in Ireland, both north and south, have been characterized by a dizzying array of political and social transformations. During these years, from some perspectives, the Republic can appear to have moved from the conservative and insular economic and political gestures of the mid-twentieth century to a more open-armed embrace of globalism and progressive social policies in the twenty-first, while, following the violence of the Troubles, the North has achieved a measure of peace and stability with the 1998 Belfast/Good Friday Agreement, even as Brexit threatens to undermine those hard-won achievements. The analysis of women's fiction that follows in this book endeavors to deepen and complicate such sweeping historical narratives, to illuminate their hidden features as experienced and understood by individual female characters. By attending closely to fictional depictions of female interiority during these years, this study explores how women writers have employed the modernist mode to depict the understanding of and response to such circumstances. This includes conditions specific to Ireland (such as wartime neutrality or the Troubles) as well as ones more general (such as migration or class struggle), both those positive (such as first love or the pleasures of summer camp) and pernicious (such as childhood sexual abuse or political violence). This approach can help to explain how and why certain literary frameworks persist across almost a century of Irish women's writing, as well as why certain cultural conditions, good and bad, appear intractable. The methodology provides readers a useful feedback loop: we can understand contemporary

---

[46] Paige Reynolds, "Bird Girls: Modernism and Sexual Ethics in Contemporary Irish Fiction," *Modernism and Close Reading*, 173–190.

conditions better when we isolate a particular body of work, we can understand a particular body of work better when we isolate contemporary conditions.

This logic informs the book's organizational structure. Chapter One turns to short fiction, skipping across decades, to examine the ongoing tactical use of the stubborn mode of modernism in representations of female subjectivity. Elizabeth Bowen's "Summer Night" (1941), set during Irish neutrality of the Second World War, Maeve Kelly's "Morning at My Window" (1972) and Evelyn Conlon's "Taking Scarlet as a Real Colour or And Also, Susan ..." (1993) both written in the midst of specific moments of feminist urgency for Irish women, and June Caldwell's "SOMAT" (2015), published amid the abortion rights debates that preceded the repeal of the Eight Amendment of the Irish Constitution, demonstrate how women writing in the aftermath of high modernism repurpose its experiments, seeking in part to amend the early movement's masculinist bias. In their representations of neglected aspects of female subjectivity, they engage with modernist heavyweights such as Joyce and Eliot, but they also mine from Russian theater and popular romance, among other surprising sources.

I then place evocative constellations of novels and short stories in chapters organized around four experiences generally understood as ordinary and largely, though not exclusively, internalized: praying, daydreaming, logging off from digital technologies, and reading. Rather than focus on an individual writer or text, each chapter centers on a particular experience that is regularly, almost obsessively, represented in Irish women's contemporary writing to identify how modernism is engaged and adapted to stage broad concerns ranging from the ethical to the secular, the affective to the material, the personal to the collective. Across these decades, female interiority as depicted through the modernist mode has served different purposes. In the mid-twentieth century, fiction that exposed to readers the private operation of female consciousness stood at odds with the efforts of the Catholic Church and state to stunt the roles available to women. Its radical quality came from making private experience public, from a resistance to local institutional pressures that sanctioned and celebrated the suppression of female experience. By the early twenty-first century, the fictional depiction of women's consciousness does a volte face: it often employs modernist form to resist endeavors to reveal entirely female private experience, endeavors that are often global and technological, to advocate the benefits of privacy.

The first of the four chapters to explore these changes is focused on praying. After independence, Catholic doctrine in the south blatantly informed state practice and powerfully influenced everyday life throughout the new nation. As seen in Chapter Two, the form and logic of religious prayer saturate Kate O'Brien's *The Land of Spices* (1941), Mary Lavin's short fiction of the mid-twentieth century, Emma Donoghue's *Hood* (1995), and Eimear McBride's *A Girl Is a Half-formed Thing* (2013). In these works, familiar modernist tactics—repetitions, obfuscations, invocations of ritual—demonstrate how Catholicism literally

26 INTRODUCTION

and figuratively interferes with women's daily lives. Chapter Three attends to daydreaming. Modernist technique, most obviously stream of consciousness, has frequently been employed to make visible and public the reveries of women. Irish women's contemporary fiction uses such tactics to emphasize the ways in which real life intrudes on and reshapes this imaginative practice. In *Night* (1972), which riffs off the narrative techniques depicting Molly Bloom's ruminations in *Ulysses*, Edna O'Brien demonstrates the limits of feminism and the sexual revolution both in revamping individual psychology as well as in reworking modernist form. At the cusp of the twenty-first century, Ireland grappled with cultural alterations arising from the newfound affluence of the Celtic Tiger, widespread revelations of childhood sexual abuse across the island, and the promise of peace in Northern Ireland. Anne Enright's *The Gathering* (2007) and Deirdre Madden's *Molly Fox's Birthday* (2008) focus on female characters in the throes of these contemporary conditions, adapting stream of consciousness to portray how the twenty-first century's flush of goods and capital altered the reveries of Irish women.

Chapter Four examines the acceleration of time and the tsunami of information available with new media technologies, looking at how women writers represent "logging off" in pursuit of slow time and privacy. Novels such as Éilís Ní Dhuibhne's *The Dancers Dancing* (1999) and Claire-Louise Bennett's *Pond* (2015) use modernist tactics, including those adopted and adapted from the modernist short story, to represent female characters who retreat to rural sites and thus might evade the incursions of modernity and technology on their private lives, while Louise O'Neill's dystopian young-adult novel *Only Ever Yours* (2014) concocts an environmentally devastated and technologically managed Ireland that allows women no privacy at all. Chapter Five then turns to the topic of how contemporary fiction by Irish women writers has pushed the stubborn mode more aggressively into public awareness and ponders further its political and ethical payoff. The critical and commercial success of Sally Rooney's *Normal People* (2018) and Anna Burns's *Milkman* (2018) exposes, from the vantage of the present moment, the logics that invite Irish women's writing to enter mainstream conversations, but preclude it from fully inhabiting them. These novels, making use of modernism in different historical settings, provocatively identify intransigent problems encountered by women, even those alert to possible freedoms of the global present. They focus in particular on the act of reading to underscore the complex if familiar brew of liberties and limitations that inform the lives of women, even today, in Northern Ireland and the Republic. As I argue, their attention to reading elucidates the changing textures of female privacy in a way that speaks powerfully to young adults in the humanities classroom, and thus provides a valuable example of the ethics of the stubborn mode at work in the present day.

In its coda, *The Stubborn Mode* makes a move frequently found in accounts of modernism and Irish writing. Centered on women's fiction, this study concludes by offering a short representative reading of a text by a writer of the opposite sex to suggest the analytical possibilities made available by its larger arguments. This gesture is deliberately mischievous, but it suggestively demonstrates what opens up when we use a tradition of women's writing as a vehicle for evaluating writing by men, rather than the other way around. Voiced by a male protagonist, Mike McCormack's *Solar Bones* (2016) employs a first-person stream-of-consciousness narrative powerfully influenced by modernism, and addresses many of the same quotidian concerns explored by the women's novels studied here. Such congruencies in content, as well as in form, speak to the abiding influence of modernist representations of female interiority. They also suggest that McCormack is in dialogue not only with the experiments of Joyce and other male modernists, but also with a tradition of Irish women's writing and performance, influences that he acknowledges but that too often have gone unnamed and uncited, neglected or dismissed by others.

With its detailed attention to how contemporary Irish fiction helps to explain the hidden workings of female consciousness, this book reveals how and why modernist technique has been employed with increasing intensity and vigor to represent women's private lives in Ireland. The stubborn mode of modernism is diachronic and holds the traces of its historical past, even as it is reworked to suit the present day. But it is also synchronic, and its critical energies are released, as many instances in this book demonstrate, when its forms and strategies collide. In contact with modernism, prayer becomes something like its opposite, an inwardly-directed litany focused on emotions linked to personal affection and sexual desire; romantic reverie, a vessel long imagined as evacuated of modern worldly concerns, becomes stuffed with objects to accommodate consumer culture's saturation of imaginative and emotional life; the elective act of logging off from new digital technologies is underwritten by the impossibility of privacy in a surveilled media culture; the close reading of literature and performance inspires meaningful personal insights, but at best seems capable of inciting only modest societal interventions.

The wide-ranging collection of authors and texts on view might appear to indulge the "associative mania" that Frank O'Connor bemoaned in Joyce's *Finnegans Wake*.[47] Instead, this assortment seeks to demonstrate how broadly the everyday experiences and concerns under consideration shape the form and content of contemporary Irish women's writing across nearly a century. The aesthetic and experiential continuities unfurled here are an endeavor to historicize the present, to offer a tool that encourages the critical distance scholars like Peter Boxall, Eric Hayot, Theodore Martin, and Michael North, among others, correctly observe we struggle to obtain in studies of contemporary literature.[48] The chapters

[47] Frank O'Connor, "Introduction to *A Portrait of the Artist as a Young Man*," *A Frank O'Connor Reader*, ed. Michael Steinman (Syracuse: Syracuse University Press, 1994), 341–345, 342.
[48] Peter Boxall, *Twenty-First-Century Fiction: A Critical Introduction* (Cambridge: Cambridge University Press, 2013); Eric Hayot, "Critical Distance and the Crisis in Criticism," 2007, *Erichayot.org*

28 INTRODUCTION

constellate twentieth-century texts, from which we have more remove, with those written in the more immediate past of the twenty-first century. We better understand the persistence of particular cultural problems—the religious repression of women, the unease triggered by female reverie, the threats posed to privacy by the ubiquity of new technologies, the internalized sexism that combines with external structures to hinder women from fully exercising their freedoms—when we trace them through time, seeing how they morph in the face of changing historical conditions. This approach may help to explain how and why modernist technique has been employed of late to represent women's private lives in Ireland.

The shape of this project also reflects my desire to champion a body of work that is engaging to read, as well as politically and socially significant. Picking up the theme of activism running through Irish women's modernism, this book is driven by a straightforward premise: we need to be reading and teaching more regularly the writers studied here. So while *The Stubborn Mode* demonstrates the benefits of awarding close critical attention to women writers from one national and linguistic tradition, its aims are expansive. During the twentieth century, women in Ireland existed in the midst of conservative and regressive mores enforced by the church and state, and these have helped to obscure their contributions to the vaunted tradition of modern literature. These unique conditions help to reveal how and why Irish women's writing has been neglected. But these writers are not alone; their neglect is not the incongruity of a particular national tradition, nor is their concealment a historical anomaly. By slowly and attentively returning to these books, we can better account for why so many women writers have gone missing. We might say that Djuna Barnes is too hard, or Danielle Steele is too easy. Yet it is outrageous that we have lived, and in some instances continue to live, in a critical and pedagogical world where so many women writers are slotted into short dedicated chapters of scholarly publications, or consigned to being read strictly as another recuperative project. Many reasons could be used to explain why we're not talking enough about these writers, these books—but I am hoping this study, with its concentration on Irish women's contemporary fiction, offers us fewer excuses to turn away once again from women's writing as we continue to explore what modernism or the contemporary means.

(blog); Theodore Martin, *Contemporary Drift: Genre, Historicism, and the Problem of the Present* (New York: Columbia University Press, 2017); Michael North, *What Is the Present?* (Princeton, NJ: Princeton University Press, 2018).

1

Refashioning Modernism

(Elizabeth Bowen, Maeve Kelly, Evelyn Conlon, June Caldwell)

The Irish writer Mary Colum, who circulated among modernism's architects and purveyors at home and abroad, was among the most incisive of that movement's early critics. And like her peers Eliot and Woolf, she cited the tactic of poaching from the past as a signal attribute of modernism by noting, "There is a new development, one writer influences another; one branch of knowledge influences another, something is added to already existing forms and materials ... Literary innovations, literary discoveries are the invention of writers thoroughly trained in the past of literature."[1] Nonetheless, an anxiety about the fiction of Irish women writers engaged with modernist precedents runs rife through the twentieth century. This attitude is captured, in one of many examples lurking in the archives, by the critical response to a 1954 special issue of *Irish Writing: The Magazine of Contemporary Irish Literature*. This periodical, founded in 1946 by David Marcus and Terence Smith, played a pivotal role in promoting new writers and advancing contemporary writing in Ireland. Despite the fact that its opening editorial statement invokes the hackneyed nationalist trope conflating Ireland as woman, *Irish Writing* (published until 1957) liberally peppered its issues with new work by Irish women—as well as with reviews of literary criticism on modernism and modernists.

In June 1954, the "Women Writers' Issue" showcased selected new work by Elizabeth Bowen, Mary Lavin, and Kate O'Brien, among others. However, the range and diversity of these pieces failed to impress the *Irish Times* critic "Thersites," the pseudonym of the civil servant Thomas Woods. His assessment of this special issue opens by announcing a "benevolent neutralist attitude" since there is "no reason at all why ... women should not make good writers."[2] The review, written in a playful but patronizing tone, expresses a genuine hostility toward the notion of women writers as a category of analysis, a category it regards as no more valid than one

---

[1] Mary Colum, "Criticism," n.d., typescript, Padraic and Mary Colum Collection, New York: Binghamton University. Cited in Denise A. Ayo, "Mary Colum, Modernism, and Mass Media: An Irish-Inflected Transatlantic Print Culture," *Journal of Modern Literature* 35:4 (Summer 2012): 107–129, 117.

[2] Thersites (Thomas Woods), "Private Views," *The Irish Times (1921–Current File)*; July 31, 1954; ProQuest Historical Newspapers: *The Irish Times* and *The Weekly Irish Times*: 6.

Modernism in Irish Women's Contemporary Writing. Paige Reynolds, Oxford University Press. © Paige Reynolds (2024).
DOI: 10.1093/9780191990540.003.0002

30 REFASHIONING MODERNISM

for writers bound by "their red-headedness or their gap-toothedness." Thersites cavalierly dismisses Lavin's short story as "blurred all through," K. Arnold Price's story as having "all the exotic impact of a dull thud," and Mary Beckett's story as "a slice of indigestible whimsy." Easily dismissed as mid-century polemic, this review nonetheless offers revealing insight into the vexed relationship between women writers and the modernist tradition when Thersites takes particular exception to the work of the, even then, critically venerated Bowen. He observes, "only a few pages of Miss Bowen's prose are enough to make me feel that I have forgotten to fasten my safety-belt." But rather than celebrate her innovative representation of modern temporality, Thersites instead describes her style as merely "a *reductio ad absurdum* of that of the well-known male author, Henry James."

Thersites was not alone in his negative opinions about women writers who engage the modernist mode, nor is such bias a bygone problem. The long career of Edna O'Brien offers a textbook case of this critical inclination. Her novel *Casualties of Peace* (1966) is written in the staccato prose of Hemingway; *Night* (1972) reworks the stream of consciousness from Joyce's "Penelope" chapter in *Ulysses*; her 1990s trilogy of novels based on real-life crises in contemporary Ireland, *House of Splendid Isolation* (1994), *Down by the River* (1997), and *Wild Decembers* (1999), invokes a laundry list of modernist technique. As she explained in a 1975 interview, for adopting such tactics "in Dublin, I have a nickname among some of the intellectuals. It's 'the bandwagon.' It's supposed to mean that I climb on bandwagons, that I'm a whore."[3] The metaphor of "the bandwagon" dismisses O'Brien's experiments, suggesting that she is uncritically following rather than setting aesthetic trends, and to call her a "whore" announces, in overtly sexual and sexist terms, that she has compromised literary experiment for material gain.[4]

These examples manifest that the portability of the stubborn mode often has provided an excuse to label the modernism found in Irish women's fiction imitative or derivative, even morally suspect. This chapter will turn that critical habit on its ear by examining four short stories published across the past century that refashion the precepts of modernist interiority to represent Irish women in their contemporary moment. Published in 1941 and set during Irish neutrality, Elizabeth Bowen's "Summer Night" questions modernism's promise to "make it new" and underscores the limitations of any literary project seeking to capture accurately the vagaries of female consciousness. In the later decades of the twentieth century, Maeve Kelly's "Morning at My Window" (1972) and Evelyn Conlon's

---

[3] John Corry, "About New York: An Irish View of City's Charms," *New York Times (1923–Current file)*; January 10, 1975; ProQuest Historical Newspapers: *The New York Times*: 25.

[4] Both terms expose a larger cultural anxiety, stoked by O'Brien's professional success and celebrity, about Irish women writers evident even now. See Dawn Miranda Sherratt-Bado, "*The New Yorker's* Edna O'Brien Profile is Sexist and Cold-Hearted," *Irish Times*, October 16, 2019, https://www.irishtimes.com/culture/books/the-new-yorker-s-edna-o-brien-profile-is-sexist-and-cold-hearted-1.4051169. See also Maureen O'Connor, *Edna O'Brien and the Art of Fiction* (Lewisburg, PA: Bucknell University Press, 2021).

"Taking Scarlet as a Real Colour or And Also, Susan ..." (1993) overtly rework the familiar strategies of modernist interiority. By speaking directly to the iconic experiments of Eliot and Henry Miller, these stories call out a masculine modernism that fails fully or even accurately to represent the contours of female subjectivity, particularly as the daily lives of Irish women were being reshaped by new professional and sexual freedoms. In the twenty-first century, June Caldwell's "SOMAT" (2015) retrofits Joyce's modernism to depict a stubborn problem that continues to shape contemporary experience—in this instance, the life-or-death issues tied to reproductive freedom.

Not simply copycats, these writers insist on the political energies emanating from the stubborn mode of modernism, energies they set loose by refashioning the movement's formal tactics, recasting its familiar themes, and calling out its vexed history. These stories insist that readers attend closely to the thoughts and experiences of female protagonists, that we labor to understand the workings of their consciousness in the face of structures (even rhetorical ones) that refuse easy access. By renovating modernist representations of interiority, these writers ask readers to bear witness to female experiences that have long been repressed, neglected, and ignored. From the vantage of the contemporary, they expose high modernism's intention to stand apart from culture and society, an ambition many Irish women writers regarded as dubious from the movement's inception, as a fallacy and a failure.

Modernist Interiority in Irish Writing

In the late nineteenth and early twentieth centuries, the widespread political, social, and cultural contributions of Irish women suggested that a newly independent Ireland, imagined in the 1916 Proclamation of the Irish Republic as serving "Irishmen and Irishwomen," might be a forerunner in the advancement of women's rights and recognition.[5] As the nation coalesced, the upending of instantiated colonial power structures offered some real promise that similar structures of power related to gender also might be challenged and reworked. But this promise was not kept. By and large, the immediate decades after high modernism saw Irish women barred from the public life of the nation that their political and cultural activism

---

[5] For accounts of women's activism during these decades, see Mary Colum, *Life and the Dream* (New York: Doubleday, 1947); James and Margaret Cousins, *We Two Together* (Madras: Ganesh & Co., 1950); R. F. Foster, *Vivid Faces: The Revolutionary Generation in Ireland, 1890–1923* (London: Penguin Press, 2015); Sinéad McCoole, *No Ordinary Women: Irish Female Activists in the Revolutionary Years, 1900–1923* (Dublin: O'Brien Press, 2003); Senia Pašeta, *Irish Nationalist Women, 1900–1918* (Cambridge: Cambridge University Press, 2013); Margaret Ward, *Unmanageable Revolutionaries: Women and Irish Nationalism* (London: Pluto Press, 1995).

32 REFASHIONING MODERNISM

had helped to create.[6] The 1922 Free State Constitution had guaranteed equal rights and equal opportunities to all citizens, but in subsequent decades, political and ecclesiastical forces sought to define women by their place in the domestic sphere. Women's public roles were heavily constrained, as evident in the Civil Service Regulation Bill (1925), the institution of the marriage bar (1932), and the Conditions of Employment Bill (1935), all of which prohibited Irish women who married from employment in the public sector, and thus from holding occupations ranging from factory work and teaching to civic administration and museum curation. The desire to render women private rather than public citizens, to define them primarily by their maternal and domestic roles, appears vividly in Article 41 of the 1937 Irish Constitution, which promises to "protect the Family" and its "inalienable and imprescriptible rights, antecedent and superior to all positive law" (41.1) and further situates women in the private realm, insisting that the state will ensure that "economic necessity" will not require them "to engage in labour to the neglect of duties in the home" (41.2).[7]

The attempts to hold Irish women to the private sphere, which lasted late into the twentieth century, affected experimental writing. In particular, the experiments of modernism seeking to depict consciousness, the private world of the individual, took on particular significance for Irish women writers who strove to represent the nuance and complexity of female experience that the state and church aspired to reduce to motherhood. Whereas modernist fiction frequently tracked the movement of women into the public sphere, Irish writers in the wake of modernism were often tracking the reverse, the movement of women into the home or convent. This trajectory helps to explain an ongoing commitment to female interiority rendered through modernist modes in Irish women's contemporary fiction. Modernism provided the formal structures necessary to represent the inchoate and incommensurable experiences of women that had been written out of public narrative—its allure stemming in part from its reputation as foreign and inherently subversive, at odds with the values of the new state. Tools including stream of consciousness, shifting points of view, and non-linear narratives allowed writers to consider the lives of women, both urban and rural, who found themselves erased from a pastoral, anti-modern national vision and isolated from meaningful roles in public life. Taking inspiration from modernist fiction that stressed the authority of a character's perceptions, that represented individuals as isolated and

---

[6] See for instance, Myrtle Hill and Margaret Ward, "Conflicting Rights: The Struggle for Female Citizenship in Northern Ireland," *Women and Citizenship in Britain and Ireland in the Twentieth Century*, eds. Esther Breitenbach and Pat Thane (London: Continuum, 2010), 113–138; Senia Pašeta, "Peace and Protest in Ireland: Women's Activism in Ireland, 1918–1937," *Diplomacy and Statecraft* 31:4 (2020): 673–696; and Maryann Gialanella Valiulis, *The Making of Inequality: Women, Power, and Gender Ideology in the Irish Free State, 1922–1937* (Dublin: Four Courts Press, 2019).

[7] Ireland, *Bunreacht Na hÉireann (Constitution of Ireland)* (Dublin: Oifig an tSoláthair, 1937).

MODERNIST INTERIORITY IN IRISH WRITING   33

unreliable, permeated by sensation and setting, these writers could draw attention to women struggling with desire, alienation, incoherence.

In form and content, modernist fiction provided the means to depict intellectual and emotional responses incompatible with the "happy, vigorous, spiritual" national ideal embodied by the "laughter of comely maidens" famously celebrated in Éamon de Valera's St. Patrick's Day radio speech from 1943, "The Ireland We Dreamed Of."[8] It is a literary-historical truism that writing of the late nineteenth and early twentieth centuries inordinately reflected and responded to changing social conditions for women, in particular to the heightened visibility and autonomy of middle-class women as they gained increased access to the public sphere. The representation of female interiority was central to early modernism and, as Tamar Katz has shown in her study of English fiction from that period, these representations were shaped by then contemporary notions of femininity and understandings of human psychology, among other social and historical factors.[9] Building on the psychological discoveries of William James and the literary experiments of Henry James and Dorothy Richardson, among others, modernists developed formal strategies and styles to depict the interior workings of the mind: extensive and detailed attention was awarded to the physical and sensory perceptions of characters, and their mental peregrinations became as important as plot, with narrative perspectives and temporalities manipulated to reflect and validate the intensities of individual experience. These tactics remained of particular value to Irish women writers, who struggled throughout the twentieth century with policies, practices, and beliefs that endeavored to stunt the liberalizing influence of modernity on female autonomy. By bringing to the page, to the public eye, the contours of female consciousness, these writers sought to maintain the energies of the activism that had informed their earliest modernist interventions.

Yet as the years marched forward, these women writers faced an evolving set of critical biases that undermined the authority of their experiments and denigrated their focus on the subjective experiences of Irish women, particularly those from the middle classes. The formal accessibility and topical moral concerns of Irish women's fiction during the mid-twentieth century resonate with the canon-shaping literary ideals espoused by F. R. and Q. D. Leavis. However, the concomitant attention of Irish women's fiction to individual subjectivity placed this body of work outside of the mid-century critical mainstream. Further, a skepticism concerning fiction and its representation of individual subjectivity

---

[8] Éamon de Valera, "The Ireland That We Dreamed Of" (1943), *Speeches and Statements by Eamon de Valera, 1917–1973*, ed. Maurice Moynihan (New York: St. Martin's Press, 1980), 466–469, 466. The adjective "comely" mistakenly replaced that of "happy" in subsequent reports of this speech: on its consequences, see Damien Keane, *Ireland and the Problem of Information: Irish Writing, Radio, Late Modernist Communication* (University Park, PA: The Pennsylvania State University Press, 2014), 2–5.

[9] Tamar Katz, *Impressionist Subjects: Gender, Interiority, and Modernist Fiction in England* (Champaign, IL: University of Illinois Press, 2000).

34   REFASHIONING MODERNISM

contributed to the devaluation of the novel by Irish critics across much of the twentieth century. In his influential study *Synge and Anglo-Irish Literature* (1931), for
example, the critic Daniel Corkery would dismiss the novel as "little else than an
impassioned study of the reaction of individual souls to their social environment"
and identify modern poetry and drama as the basis for a "normal and national"
literature.[10] His influential litmus test for worthy Irish literature required representations of "(1) The Religious Consciousness of the People; (2) Irish Nationalism;
and (3) The Land," defining consciousness as shared religious belief, rather than
individual perception.[11]

Later in the twentieth century, influential Marxist critics argued that literature
attending largely to the psychological realm was complicit with the pernicious
logics of privatization, liberal individualism, and bourgeois privilege. In Fredric
Jameson's formulation, as merely one example, a focus on the private, psychological world distracted from the realities of the alienated, market-focused present
and threatened political collectivity.[12] In contemporary Irish fiction, a sustained
engagement with modernist modes of representing female subjectivity might
threaten to replicate and condone perceptions of women as solipsistic and selfish,
rather than as attentive to and engaged with crises plaguing the external world. It
might also, as such critics have argued, risk diffusing or even refusing the external factors that shape individual psychology. But the bourgeois fantasy that the
home is a private, apolitical space does not hold up well in an Irish Republic
where the political document of the Constitution situates women in the home,
or in a Northern Ireland where Troubles-era internment saw domestic spaces vio-
lated for political ends. Admittedly, in Irish fiction employing the modernist mode,
female characters across classes may be shown to hold a diffuse or oblique engagement with their surrounding political and social conditions. Yet the complexities
and contradictions characteristic of modernist interiority, made even more visible
through insistent replication and refashioning, allow these writers to push back
against a limited and limiting tradition of female representation.

The Many Modes of Elizabeth Bowen

The twentieth century was hard on Irish women's fiction: the novel had little place
in the Revival; early twentieth-century experiments heavily tinctured with realism
were seen as outside, even explicitly at odds with, the remit of modernism; the naturalist fiction most representative of the mid-century Counter-Revival focused on

---

[10] Daniel Corkery, *Synge and Anglo-Irish Literature: A Study* (Cork: Cork University Press, 1931),
18, 3.

[11] Ibid., 19.

[12] Fredric Jameson, *The Political Unconscious: Narrative as a Socially Symbolic Act* (Ithaca: Cornell
University Press, 1981), 221–222.

a public and political world from which Irish women largely had been barred; a bias against commercial and confessional fiction in the later decades of the century undermined the authority of women's writing. But these women themselves shoulder some of the blame for their exclusion from the inventory of modernist writers. Even as they invoked its experiments, most refused to champion the logics of high modernism and deliberately placed themselves on its margins. Their early public activism helps in part to explain an ongoing resistance to codified definitions of modernism insisting that the work of art was autonomous. Iris Murdoch, for example, was notoriously dismissive of such principles that would come to define literary modernism, asserting that "The work of the great artists shows up 'art-for-art's sake' as a flimsy frivolous doctrine. Art is for life's sake ... or else it is worthless."[13] Murdoch's commitment to its strategies suggests that she, like many of her peers, understood that modernism was more than simply involuted aesthetics.

Many Irish women writers, committed to what were or would become defining characteristics of high modernism, such as formal experiment or cosmopolitanism, vehemently insisted on the social nature of the movement and its writing. In a 1944 essay for *The Bell*, Elizabeth Bowen eulogized her childhood friend Mainie Jellett, noting that their last conversation centered on the work of Dorothy Richardson, "whose strain of genius has not yet been enough recognized by the world."[14] She reads Jellett's essay "An Approach to Painting" (1942) as confirmation of her belief that "an artist's natural place is in the heart of human society" (116). She further cites Jellett's contention that the artist's "gifts are vitally important to the mental and spiritual life of that majority. Their present enforced isolation from the majority is a very serious situation and I believe it is one of the many causes which has resulted in the present chaos we live in" (117). As academic definitions of modernism coalesced, these writers refused its perceived remove from political and social concerns; instead, as Anne Fogarty has observed, their "political activism served as a spur for their experimental writing that has palpable modernist hallmarks."[15]

The place of Irish women on the outskirts of modernism was secured further by their interleaving of more popular modes and genres with the movement's innovations. Critics have ascribed Bowen's belated recuperation in part to the fact that

---

[13] Iris Murdoch, "The Sublime and the Good" (1959), *Existentialists and Mystics: Writings on Philosophy and Literature*, ed. Peter Conradi (London: Chatto, 1997), 205–220, 218. Cited in Frances White, "'Despite Herself': The Resisted Influence of Virginia Woolf on Iris Murdoch's Fiction," *Iris Murdoch Connected: Critical Essays on Her Fiction and Philosophy*, ed. Mark Luprecht (Knoxville: University of Tennessee Press, 2014), 3–28, 12.

[14] Elizabeth Bowen, "Mainie Jellett" (December 1944), *People, Places, Things: Essays by Elizabeth Bowen*, ed. Allan Hepburn (Edinburgh: Edinburgh University Press, 2008), 115–120, 116. Subsequent references parenthetical.

[15] Anne Fogarty, "Women and Modernism," *The Cambridge Companion to Irish Modernism*, ed. Joe Cleary (Cambridge: Cambridge University Press, 2014), 147–160, 148.

36 REFASHIONING MODERNISM

readers and critics were discomfited by her refusal to settle neatly in one stylistic camp: according to these assessments, her prose appears to break a contract between familiar forms and themes that appeal to readers and the less conventional properties that alienate them.[16] A critic of modernism's solipsism, Bowen was among the most astute masters of the stubborn mode, one who understood its ability to showcase hidden aspects of consciousness and productively unsettle readers. Her tactical amalgamation of familiar literary modes and genres is evident in the juxtapositions of modernism and the Gothic that characterize stories such as "The Demon Lover" (1945) and "Hand in Glove" (1952), or in the interplay of modernism with the conventions of the Big House novel in *The Last September* (1929) or the spy novel in *The Heat of the Day* (1948). For many years, her complicated relationship to modernist technique saw her prose dismissed as "an imperfect approximation" of Woolf, but thanks to a surfeit of astute scholarship, Bowen's status and stature as a modernist or late modernist writer have been secured.[17]

Bowen's long career offers salient demonstrations of how Irish women writing in the wake of modernism deployed this stubborn mode to intervene in culture. As merely one example, the short story "Summer Night" (1941), set in the Republic during the Second World War, juxtaposes various literary forms to explore the psychic effects of Irish neutrality on a group of affluent Anglo-Irish characters.[18] Told from the third-person point of view, and rich with the abstractions and symbolism characteristic of Bowen's prose, this story constellates the perspectives of its multiple characters as they respond to life under neutrality. The story opens as Emma anxiously drives away from her family—her husband (called the Major), their two daughters, and the Major's Aunt Fran—to meet her married lover, Robinson. During her journey, Robinson is visited in his country home by two locals, Justin and his deaf sister Queenie.

The scenes that compose this story, written in free indirect discourse, shift among the thoughts and experiences of the characters and are deeply influenced

---

[16] See Anne Fogarty, "'A World of Hotels and Gaols': Women Novelists and the Space of Irish Modernism, 1930–1932," *Modernist Afterlives in Irish Literature and Culture*, ed. Paige Reynolds (London: Anthem Press, 2016), 11–22, 20; Brook Miller "The Impersonal Personal: Value, Voice, and Agency in Elizabeth Bowen's Literary and Social Criticism," *Modern Fiction Studies* 53:2 (Summer 2007): 351–369; Sinéad Mooney, "Unstable Compounds: Bowen's Beckettian Affinities," *Elizabeth Bowen: New Critical Perspectives*, ed. Susan Osborn (Cork: Cork University Press, 2009), 13–33, 17; Susan Osborn, "'How to measure this unaccountable darkness between the trees': The Strange Relation of Style and Meaning in *The Last September*," *Elizabeth Bowen: New Critical Perspectives*, 34–60, 41. On the merger of high and low forms in women's fiction, see Nicola Humble, *The Feminine Middlebrow Novel, 1920s–1950s: Class, Domesticity, and Bohemianism* (Oxford: Oxford University Press, 2001).

[17] Osborn, 37. For readings of Bowen as modernist, in addition to those cited elsewhere, see Keri Walsh, "Elizabeth Bowen, Surrealist," *Éire-Ireland* 42:3–4 (Fall/Winter 2007): 126–147, and Siân White, "Spatial Politics/Poetics, Late Modernism, and Elizabeth Bowen's *The Last September*," *Genre: Forms of Discourse and Culture* 49:1 (2016): 27–50.

[18] For a reading of the story set in the context of neutrality, see Clair Wills, *That Neutral Island: A Cultural History of Ireland during the Second World War* (Cambridge: Belknap Press, 2007), 174–176.

by modernist literary impressionism. This strategy, used by James, Conrad, and Woolf in their fiction, is employed to represent, in the words of Jesse Matz, a form of perception based "not in sense, nor in thought, but in the feeling that comes between; not in the moment that passes, nor in the decision that lasts, but in the intuition that lingers."[19] Bowen's canny use of impressionism—as well as other modernist formal tactics including narrative dislocation and elliptical prose—captures the ennui, frustration, and anxiety that characterize daily life under neutrality for all of the characters. Yet even as she employs these forms, Bowen mocks any pretense that modernism remains ground-breaking. During his visit to Robinson's home, Justin muses on the effect that the Second World War has had on contemporary life and vehemently insists, "'we should have to find a new form ... A new form for thinking and feeling.'"[20] In the summer of 1940, this male character champions the modernist credo "make it new," decades after its initial iteration. In the context of the story as a whole, Justin's proposal that a "new form" might combat wartime enervation rings false—especially as Bowen deploys "old forms" to shed new light on the too-familiar problem of a European society wracked by war.

In particular, Bowen's juxtaposition of modernism and popular romance throughout "Summer Night" offers a stunning account of the complicated nature of privacy for Irish women. As the story concludes, each of the characters remains unsettled and insecure: Emma and Robinson's affair is not proceeding smoothly; Emma's household in her absence is plagued by anxiety and upset; Justin is distraught after his frustrating visit with Robinson. Queenie alone seems fine. The final paragraphs of the story depict her in her bedroom, where she retreats into a nostalgic reconstruction of a long-ago romantic encounter, a private fantasy in which she merges past and present by substituting Robinson for the suitor of her youth. This story's dense cogitation on wartime neutrality has the storybook ending of a popular romance, but one that, while temporarily consoling, is strictly imaginative and individual. By ending this way, with Queenie's impressions as she smiles at rest in her bed alone, Bowen conflates the indeterminate endings of modernist fiction and the neat closure of romantic fiction. These dissonant literary forms in play suggest their simultaneous pleasures and perils: modernism offers impressions rather than strategy; romantic fiction allows for the fulfillment of desires and ambitions, but turns inward to couples rather than outward to communities. In this story, neither modernism nor romantic fiction comes out looking like the answer. It is not, to paraphrase Justin, that we need a new form to reflect new social ills; instead, Bowen powerfully demonstrates that we can simply juxtapose old forms to stoke new meaning. Through its depictions of female

---

[19] Jesse Matz, *Literary Impressionism and Modernist Aesthetics* (Cambridge: Cambridge University Press, 2001), 1.

[20] Elizabeth Bowen, "Summer Night," *The Collected Stories of Elizabeth Bowen* (New York: Ecco Press, 1989), 583–608, 589.

38 REFASHIONING MODERNISM

interiority, "Summer Night" showcases the fault lines of privacy in Ireland and renews seemingly exhausted modes to unsettle and engage readers in a critique of contemporary culture.

Bowen's attention to the representation of female interiority drew from European traditions of realism, perhaps most obviously in her commitment to the omniscient point of view.[21] But her fiction, here and elsewhere, exposes another powerful influence—that of nineteenth-century Russian realism, with its experiments in psychological verisimilitude. Like other Irish women writers, she aligned its crucial impact on her fiction with that of modernism. In an interview on her influences, Bowen discussed the productive "shock" of American modernists on her writing—how Hemingway's "technique, seemed to us revolutionary," how Faulkner "changed our idea of fiction"—and she nods, as well, to lessons learned from continental European writers.[22] But she ends the interview by citing the importance of Russian writers, observing, "fuel was added to our creative wish as translation from Russian—Tolstoy, Turgenev, Chekhov—came pouring in."[23]

That any Irish writer might find inspiration in a Russian literary tradition focused on the representation of rural farming families, a vanishing aristocracy, and heavy drinking may seem unsurprising. Yet as noted by a surfeit of Irish women writers, Russian realism's experiments in psychological expression complemented those offered by high modernism.[24] Russian realism provided them an alternative model for experiments in the representation of female interiority, one that might work in tandem with the more overt and alienating ones provided by

[21] See Elizabeth Bowen, "Notes on Writing a Novel," *Orion: A Miscellany, No. 2*, eds. Rosamond Lehmann, C. Day Lewis, Denys Kilham Roberts (London: Nicholson and Watson, 1945), 18–29.

[22] Elizabeth Bowen, "A Matter of Inspiration," *People, Places, Things: Essays*, ed. Allen Hepburn (Edinburgh: Edinburgh University Press, 2008), 263–267, 267.

[23] Ibid.

[24] Murdoch spent her college years translating into English Pushkin, Gogol, and Lermontov, as well as reading Proust, Woolf, and "great writers" such as "Shakespeare—Tolstoy—James Joyce—for the last of whom I'm feeling an enormous enthusiasm." See Peter J. Conradi, *Iris Murdoch: A Life* (New York: Norton, 2001), 153. In 1963, as part of the European Community of Writers, Kate O'Brien made a pilgrimage to Leningrad and Moscow, where she visited Tolstoy's country estate and Chekhov's home. See Eibhear Walshe, *Kate O'Brien: A Writing Life* (Dublin: Irish Academic Press, 2006), 139. Lavin cited Chekhov as her greatest influence, followed by Willa Cather and Marguerite Duras. See Mary Lavin, interview with Tom Gullason, November 3, 1967, Mary Lavin Papers, ML/5/3 dft. A, p 21–22. Courtesy of UCD Special Collections. Edna O'Brien habitually cites the influence of Chekhov, as in David Haycock, "Edna O'Brien Talks to David Haycock about Her New Novel, *A Pagan Place* (1970)," *Conversations with Edna O'Brien*, ed. Alice Hughes Kersnowski (Jackson, MS: University Press of Mississippi, 2014), 8–12, 10. Discussing *Fox, Swallow, Scarecrow* (2007), her adaptation of Tolstoy set during the Celtic Tiger, Ní Dhuibhne explained her desire to parallel "the newness of the train in *Anna Karenina* with the newness of the Luas [rail system in Dublin]." See Ciaran Carty, "Éilís Ní Dhuibhne: A Compelling Voice in Anyone's Language," *Irish Times*, April 27, 2016. In 2014, McBride noted "her interest in Russian writers, especially Dostoevsky and Chekhov." See Susanna Rustin, "Eimear McBride: I Wanted to Give the Reader a Very Different Experience," *The Guardian*, May 16, 2014. Catherine Brady, Cláir Ní Aonghusa, Kate O'Riordan, and Maura Stanton cite Russian authors, Chekhov in particular, in Caitriona Moloney and Helen Thompson, eds., *Irish Women Writers Speak Out: Voices from the Field* (Syracuse: Syracuse University Press, 2003), while in 2016 Lucy Caldwell adapted Chekhov's *Three Sisters*, setting the play in post-ceasefire Belfast, and Marina Carr adapted Tolstoy's *Anna Karenina* for the Abbey Theatre.

Anglo-American and continental modernisms, and they appreciated its commitment to character and atmosphere over plot and setting, as well as its self-aware response to social problems. So while Frank O'Connor, Seán Ó Faoláin, and Máirtín Ó Cadhain drew from work rooted in the gritty peasant lives of Gogol and Turgenev, women writers often turned instead to writerly representations of the enervated middle and aristocratic rural classes.[25] Of additional importance, realism in Russia was not simply textual; it was identified with the theater of Aleksey Pisemsky, Alexander Ostrovsky, and Anton Chekhov, among others. The psychological realism of such drama was geared expressly for public consumption, associated with the founding of influential institutions such as the Moscow Art Theatre and the development of innovative performance theories. These Irish women writers were in tune with the possibilities made available by the public and performative displays of psychological realism, the grounds of these Russian experiments.

The Limits of Masculinist Modernism in Maeve Kelly

Throughout much of the twentieth century, the church, state, family, and market colluded to privatize the lives of Irish women, to conceal and deny experiences good, bad, and indifferent that were incommensurable with their logics: to deny skepticism and doubt, to cast aspersion on desire and self-sufficiency, to explain away suffering and isolation. As the story goes, women in the Republic were allowed a more public role only with the 1959 ascension of Seán Lemass and his government's more outward-looking social and economic policies. Throughout the century, women's groups regularly protested government restrictions, but they had little meaningful influence until the First Commission on the Status of Women was established in 1970. With the emergence of second-wave feminism, increased access to education, and Ireland's 1973 entrance into the European Economic Community (EEC), social and cultural changes followed as attitudes shifted, certain regulations were dismantled, and more women entered the workforce.[26] During these years, Irish women writers employed modernist tactics and themes in their fiction to bring to light the psychic consequences of such transformations. In the quest to reach readers, realism, with its focus on the individual in society, remained for them a useful tool, and as Bowen's work across these decades demonstrates, user-friendly literary genres such popular romance or spy fiction helped to mediate modernism's more alienating qualities but without compromising its substance. As readers increasingly became schooled in and adept at

[25] On these influences for O'Connor and Ó Faoláin, see Frank Shovlin, *The Irish Literary Periodical: 1923–1958* (Oxford: Oxford University Press, 2003), 44.

[26] See Éilís Ní Dhuibhne, introduction, *Look! It's a Woman Writer!: Irish Literary Feminisms 1970–2020*, ed. Éilís Ní Dhuibhne (Dublin: Arlen House, 2021), 13–33.

40 REFASHIONING MODERNISM

unpacking modernism, these writers more unabashedly began to deploy this mode to expose and examine the knotty contours of female interiority.

As critical constructs of modernism took hold, and feminist critique gained traction, these writers also became more explicit in their complaints about modernism's masculinist bent. In her assessment of gender bias in the Irish literary field, Anne Enright has pointed out that in reviews, "Irish men writing about women are sometimes praised for their insight, as though this was something women themselves were incapable of saying for themselves."[27] A century before, modernist women writers had called out a similar problem, identifying prejudices and citing the shortcomings of male representations of female subjectivity. For example, at the cusp of the twentieth century, in novels such as *A Drama in Muslin* (1886) and *Esther Waters* (1894), George Moore portrayed the experiences of women—often bleak, and culminating in some sort of personal tragedy tied to era's constraints on gender and sexuality—through a much-praised psychological realism that melded naturalist determinism with modernist impressionism. Yet despite his rejection of Victorian conventions and beliefs, and his celebrated formal experiments, assessments of Moore's innovations voiced by women writers suggest they regarded his representations of female interiority as necessarily limited by his gender. As Stephen Regan reports, both Virginia Woolf and Katherine Mansfield admired *Esther Waters* but deemed it lacking in emotion, with Woolf admiring the novel's provocation of a "new way of feeling and seeing" and its formal "shapeliness, style" but ultimately claiming it was "without a heroine" since Moore could not "project Esther from himself."[28]

Maeve Kelly's short story "Morning at My Window" (1972), an interior monologue written from the point of view of an Irish migrant nurse working in mid-twentieth-century London, addresses similar concerns. First published in *New Irish Writing*, the story opens with an epigraph, the final stanza of T. S. Eliot's "Morning at the Window," which reads:

> They are rattling breakfast plates in basement kitchens,
> And along the trampled edges of the street
> I am aware of the damp souls of housemaids
> Sprouting despondently at area gates.

---

[27] Anne Enright, "Call Yourself George: Gender Representation in the Irish Literary Landscape," *No Authority: Writings from the Laureateship* (Dublin: University College Dublin Press, 2019), 73–87, 85. For fiction by Irish men centered on female experience that adopts and adapts modernist forms and themes, see John McGahern's *The Barracks* (1963), Roddy Doyle's *The Woman Who Walked into Doors* (1996), or Colm Tóibín's *The Testament of Mary* (2012); Joseph O'Connor's *Ghost Light* (2010), Gavin McCrea's *Mrs. Engels* (2015), and John Banville's *Mrs. Osmond* (2017) are among those that engage modernism as a context.

[28] Virginia Woolf, "George Moore," *Death of the Moth and Other Essays* (New York: Harcourt, Brace & Co., 1942), 160, 157. Cited in Stephen Regan, "Note on the Text and Reception," George Moore, *Esther Waters*, ed. Stephen Regan (Oxford: Oxford University Press, 2012), xxxii–xxxix, xxxvii–xxxviii.

Published in *Prufrock and Other Observations* (1917), this poem as a whole reflects the popular understanding of Eliot as an architect of new forms, a pessimistic chronicler of his contemporary moment, and a misogynist. In her story, Kelly directly writes back to Eliot, having her protagonist immediately correct his representation of working women:

> Mr Eliot was aware of the damp souls of housemaids, sprouting despondently at area gates. What a pity, said I to myself, that he was not aware of the damp souls of student nurses drenched in despondency, drowned in their own misery and asphyxiated by the sadness of others. I soon shall have no soul left, or if I have it will be so narrowed and cicatriced by the scarifying experiences of my days that it will not be worth a passing thought, a line of doggerel, or a verse from a poem.[29]

The modernist mode in which the story's unnamed narrator is fluent exposes the difficulties of her demanding position as a trainee nurse, as well as articulating the complexities and contradictions of her interior life. In this story, her impressions of one morning on the hospital ward are depicted in stream of consciousness, riddled with interruptions from the outside world that are seamlessly woven into the prose. The interior monologue jockeys between external demands for her attention—in particular, those from needy patients, insulting doctors, and fellow nurses—and her internal responses. Amid these duties, she struggles not to deny or contain her unruly thoughts as they unfold, but instead to safeguard them. As she notes during her lunch break, "The mind must have chaos for creating. Out of disorder comes order. Out of order comes routine. Out of routine comes stagnation, out of stagnation comes corruption, out of corruption comes death. DON'T THINK, NURSE. NURSES ARE NOT MEANT TO THINK, ONLY TO OBEY" (34). Modernism's familiar forms make vivid her efforts to maintain a rich inner life amid the scutwork and burdensome emotional labor that define feminized professions such as nursing.[30] However, while the story's broken prose and unconventional punctuation convey the immediacy of the narrator's impressions, they also suggest that such impressions are inchoate and fragile—that the contemplative state necessary to preserve her "soul" is under assault. Amid a cascade of professional demands, exacerbated by the lack of respect she is accorded by virtually everyone whom she encounters, she struggles to sustain the internal analysis that allows her "to preserve identity" (34).

---

[29] Maeve Kelly, "Morning at My Window," *Orange Horses* (Dublin: Tramp Press, 2016), 25–34, 25. For accounts of Irish women's emigration to England, see Clair Wills, *The Best Are Leaving: Emigration and Post-War Irish Culture* (Cambridge: Cambridge University Press, 2015) and *Lovers and Strangers: An Immigrant History of Post-War Britain* (London: Allen Lane, 2017).

[30] For additional context, and a reading of Kelly's *Florrie's Girls* (1989), see Tony Murray, "Writing Irish Nurses in Britain," *A History of Irish Working-Class Writing*, ed. Michael Pierse (Cambridge: Cambridge University Press, 2017), 195–208.

42   REFASHIONING MODERNISM

A masculine modernism—embodied here by the work of Eliot—might appear in "Morning at My Window" to be a straw man, one easily dismissed thanks to its casual misrepresentation of female experience and its entire neglect of female interiority. But instead, Kelly uses Eliot to demonstrate how modernist precedents offer still relevant tools that must be recalibrated to suitably capture the contemporary experience of Irish women. From the outset, as Simon Workman notes, the switch from "the window" to "my window" in the title insists on a woman as observing subject rather than observed object.[31] Further, the story concludes with the narrator's question, "Mr Eliot, what were you doing wasting your time at area gates?" (34) She understands what this modernist poet missed by lurking on the edges of the "scarifying experiences" that constitute the lives of working women, but this image lifted from Eliot's poem offers an invitation as well by suggesting that the real work happens behind this metaphorical gate, in the murky interior of female consciousness.

Such a message has particular potency for Ireland, where a tight focus on the intricacies of female consciousness counters a legacy of flat and facile literary tropes of womanhood that, as Katherine Martin Gray points out, "have been absorbed by political discourses, which then recast them as patriotic emblems: the process has limited possible identities for Irish women to those represented in an archaic national identity."[32] The list of these stereotypes is a long one, including among them "Cathleen ni Houlihan, the winsome colleen, the *shan van vocht*, tragic Deirdre victimized by love and war, the insatiable Mother Ireland who demands the blood of her sons to maintain her wars, the spéirbhean, Maeve the warrior queen, and dark Rosaleen" (269). In Ireland, modernist experiment across genres sought to destabilize these ideals, and Grey cites in particular the depictions of complicated women in works by Synge, Joyce, and Beckett, but notes such rebuttals "were strongly resisted by traditional Irish popular taste ... [though the] belated acceptance of these twentieth-century works has undoubtedly helped to undermine the aestheticized image of Irish woman" (270). So here, another promising example of the deferred accommodation of modernist experiment helping eventually to unsettle long-standing cultural misperceptions. And yet what remains surprising, as will become evident in readings across the subsequent chapters, is the stunning durability of these tropes in women's fiction, and how powerfully and persistently they continue to affect the self-perception of female characters.

A focus on modernist interiority is not without risk for contemporary Irish women writers. In the quest to render immediacy and intensity, to insist on

---

[31] Simon Workman, "A Life of One's Own," *Orange Horses*, v–xx, xviii.

[32] Katherine Martin Gray, "The Attic LIPs: Feminist Pamphleteering for the New Ireland," *Border Crossings: Irish Women Writers and National Identity*, ed. Kathryn Kirkpatrick (Tuscaloosa: University of Alabama Press, 2000), 269–298, 269–270. For an account of such logics in Northern Irish women's fiction, see Michael L. Storey, *Representing the Troubles in Irish Short Fiction* (Washington, D.C.: The Catholic University of America Press, 2004), 179–207.

the primacy of perception in their representations of experience, these works often valorize doubt, the quality Salman Rushdie famously cited as "the basis of the great artistic movement known as Modernism."[33] High modernism, arising in concert with various discoveries that undermined faith in long-standing religious and moral precepts, often depicted characters riddled with doubt in order to help illuminate the fault lines in cultural certitudes. In Joseph Conrad's *Heart of Darkness* (1899), as merely one renowned example, Marlow's tale of his experiences in colonial Africa are marked by confusion about what he sees and encounters in the Congo, and this uncertainty provides one register of his larger skepticism about imperialism and his complicity in that project. Such modernist self-questioning percolates throughout Irish fiction, even in works written after modernism. Richard Kearney, for example, reads the self-reflexive fiction of writers such as John Banville and John McGahern as a direct response to modernism, contending "these authors share with Joyce and Beckett the basic modernist project of transforming the traditional narrative of *quest* into a critical narrative of *self-questioning*."[34]

Contemporary Irish women writers, writing from a postcolonial as well as a post-national context, clearly understand modernist doubt as a valuable device for critique, but they also must aver the reality of the particular conditions they seek to represent.[35] That is, they need to assert that institutional religion actually limits the authority of women; sexual and physical harassment and abuse in fact happen; political parties and government policies literally are dominated by male voices and masculinist logics; digital technologies really do compromise rights of privacy; universal gender equality does not exist. To render such conditions entirely subjective, to filter them entirely through one woman's consciousness, threatens to undermine their veracity in a culture that, as we have seen vividly in the era of #MeToo, often represents and too easily understands female experience as a fiction, the subjective interpretation of an imagined experience. The unreliable female narrator, for example, can be deeply problematic when accounts of female

---

[33] Cited in Laura Marcus, "The Legacies of Modernism," *The Cambridge Companion to the Modernist Novel*, ed. Morag Shiach (Cambridge: Cambridge University Press, 2007), 82–98, 90. For an overview of modernist doubt, see Ariane Mildenberg, "'Hooks' and 'Anchors': Cézanne, the Lived Perspective, and Modernist Doubt," *Understanding Merleau-Ponty, Understanding Modernism*, ed. Ariane Mildenberg (London: Bloomsbury, 2018), 59–72.

[34] Richard Kearney, *Transitions: Narratives in Modern Irish Culture* (Manchester: Manchester University Press, 1988), 83. Neil Murphy examines modernist doubt after modernism in *Irish Fiction and Postmodern Doubt: An Analysis of the Epistemological Crisis in Modern Irish Fiction* (Lewiston: Edward Mellen Press, 2004).

[35] For a reading of contemporary Irish fiction as post-nationalist, see Eve Patten, "Contemporary Irish Fiction," *The Cambridge Companion to the Irish Novel*, ed. John Wilson Foster (Cambridge: Cambridge University Press, 2006), 259–275. On modernism and female narrative authority, see Siân White, "'Stories Are a Different Kind of True': Gender and Narrative Agency in Contemporary Irish Women's Fiction," *The Edinburgh Companion to Irish Modernism*, eds. Maud Ellmann, Siân White, and Vicki Mahaffey (Edinburgh: Edinburgh University Press, 2021), 351–367.

experience past and present are already cast in doubt by a society whose structures of power might benefit from their being undermined.

As a result, in their efforts to capture the moves between inward and outward experience, these Irish women writers refuse to relinquish entirely realism's commitment to a recognizable and concrete shared reality—even as they embrace the unknowable and ephemeral individual impressions of that reality lauded by modernism. By interweaving modes, they engage others more readily and more broadly in their depictions of individual experience, seeking witnesses both inside and outside of the text. As well, these writers, concerned that modernist solipsism threatens an ethical dead-end for women, and channeling the awareness of audience that characterized early modernist practice in Ireland, often craft an interior monologue that gestures to the outside world, a point noted by Derek Attridge and Susan Cahill.[36] This is one of many tactics seeking to make outsiders, fictional characters within the text as well as readers outside of it, alert to and complicit in the individual peregrinations, observations, and revelations recorded in the narrative. Another is the frequent presence of a female narrator, sometimes a writer herself, who is conscious of her authority in constructing and sharing her story, who acknowledges the doubt and instability in her narrative while insisting simultaneously on the veracity of the experiences and emotions she recounts. Such gestures suggest a melding of the public address that characterized early twentieth-century Irish women's modernism with the meta-textuality of postmodernism in order to produce a discerning interiority highly aware of an audience. This ambiguous divide separating private consciousness from public record allows these characters to appear to operate both inside and outside of history.

Voicing Female Sexuality in Evelyn Conlon

In the wake of high modernism, Irish women's fiction has kept a keen eye trained on female interiority, consistently employing the movement's familiar themes and experiments in its representations of consciousness. But such a commitment has not always met with warm embrace, particularly when depicting sexual matters, as formal and informal censorship endeavored to stunt more transgressive representations of the private lives and thoughts of women. In Ireland, the practices of the Committee on Evil Literature, established in 1926, and the 1929 Censorship of Publications Act, were intended to prohibit access to literature that might threaten a corrupting foreign influence, undermine social cohesion, and trouble accepted standards of morality. Notably, Radclyffe Hall's *The Well of Loneliness*

---

[36] Derek Attridge, "Foreword," *Joycean Legacies*, ed. Martha Carpentier (London: Palgrave, 2015), vii–xx, xv; Susan Cahill, "Post-Millennial Irish Fiction," *The Oxford Handbook of Modern Irish Fiction*, ed. Liam Harte (Oxford: Oxford University Press, 2020), 603–619, 611–612.

(1928) and studies by Margaret Sanger and Marie Stopes were among the first books banned in Ireland, revealing that the censorship board targeted texts by women that expanded perceptions of gender and sexuality, and that now are widely understood as formative to modernism.[37] But even as the strict censorship of literature became increasingly uncommon following the Censorship of Publications Act (1967), Graham Masterson's guide *How to Drive Your Man Wild in Bed* (1976) was banned in 1985, which suggests the state's lingering attempts to control the erotic lives of its citizens.[38]

Evelyn Conlon's "Taking Scarlet as a Real Colour or And Also, Susan ..." (1993) was published in a moment in which Irish women were gaining belated access to certain freedoms they previously had been denied. In the late twentieth century, many of the long-standing laws that buttressed the patriarchal fantasy of spatial privacy in Ireland began to fall, prompted in part by the Republic's 1973 entrance into the European Economic Community. Conlon's story tacitly acknowledges these changes as well as the relatively new authority awarded to Irish women in managing private concerns related to female sexuality and reproduction.[39] In it, modernist form acknowledges and accommodates such political and cultural transformations, using fragmentation and indeterminacy to showcase their uneven outcomes for individuals. The seemingly outdated quality of modernism here provides a reminder of the ways that female autonomy has presented a stubborn problem for conceptions of Irish citizenship and subjecthood. The female narrator's messy, quasi-public articulation of her thoughts, feelings, and experiences reflects the visible breakdown of dated policies and practices seeking to contain and shame women for their sexual proclivities and activities.

Written in a single sustained paragraph, this short story set in 1990s Dublin captures one side of a conversation between two women in a bar. Delivered by the unnamed female narrator to an interlocutor named Susan, the associative first-person monologue ranges across an array of topics from the speaker's enthusiasm for candles to her assessment of journalism, but centers mostly on the topics of literature and sex. Throughout, the speaker criticizes male writers for their inability to pay attention, to see beneath the surface of female experience. As she observes,

---

[37] Among the authors and books considered in this study, several were banned, including Kate O'Brien's *The Land of Spices* in 1941 for its reference to male homosexuality, and Edna O'Brien's *The Country Girls* in 1960 for its representations of female sexuality. Yet only printed material fell under the edict of the Censorship of Publications Act, so a writer such as Maura Laverty, whose novels were banned in the 1940s, could stage her progressive plays at Dublin's Gate Theatre.

[38] See Conor Gallagher, "Publications on Abortion Coming Off Banned Books List," *Irish Times*, July 19, 2019, https://www.irishtimes.com/news/health/publications-on-abortion-coming-off-banned-books-list-1.3960794.

[39] These include the outcomes of "McGee vs. Attorney General" (1973) and "Attorney General vs. X" (1992) that advanced reproductive rights in Ireland, as well as a 1983 referendum that secured, by 66.9% of the vote, the Eighth Amendment of the Irish Constitution equating the right to life for a woman and her unborn child, but resulted in the defeat of referenda seeking further to restrict abortion rights. For additional context, see Diarmaid Ferriter, *Occasions of Sin: Sex and Society in Modern Ireland* (London: Profile Books, 2009).

46 REFASHIONING MODERNISM

"The books made us saints, cheap, plastic saints with lack of love, or they called us scarlet, but they didn't see it as a real colour. No Irish book ever told me about love ...."[40] Written during a period of changing social values in Ireland, signaled in part by the 1990 election of Mary Robinson as the county's first female president, the story takes the speaker's private insights and renders them public speech, in part to advance a relatively straightforward feminist message that the provocative content of female consciousness can be articulated best by women.

"Taking Scarlet as a Real Colour or And Also, Susan ..." offers a textbook case of the stubborn mode used to display stubborn problems, among them the misrepresentation of female sexuality. This story reworks the animated stream of consciousness found in Joyce's "Penelope" chapter and similarly is rife with shocking sexual terms, controversial views on morality, and detailed memories of the speaker's erotic encounters. But outside of her bedroom, Conlon's character vocalizes and shares her experience in a public setting with a female confidant who is awake and responsive, if wary of her companion's volubility. The intersubjectivity conveyed through narrative form in Bowen and Kelly is represented here through the narrator's account of a conversation in which her musings are articulated and made known to another. Thus, a more apposite modernist forbear might be the latter portion of "A Game of Chess" from Eliot's *The Waste Land* (1922), which likewise reconstructs one side of a conversation shared between two women in a pub. In that scene, Eliot's speaker relates to her silent companion a conversation shared with a third woman named Lil, whose husband has recently returned home from the First World War. Here, Eliot grants the microphone to a female speaker, but she uses it to recapitulate and reinforce familiar structures of power that restrict and harm women: the speaker reports warning Lil to get false teeth to improve her appearance and thus to secure her husband's fidelity, she divulges that Lil has been ravaged by an abortifacient, she embodies a competitive rather than cooperative ethos. Ranging across issues tied to sexuality, this monologue reflects Eliot's larger indictment of the deleterious effects of the biological, the social, and the technological on modern life.

Not simply a renovation of familiar high modernist texts written by men, Conlon's story also writes back to a tradition of Irish women's fiction that itself writes back to modernism. It suggestively revises Mary Lavin's short story "Sarah" (1943), which depicts the tragic tale of its titular protagonist, an unwed mother and domestic worker who dies after being cast out of her home as retribution for her perceived sexual and moral transgressions. In Conlon's story, the protagonist offers a riposte

---

[40] Evelyn Conlon, "Taking Scarlet as a Real Colour or And Also, Susan ...," *Telling: New and Selected Stories* (Belfast: Blackstaff Press, 2000), 45–57, 54. Subsequent references parenthetical. This story is the second in a trilogy that includes "Susan—Did You Hear ..." (1987) and "Furthermore, Susan" (2000). On Conlon, see M. Teresa Caneda-Cabrera, ed., *Telling Truths: Evelyn Conlon and the Task of Writing* (Oxford: Peter Lang, 2023).

to this oppressive but familiar cultural dynamic. She recalls the story of a prostitute named Gladys, with "rakes of children ... [who] looked like the shopkeepers, the farmers, the labourers, the van drivers" (46). However, unlike that of Sarah, Gladys's story ends happily, after the men of the community come to fear exposure and "stopped turning up, but it was great for Gladys because they kept paying her, to keep her mouth shut, so she always had enough money to rear their children" (47). Gladys has the authority to manage her secrets and use them to improve her fate and that of her children.

Like many characters in Irish women's contemporary fiction, Conlon's narrator is an avid reader, but one who believes that books have failed her. She inaugurates the story by announcing, "I'll tell you what it says in books, Susan," then offers a record of her insights, observations, and personal experience as a counter-narrative to what she perceives as the great failure of literature, its inaccurate portrayal of women (45). As she tells Susan, "I still think of those books as the letters of a lover who turned out to be a fraud. What they didn't say about us is bad enough until you find out what they did say; yet, bad as that is, there is nothing worse than what they didn't say" (48). She then explicitly calls out modernism's masculinist bias. Near the close of the story, the speaker launches into the contents of a letter she once imagined writing directly to the American writer Henry Miller, asking, "Mr Miller, why is it that you cannot bear us to enjoy it as much, or even worse, more than you?" (55) Banned in the United States for obscenity, Miller's formally experimental novels such as *Tropic of Cancer* (1934) and *Tropic of Capricorn* (1939) represented for many the transgressive possibilities of experimental form in their representation of sexuality. But here, through her list of Miller's evident failures to depict accurately female desire, Conlon's speaker reveals his experiments to be neither inherently progressive, nor revolutionary in their insights.

Despite its trenchant feminist critique, Conlon's story is no full-throated celebration of the narrator's observations, no sure-footed assertion that representations of female interiority have a secure platform in the late twentieth century. An authoritative female speaker gives immediate and unfiltered voice to her insights and experiences and as such makes visible the vagaries of female consciousness— but in the form of a lecture to which the silent Susan must bear witness.[41] The narrative captures only the speaker's words, though she alludes to Susan's questions and comments, and she repeats Susan's name throughout her monologue; this repetition serves as a form of grounding, roping Susan's attention to the narrative and reminding readers of the presence of an interlocutor. Not only does the speaker doubt the attention of her audience amid these shocking revelations, she

---

[41] In one account of this narrative as "political monologue," Conlon identifies Susan as "the imaginary woman we need to address." See Caitriona Moloney, interview, "Evelyn Conlon," *Irish Women Writers Speak Out*, 17–29, 23.

48 REFASHIONING MODERNISM

suspects she would not receive full credit for her literary imagination if she were to write. She imagines authoring a book in which she admits, "I have slain my children, sent my sons to war, peed in a cup in a guesthouse ... made love with a dog" (49). She understands, as Susan warns, she'd need to be "careful" with such a tale. But she also understands its value: "There are people in books who take their tragedies out to have a look at them, or they take their hearts out to throw them away because of the trouble they've caused. Me? I'd take the whole lot out just to have a peep and if it turned into a gawk ... well. Nothing wrong with a genuine gawk as long as you don't start looking for answers" (50).

The narrator's imagined mode of writing here resonates with Karen Zumhagen-Yekplé's notion of the modernist "counter-epiphany" in *Ulysses*, in which Joyce's "*counter-epiphanic* aesthetic strategies ... are ultimately directed not at grasping after fleeting epiphanic insights but at getting readers to make a more lasting change, one that depends on imaginatively considering what it would be like to step back from our questions and let go of our quests for answers."[42] Comfortable with exposure and indeterminacy, and aware that others might call into question her writerly imagination, the narrator announces she nonetheless can risk sharing the provocative intimacies of her story with a larger audience. And yet, as Conlon makes clear, obdurate limitations for Irish women who imagine such risks remain—in part because, in this short story, the female narrator's book and even her letter to Miller remain unwritten and unpublished and unread. As represented in Conlon's reworking of modernism, the epiphany thinks it can solve the stubborn problem, but the counter-epiphany knows better.

Joyce's Afterlife

As Conlon's story reveals, Joyce's modernism represents one strain vividly apparent in Irish women's contemporary writing, another instance of formal tactics that linger well past their perceived prime or seeming relevance. Accounts of his influence are easy enough to find. Elizabeth Bowen eulogized his work in an essay for *The Bell* entitled "James Joyce" (1941), and Mary Colum with her husband Padraic Colum wrote the study *Our Friend James Joyce* (1958). Edna O'Brien, who cites him as her formative inspiration, has written a short biography entitled *James Joyce* (1999) for the Penguin Lives series, and regularly muses on his writing in critical introductions and press articles, while Anne Enright had asserted "Joyce made everything possible."[43] His lasting impact on women's fiction is evident:

---

[42] Karen Zumhagen-Yekplé, *A Different Order of Difficulty: Literature after Wittgenstein* (Chicago: University of Chicago Press, 2020), 170.

[43] David Mehegan, "For This Writer, Identity Is Subject to Change," *Boston Globe*, February 27, 2008, http://archive.boston.com/ae/books/articles/2008/02/27/for_this_writer_identity_is_subject_to_change/?page=2.

JOYCE'S AFTERLIFE   49

Kate O'Brien, Mary Lavin, and Éilís Ní Dhuibhne have reworked his notion of the epiphany[44]; Edna O'Brien and Deirdre Madden have authored stream-of-consciousness novels with protagonists that clearly owe a debt to Molly Bloom (and are discussed in Chapter Three); and Irish women writers have invoked and adapted the "bird girl" scene from *A Portrait of the Artist as a Young Man* (1916) in their novels.[45] His shadow looms large over other genres of contemporary writing as well, with Mary Manning having adapted his *Finnegans Wake* (1955) and "Ivy Day in the Committee Room" (1966) for the stage, and Eavan Boland having claimed Joyce as a "presence" in her poetry due to her instinctive awareness of his innovations.[46] Even now, the capacity of his work to reflect and refract the present moment is apparent in edited collections that invite writers to reimagine his stories, such as Oona Frawley's *New Dubliners* (2005) and Thomas Morris's *Dubliners 100* (2014), or in novels that deliberately recapitulate aspects of *Ulysses*, such as Mary Costello's *The River Capture* (2019), or reimagine his biography, such as Nuala O'Connor's *Nora: A Love Story of Nora and James Joyce* (2021) and Mary Morrissy's *Penelope Unbound* (2023), or in public lectures that celebrate his influence.[47] These demonstrate the unique traction of Joyce's innovations and provocatively suggest how contemporary themes continue to be well represented through them—a fitting tribute, given his own use of historical sources ranging from classical myth to erotic potboilers.

Joyce is necessarily a figure with whom contemporary Irish women writers engage, whether it is Eimear McBride labeling him "my hero," or Claire-Louise Bennett refusing him as an influence.[48] For over a century, his modernism has provided them a variety of useful tools. Joyce gave enormous credibility to

[44] On O'Brien and the epiphany, see Mary Breen, "Something Understood?: Kate O'Brien and *The Land of Spices*," *Ordinary People Dancing*, ed. Eibhear Walshe (Cork: Cork UP, 1993), 167–190; on Lavin, see Anne Fogarty, "Discontinuities: *Tales from Bective Bridge* and the Modernist Short Story Tradition," *Mary Lavin*, ed. Elke D'hoker (Dublin: Irish Academic Press, 2013), 49–64; on Ní Dhuibhne, see Carty.

[45] Jane Elizabeth Dougherty, "'Never Tear the Linnet from the Leaf': The Feminist Intertextuality of Edna O'Brien's *Down by the River*," *Frontiers: A Journal of Women Studies* 31:3 (2010): 77–102; Paige Reynolds, "Bird Girls: Modernism and Sexual Ethics in Contemporary Irish Fiction," *Modernism and Close Reading*, ed. David James (Oxford: Oxford University Press, 2020), 173–190.

[46] Eavan Boland, "James Joyce: The Mystery of Influence," *Transcultural Joyce*, ed. Karen Lawrence (Cambridge: Cambridge University Press, 1998), 11–20, 13.

[47] See Eimear McBride, "Joyce, Joy, and Enjoying *Ulysses* Still," *Irish Times*, December 17, 2022, https://www.irishtimes.com/culture/books/2022/12/17/eimear-mcbride-joyce-joy-and-enjoying-ulysses-still/; and Sally Rooney, "Misreading *Ulysses*," *The Paris Review*, December 7, 2022, https://www.theparisreview.org/blog/2022/12/07/misreading-ulysses/.

[48] Eimear McBride, "My Hero: Eimear McBride on James Joyce," *The Guardian*, June 6, 2014, https://www.theguardian.com/books/2014/jun/06/my-hero-eimear-mcbride-james-joyce; Emma Nutall, "Claire-Louise Bennett on Debut Collection, *Pond*," *The Skinny*, November 20, 2015, https://www.theskinny.co.uk/books/features/claire-louise-bennett-pond-fitzcarraldo-stinging-fly. For writers such as these, Barry McCrea regards Joyce's traction as one manifestation of the longer influence of the language question in "The Novel in Ireland and the Language Question: Joyce's Complex Legacy," *Logos: A Journal of Modern Society and Culture* (2022), https://logosjournal.com/2022/the-novel-in-ireland-and-the-language-question-joyces-complex-legacy/.

50 REFASHIONING MODERNISM

representations of the everyday experience of Irish men and women, particularly those of the middle classes. This focus, which had appeared throughout Irish women's realist fiction of the nineteenth century, was suddenly, with Joyce, situated in the white-hot nucleus of high modernism. In a 1969 lecture given to a group of young painters, Kate O'Brien cited Joyce as "someone with whom you will have reckon," celebrating his use of stubborn modes, as when she praises the modernist *Ulysses* for "its cold and deadly realism ... miles ahead of any of the avant garde stuff nowadays coming out of France and England."[49] His writing is, as she notes, "instructive indeed for anyone who hopes to write a novel, or even a short story, to observe how Joyce can set down the dullest trivialities of an impoverished life—and not once or twice, but making of them his whole theme ... and make you see them, and hold them, in a cold kind of light that immortalises them" (9). The situatedness of his experimental fiction, which details the Dublin quotidian down to the trash floating in the Liffey, the lemon soap on its store shelves, the lace on Molly's underwear, set the pace for an ongoing commitment to rendering for international readers the sited and intimate specifics of ordinary Irish life.

Joyce's distinctive brand of modernism had, and has, much to offer Irish women writers in his wake. What was once regarded as too private, too trivial, too outside the ambit of the national, when filtered through his ratified experiments, finally could be perceived by critics and readers as more substantial and admirable. He provided a productive, and critically venerated, compromise between realism's telling and modernism's showing, realism's forward-moving plots and modernism's fluctuations driven by consciousness. There were other important lessons made available: Molly Bloom's extreme interior monologue offered new representational strategies to give voice to the complexity of Irish female experience; his fearless depiction of female sexuality offered a template from which to draw; his outsider status and sense of alienation resonated with Irish women placed on the margins of their culture; his scandalous reputation served as a magnet for public attention, drawing notice even from those unable to parse his fiction.[50]

These characteristics would be invaluable to those seeking to showcase the intricacies of female consciousness. As Seamus Deane has asserted, *Ulysses* is a novel that makes "the activity of thought ... the central and the determining influence on the form."[51] But the repeated recapitulation and revision of Joyce's formal experiments, and their escalated familiarity to readers, also help to illuminate what might

---

[49] Kate O'Brien, "James Joyce and *Ulysses*," October 1, 1969, typescript of speech given at Canterbury College of Art (Box 4, Folder 6D), 21 pp., 1, 6. Courtesy Charles Deering McCormick Library of Special Collections and University Archives, Northwestern University Libraries.

[50] On Joyce's changing reception, see Kathleen McCormick, "Reproducing Molly Bloom: A Revisionist History of the Reception of 'Penelope,' 1922–1970," *Molly Blooms: A Polylogue on "Penelope" and Cultural Studies*, ed. Richard Pearce (Madison: University of Wisconsin Press, 1994), 17–39.

[51] Seamus Deane, *Celtic Revivals: Essays in Modern Irish Literature, 1880–1980* (London: Faber & Faber, 1985), 76.

be perceived, and has been perceived by some critics, as certain limitations in his representations of women. Much of his work centers on the social world of men, placing women on its outskirts. Even as they command male attention, these women remain ciphers, figures who often are lost in their thoughts such as Gretta observed from a distance by her husband Gabriel, or Molly silently reviewing the events of her life as her husband Leopold sleeps. As Edna O'Brien once noted of Anna Livia Plurabelle, "We do not get inside her mind or know the registers of her disenchantments as she passes from youth to age, except for a rare and piercing lamentation—'Is there one who understands me?'"[52] In Joyce's fiction, the limitations of male characters are often revealed by his pinpointing their inability to fully recognize and understand the complex interior lives of women. It seems such inadequacies, as much as Joyce's inventions, provide fodder for Irish women writers in their depictions of female experience.

As a result of his profound influence, and our desire to have an easy referent for Irish experimentation, Joyce has overshadowed other modernist influences on Irish women's writing, influences that this and subsequent chapters tease out. However, an affiliation with Joyce provides these writers a valuable shorthand for marketing, as well as a measure of aesthetic credibility and intellectual gravitas that might counter condescending or dismissive attitudes toward their experimental fiction.[53] The jackets of books evidencing even a hint of high modernism are spattered with quotes that celebrate their taking "a cool nod at Joyce" (as seen in a blurb for Anakana Schofield's 2012 novel *Malarky*) or being "like Joyce's *Dubliners*" (as seen on Lucy Caldwell's 2016 collection *Multitudes*). Rare is the experimental women's novel that is not suggestively associated with Joyce in book reviews or interviews, and literary critics regularly note the influence of his themes and structures on Irish women's writing. A *New Yorker* profile of Sally Rooney, for example, paralleled the female protagonists Frances and Bobbi from *Conversations with Friends* (2017) with Stephen and Cranly from *A Portrait of the Artist as a Young Man*, asserting "Capitalism is to Rooney's young women what Catholicism was to Joyce's young men, a rotten national faith to contend with."[54] Joyce's ongoing influence even surfaces on occasion in the narratives themselves, as in

---

[52] Edna O'Brien, "How James Joyce's Anna Livia Plurabelle Shook the Literary World," *The Guardian*, January 27, 2017, https://www.theguardian.com/books/2017/jan/27/edna-obrien-how-james-joyces-anna-livia-plurabelle-shook-the-literary-world.

[53] In her study of Eimear McBride's fiction, Ruth Gilligan argues that an association with the "deceased males" of high modernism undermines the "unique talent" of experimental women writers and risks their continued neglect, a claim this study as well as recent work by Carey Mickalites and Doug Battersby refutes. See Ruth Gilligan, "Eimear McBride's Ireland: A Case for Periodisation and the Dangers of Marketing Modernism," *English Studies* 99:7 (2018): 775–792; Carey Mickalites, *Contemporary Fiction, Celebrity Culture, and the Market for Modernism: Fictions of Celebrity* (London: Bloomsbury, 2022), 163–175; and Doug Battersby, *Troubling Late Modernism: Ethics, Feeling, and the Novel Form* (Oxford: Oxford University Press, 2022), 217–251.

[54] Alexandra Schwartz, "A New Kind of Adultery Novel," *New Yorker*, July 24, 2017, https://www.newyorker.com/magazine/2017/07/31/a-new-kind-of-adultery-novel.

52 REFASHIONING MODERNISM

Rooney's *Beautiful World, Where Are You*, when Alice is interviewed at a literary festival in Rome and asked "questions about feminism, sexuality, the work of James Joyce, the role of the Catholic Church in Irish cultural life," or when Eva Kenny's protagonist in "Christmas Story" (2022) shares her interpretation of "The Dead" while she and her Tinder match stroll the streets of Covid-era Dublin.[55]

This provocative (and generally complimentary) association also can be a burden to women seeking a new idiom. As a result, even a Joyce enthusiast like McBride can give voice to an ambivalence about his forms: "The Joyce thing has become problematic. Like many, or most, Irish writers, Joyce has been a big influence, partly because I've never been particularly interested in social realism. Reading *Ulysses* was like someone opening the gate and saying: if you have the virtuosity, there is nothing you cannot do with this form. I think Joyce's barbarism gave me the chutzpah to try. But it was never about imitating him. I remember sitting down to write *Girl* and feeling Joyce was on the outside. He and I are looking for different things. His work is about the extension of the human into the universe, mine is about human vulnerability and fallibility."[56] So while clearly engaged with modernism, that of Joyce as well as others, these writers nonetheless refuse to embrace the mode as a pat categorization.

Modernism Now for June Caldwell

Contemporary fiction written in the modernist mode and focused on female interiority offers an alternative narrative to reductive paradigms of Irish womanhood, one that might normalize psychic complexity and sanction unconventional manifestations of privacy. Such an intention underscores the activism hard-wired into Irish women's use of modernism across more than a century. Their linking of form and ethics chimes with Derek Attridge's claims for J. M. Coetzee's fiction as a response to contemporary historical and national conditions. Attridge contends that political exigencies in late twentieth-century South Africa triggered a "suspicion of anything appearing hermetic, self-referential, formally inventive, or otherwise distant from the canons and procedures of the realist tradition."[57] Literature was, in that particular historical moment, in that particular country, expected to be interventionist, to speak directly and immediately to the political context, and

---

[55] Sally Rooney, *Beautiful World, Where Are You* (New York: Farrar, Straus and Giroux, 2021), 95; Eva Kenny, "Christmas Story," *Irish Times*, December 27, 2022, https://www.irishtimes.com/culture/books/2022/12/27/christmas-story-a-new-story-by-eva-kenny/.

[56] Kate Kellaway, "Eimear McBride: Writing is Painful—but It's the Closest You Can Get to Joy," *The Observer*, August 28, 2016, https://www.theguardian.com/books/2016/aug/28/eimer-mcbride-interview-lesser-bohemians-writing-never-stops-being-painful.

[57] Derek Attridge, *J. M. Coetzee and the Ethics of Reading* (Chicago: University of Chicago Press, 2004), 1.

these expectations shaped the form of the novel. According to Attridge, only after the end of formal apartheid and the establishment of a democratic government in 1994 could readers welcome South African fiction that veered from realism. In contrast, Joyce has provided writers in Ireland a canonical and thus navigable route to experimentalism in fiction, but one supple and capacious enough to adjust to contemporary conditions—one that can dodge the readerly suspicion Attridge identified in the South African literary tradition.

Nonetheless, critics and readers only embraced the modernist mode in Irish women's fiction in the twenty-first century after the island's material and economic conditions had transformed. Since the advent of the twentieth century, Irish social history has appeared to advance erratically—the century's early years filled with political insurrections and progressive gender politics whose promise was stymied by regressive policies at a post-war moment that witnessed other European countries embrace, albeit awkwardly and unevenly, a forward-looking modernity. A rush of socially progressive change in the Republic was compressed into the close of the twentieth century and dawn of the twenty-first. In 1979, contraception became legal to married couples; in 1985, the importation of condoms was decriminalized; in 1993, homosexuality was decriminalized; in 1996, divorce was legalized. In 2015, Ireland became the first country to legalize same-sex marriage by popular vote, and a constitutional ban on abortion put in place in 1983 was jettisoned, again by a referendum, in 2018. In concert with these transformations, shocking abuses enabled and concealed by the Catholic Church came to public notice, and a large swath of the population began to question and even spurn the religious beliefs and practices that had ordered Irish life for centuries.

During the twentieth century, Bowen's "Summer Night" used the stubborn mode to shed new light on Irish neutrality, Kelly's "Morning at My Window" to examine migrant Irish women's labor, and Conlon's "Taking Scarlet as a Real Colour or And Also, Susan ..." to reflect the altered social norms and moral codes of Ireland under the European Union. Irish women's writing in the twenty-first century similarly employs now familiar experiments to consider and represent cultural transformations. In a political context, the "Repeal the Eighth" movement successfully marshaled support for the 2018 revocation of the Irish Constitution's Eighth Amendment, which effectively prohibited abortion. This campaign consolidated artists, activists, and intellectuals, among many others, in an endeavor to render this medical procedure, one often kept secret for reasons both legal and personal, more accessible and acceptable. During Repeal, Irish women writers advocated abortion rights in fora ranging from public demonstrations to literary anthologies—a tactic in tune with the social and political activism of the early twentieth-century avant-garde. At the 2016 "Theatre of Change" symposium held on the stage of the Abbey Theatre, for instance, the Irish academic Susan Cahill described her own experience obtaining an abortion, an intimately

54 REFASHIONING MODERNISM

personal narrative that was published in the *Irish Times* as well as posted on YouTube.[58] In the twenty-first century, such representations of female experience once found largely in the pages of fiction could surface in the confessional writing and performances of Irish women easily accessed online by international audiences.

As the intimacies of women's private lives have become more readily public, modernism has been adapted to expose those aspects of experience that might otherwise elude readers and audiences while still insisting on their complexities. During Repeal, experimental fiction provided a valuable complement to more comprehensible representations of abortion restrictions and their consequences. In their account of women's writing after the Celtic Tiger, Claire Bracken and Tara Harney-Mahajan note that "experimentation is a marked feature of contemporary women's writing, where it is deployed to take on themes of immense social importance—implicating, in particular, gendered bodies."[59] They cite, as one example, the work of June Caldwell, whose short story "SOMAT" (2015) describes, from first-person point of view of a fetus, the experience of a mother artificially kept alive so that her baby might be harvested. A close look at "SOMAT" brings to light the ethical implications of the resurgence of modernism in twenty-first-century Irish women's fiction. A critique of the Eighth Amendment, and its equating of the life of the mother and her unborn child, this story is written in the modernist mode. Its stream-of-consciousness narrative compresses fragmented sentences, inverts syntax, and juxtaposes scraps of unindicated dialogue, leaving the reader to piece together events and perspectives. With its staccato prose and unsettlingly graphic details, the story refuses the easy sympathetic identification that might be stimulated by gentler considerations of reproductive rights, such as those found in Maeve Binchy's *Light a Penny Candle* (1982) or Marian Keyes's *The Break* (2017). Modernism here underscores a contradiction of the contemporary moment. Certain topics, once taboo, are now candidly described and discussed, but nevertheless continue to elude full understanding. As such, modernism invoked well after its debut—with its deliberate obfuscations and its attendant interpretive difficulties still in place—continues to remind us of the ineluctable aspects of human experience.

"SOMAT" bears the hallmarks not only of modernist form, but also of the activism that infused the movement's early years in Ireland. When this story was first published, the topic of abortion in Ireland dominated public debate, and Caldwell drew her story from actual accounts of women who were kept on life support to sustain the life of a fetus. As she noted, "I wanted to write a story that reflected

---

[58] Susan Cahill, "My Abortion Was Not Remotely Traumatic," *Irish Times*, February 21, 2016, http://www.irishtimes.com/life-and-style/people/susan-cahill-my-abortion-was-not-remotely-traumatic-i-have-no-regrets-1.2542740.

[59] Claire Bracken and Tara Harney-Mahajan, "A Continuum of Irish Women's Writing: Reflections on the Post-Celtic Tiger Era," *LIT: Literature Interpretation Theory* 28:1 (January 2017): 1–12, 8.

the trajectory of horror and I felt that it was best told from the fetus's perspective, to highlight the hideousness. After spending years in journalism and being restricted on what you could say and how you could say it, I firmly believe that fiction can be more effective, more politicised."[60] The popularity of this story, which was named a "favourite" in *The Sunday Times*, suggests that readers of Irish fiction in 2015 were prepared for a more experimental representation of contemporary events, just as Attridge found in South Africa following apartheid.[61] The ethical implications of Caldwell's modernist experiment are suggestive. Because the plot reflects and reworks real-life events, her invocation of modernism's formal complications might provide a prophylactic against the more insidious aspects of contemporary public narrative, which in its quest to communicate to broad audiences, threatens to flatten representations of female experience or to sensationalize their suffering as "clickbait."

From the outset, the story's title can be interpreted as revivifying modernist tactics thanks to its unconventional typography, its reference to classical tradition, and its fragmentation: "SOMAT" comes from the Greek word "soma," meaning body. Generally used in English as a prefix, it is the fragment of a whole. Even in its more common usage, as in the word somatic, which means related to the body rather than the mind, the root "soma" is merely a part of the word, one that cannot stand alone. This story is rife with parts that are dependent but cannot function appropriately either autonomously or mutually. Most obviously, the mother is a body without a functioning brain, and the fetus must depend on her body to survive to birth. As well, the medical system, church, and state collude to make a decision about the welfare of the mother and fetus without respect for the wishes of the family. The fetus alone gives dispassionate voice to the jarring facts of the mother's situation, noting, "She does not look good ... a piece of mould growing from her head that looks like a clouded wedding bouquet."[62] Here, in light of the title's Greek root, a potential perversion of the mythic origins of Athena, the goddess of wisdom born from the head of Zeus, reminding readers by contrast of the realities of gestation for the human body through the modernist tricks of classical allusion and imagery calculated to shock.

The events of Caldwell's plot become clear only as the in-utero narrator, who opens the story by announcing "I was a controversial case," patches together bits

---

[60] Catherine Dunne, interview with June Caldwell, May 24, 2017, https://www.catherinedunne author.com/june-caldwell-room-little-darker-interview/.

[61] Katy Hayes, "Women's Writes," review of Sinéad Gleeson, *The Long Gaze Back: An Anthology of Irish Women Writers, The Sunday Times*, September 6, 2015, https://www.thetimes.co.uk/article/womens-writes-znb8gnn9czb. The story later appeared in Caldwell's collection *Room Little Darker*, which was chosen as the March 2018 "book club" selection by the *Irish Times*. See https://www.irishtimes.com/culture/books/room-little-darker-by-june-caldwell-is-march-s-irish-times-book-club-choice-1.3412763.

[62] June Caldwell, "SOMAT," *Room Little Darker* (Dublin: New Island Books, 2017), 81–92, 86. Subsequent references parenthetical.

56 REFASHIONING MODERNISM

of discussions overheard and perceptions understood from the outside world (83). The interior monologue is interspersed with fragments of dialogue recounting various positions on the case articulated by family members, doctors, nurses, hospital administrators, politicians, the church, and the press. Amid the debates about the fate of mother and fetus, which unfold outside and around the maternal body, the narrative voice aggressively draws attention to the protagonists' interiority. By doing so, "SOMAT" suggests persistent limitations not only for female authority but also for female expression in Ireland, even today. Voiced in utero, a male point of view captures and articulates the mother's experience, and she is represented largely through recapitulated words of comfort directed to her unborn child, her voice kept alive but stuck in a traditional maternal register. The mother, whose body is at the center of this debate, lacks the authority, even in fiction, to claim and convey her own story. Here, as so often in the works studied across this book, form follows function: this is the account of an Ireland that, even in the twenty-first century, relies on male voices to communicate, and patriarchal perspectives to determine, female experience. In addition, as the story critiques the system that fails to protect the mother, by awarding full consciousness to a fetus, Caldwell underscores the ethical quandaries at the heart of debates about abortion: through her sentient narrator, she acknowledges the side of the debate that grants an unviable fetus fully human status before birth. Not only are the bodies here not functioning, and the systems that created and sustain this heart-breaking situation clearly defective, but also, the story suggests, broken as well are discourses that fail to acknowledge the complexities on both sides of this issue.

"SOMAT" is one instance among many found throughout contemporary Irish women's writing in which difficult forms are invoked to depict difficult problems, in which the complexities of female experience are underscored or even heightened by the deployment of deliberately challenging literary strategies. During the late twentieth and early twenty-first centuries, Irish women's writing has helped to dismantle the logics of secrecy and shame about experiences once kept private, and used literary form to introduce new levels of complexity to contentious issues we might now regard as familiar and even resolved. As widespread injustices in Ireland have been revealed and scrutinized, often on digital platforms, many of these writers have embraced the modernist mode to expose and underscore the intricacy and distinctiveness of individual female subjectivity, keeping their eye on singular private experiences in the midst of crises now rendered glaringly public.

In this story, time-honored tactics associated with modernism heighten the recognition that, even today, in matters tied to reproductive health women's desires often are unheard, their bodies controlled by others, their experiences erased in public discourse. As such, Caldwell echoes the concerns of early twentieth-century modernists including Jean Rhys and Katherine Mansfield. But "SOMAT" is also in dialogue with the innovations of Joyce and suggestively evokes "Oxen of the Sun," the chapter from *Ulysses* set in the National Maternity Hospital, which documents the arduous final hours of Mina Purefoy's three days of labor. Like Eliot's "Morning at the Window," Joyce's chapter willfully portrays women as objects rather than subjects, situating the chapter's point of view at a remove from the women in the hospital. The narrative focus rests not on Purefoy, nor on the experience of the nurses or other female patients, but instead on Bloom and a group of raucous medical students and their companions in the hospital waiting room. A set of drunken discussions among the men unfolds in the waiting room and disturbs the female patients. Among these, they debate whether to privilege the life of the mother or the child in a complicated delivery and note that while the Catholic Church insists that the life of the child be prioritized, the law (in 1904, when the novel is set) offers no such direction.

"Oxen of the Sun" is generally understood as the most challenging chapter of *Ulysses*. An audacious history of form, it capitalizes on the logics of the stubborn mode: it uses the recognizable forms and tropes of past literature to advance its message. In this chapter, outdated language and literary traditions capture present-day conditions, in part to signal outdated attitudes and approaches. It is comprised of thirty-two episodes that track the development of the English language, each drawn from precedents ranging from ancient Roman prayer to contemporary slang. The interpretive difficulty presented by such linguistic experiments suggestively nods to Purefoy's physical labor, understood as "none so hard," and to the general condition of pregnancy and birth, "that allhardest of woman hour."[63] But the chapter's parodies also suggest the inability of masculine perspectives to comprehend the corporeal and emotional realities of childbirth, to take this female experience seriously, including that of Bloom who respects its sanctity. The drunken young men in the waiting room—like those who buzz around the pregnant body in "SOMAT"—are clueless, unable or refusing to grasp what unfolds in a different room, in a different body, in a different consciousness. Each of the many literary forms from across centuries invoked by Joyce fails to account fully for what such women endure. Caldwell's story, by employing modernism in the twenty-first century, reveals that similar failures span into the present day. If Bloom skirts the ensuing debate over saving mother or child, noting that the church profits financially from a baptism as well as a funeral, "SOMAT" suggests the further profits, material and ideological, now relevant to the contemporary case documented in its story. Joyce's chapter culminates in a babbling chorus of drunken slang and dialect that he associates with cultural disintegration and chaos, but Caldwell's story throughout insists that the careful administrative language of medical bureaucrats, church representatives, government officials, doctors, and public relations staff registers the next stage of cultural decline.

---

[63] James Joyce, *Ulysses* (New York: Vintage, 1986), 316, 315.

Modernist Expertise

In the twenty-first century, the artful refashioning of modernism, and in particular a creative relationship to its difficulties in the representation of female subjectivity, have granted many Irish women writers a fast pass to professional authority and legitimacy. Their refashioning of a notoriously difficult modernism might be the opposite of the method identified by Melanie Micir and Aarthi Vadde in their account of "obliterature," in which they celebrate amateurism for its resistance to the "the gendered formation of literary value" and draw attention to "the casual, minor, repurposed, and ephemeral writing expelled from literary criticism's traditional purview."[64] The women writers studied here are interested in expertise, in adroitly performing the dominant codes of modernism for readers in a culture that disavowed their talent and expertise. Such a commitment may reflect their long and distinctive national literary tradition: as postcolonial writers, Irish women are inheritors of a tradition powerfully shaped by the centuries-old contest between the English and Irish cultures. These writers readily appreciate the distinctive and influential cultural products born of such tension, understanding that the vaunted corpus of Irish writing in English was forged in part from the dynamic, fraught interactions between the languages and literatures of colonizer and colonized. They are practiced in adopting and adapting the language, as well as the aesthetic forms, of the more powerful to give voice to the less powerful: as such, the "native" language of women's expression might be in productive tension with the "imperial" language of a male-inflected modernism. Likewise, modernism awards gravitas to their representations of female interiority, to the experimental depictions of the private self that the church and state worked so hard to sequester and silence. Such expertise, as the following chapters will demonstrate, has allowed them in the wake of high modernism to capture the nuance and complexity of female interiority, and to make public for an international readership their ruminations on a variety of quotidian and nationally distinctive experiences.

---

[64] Melanie Micir and Aarthi Vadde, "Obliterature: Toward an Amateur Criticism," *Modernism/modernity* 25:3 (2018): 517–549, 520.

2

Praying

(Kate O'Brien, Mary Lavin, Emma Donoghue, Eimear McBride)

For roughly a century, Irish women writers have refashioned the strategies of modernist interiority to reflect unfolding experiences of female privacy. In their fiction, they make visible the hidden vagaries of consciousness with the intent of demonstrating the crucial value of the private world for Irish women in a culture dominated and shaped by formidable institutions and hierarchies. Given the imbrications of private and public experience I describe in Chapter One, it becomes clear that this dedicated focus on female subjectivity represents neither an uncritical retreat into the private world of the novel, nor a reflexive return to exhausted models of modernist subjectivity, nor a total capitulation to neoliberal formulas of hyper-individualism. Instead, these writers regard the fictional depiction of these women's intimate and imaginative negotiations with powerful forces, old and new, as one means to recapture and fortify the private world against stubborn problems including the demand for social conformity, the imposition of institutional imperatives, and the lure of bland consumerism. The long history of the modernist mode accentuates the traction of time-honored attitudes and behaviors, reminding readers that to discard, or even alter, established practices and forms is difficult work. The intransigence of modernism, the very fact that this mode continues to provide an appropriate tool to represent the interior lives of contemporary women, suggests that its representational capacities are not yet depleted, but it also implies that traditional ways of thinking and being die hard.

The assertion that religion, the belief and worship of a higher power, is among the external factors that have had a potent effect on subjectivity will likely come as little surprise. In the wake of high modernism, Irish women writers often have turned to prayer as one means to explore the relationship between religion and consciousness. Prayer, described by William James in *The Varieties of Religious Experience* (1902) as "the very soul and essence of religion," has prehistoric origins and endures into the present day as both a rhetorical form and a cultural practice.[1]

---

[1] William James, *The Varieties of Religious Experience: A Study in Human Nature* (New York: Modern Library, 1902), 454. For a synthetic overview, see Philip Zaleski and Carol Zaleski, *Prayer: A History* (Boston: Houghton Mifflin, 2005).

Modernism in Irish Women's Contemporary Writing. Paige Reynolds, Oxford University Press. © Paige Reynolds (2024).
DOI: 10.1093/9780191990540.003.0003

60 PRAYING

The high modernism of the early twentieth century kept a close eye on religious prayer, as seen in modernist classics by T. S. Eliot, William Faulkner, Zora Neale Hurston, and Virginia Woolf, among others, suggesting its continued significance amid the ascent of Western secularism.[2] Irish modernism was especially inflected by religious concerns and often integrated prayer into its narratives of daily life, owing in part to the pervasive influence of Catholic belief and practice across the island. Prayer vividly emerges, for example, in Wilde's *De Profundis* (1897), Joyce's *A Portrait of the Artist as a Young Man* (1916), Yeats's "A Prayer for My Daughter" (1919), and Beckett's *Dreams of Fair to Middling Women* (1932). Modernism features a rich cast of characters, both real and fictive, who strive to revoke entrenched socio-cultural norms tied to religion in pursuit of new ways of thinking and being. However, as seen in these examples, they rarely manage to neatly or entirely cast aside religion and the sacralized ritual of prayer.

The Catholic Church's power over the Irish imaginary has been executed in part through its disciplining of prayer, a force that has landed most heavily on the artificially privatized experience of women. Representing prayer through the familiar tactics of the modernist mode, Irish women writers draw attention to the ways that female consciousness submits to, as well as eludes, organized religion. In Kate O'Brien's novel *The Land of Spices* (1941), Mary Lavin's short stories, Emma Donoghue's *Hood* (1995), and Eimear McBride's *A Girl Is a Half-formed Thing* (2013), prayer surfaces in the narrative as public practice and as private meditation. These writers acknowledge the unfathomable nature of prayer and provide readers sophisticated and sympathetic accounts of this practice, even as they critique how it creates a specious feeling of individual well-being and binds practitioners uncritically to an institution. Their characters worship collectively at mass and individually in imagined colloquy; they recite familiar devotions and craft unique entreaties to God. In all of these works, prayers are incorporated directly into the narrative, with verbatim excerpts of Catholic prayers of petition, thanksgiving, confession, supplication, and adoration interspersed throughout. The pervasive reproduction of canonical prayers in women's fiction accurately represents the effectively systematized nature of religious practice in modern Ireland, as well as conveying the powerful influence of prayer on the interior lives of female characters. Even outside of religious worship, the thoughts of female characters are frequently inflected with its formal features: the presence of an imagined interlocutor, routine verbal phrases and patterns, desires voiced with the hope of response and fulfillment.

For these writers, prayer not only operates as a thematic concern or plot device but also shapes their representations of female consciousness. As a rhetorical

---

[2] For accounts of modernism and religion, see Suzanne Hobson, *Angels of Modernism: Religion, Culture, Aesthetics 1910–1960* (Houndsmill Basingstoke: Palgrave Macmillan, 2011); Pericles Lewis, *Religious Experience and the Modernist Novel* (Cambridge: Cambridge University Press, 2010); David Sherman, "Woolf's Secular Imaginary," *Modernism/modernity* 23:4 (2016): 711–731.

form, prayer can seem predetermined, both ahistorical and ritualistic, but the female characters in these novels attempt, with varying success, to adopt and adapt that fixed form to suit their distinctive personal and social conditions. For Kate O'Brien, prayer unevenly provides her main adult protagonist, a Catholic nun in early twentieth-century rural Ireland, a beneficial feeling of communion with the divine, as well as inspiring therapeutic self-knowledge. In her short fiction, Mary Lavin offers a darker assessment of prayer: for many of her characters living in mid-twentieth century Ireland, it instantiates problematic habits of being, and its mystifications thwart the comprehension necessary for self-protection and personal happiness. For Emma Donoghue, prayer retains its authority and influence in the life of her lesbian protagonist living in late twentieth-century Dublin, but can be adapted more freely to individual experience. All of this fiction has a measured engagement with modernist experiment, holding onto the clarity promised by realism to counter the enigmas of the prayer it represents and frequently critiques. Writing in the twenty-first century, in the wake of high-profile exposures of sexual abuse by Catholic clergy and in Catholic institutions, Eimear McBride tosses realism aside to reveal how the qualities of obfuscation and mystery that characterize modernism and prayer become embodied, powerful—and lethal. Through an aggressive display of modernist form, which still carries the weight of rebellion and resistance, the invocations of prayer in *A Girl Is a Half-formed Thing* lay bare the distortions and failures of Christian belief and practice in the face of real human suffering.

These representations of prayer underscore religion's traction not only on female subjectivity, but also on literary form. In her theory of form, Caroline Levine contends, "Forms will often fail to impose their order when they run up against other forms that disrupt their logic and frustrate their organizing ends, producing aleatory and sometimes contradictory effects."[3] Levine's use of the term "collision" to describe these effects seems enormously valuable in its evocation of the energies produced when forms interact.[4] By placing prayer in dialogue with literary realism and modernism, these writers invite a consideration of Catholicism's powerful hand in shaping contemporary female experience and subjectivity. Published amid decades that saw Catholic doctrine manipulated to limit the public roles available to Irish women, the fiction under review in this chapter is particularly interested in exploring when and how prayer fails its female supplicants. In this endeavor, the formal juxtaposition of prayer and modernist technique—the earnestness of traditional religious devotions seemingly at variance with the ironies of modernism's innovative aesthetics—is productively

---

[3] Caroline Levine, *Forms: Whole, Rhythm, Hierarchy, Network* (Princeton: Princeton University Press, 2015), 7.

[4] See Jonathan Kramnick and Anahid Nersessian, "Form and Explanation," *Critical Inquiry* 43 (Spring 2017): 650–669, and Anahid Nersessian, "What Is the New Redistribution?," *PMLA* 132:5 (2017): 1220–1225.

62 PRAYING

disconcerting and thus demands attention. What are the limits of these forms for female self-understanding and self-expression, what are their latent possibilities? By inviting such questions, these works rejuvenate and sustain the critical energies of activism that characterized the interventions of Irish women modernists from the late nineteenth and early twentieth centuries.

Failed Prayer in *The Land of Spices*

Kate O'Brien was an early master of the stubborn mode, a writer whose savvy, persistent use of realism has invited critics to regard her, mistakenly, as a failed modernist. Declan Kiberd, for example, has suggested that O'Brien can be found "objecting to the modes of the realist novel which she ultimately cannot transcend."[5] He attributes the interior monologues found in her novel *The Ante-Room* (1934) to the model set by *Ulysses*, but contends "the device is so sparingly and so cautiously used ... as to constitute a regression to nineteenth-century modes."[6] Other scholars have acknowledged the influence of Joyce's modernism on *The Land of Spices*, with most reading the novel as a riposte to *A Portrait of the Artist as a Young Man*.[7] But O'Brien also drew lessons from other modernists, ranging from Ibsen to Woolf. She had a uniquely capacious and supple understanding of Irish modernism, as evidenced in her lecture "Ireland and Avant-Gardisme," in which she singled out Wilde, Shaw, Yeats, Synge, O'Casey, Joyce, and Beckett as "sheer and unaffected <u>Avant-Garde</u> unschooled Avant Garde. Simply the thing itself— accidental. Individual—a new way of crying out loud."[8] In this essay, she also counted unusual suspects such as Swift, Gregory, and Douglas Hyde among the Irish avant-garde, including in her innovative assessment an eighteenth-century satirist as well as two icons of the Revival whose trademark was not, at the moment of her writing, radical experiment.

As critics have demonstrated, O'Brien consciously employed modernism throughout her long career, even as she remained simultaneously committed to the aesthetic and social possibilities inherent to realism.[9] Across her work, she grappled with the consequences of Catholic belief and practice for her characters,

---

[5] Declan Kiberd, *Irish Classics* (Cambridge, MA: Harvard University Press, 2001), 562.

[6] Ibid.

[7] See Mary Breen, "Something Understood?: Kate O'Brien and *The Land of Spices*," *Ordinary People Dancing: Essays on Kate O'Brien*, ed. Eibhear Walshe (Cork: Cork University Press, 1993), 167–190; Adele Dalsimer, *Kate O'Brien: A Critical Study* (Boston: Twayne, 1990); and Elizabeth Foley O'Connor, "Kate O'Brien, James Joyce, and the 'Lonely Genius,'" *Joycean Legacies*, ed. Martha Carpentier (Houndmills Basingstoke: Palgrave Macmillan, 2015), 11–32.

[8] Kate O'Brien, "Ireland and Avant-Gardisme," typescript, 12 pp., Kate O'Brien Papers (P12/157), 6. Courtesy Special Collections, Glucksman Library, University of Limerick.

[9] See Aintzane Leggareta Mentxaka, *Kate O'Brien and the Fiction of Identity: Sex, Art, and Politics in Mary Lavelle and Other Writings* (Jefferson, NC: McFarland and Co., 2011) and essays in Paige Reynolds, ed., Special issue on Kate O'Brien, *Irish University Review* 48:1 (Spring/Summer 2018).

both Irish and European, and she placed prayer, as text and ritual, at the center of several novels. In her first novel *Without My Cloak* (1931), prayer infuses the actions and thoughts of its characters, as when a homesick Christina offers a "fantastic prayer" to the sanctuary lamp in an American church, and reveals it to be a means of powerful and pervasive expression.[10] Even outside of the Catholic tradition, prayer here provides the characters a way of registering daily experience, as when Denis understands the shadow of a tree in golden light as "like a Mussulman's praying carpet."[11] Other novels reveal the influence of prayer as a template for aesthetic organization. *Pray for the Wanderer* (1938) takes its title from a Marian hymn, for example, and the plot of *The Ante-Room* is ordered by rigidly structured prayers and rituals over three days as the Mulqueen family anticipates the death of its matriarch. O'Brien's fiction often illustrated the lives of characters drawn from Ireland's Catholic middle classes, dissecting the ways in which national, economic, and religious norms shaped, and sometimes distorted, their experiences.[12] While sympathetic to Catholicism, she was also deeply critical of the ideological constraints its beliefs and practices placed on its adherents, and her characters' ambivalence about the efficacy of prayer frequently provided a register for her own conflicted relationship with religious faith and institutions.

Published in 1941, *The Land of Spices* is perhaps O'Brien's best-known depiction of a middle-class milieu in Ireland profoundly influenced by Catholic social thought and practice. Set in early twentieth-century Mellick (a fictive town based on Limerick), the novel chronicles the relationship between Helen Archer, known also as *Mère Hélène*, the Reverend Mother of the *Compagnie de la Sainte Famille*, and Anna Murphy, a young Irish student who attends the convent school. It offers a third-person chronological narrative that runs from 1904 to June 1914 and is amply peppered with flashbacks, tracing Anna's life from age six until she prepares to enter university. Experimenting with how prayer might be represented in fiction, O'Brien explores the imbrication of the transcendent and the everyday in female consciousness. When woven into narrative prose, prayer can be decontextualized and defamiliarized, the collision of the forms producing a kind of alienation effect that invites readers to interrogate rhetorical habits that might otherwise go unexamined. The habitual appearance of well-known prayers and poems throughout the novel's interior monologues reminds readers that external aesthetic and liturgical forms shape and even govern the consciousness of the

---

[10] Kate O'Brien, *Without My Cloak* (London: Virago Press, 1987), 407.

[11] Ibid., 305.

[12] See Michael G. Cronin, *Impure Thoughts: Sexuality, Catholicism, and Literature in Twentieth-Century Ireland* (Manchester: Manchester University Press, 2012), 82–113; Eamon Maher, "Love, Loss of Faith, and Kate O'Brien," *Doctrine and Life* 49:2 (February 1999): 87–97; Sharon Tighe-Mooney, "'Nun, Married, Old Maid': Kate O'Brien's Fiction, Women, and Irish Catholicism," PhD Thesis, Maynooth University, Ireland (October 2009).

64 PRAYING

female characters. These forms can hamper—or facilitate—personal insights and self-expression by providing familiar vessels for the characters' unfamiliar, and sometimes unsettling, emotions and thoughts.

Just as some modernists imagined that classical allusion might help to contain and manage the excesses of modernity, O'Brien suggests that prayer provides a mechanism through which her female protagonists might contain and manage the vagaries of consciousness. And yet the novel's title immediately suggests otherwise. *The Land of Spices* alludes to George Herbert's metaphysical poem "Prayer (1)," a consideration of the mysteries of prayer whose final line defines prayer as "The land of spices; something understood."[13] Like many of her peers, O'Brien was alert to and influenced by "The Metaphysical Poets" (1921), Eliot's essay championing these poets for their embrace of paradox, for their ability to suture thought and feeling, form and content. With its surfeit of metaphors and sensations seeking to describe the manifold qualities of prayer, Herbert's poem underscores the limitlessness of this form. From the outset, given its title, *The Land of Spices* likewise suggests that we can never fully understand the mysteries nor grasp the range of possibilities embedded within prayer. In this novel, O'Brien interlaces structured prayers, ones sometimes rehearsed for centuries, with the internal monologues of her female characters. The oblique nature of prayer for O'Brien, as for many writers in her wake, renders it a fitting means by which to explore the similarly unfathomable properties of female subjectivity. Prayer allows her to consider the mysteries that inform ordinary human experience, such as desire, betrayal, friendship, and faith—as well as to demonstrate instances in which prayer, and its many promises, fail those who embrace it.

The depiction of female interiority in the Catholic community of *The Land of Spices* reflects an important historical transformation in religious belief and practice. In their influential studies of secularism, both Charles Taylor and Talal Asad have identified, as one of the hallmarks of modernity, the shift of religion from public practice to interior faith.[14] This transition appears in the novel's plot and characterization, but also via its literary devices. Free indirect discourse allows O'Brien to move between the inchoate thoughts of her female characters, which are often provided through interior monologue, and the more faithful representation of exterior realities provided by an omniscient narrator. Though written in the immediate wake of high modernism, the novel does not employ full-throttle stream of consciousness to depict the subjectivities of its female protagonists, even as O'Brien pulls from the innovations of Joyce and Woolf, among others.[15]

---

[13] George Herbert, "Prayer (I)," *The Complete English Poems*, ed. John Tobin (London: Penguin Books, 1991), 45–46, 46.

[14] Charles Taylor, *A Secular Age* (Cambridge: Harvard University Press, 2007); Talal Asad, *Formations of the Secular: Christianity, Islam, Modernism* (Stanford: Stanford University Press, 2003).

FAILED PRAYER IN *THE LAND OF SPICES*   65

Instead, her commitment to free indirect discourse gives order and shape to the representation of female consciousness, much like the rhetorical form of prayer gives order and shape to communication with a higher power.

The Land of Spices places the stories of Helen and Anna in parallel, moving between their lives as they grapple with various personal crises—most poignantly, the deaths of Helen's father and of Anna's brother. These twinned bildungsromane are interwoven. However, pulling out Helen's strand of the novel highlights how O'Brien deploys prayer to showcase not only the dynamic interchange between realism and modernism but also the full range of this protagonist's consciousness. *The Land of Spices* is structured largely from a series of Helen's interior monologues. As an English nun in Ireland, she struggles with her faith and her professional identity. She strains to accept the patriarchy that drives the Catholic Church and Irish nationalist politics of this period, as well as the values of "*la pudeur et la politesse*" (modesty and good manners) espoused by her order. The novel's central conflict is revealed amid her prayers and ruminations centered on a traumatic event in her youth that propelled her entry into religious life. At age eighteen, she covertly observed "the embrace of love" shared between her beloved father and his young male student Etienne.[16] In the wake of this revelation, she rejects the cosmopolitan life that her father represents to join a religious order.

In this novel, O'Brien's formal choices draw attention to the disciplinary logics of the Catholicism that shaped daily life in Ireland as well as their effects on individual psychology. Throughout, Helen wrestles with the contradictions and excesses given voice in religious prayer; she is repeatedly described as "detached" and seen attempting to repress or reluctantly puzzle out the mysteries that surround her. Her interior monologues reveal that she struggles with obedience, not just to the patriarchy of the church and to the values that define her order, but also to the prayer that should order, manage, and contain her unruly consciousness. The collision between religious prayer and literary realism, evident in the novel's employment of free indirect discourse, helps to convey the increasing friction between the traditions of Catholicism and the burgeoning autonomy of women. As Tom Inglis describes in his influential study *Moral Monopoly*, the Catholic Church in Ireland effectively regulated behavior from the mid-nineteenth century forward—thanks in part to the Devotional Revolution, which under the guidance of Cardinal Paul Cullen consolidated the authority of the church and formalized its practices.[17] This transformation increased regular attendance at mass, as well as participation in the sacraments of confession and communion, and further instantiated various

---

[15] Aintzane Leggareta Mentxaka, "Kate O'Brien and Virginia Woolf: Common Ground," *Irish University Review* 48:1 (2018): 127–142.

[16] Kate O'Brien, *The Land of Spices* (London: Virago Press, 2014), 165. Subsequent references parenthetical.

[17] Tom Inglis, *Moral Monopoly: The Rise and Fall of the Catholic Church in Modern Ireland* (Dublin: University College Dublin Press, 1998).

66   PRAYING

habits of prayer such as novenas, recitations of the Rosary, and devotions to the
Sacred Heart. These religious practices were effectively and efficiently woven into
everyday life, continuing (albeit with less regularity and fervor for many) even
after Vatican II. Amid her highly structured days in the convent, ordered by these
services and prayers in concert with administrative duties and academic lessons,
Helen struggles internally with the external discipline imposed by Catholicism on
daily life and morality.

The Land of Spices showcases, in its content as well as its form, how a devout
woman negotiates between the obedience demanded by the church and the
vagaries of individual consciousness. The title of the opening chapter, "The Holy
Habit," provocatively draws attention to the mandatory attire of nuns as well as
the conventions that shape convent life. The novel commences on Rosary Sunday, depicting a service that joins three young postulants to the order. The young
girls at the convent school attend this service and, during it, are consumed by
schwärmerei, an unbridled and excessive sentiment. Yet both Helen and the young
student Anna stand outside of the ceremony's intense affect. As Helen looks at one
young postulant, "a reflection of dry pity escaped across her prayers" (4). Prayer
should be largely identical among these worshippers, but it clearly enables two different forms of attention here: one characterized by surrender, another by Helen's
detachment.

A choir soon begins to chant the words of Teresa of Avila, eliciting further the
internal tension between Helen's prayerful self and her rational, critical self:

> Reverend Mother reflected as she listened that if Saint Teresa of Avila did in fact
> write the words now being chanted so untidily, there would be little doubt that her
> wisdom would have forbidden their devotional misuse by girls—but traditions
> were traditions, she thought wearily, and who was she to be so boldly sure of what
> Teresa would have thought? "Not for the joy that waits me ..." if prayerfulness
> was stirred in her by such perilous assertion of the love of God, who was to know
> what instant of pure devotion, perfect praise, they might not light in some fresher,
> holier, more innocent heart? (5–6)

Helen here expresses a cautious skepticism, even as these young girls leap into
faith. She refuses the mysteries of prayer—in part because the girls' sloppy performance interferes with the capacity of this hymn to induce soothing meditations,
such as those provoked for Mrs. Ramsay by the sonorous Latin mass in Woolf's To
the Lighthouse (1927). Prayer here isolates Helen from fellow feeling, confirming
not the inherent connection among worshippers but rather the inscrutability of
those composing her community and her separation from them.

Rather than a loss of self, Helen manifests in this scene the idiosyncratic individualism of modernism's outsider protagonists. Yet prayer necessarily requires
that attention be directed inward and outward. Immediately after this acute

observation, the novel sheds free indirect discourse and Helen's prayers become a direct address:

> "I have grown to be a coward and a snob in Thy service," she prayed repentantly. "Teach me to be otherwise before it is too late. Teach me to escape from the carpings of my small judgment, and to see Thy creatures sometimes with a vestige of Thy everlasting love. Make me humble, Lord; make me do Thy work from my heart, not always with this petty, miserable brain. Compel me to understand that there are a million ways of finding the favour of Thy mercy. Lord, give me charity. Give me the grace to find Thy image in us all ..."
>
> But as she prayed for herself and found momentary relief from the dryness of her own sensibility in an appeal against it, conscience reminded her that all her prayer to-day should be for the three new lives being dedicated to a work she knew to be so hard. Yet, dutifully though she turned her mind from her own need of help to theirs, thoughts of office and government crowded into it, so that the three novices were lost almost immediately in anxieties covering a whole community of nuns and a school of sixty girls. (6)

Here, the representation of her consciousness is shaped by, interrupted by, and fragmented by prayer. This passage is ordered by the structure of a traditional prayer, but the collision of prayer and interior monologue reveals that her thoughts elude its discipline.

Prayer regularly fails to help Helen master what she perceives to be unruly or verboten feelings, and that failure opens certain possibilities for liberation, imaginative and practical. Later, when she meets with a young priest named Father Conroy and his bishop, her consciousness once again resists the restraint promised by the engagement of prayer's familiar form. As the men urge her to advocate national ideals in the education of her young pupils, she resists, an ideological position that places her securely outside of nationalist interests as well as the patriarchal authority of the Catholic Church. This scene, and the chapter itself, do not conclude with her obedient acquiescence to these men and their directives. Instead, Helen sharply and critically responds to the bombastic Father Conroy, asserting 'our nuns *are not* a nation' (16). As he derides her understanding of the Irish people and their history, she observes internally that he has inspired "a visitation very strange to her—a visitation of hatred; she desired to pray against it, but under the ugly weight of feeling, could not reach the other barrier of prayer" (18). In this moment, in her psyche, Helen's authentic emotional response, not a trained obeisance, triumphs.

Across this novel, O'Brien represents prayer as a normative practice allowing for the useful negotiation between two very different affective states, swooning *schwämerei* and cold detachment. Like a literary critic outside the thrall of an absorbing novel, Helen stands outside the seductive communal and affective

68 PRAYING

pull of religious prayer. This chapter, filtered through her perspective, seemingly diminishes the affect represented by the immature girls and nuns, and offers a stern if silent rebuke to the submission demanded by male authority. To frame this in terms of the mode, the chapter places the melodrama of the nineteenth-century popular stage and surety of feeling offered by Victorian popular fiction in dialogue with the impersonality and ambiguity of modernism, awarding uneasy privilege to the latter. Yet the chapter ends with failed private prayer, a religious and linguistic act that cannot overcome "the ugly weight of feeling." Helen appears throughout the novel's opening as a detached observer, but she too falls sway to "feeling" in the first chapter's conclusion, just not the buzzy pleasure shared by her community.

"Our Father": Prayer and Parents

The Land of Spices underscores the Derridean claim that the full promise of prayer can never be obtained.[18] As Helen struggles with her youthful alienation from her beloved father, she imagines prayer as a curative. However, she finds that even her "constant, humble prayer of maturity"—no matter how "insistent or repentant"—fails to repair her past or correct her misjudgments (21). She seeks self-understanding through the vehicle of prayer, unaware that one defining point of the modernist mode in which her prayers are embedded might be its insistence that individuals can never achieve that understanding. Nonetheless, the interactions between the structure and discipline of prayer and her unmanageable personal meditations are crucial to Helen's epiphanic acceptance of her father, their troubled relationship, and his death.

In the middle of the novel, Helen receives a letter announcing the death of her father just as "[t]he bell rang for Evening Meditation" and she is "relieved by the obligation of obedience" (152). In this scene, prayer is characterized as a reflexive routine that is liberating, a welcome imposition that distracts from personal suffering. Daily rounds of prayer allow her to "hold him at bay" until alone in bed when she is "assaulted" at night by the need to recall the moment when she encountered her father with Etienne (152). Left alone, in personal prayer, she kneels "immobile and seeking grace, all night, before her memories of him," where she prays to personal memories, not to God (152). Resting in bed, "She dreaded, almost madly, what lay in wait for the next movement of her thoughts, so she escaped a minute into the present, and prayed for him as he now was, prayed that the horny good love of [his housemaid] *Marie-Jeanne's* old hands, so worn in work for him, would warm his dying hands in this dark hour and remind him, for as long as possible, of the human sympathy which he had always given, and needed, so abundantly"

---

[18] See John D. Caputo, *The Prayers and Tears of Jacques Derrida: Religion without Religion* (Bloomington, IN: Indiana University Press, 1997).

(156). Consolation comes here from thoughts of human touch, a gesture as banal as Marie-Jeanne's penitential prayers, which are described as "repeated over and over ... all through life" and focused on the minor everyday woes of burned pancakes or a headache (157). Helen warmly recalls that her father—a scholar of metaphysical poetry—would mimic these prayers, which "would make him smile with love, and trap him into his old chanting" (157). Helen can project the realized solace of prayer onto her father, as guided by a domestic worker outside of a religious order whose prayers are as routine as her household tasks.

This memory of prayer's comfortable and soothing integration into everyday life is followed immediately by the rumination that allows her to face the traumatic vision that propelled her into religious life:

> ... the picture of *Etienne* and her father ... luridly vivid ... would not leave the stretched canvas of her eyelids ... it changed, became dreadful, became vast or savage or gargoyled or insanely fantastical; how it became a temptation, a curiosity, a threat, and sometimes no more than piteous, no more than dreary, sad. She remembered how she prayed to be delivered from it, to be blind, to be stupified— and how it still moved and glittered evilly, faceless, nameless, and then again most violently identified—and every night at last, such sleep as she found came only through struggle with this image, and was broken by its glare. (165)

Here, oddly enough, is the metaphorical excess of Herbert's poem for which the novel is named, yet it arrives in a hellish vision that might seem drawn from a Gothic novel. Helen's detachment, which was demonstrated in contradistinction to the girls and nuns of the order in the novel's first chapter, has evaporated.

In this moment, fantastic imagination, represented as painfully visual (unlike the promised solace of aural prayer) takes hold of Helen's thoughts. To contain this vision, she once more begins to pray: "'Father, forgive me,' she prayed. 'Father, forgive me—I know not what I did'" (168). Here, she adapts to her own conditions the words of Christ spoken from the Cross, when he petitions God to forgive those who ignorantly betrayed and crucified him (Luke 23:34). In this moment, the obliquity of the apostrophe—her address to "Father"—makes it unclear whether she is addressing God or her biological father. Margot Backus and Joseph Valente astutely read instances of uncertainty in the novel as a register of Helen's confusion about "enigmatic signifiers," most obviously those related to human sexuality.[19] Yet this moment also embodies the mystifications at the heart of religious prayer. The constraints of prayer and the order it provides, as well as its failure to stop her painful memories and her obstreperous introspection, ultimately facilitate Helen's direct encounter with the disturbing and unresolved memories of her break with her father. In doing so, prayer facilitates her psychological healing.

---

[19] Margot Backus and Joseph Valente, "*The Land of Spices*, the Enigmatic Signifier, and the Stylistic Invention of Lesbian (In)Visibility," *Irish University Review* 43:1 (May 2013): 55–73.

70 PRAYING

The Ambivalent Epiphany

The Land of Spices concludes with a chapter entitled "Te Deum" after *Te Deum Laudamus* ("Thee, O God, We Praise"), a hymn of praise that blesses and gives thanks. The chapter follows Anna's epiphany as a young adult, when she accepts the accidental death of her beloved brother Charlie and begins to recognize the consolations that art might provide her—an epiphany that comes in the wake of Helen's securing a university education for Anna. Here, full attention shifts to Helen, who walks alone among the "formal, shaded quiet of Bishop's Walk" (288). Just as Teresa of Avila imagined the work of prayer in spatial terms in *The Interior Castle* (1577), a guide to spiritual development and prayer that fascinated O'Brien, Helen draws inspiration from the order and silence of this landscape.

This final chapter appears to cast out the psychological crises that dominated Helen's consciousness in previous chapters, replacing them with a variety of Catholic prayers and contemplative practices. These include the *Te Deum* as well as meditative walks, recitations, and visitations. As Helen considers Anna's future amid these exercises, she thinks: "Prayer would follow her; prayer always could ... Prayer could go with her, making no weight—and whether or not she remembered 'the days of the poems,' an aging nun would remember them. How sweet is the shepherd's sweet lot, from the morn to the evening he strays" (296). This final line, drawn from William Blake's poem "The Shepherd" in *Songs of Innocence* (1789), juxtaposed with Helen's celebration of prayer, once more underscores the dynamic relationship between forms in this novel (a dynamism heightened further by the fact that "The Shepherd" is an illuminated poem, juxtaposing word and image). In this scene, Helen seems entirely reconciled to the potential solace prayer might offer her as well as her young protégé. Yet that promise is best articulated by the literary form of poetry. This moment suggests that, for Helen, prayer provides a valuable tool that might constructively order and contain obstreperous female consciousness and thus inspire healing self-awareness. However, her turn to lines from Blake in this final scene matters. This allusion suggests that religious prayer alone inevitably or even necessarily fails its practitioners, a message apparent in multiple poems from Blake's *Songs of Innocence* and *Songs of Experience* (1794). These poems suggest that religious prayer distracts well-meaning citizens from the necessary critical thought and political action that might protect vulnerable subjects, such as the young boys from "The Chimney Sweeper" who are pressed into life-threatening labor. Nestled in her thoughts, Helen's literary allusion gives further testament to her latent ambivalence about prayer, as well as to the aleatory effects of out-of-time literary modes.

In his study of modern Irish poetry and Catholicism, Andrew Auge notes that the naturalism that prevailed in Irish fiction from the mid-twentieth century forward allowed for a critique of the church. But he contends that Irish fiction writers, among whom he includes Edna O'Brien as well as Seán Ó Faoláin and John McGahern, "were capable of unraveling the imposing raiment of Irish Catholicism but not of fabricating anything new or more liberating from its filaments."[20] *The Land of Spices* may appear less experimental, less abstract, less difficult than the poetry of Beckett or Denis Devlin, which similarly considered the contours of religious practice, but the formal collision of traditional prayer and indirect interior monologue in this novel similarly reflects the struggle between faith and self that Helen endures, a struggle that appears in works throughout the modernist canon. Here, O'Brien engages with social realities but judiciously uses the stubborn mode to give shape to and convey the internal struggles of her protagonist, thus giving voice—through the evident tension between the tactics of modernism's associative stream of consciousness and highly structured forms of Catholic prayer—to the frequently hidden or repressed intemperance of female imagination.

Lavin's Prayerful Obscurities

Much like O'Brien, Mary Lavin frequently represents in her fiction the unformed and associative thoughts of her female characters through an amalgamation of realist interior monologue and modernist stream of consciousness. Schooled in the intricacies of innovative fiction, Lavin wrote a master's thesis on Jane Austen, and she began a doctoral dissertation about Virginia Woolf, on the back pages of which she wrote her first short story "Miss Holland" (1938). Like others described in this study, she drew from Russian psychological realism, repeatedly citing as influences Chekhov, Tolstoy, and Turgenev—as well as Katherine Mansfield, the modernist short story writer who was an early translator and adapter of Chekhov into English.[21] Lavin throughout her career praised a diverse array of modernist writers from E. M. Forster to Katherine Anne Porter. Yet she asserted, "I'm not experimental, as Joyce and Beckett have been; that is, I'm not looking for new techniques."[22] Critics, however, disagree. As early as 1944, reviewers were linking her work to modernist experiment, with one review of her story "The Green Grave and the Black Grave" (1940) noting that it "followed a remote rhythm like Virginia Woolf's *The Waves*, and played variations upon vowel sounds out of a theme by James Joyce."[23]

---

[20] Andrew J. Auge, *A Chastened Communion: Modern Irish Poetry and Catholicism* (Syracuse, NY: Syracuse University Press, 2013), 10. For an account of Irish Catholic fiction, see Emer Nolan, *Catholic Emancipations: Irish Fiction from Thomas Moore to James Joyce* (Syracuse: Syracuse University Press, 2007).

[21] Mary Lavin, Interview with Robert and Sylvia Stephens, n.d., ML/5/6 dft. Q&A, p.1. Courtesy of UCD Special Collections.

[22] Ibid., 9.

[23] Richard Church, "Realism and Poetry," *John O'London's Weekly* (June 2, 1944): 93. ML/6/24. Courtesy of UCD Special Collections.

72 PRAYING

Lavin wrote in a historical moment in which the Catholic Church exercised astonishing power over the everyday lives of modern Irish women. As Tony Fahey notes, the church responded to the rise of individualism in the nineteenth century with "pastoral, educational and social services ... focused very much on the family."[24] Throughout much of the twentieth century, the church maintained a formidable influence on political and social issues related to morality, ranging from the state censorship of books and prohibition of dance to the management of personal matters such as divorce or access to birth control. When the Irish Constitution appeared in 1937, Article 44.1.2 announced, "The State recognises the special position of the Holy Catholic Apostolic and Roman Church as the guardian of the Faith professed by the great majority of the citizens."[25] Following independence, the influence of the Catholic Church encroached upon the administration of the practical aspects of modern life; it was the major provider of social services related to childcare, education, and health.

As the century lurched forward, writers like Lavin began more aggressively to use the modernist mode to depict, in particular, the power the Catholic Church exerted over female sexuality. Lavin invoked prayer to showcase the tension between religious doctrine and the complexities of female interiority, particularly those related to sexual desire and reproduction in Irish society. Her stories frequently center on the church's endeavors to shield young women from knowledge of social and biological realities. For Lavin, the obliquity of modernism could best render how Catholicism in post-independence Ireland censored information to control and constrain human sexuality. In her writing, prayer—as both rhetorical form and collective practice—demonstrates how the language of the church affects the everyday lives of Irish women but fails to articulate or productively alter female experience. Lavin employs the difficulties and deliberate obscurities that characterize modernist writing to reflect the Catholic Church's pernicious endeavors to keep its congregants in the dark.

Like those of O'Brien, Lavin's depictions of female consciousness are infused with the rigid formal structures of traditional Catholic prayer. Prayer's predetermined conventions elicit predictable and often regulated responses from supplicants. Any divergence from those norms exposes the unpredictable contours of female subjectivity. In Lavin's "The Living" (1958), first published in *The New Yorker*, a young boy overhears a mourning mother question the purpose and logics of prayer. He eavesdrops as she confesses to her female companion that she used to pray that her intellectually disabled adult son would die before her:

> "Wasn't it the unnatural thing to have to pray for anyway? Don't all women pray for the opposite: to die before them and not be a burthen on them? And wasn't it

---

[24] Tony Fahey, "Catholicism and Industrial Society in Ireland," *Proceedings of the British Academy* 79 (1992): 241–263, 263.

[25] Ireland, *Bunreacht na hÉireann (Constitution of Ireland)* (Dublin: *Oifig an tSoláthair*, 1937).

74 PRAYING

These stories, as they grapple with mid-twentieth-century perceptions of ordinary women's lives in Catholic Ireland, invoke modernist experiments that demonstrate their congruities with Catholic prayer. Both the modernist short story and religious prayer couch their meaning in carefully crafted forms, their outcomes open-ended and inconclusive. In her study of Lavin's first collection, *Tales from Bective Bridge* (1942), Anne Fogarty demonstrates how Lavin prolonged high modernist experiment, via her use of ambiguity and a reworked epiphany, as "a means of signposting but not fully articulating masked psychological realities"— literary tactics that sound eerily akin to the mysteries of prayer.[31] Yet such mysteries can be problematic, as these stories demonstrate, when they deviate from their sanctioned expression in set prayer or, as others of her stories suggest, when they are associated with female sexuality. Through her use of the modernist mode, Lavin often depicts women's thoughts and behaviors as obscured and repressed, reflecting the nature of the social and cultural silencing of women as orchestrated by the church.

The mystery central to Catholicism and celebrated in prayer is the divine unknown, which can provide a supernatural spur to imagination, but rarely benefits Lavin's female protagonists. In "The Nun's Mother" (1944), the middle-aged Mrs. Latimer contemplates her daughter's joining a religious order and expresses her ambivalence about her daughter's vocation through multiple variations of the phrase "it was all over" repeated throughout the story. As she and her husband ride home in a taxi from the convent, Mrs. Latimer considers how shopping will be less enjoyable without her daughter present, and she ponders Hollywood movies like *The White Sister* (1933) that valorize the nunnery. The contemporary secular world for Irish women in this story is pleasurable, but it is represented by trite activities and ideals no less constraining than the practice of prayer for being conspicuously modern. As she muses over the events of the day, Mrs. Latimer understands that time will now pass "faster and faster"—another repeated phrase—without her daughter.[32] Though other women insist she is lucky to have a religious daughter to pray for her, Mrs. Latimer rejects this consolation as "utterly absurd," noting:

She believed in prayer—to a certain extent—prayers of praise and prayers of contrition—but not prayers of petition: Dear God, please help me find my brooch—Dear God, don't let it rain today when I've no umbrella—that kind of thing. That wasn't real prayer. That she despised. And prayers for her soul's salvation, from her daughter Angela—well, that too she would frankly discount. To think of depending on the prayers of Angela. Angela! Who was in pigtails till the

[31] Anne Fogarty, "Discontinuities: *Tales from Bective Bridge* and the Modernist Short Story Tradition," *Mary Lavin*, ed. Elke D'hoker (Newbridge: Irish Academic Press, 2013), 49–64, 54.

[32] Mary Lavin, "The Nun's Mother," *The Stories of Mary Lavin*, vol. 2 (London: Constable, 1974), 43–63, 45. Subsequent references parenthetical.

a hard thing to have to bring him into the world only to pray for him to be taken out of it? Oh, it's little you know about it, and if there was a woman standing here in front me, and she had the same story as me, I'd say the same thing to her. Isn't it little anyone knows about what goes on inside another person?"[26]

Her inability, or refusal, to pray by script reads as noteworthy to this boy already schooled in the norms of this rhetorical form, an unsettling lesson that reflects his own doubts about the efficacy of prayer. As well, the mourning mother here marvels at the limitations in understanding another's subjectivity, a truth revealed by the practice of prayer. A similar dynamic appears in Woolf's short story "An Unwritten Novel" (1921), when the narrator observes Minnie Marsh in prayer and asks, "Who's the God of Minnie Marsh, the God of the back streets of Eastbourne, the God of three o'clock in the afternoon? I, too, see roofs, I see sky; but, oh, dear— this seeing of Gods! ... Minnie's God! Did he send the itch and the patch and the twitch? Is that why she prays?"[27] A common and codified practice, one that might generate fellow feeling, prayer in both stories serves to accentuate the isolation and alienation of their female characters.

In "The Living," prayer seems to hold little space for ambivalence or modes of human sympathy at odds with the ideals espoused by the Catholic Church. The dovetailing of prayer and the modernist gestures in Lavin's "A Happy Death" (1946) buoys this perspective, as well as supporting her tenet that "I think of subject and form as dependent on each other in a story."[28] In this story, which Zack Bowen has labeled "Dostoyevskian in its intensity and strangeness," the willful repetition of prayers underscores the persistence of ingrained ways of thinking.[29] The character Ella attempts to secure for her husband Robert "the grace of a happy death" by having him repeat the Act of Contrition after her.[30] Instead, on his deathbed, he wishes to apologize—directly to her and in his own words—for his limitations and to celebrate their relationship. However, Ella cannot recognize the merit of this genuine and meaningful interaction with her husband, a former librarian, because it falls outside of the religious rituals with which she has been raised. Despite evidence that her husband has died in peace, she screams and sobs as she is led from the ward, stunned that God has not heard her prayers and "vouchsafed to her husband the grace of a happy death" as outlined by religious doctrine (240).

[26] Mary Lavin, "The Living," *The Stories of Mary Lavin*, vol. 2 (London: Constable, 1974), 225–236, 231.

[27] Virginia Woolf, "An Unwritten Novel," *The Complete Shorter Fiction of Virginia Woolf*, ed. Susan Dick (New York: Harcourt, Brace and Company, 1985), 106–115, 109.

[28] Mary Lavin, Interview with Tom A. Gullason, November 3, 1967, ML/5/3 dft. C, p.31. Courtesy UCD Special Collections.

[29] Zack Bowen, *Mary Lavin* (Lewisburg, PA: Bucknell University Press, 1975), 36.

[30] Mary Lavin, "A Happy Death," *The Stories of Mary Lavin*, vol. 1 (London: Constable, 1974), 186–240, 227.

beginning of the summer? Angela, who up to her last day at home always sat so immodestly with her bare thighs showing? Oh it was hard, even now, to believe she was going to be a nun—a nun! (45)

In "The Nun's Mother," Lavin harnesses free indirect discourse to showcase Mrs. Latimer's ambivalence and anxiety triggered by her daughter's novitiate. Prayer—an act intended to consolidate, a rhetorical form intended to console—only exacerbates her feelings of sorrow, of loss, of isolation.

Lavin's short story "Sunday Brings Sunday" (1944) offers a particularly trenchant critique of prayer and the dark consequences that might stem from its routines and its linguistic obscurity. The story chronicles the move into young adulthood by Mona, "a good girl and very biddable," as she turns sixteen.[33] Recognized by the local community for her diligence and piousness, she begins to work for a local doctor and takes up with a boy named Jimmy. Mona's partial knowledge and passive acceptance, both qualities of virtuous Catholic prayerfulness, have disastrous consequences when applied to the biological reality of sex. Mona and Jimmy spend time together in a local haystack, sharing moments of sexual foreplay that she perceives only as his voice becoming "thick" (107) or his hands getting "sweaty and clumsy" (108) while they interact. Her passivity and innocence enable "the dreadful thing" (109), as she understands it, to unfold when she and Jimmy ostensibly are "only pushing and shoving and having fun" (114). This sexual encounter has a predictable outcome: Mona becomes pregnant. In the story's final scene, she sits in the Sunday service feeling ill, only dimly aware of her "sin" and its manifold consequences. Her attention in this moment shifts from the structured mass, and she slips into nightmarish reverie. In her imaginative vision, the "year" of Sundays comes rushing into the church, and she sees herself floating away in the darkness and muck that symbolize her limited understanding as well as her sense of impending doom.

A self-described Catholic writer, Lavin uses prayer in "Sunday Brings Sunday" to showcase accepted religious attitudes and customs that endure to the detriment of young women like Mona. Throughout, prayer is portrayed as one in a series of seemingly harmless but ultimately deadening and even dangerous routines. The story opens with a white-faced curate with "vacant" (91) eyes urging his congregants, whom he accuses of having "slipped out of this pious practice" (92), not to abandon the "habit of prayer" (93). In his sermon, prayer is condoned as a "duty" and an "efficacious means of obtaining favours" (91). This "habit," he urges, must be passed down by parents to children, and he insists that no one make the "great mistake" of being ashamed to pray publicly (91). Lavin fills this opening scene with deliberately recurrent words and images: phrases such as "prayer is an efficacious

---

[33] Mary Lavin, "Sunday Brings Sunday," *The Stories of Mary Lavin*, vol. 2 (London: Constable, 1974), 91–116, 104. Subsequent references parenthetical.

thing" and words including "vacant" appear repeatedly; she describes the curate as relentlessly knotting and unknotting the cord tied to his stole; congregants are likened to actors performing the same play each night. The exodus from mass is attended each and every Sunday by the "half-crazed" Mad Mary, who continually shrills, "Sunday brings Sunday, as ever is and as ever was!" (95), and local boys who regularly flirt with girls leaving church.

In "Sunday Brings Sunday," prayer fails Mona and that failure brings no possibility of liberation, as it does for O'Brien's Helen Archer. As such, this story offers a dark feminist critique of religious practice. The priest has repeatedly insisted in his sermons that prayer is "the most efficacious means of ensuring that we do not stray from the state of sanctifying grace" (93). Yet the diligent instruction on prayer and the act of prayer itself cannot help Mona "avoid sin" (115) as she had been promised—or undo its consequences. Through its invocation of modernism, the story also points to the limitations of prayer by problematizing the enigmatic. Difficulty and even inscrutability are vaunted characteristics of high modernism, but they have dire consequences for women's real lives in mid-twentieth-century Ireland. This story sheds light on why Lavin, a writer well-versed in the tactics of literary high modernism, might have been reluctant to fully embrace the movement's obfuscating experimentation, even as the conclusion of this particular story slips fully into impressionism and abstraction. Mona, the story suggests, needed someone to explain with clarity and precision the details and outcomes of sex and human biology, but she was left instead with the mysteries of prayer.

Perhaps due to her long-standing commitment to religious themes, Lavin has little or no place in discussions of Irish modernism, but she is also marginalized by those who seemingly might embrace her as a Catholic writer. When asked in a 1967 interview why she was ignored by the "Catholic world," Lavin responded: "I don't know. Perhaps in spite of the fact that I was scrupulously orthodox Catholic in my private life, there was little evidence of this in my writing, and since one's writing has so many roots in the unconscious perhaps there was even evidence of the strong critical view I always took of many things in the religion to which I was still deeply and openly committed."[34] Her "strong critical view" often turned itself to how Catholic teaching perniciously affects sexuality, a common theme for Irish women writers, and the intractability of prayer, its inability to accommodate or adjust to women's experiences. As the history of the stubborn mode shows, this was no way for an Irish woman writer to earn critical esteem in the twentieth century.

---

[34] Mary Lavin, Interview with Tom A. Gullason, November 3, 1967, M/5/3 dft. A, p.15. Courtesy UCD Special Collections.

Sex and Prayer in *Hood*

Prayer in more recent fiction by Irish women writers is not always a failure. Nor does it inevitably serve as a pernicious tool with which to thwart political action or hamper individual autonomy, or to constrain and condemn female sexuality and encourage shame. Such altered representations of prayer may reflect a more secular Irish society. In 1973, after a referendum with an almost 85 percent majority, the article subsection sanctioning the special position of the Catholic Church was removed by the Fifth Amendment of the Constitution Act (1972). The secularism characterizing modernity and modernism was ratified by a vast array of citizens in the Republic. However, daily practice was slower to see the effects of secularization. Many hospitals, and over 90 percent of the country's state-funded primary schools, continue to be managed by religious orders. Nonetheless, the late twentieth century saw progressive ideals begin to take hold, with referenda supporting the decriminalization of homosexuality (1993) and the legalization of divorce (1996). These efforts have undone long-standing prohibitions and further dismantled church authority, yet the customs of Catholic devotion endure. Even today, the Angelus chimes regularly at 6 a.m. and noon on RTÉ radio and at 6 p.m. on television before the evening news, inviting individuals to pause and recite the angel Gabriel's greeting to Mary and echo her response.

In her *Hood* (1995), Emma Donoghue responds to the obduracy of religious practice amid these cultural changes when she invokes prayer to showcase the uneven nature of mourning for her protagonist Pen, a young lesbian whose lover Cara has unexpectedly died in a car accident. The novel is organized into seven chapters, each following a single day of Pen's everyday life in the wake of Cara's death, and each interleaved with flashbacks to their relationship. In it, prayer and innovative interior monologue once more collide to depict the intricate nature of female sexuality. While attending Cara's funeral mass, Pen notes, "The priest's clichés were turning my stomach; listen out for it, yes, 'cut off in the bloom of her youth.'"[35] Faced with this enervated language, the thirty-year-old Pen covers her face and plugs her ears, recalling how as a young girl she used to spend mass absorbed in "the most lurid of sexual fantasies" (135). Mass and the restrictions of Catholic observance, such as when she would "try giving up masturbation for Lent" (136), prompt an instinctive resistance from Pen. But importantly, these same restrictions allow for imaginative and erotic pleasure because "the church was the perfect environment for what they still called impure thoughts in those days. Perhaps because the body was so limited in its movements, so dulled and contained, that the mind ran riot" (136). From this training, she discovered with

[35] Emma Donoghue, *Hood* (New York: Harper Perennial, 2011), 135. Subsequent references parenthetical.

78   PRAYING

Cara how "a demanding hand could metamorphose into an angelic tongue, or vice versa, and I could float free of the literal" (136).

The rhetorical form of prayer is efficacious (to use Lavin's term) only when its language and structure are adapted to Pen's personal experience. At the end of this service, the monsignor asks the mourners to join in reading "St. Patrick's Breast-plate," a prayer of protection attributed to Ireland's patron saint. Pen uses her voice to resist the imperatives of the church and nation that refuse to acknowledge her relationship with Cara. "I began obediently," she notes, "my voice blending into the muted clamour of voices, but found I had slipped into 'Cara be with me'" (140). She replaces "Christ" with her lover's name in this prayer, believing that no one will notice and that God will not mind. The language and practice of prayer reveal themselves to be supple enough to accommodate her sorrow. But the repetitions of prayer fail to offer her consolation, nor do her entreaties bring Cara back to life.

The collision of forms represented here heightens the distinction between the body and spirit. In her revised prayer, Pen chants, "Cara within me/Cara behind me/Cara before me" (140), which only serves to highlight Cara's bodily absence and to invite more recollections of their relationship, now lost forever. The scene volleys between articulated lines of prayer and parenthetical memories of sex:

> Cara beneath me
> (I could see her now, her face crushed into the pillow, the long notched bow of her spine under my thighs)
> Cara above me
> Instead of a final hymn, the Monsignor asked us to join in (her ever-young nipples dancing over my eyelids)
> Cara in quiet
> Cara in danger
> Cara in hearts of all that love me
> Cara in mouths of friend and stranger (141)

The two forms, public prayer and internal monologue, petition and bereavement, are vividly irreconcilable on the page. Pen ends the prayer by going silent, "paral-ysed" because "I wanted her to be in nobody's mouth but mine" (141). For Pen, the erotic embodiment floating through Catholicism makes her misperceive prayer as an easy place in which to slot her sexual desires, a form to accommodate the mys-tery of love and the obliquity of a closeted relationship that cannot yet be named. She blows open the prayer, revealing it to be a less intransigent form than imag-ined, something a young woman can single-handedly alter to suit her individual needs and her contemporary conditions. But that defamiliarization cannot strip the prayer entirely of its tenacious qualities nor its history. Pen's entreaties go unan-swered; she is refused any promised solace; and this mantra remains associated with a religion that fails to recognize her sexuality. Prayer in this context still fails her, but in that failure generates a different kind of success.

SEX AND PRAYER IN *HOOD* 79

Even in light of Donoghue's experimental structure and punctuation in this portion of the novel, as Pen here sutures sexual desire and religious practice (as Molly Bloom had before her), it might be a leap to label *Hood* as fiction broadly characterized by modernism. It centers on an experience of sexuality perceived as transgressive, like many modernist works, and it is formally organized as a series of daily first-person entries, akin to Stephen's diary in the final pages of *A Portrait of the Artist as a Young Man*. Yet Donoghue relies most on a "conservative" realism to ground her intimate account of queer love in contemporary Ireland. Accessibility matters: this is an instance of a woman writer communicating female sexuality clearly and engagingly to her audience—a tactic I have argued is integral to the activism and ethics of the stubborn mode. In this scene, she defamiliarizes prayer, divesting it of its strict association with a Catholicism that discounts her identity and experience, while maintaining the sacred and sensory pleasures of its form.

Toward the novel's conclusion, a secular ceremony celebrating Cara seems to promise more comfort and connection. Pen finds consolation in "the ritual thingy" (292) hosted by a women's support group in which Cara's friends share Irish songs, testimonies about Cara, and Adrienne Rich poems. During this ceremony, a "hippy" begins the pagan chant "We All Come from the Mother": "hoof and horn/hoof and horn/all that dies will be reborn" (294). Pen joins in quietly, finding the chant "hypnotic" (295). But the novel's conclusion does not neatly replace Catholic prayer with poetry or pagan chant as the possible remedy for Pen's grief. When biscuits are passed among the women after the ceremony, Pen refuses the suggestion that they represent Cara, though she tells the women "Take. Eat." (296), mimicking the blessing of communion. Likewise, she tells Cara's friend Jo that she still communicates with Cara, noting, "it's like talking to God. You have to sort of guess the answers. Pick up the mood" (303). Jo snorts with laughter, replying, "'I gave all that prayer business up decades ago ... Decided it was all in my head'" (303).

Ultimately, Pen regards prayer as another incomprehensible experience among others in the week following Cara's death, but one that helps to inspire an epiphany at the novel's close when she determines to come out to her mother. Even then, Pen remains alert to prayer's contradictions, its reflexive language and its tantalizing promise of transcendence, as she hears her mother's "ritual answer" in response to her request for tea (307). "All these familiar lines," Pen notes, "made it so difficult to begin anything new" (307). Yet the "familiar lines" also suggest the recognizable structure of the sacrament of confession, which here is embraced and reworked to prompt and enable a reconciliation between Pen and her mother, as well as between Pen's private and public personae.[36] Pen ends the novel ready to tell her mother "a very long story" (309) about her identity, to voluntarily claim her own private experience and articulate it publicly in her own voice. Yet the reader is not

---

[36] On the Catholic confessional imagination in Joyce, see Jonathan Mulrooney, "Stephen Dedalus and the Politics of Confession," *Studies in the Novel* 33:2 (Summer 2001): 160–179.

80 PRAYING

given access to this conversation, which falls after the novel concludes. This open ending, a feature of the modernist mode, resonates with the nature of prayer, which similarly refuses to provide neat closure to the mystery of human experience.

The Ethics of Prayer in *A Girl Is a Half-formed Thing*

Like other works studied in this chapter, Eimear McBride's debut novel *A Girl Is a Half-formed Thing* (2013) depicts a female protagonist in Ireland who seeks from prayer more than she can obtain in a narrative style that registers the fracturing of consciousness occasioned by that deficiency. Set in the late twentieth century, this novel catalogs, from the unnamed girl's first-person point of view, a life marked by two decades of ongoing trauma and abuse. Her older brother has a chronic brain tumor; her father has abandoned the family; her mother's attention is commandeered by fundamentalist Catholicism. When she is thirteen, the girl's uncle seduces her, propelling her into an affair with him that lasts her entire life, and this rape initiates a subsequent series of increasingly abject and violent sexual encounters with other men. The novel concludes with her brother's death, and in its wake, her own suicide by drowning. As critics have noted, these harrowing experiences, and the protagonist's responses to them, are conveyed through a laundry list of modernist technique, including broken syntax, unclear referents, narrative fragmentation, and stream of consciousness.[37]

When *A Girl Is a Half-formed Thing* first appeared, it was greeted with rhapsodic praise—a far cry from the dismissive assessments that previously had dogged Irish women writers employing the modernist mode. This immediate acclaim may be explained, in part, by the distinctive capacity of the modernist mode to represent the complexities of childhood sexual abuse. Across the late twentieth and early twenty-first centuries, readers have witnessed shocking widespread public revelations about the systemic and sustained abuse of children in Catholic institutions, and have been made aware of childhood sexual abuse more generally through advocacy groups such as One in Four, a non-profit named for the fact that one in four Irish citizens has suffered such violence.[38] With its deliberately challenging

[37] See, for example, Derek Attridge, "Foreword," *Joycean Legacies*, vii–xx; Katarzyna Bazarnik, "A Half-Formed Thing, a Fully Formed Style: Repetition in Eimear McBride's *A Girl Is a Half-Formed Thing*," *Studia Litteraria Universitatis Iagellonicae Cracoviensis* 13:2 (2018): 77–88; Ruth Gilligan, "Eimear McBride's Ireland: A Case for Periodisation and the Dangers of Marketing Modernism," *English Studies* 99:7 (2018): 775–792; Carey Mickalites, *Contemporary Fiction, Celebrity Culture, and the Market for Modernism: Fictions of Celebrity* (London: Bloomsbury, 2022), 163–186; Paige Reynolds, "Bird Girls: Modernism and Sexual Ethics in Contemporary Irish Fiction," *Modernism and Close Reading*, ed. David James (Oxford: Oxford University Press, 2020), 173–190; Aran Ward Sell, "Half-Formed Modernism: Eimear McBride's *A Girl Is a Half-Formed Thing*," *Hungarian Journal of English and American Studies* 25:2 (June 2020): 393–413.
[38] Such abuses have been recounted in a wealth of astute scholarly critique: see Margot Gayle Backus and Joseph Valente, *The Child Sex Scandal and Modern Irish Literature: Writing the Unspeakable* (Bloomington, IN: Indiana University Press, 2020); Sarah-Anne Buckley and Caroline McGregor,

THE ETHICS OF PRAYER IN *A GIRL IS A HALF-FORMED THING* 81

formal tactics that refuse ready comprehension and neat interpretation—along with its concentration on individual interiority—this novel's modernism insists on the intricacy of the experience of abuse for each victim. As well, despite being endemic, such abuse often goes unrecognized and therefore continues unaddressed, unpunished, and unchecked. Modernism's formal complexity demands from readers intense and concentrated attention in order to witness the intimate violence McBride depicts. This novel is a difficult read, both intellectually and emotionally taxing, even as its literary tactics are familiar and the abuses it represents age old.[39] A strategic use of the stubborn mode of modernism thus highlights important factors that make the sexual abuse of children a stubborn problem, one difficult to identify, one we cannot yet manage to solve and eradicate.

The representation of sexual abuse is not the lone project of this novel. In interviews, McBride has explicitly confirmed the continued relevance and messy capaciousness of the modernist project, asserting, "[T]here is more in this tradition than we have been led to believe. Everyone thinks modernism is dead and done, because there's *Finnegans Wake* and Beckett and they've tied everything up neatly. I really don't think they have tied everything up neatly."[40] In *A Girl Is a Half-formed Thing*, McBride untangles and reanimates modernism by using one of the oldest rhetorical forms available: prayer. Like other writers in this chapter, she repurposes prayer to interrogate the effects of religion on female consciousness. Throughout this novel, religious utterances appear not only in everyday life as profanity and invective, or as expressions of pleasure and anger, but also in formal acts of individual prayer and collective worship. The girl's internal monologue is suffused with set prayers, liturgical as well as devotional, and these help to demonstrate how deeply internalized the logics of Catholicism are, even in those who overtly and aggressively reject them. This suggests that prayer and the beliefs that

---

"Interrogating Institutionalisation and Child Welfare: The Irish Case, 1939–1991," *European Journal of Social Work* 22:6 (2019): 1062–1072; Emilie Pine, Susan Leavy, Mark Keane, Maeve Casserly, and Tom Lane, "Modes of Witnessing and Ireland's Institutional History," *Irish Literature in Transition* (1980–2020), vol. 6, eds. Eric Falci and Paige Reynolds (Cambridge University Press, 2020), 278–294. For studies of childhood trauma in *A Girl Is a Half-Formed Thing*, see Susan Cahill, "A Girl Is a Half-formed Thing?: Girlhood, Trauma, and Resistance in Post-Tiger Irish Literature," *LIT: Literature, Interpretation, Theory* 28:2 (2017): 153–171, and Anne Fogarty, "'It was like a baby crying': Representations of the Child in Contemporary Irish Fiction," *Journal of Irish Studies* 30 (October 2015): 13–26. Links between Catholicism and the girl's sexual abuse are noted by Clair Wills in "Edna O'Brien and Eimear McBride," *Irish Literature in Transition* (1980–2020), 295–303.

[39] This tension between feeling and thinking was identified by me in "Trauma, Intimacy, and Modernist Form," rev. of Eimear McBride, *A Girl Is a Half-formed Thing* (Coffee House Press, 2013), *Breac: A Digital Journal of Irish Studies* (September 2014), http://breac.nd.edu/articles/trauma-intimacy-and-modernist-form/, but subsequently simplified in some critical summaries as suggesting that the intellectual work demanded by the book's modernist form strictly "acts to reduce our emotional involvement with novel." See Derek Attridge, "Modernism, Formal Innovation, and Affect in Some Contemporary Novels," *Affect and Literature*, ed. Alex Houen (Cambridge: Cambridge University Press, 2020), 249–266, 261.

[40] Susanna Rustin, "Eimear McBride: 'I wanted to give the reader a very different experience,'" *The Guardian*, May 16, 2014, http://www.theguardian.com/books/2014/may/16/eimear-mcbride-girl-is-a-half-formed-thing-interview.

82 PRAYING

undergird it continue to shape the psychological life of the narrator long after she has shed the church's rituals and observances. It also intimates that religious practice, and prayer in particular, cannot be disentangled from the horrifying injuries and injustices endured by the girl at the center of this novel.

Prayer and "Empty Spaces"

Modernism, in general thematic terms, is often understood as a reaction against established religious, political, and social views. The powerful gesture McBride makes, in her insistent repetition of themes found in modernism's critiques of Catholicism, demonstrates how religious habits of thinking endure even after its institutions are degraded and dismantled. In 1984, according to Roman Catholic Archbishop Diarmuid Martin of Dublin, nine in ten citizens identified as Catholic, and six in ten attended mass once a week, roughly twice the level found elsewhere in Europe.[41] This number fell precipitously following a tsunami of late twentieth-century scandals exposing abuses by the Catholic Church. These included revelations in the early 1990s that revered Irish clerics Bishop Eamon Casey and "The Singing Priest" Michael Cleary had concealed romantic relationships and fathered children, the arrest in 1994 of the Belfast priest Brendan Smyth for the serial molestation of children over four decades, and the ongoing revelations of widespread abuses in Catholic-run institutions including Magdalene laundries, industrial schools, orphanages, and primary schools. Despite these revelations, and the fact that by 2011, only 18 percent of the Irish attended mass, fully 84 percent of those polled in the Republic continued to identify as Roman Catholic.[42]

Like the modernists reacting to the trauma of the First World War, McBride in this novel responds to these astonishing contemporary conditions in Ireland. Her unflinching embrace of modernist difficulty in depictions of prayer conveys a skepticism that the hegemonic effects of this practice can be punctured (because it remains resistant to generative adaptation), as well as a distrust in the liberating capacities of female subjectivity (because it changes nothing for the better). *A Girl Is a Half-formed Thing* is aggressively allusive, nodding to Catholic prayer and early twentieth-century modernism in almost equal measure. Together, they insist on the embodied intensities of the narrator's experiences, which are portrayed as vexed and painful from the novel's outset. Within the first pages, McBride imports prayer into the representation of her protagonist's in utero consciousness. Snippets of the mother's overheard prayers, offered on behalf of her young son during his

---

[41] Diane Winston, "Irish Catholics Continue to Flee the Church," *Global Post*, March 26, 2013, https://www.pri.org/stories/2013-03-26/irish-catholics-continue-flee-church.

[42] Central Statistics Office (Ireland), *This Is Ireland: Highlights from Census 2011* (Dublin: Stationary Office, 2012): 42, https://www.cso.ie/en/media/csoie/census/documents/census2011pdr/Census_2011_Highlights_Part_1_web_72dpi.pdf.

first round of brain surgery, appear amid the unborn narrator's perceived physical sensations: "Gethsemane dear Lord hear our prayer our. Please. Intercession. Night in hospital beds. Faces on the candlewick. Lino in the knees. Please don't God take. Our. Holy Mary mother of all, humbly we beseech thee."[43] By calling out Gethsemane, the garden where Christ prayed the night before his crucifixion, McBride immediately suggests the inability of prayer to alter circumstance, in particular the potential suffering and death of a beloved son. Further, this early prayer imbricates physical suffering and prayer—even before the protagonist is born. The unclear referent "our" links mother and child, intimating that the mother's petitions on behalf of her son are shared by and come at a cost to her daughter. As they wait in hospital, the girl meanwhile understands her father is "Somewhere there. I think" (4). His present-absence signals another central theme of the novel, evident after his total abandonment: "Our empty spaces where fathers should be. Whenabouts we might find them and what we'd do to fill them up" (5).

Prayer in this novel is often associated with the desire for a loving and authoritative patriarch. Those spaces vacated by "fathers"—the deliberate abstraction referencing her biological father, as well as the Christian God—are inadequately occupied by sexual activity and prayer. That paternal void first is filled imaginatively by the girl's maternal grandfather, whose arrival for a visit when she is young is marked by her announcement: "Come in God and sit down" (13). She describes her grandfather's religious devotion in a way that fuses everyday practice with sex and worship:

They were true God fearing in for a penny in for a pound. Milk-soaked mackerel for every Friday night. Mass every morning for all children over three and the wrath of God for anyone saying Jesus out loud or even in your head. For what's unsaid's as bad as, if not worse. Saturday til afternoon dedicated to praying with his wife—when none of the little could enter without a big knock. Such worshipping worshipping behind the bedroom door. With their babies and babies lining up like stairs. For mother of perpetual suffering prolapsed to hysterectomied. A life spent pushing insides out for it displeased Jesus to give that up. (14)

This passage conflates prayer and sex, with the language of prayer obscuring the reality of sex. The religious routines of mackerel "every Friday night" and mass "every morning" are represented as akin to the automatism of her grandparent's sexual relations, which unfold every "Saturday til afternoon ... worshipping worshipping behind the bedroom door." Both routines end badly for women, awarding them a life of "perpetual suffering." Moreover, when the grandfather later instructs the children that "Your body is a temple for Christ" (17), he represents

---

[43] Eimear McBride, *A Girl Is a Half-formed Thing* (New York: Hogarth, 2015), 4. Subsequent references parenthetical.

84   PRAYING

the body as a receptacle to be occupied by the authority of a masculine Christ, prompting an early confusion about what might "fill" the girl.

The grandfather is aligned with a traditional Catholicism, one that translates marital sex into routinized suffering, parental love into corporal punishment. Like a disembodied but omnipotent god, he shapes the family's behavior even in his absence. After his departure, the mother converts her father's rhetorical violence into action and beats her children. A connection between prayer and pain, endorsed by these authority figures, informs the girl's larger understanding of religion. At mass, she perceives, once again, church ritual and prayer as physically painful: the service is hot, her feet and knees hurt on the kneeler, misbehavior makes church "a dangerous place for smacking" (23). When she arrives home, she defaces an image of Christ, marking him with "a million gushing cuts" and "blood down between his legs" (24–25). When her brother finds her artistic alteration of "good suffering Jesus" (24), he labels the defaced image "dirty" and warns his sister she'll "be going down to the hot place" (25). The repetitions of prayer and worship are recapitulated in cycles of familial violence, displaced and adapted, but stubbornly repeated.

The mother is the religious force in the household who imposes the quotidian rituals of prayer and worship amid their family chaos. Yet ironically, her religious commitments, in particular to her non-liturgical female prayer group, remove her from the home and blind her to the needs of her children. The mother becomes swept up in the Catholic Charismatic renewal of the 1970s and 1980s, an embrace of Marian devotional practices that reflected larger social trends of the late twentieth century in Ireland, particularly the resistance to fast-changing social norms.[44] This focus on the symbolism and veneration of Mary, the mother of Christ, suggests particular gendered restraints against which the protagonist struggles. Marian prayers such as the Rosary are spiritual devotions that rely heavily on monotonous repetition. These repetitions stand in contrast to the more dialogic meditative practices of Ignatian prayer, imagined as a colloquy with God, which wend their way through Joyce's novels. The novel's attention to Mary, in concert with the representation of a suffering young woman, also provides a suggestive reminder of jolting historical incidents in Ireland. In 1984, at the foot of a statue of Mary situated in a grotto in Granard, Co. Longford, a fifteen-year-old schoolgirl named Ann Lovett died giving birth to a stillborn child. One year later, in a grotto located in Ballinspittle, Co. Cork, witnesses claimed to have observed a spontaneously "moving statue" of Mary, which drew hordes of pilgrims to the site and prompted similar reports of moving statues throughout Ireland. These events, which commanded national attention, not only point to the continued relevance of

---

[44] See Auge 194–216, and James S. Donnelly, "Opposing the 'Modern World': The Cult of the Virgin Mary in Ireland, 1965–85," *Éire-Ireland* 40:1 (2005): 183–245.

PRAYER AND "EMPTY SPACES" 85

Marian devotion in Irish culture but also underscore the traction of Mary's legacy of silent suffering and sacrifice into the present day.

So although the "empty spaces" to be filled in the girl are powerfully associated with fathers, actual and symbolic, the girl's mother plays a crucial role in how she understands religion and prayer. In Joyce's *Ulysses*, Stephen Dedalus refuses to kneel beside his mother's bed as she lies dying. Those around Stephen, most particularly the aggressively ironic Buck Mulligan, are puzzled by his adamant refusal to accede to his mother's wishes, to pray in order to give her comfort. This scene, often read as a sign of Stephen's commitment to his individuality and his art, also registers the power of prayer: his refusal to perform this act is a testament to its force. In this moment, Stephen announces a separation from his mother, and in doing so, repudiates the dissolution of boundaries that prayer demands. In contrast, *A Girl Is a Half-formed Thing* opens with the unborn protagonist anticipating her arrival into a world already malformed by her brother's illness and the collateral suffering that stems from this familial trauma. There is no physical distinction between herself and her mother in these early pages, and in the womb the mysteries of prayer are metrical and soothing, nurturing to the entire family. The narrator recalls her time in the womb as characterized by pleasant and unifying routines: "Learning you Our Fathers art. And when you slept I lulled in joyful mysteries glorious until I kingdom come" (5). In contrast, her birth is represented as traumatic separation, a "Dividing from the sweet of mother flesh that could not take me in again" (6). This biologically determined event initiates her lifelong pursuit of the comforts and consolations experienced in the womb, perhaps because it is the lone instance from this novel in which an adult guardian naturally and instinctively protects the girl from harm.

The novel's fixation on Mary also suggests the problematic conflation of women with objects. This conflation becomes vividly evident when, as an early adolescent, the protagonist shatters a statue of the Virgin Mary, a figurine from Lourdes circulated in rotation among the members of her mother's prayer group. As she and her mother carefully transport the statue to its next home, her mother tells her in the car that teachers think her brother may be "subnormal" (47). In response, the protagonist repeatedly belts the "Blue blond gold" statue of Mary against the car dashboard: "Take it. Take that. Take that" (48). She destroys the statue, thinking, "Fuck that virgin onto the tarmac" (48). The shame stemming from the girl's earlier mistreatment of her brother provokes a violent outburst that manifests in damage to a religious icon, similar to an earlier moment in which she defaced the image of Jesus. The destruction of the Virgin Mary—described by the profanity "fuck"—also expressly links violence against women, even against an inanimate statue of Mary, to a form of comfort and connection. After this incident, the girl weeps and her mother, uncharacteristically, soothes her; the violence has triggered a rare moment of loving solace from her parent.

False Comfort: Rape and Ritual

In the early sections of the novel, prayer is interwoven among the thoughts of the child protagonist to suggest how its logics will shape her future: prayers are uttered in adversity, and they are frequently tied to desire. The performance of prayer is not consoling, but instead associated with physical pain and suffering. It is imagined as a vocative, connective expression, but when fused with the fragmented consciousness that pulls from modernist technique, the interruptive nature of the prayers and their oblique language serve only to highlight the girl's isolation and the vacuum left by "our father"—a vacuum filled by the unexpected visit of a malevolent grandfather, rather than the consistent presence of a loving God or parent.

This association of violence and comfort, prompted by the girl's religious background and articulated in prayer, becomes acutely visible when she becomes sexually active at age thirteen, after she is raped by her uncle during his visit to her family's home. The protagonist's initial teenage infatuation with her attentive uncle is infused with prayer, suggesting that she cannot distinguish between the different forms of boundary crossings invited by religion and by sexual intimacy. Her desire for affection can be understood only as something mystical and excessive, and something that must come from a powerful male figure. When she first senses her attraction to her uncle, she perceives it as purely physical, even painful: she regards desire as akin to smoke coughed out, vomit expelled, the roast of a sunburn or sunstroke (57). When she subsequently identifies these feelings as "lust," and therefore a prompt for "mortal sin," her consciousness immediately shifts into an unadulterated recitation of the Lord's Prayer, ending with "lead us not into temptation but deliver us from evil" (57). This prayer fails. Soon after, her uncle kisses and fondles her, and she retreats alone to a nearby lake, considering the transformation this encounter has triggered. The passage records in great detail the sensory experience of her moving into the cold, murky water. She explicitly understands this as a self-baptism, thinking, "I'll put my head in for discreet baptise ... I sink baptise me now oh lord and take this bloody itch away for what am I the wrong and wrong of it always always far from thee. Ha" (62). She imagines this baptism as washing her clean of sin, but the ritual necessarily also signals rebirth, her transition from child to adult. As she exits the lake, she observes, "I don't think I will be clean now. Think instead I'll have revenge for lots of all kinds of things. The start is. That is love" (64). She returns to her home, where her uncle subsequently rapes her.

In the final chapter of *Ulysses*, Molly's reverie offers unmediated access to an account of sexual desire that provides evidence of her age and maturity. Her relationship to the church, with its patriarchal authority embodied by priests as well as by a disembodied God, is both distanced and ironic, and her free-flowing reverie moves seamlessly between her own pleasurable sensation and the futile attempts of the church to control her behaviors. As Molly recalls,

FALSE COMFORT: RAPE AND RITUAL   87

I hate that confession when I used to go to Father Corrigan he touched me father
and what harm if he did where and I said on the canal bank like a fool but where-
abouts on your person my child on the leg behind high up was it yes rather high
up was it where you sit down yes O Lord couldnt he say bottom right out and have
done with it what has that got to do with it and did you whatever way he put it I
forget no father and I always think of the real father what did he want to know for
when I already confessed it to God he had a nice fat hand the palm moist always I
wouldnt mind feeling it neither would he Id say by the bullneck in his horsecollar
I wonder did he know me in the box I could see his face he couldnt see mine of
course hed never turn or let on still his eyes were red when his father died theyre
lost for a woman of course must be terrible when a man cries let alone them Id
like to be embraced by one in his vestments and the smell of incense off him like
the pope besides theres no danger with a priest if youre married hes too careful
about himself then give something to H H the pope for a penance.[45]

Here the obliquity surrounding sexual topics that penalized so many of Lavin's
young female characters becomes, when articulated by Father Corrigan and recapitulated by Molly, a source of humor and even disdain, as well as the basis
for further erotic imaginings and considerations of the consequences of sexual
transgression, all notions that remain safely ensconced in Molly's imagination.

The first-person account of sex and desire voiced by McBride's young protagonist relies largely on her immediate sensory experiences, and in it she frequently
resorts to the abstruse prayerful language provided to her by the church. A rhetorical form with intention, prayer summons something into being. Here, she appears
to will this sexual initiation into being because she wishes to fill the "empty space"
left by her father. The intensity and enigmatic nature of prayer becomes too easily
confused with similar properties she experiences through sexual abuse. Like sex,
the powers of Catholic ritual and prayer are complex, profound, transformative—
and entirely too much for a thirteen-year-old girl. The fusion of prayer and
modernist form thus showcases the necessary limitations of the protagonist, who
cannot articulate fully or accurately what has transpired during and after this
rape. She can identify this act as a turning point, an epiphany of sorts. But she
cannot fully understand or manage its consequences. So, for instance, when she
subsequently initiates a sexual encounter with a naïve teenage boy, she mistakes
her authority as ultimate, asking and answering her own question: "What am I?
God." (78).

In the depiction of sexual violation and its consequences, *A Girl Is a Half-
formed Thing* highlights the risks and pleasures of prayer. As a rhetorical form that
requests connection with an abstracted higher power, prayer invites that divine

---

[45] James Joyce, *Ulysses* (New York: Vintage, 1986), 610.

88 PRAYING

power into the embodied self. It demands a radical openness in order to render the petitioner "one with God." This suggests a similarity between prayer and modernism, made evident when their forms collide. Modernist representations of the individual are characterized by the permeability of the self. Further, readers are invited into the unmediated private consciousness of an individual character through tactics such as stream of consciousness. A classic realism—with its narrative authority, its cogent structure, its lucid sentences—might offer a buffer, some sense that an outside authority observes, orders, and controls these events. But McBride refuses readers this distance. The pernicious modes of boundary crossing and unhealthy integration that characterize the protagonist's adolescence, when rendered in the modernist mode, feel disturbingly immediate and intimate, even as the calculated artistry of McBride's writing simultaneously reminds us of the traditions from which she draws. Both can be true.

The Stolen Child

Just as the protagonist works to refashion the rite of baptism in the middle of the novel, she attempts to transform the sacred language of prayer in the novel's fifth and final section, entitled "The Stolen Child." This section depicts the death of her brother and the attendant distress of the now university-age protagonist, which culminates in her suicide by drowning. "The Stolen Child" is entirely awash in the practice and language of prayer, ranging from the mother's incessant "scalding prayers" (179) over her dying son and the "jangle praying swaying" (180) of a visiting prayer group, to prayers of thanks before dinner (186), the priest's administration of extreme unction (205), and the litanies of mourners at the wake. In this section, prayer and physical suffering remain interwoven in the girl's mind. As the mother keeps vigil by her son's bed, the protagonist observes, "She sits with you. That night I hear. Hail holy queen hail our life our sweetness and our hope to thee do we fly poor banished children. Of Eve. And in the morning. She is there. Cross her legs with her book down. Rosary wound like rope. Pulling in her skin going white til blue" (198). The nourishing repetitions of the Rosary, enabled by the beads and the attendant prayers celebrating Mary's veneration of her son, have transformed the Rosary into a suffocating instrument of torture.

This final section is also replete with horrifying and graphic accounts of brutal sex, which are woven through with snippets of prayers and religious imagery. When her uncle sneaks into her bedroom as they await her brother's imminent death, she resists his sexual overtures but then succumbs and feels in her orgasm the complicated pleasure of their encounter. Afterward, she ends with prayer: "Now peel his body off to kneel and while he will stay off I pray. Pray this will all be gone" (185). Later, when the protagonist seeks out a violent sexual encounter with a filthy vagrant, her uncle discovers them. He beats the vagrant, while the protagonist's stream of consciousness aligns her with Christ's suffering. As her uncle drags her away, she feels the Christ-like "burn on nettles and thorns barbwire" (190). And when the uncle bites her breast in anger, blood rises to the surface of her white skin. This recalls the Christian symbolism of the pelican, who wounds its own breast to feed blood to its starving brood, in which the bird comes to represent Christ, who sacrificed himself for the redemption of his followers. The simulated act of ritual sacrifice—as with the self-baptism that initiated her sexual life—fails to provide her transcendence or nourish those around her, confirming the inaccessibility of this ideal.

The brother's wrenching deathbed scenes perversely provide almost a respite from the raucous, terrifying sexual encounters with her uncle and the vagrant cataloged by the protagonist. During her brother's final days, the girl elects, on the advice of her mother, to attend mass. Here, she again is filled by prayer and its habits:

> Sunday go. Sit rove praying. Not like when I was little long ago though, when I was some other thing. I bow my head. But the words of prayers are come coming into me as I have never been gone. Gone from praying or the house of God. You take away the sins of the world. Have mercy on us. Lamb of God you take away the sins of the world. Have mercy on us. Lamb of God you take away the sins of the world. Grant. Us. Peace. Fill my shallow breathing. What I could be. Be granted peace. After all this. After all I am Mary Magdalenish. I would wash with my hair, wash away sins. Lord I am not worthy to receive you but only say the word and I shall be healed. (202)

Once more, her perceptions and feelings are filtered through familiar prayers, which are now directed to the "you" of God, not to her brother. Amid these prayers, she invokes Christian saints to obtain further consolation. Mary Magdalene, according to the Gospels, traveled with Jesus and the disciples, and witnessed his crucifixion, burial, and resurrection; Mary Magdalene is sometimes confused, as she is by the protagonist, with the "sinful woman" who anoints Christ's feet with her hair (Luke 7:36–50). This reference aligns the alienated protagonist not only with a trans-historical community of "fallen women" awarded forgiveness, but also with the generations of Irish women incarcerated in the infamous Magdalene laundries, Catholic institutions that detained women accused of sexual transgression. This prayer, and the association with Mary Magdalene, provide the narrator temporary solace. With communion having offered her grace, she exits, experiencing what appears to be a genuine reprieve from suffering: "after go in peace to love and serve the Lord, thanks be to God" (202).

On exiting the church, however, she immediately encounters the vagrant with whom she had the previous violent, anonymous sexual encounters by the lake. His entreaty literally interrupts the feeling of mercy conditionally awarded to her by

90 PRAYING

mass: "After communion, after go in peace to love and serve the Lord, thanks be to God I step out of the church. Immaculate blue sky. If I carry my state of grace Hello girleen I thought it was you" (202). His catcalls replace "grace" with "shame" (202) and wash away the relief and acceptance temporarily provided by the Catholic mass, thus confirming the evanescence of a ritual that promises enduring sustenance. The catcalls are a sordid version of the manic repetitions of Lavin's Mad Mary who chanted outside of the town's mass in "Sunday Brings Sunday." Written roughly a half century apart, these two works depict traumatized female protagonists who leave mass and encounter an articulated response to their prayers offered in church, albeit not a response from a beneficent God but one thrust on them by troubled individuals on the margins of society. In both cases, such a response heightens the suffering of these young women.

This contest, this battle of will between the girl and God that began in utero, continues to shape her consciousness. As the novel draws to a close, the account of practical activities, of taking care of her brother and preparing for his funeral, are riven with phrases and passages drawn from prayer. These prayers, in dialogue with McBride's invocation of modernism, overtly demonstrate the failures of the church and its system of belief for the protagonist. As she waits and watches for her brother's death, for instance, she thinks, "Jesus is coming. Jesus will be here soon. I'll rip his arms. I. Won't have God's son here I. Won't. Jesus will lose you. This time I say I'll win. I. Will. Make you safe this time" (206). She works to alter prayer, to fragment it, to reshape it, but prayer remains recalcitrant, obdurate in its refusal to provide her consistent and meaningful protection or succor. After her brother's death, she breaks into tears, again offering her own revised prayer that beseeches, "Your will be done not mine no let mine let mine" (211). She can rework this rhetorical form, but she cannot alter the outcome of real-life events. The random but pervasive infusion of prayer throughout the narrative demonstrates her lack of control, as well as her inability to excise its logics tethering love to suffering and sacrifice.

The conflation of her brother and Christ in this final section of the novel is not subtle. As the mourners wait for the undertaker, she thinks, "My brother. My Son" (203). In the immediate wake of his death, her thoughts still infused by the language of prayer and worship, she cries and queries, "Who am I talking to? Who am I talking to now?" (212). She announces the vacuum left by her dead brother, as well as by the silent interlocutor of Catholic faith. The loss of her brother propels her into even more aggressively self-destructive behavior, as she races again to the vagrant's waterside hideout. As she seeks him out, she chants "my will be done" (215), appropriating the language, and seemingly the agency and authority, of God. But once at the lake, the vagrant brutally rapes her. Bleeding, beaten, and covered in vomit, she returns home where her mother shames her, and as she climbs the stairs to her bedroom, she hears the collected group of mourners praying behind the closed door of her brother's room. But their prayers fall flat, merely recorded and entirely unintegrated into her stream of consciousness. The promise of a Lord who will attend his followers through every hardship is completely at odds with the narrator's exile and her separation from her brother.

In her review of McBride's second novel, *The Lesser Bohemians* (2016), Jacqueline Rose asserts, "What fucks up language is fucking—good, bad or indifferent."[46] In this novel, what fucks up language is praying. In the final moments of the novel, the habits and language of prayer entirely fall apart, as do the embodied repetitions that have characterized sex throughout the narrative. After overhearing the prayer in her brother's bedroom, the protagonist goes to the bathroom to cleanse herself. Her uncle enters the bathroom, ostensibly to care for her wounded body, but instead he offers her the "comfort" (221) of sex, the perfunctory and toxic solace he knows to offer, the perfunctory and toxic solace she habitually accepts. In this scene, the language entirely collapses: the capital "I" of her narrative shifts to the lower-case "i" and phrases become even shorter, more halting, more punctuated, more abstruse. Without her brother, or the fictions of faith to sustain her, her self—still unnamed—cannot be articulated. The next day, with the prose returning to its previous fragmented style, her mother condemns her: "Well my girl, you may look down your nose at my beliefs and friends but I wasn't out throwing myself on every man passing while my brother was dying. You are disgusting. You are. Sick in the head" (224). This insult obviously links her with her brother, who has just died of a brain tumor. But as the thoughts running through the protagonist's "head" and chronicled in stream of consciousness have demonstrated, the separation her mother identifies between "belief" and promiscuity are not as distinct or impermeable as she contends. The conflation and overlap between religion and sex—and most important, the rhetorical and logical similarities between their expression and representation in this novel—are irrefutable.

The Perils of Reverence

When the protagonist, at the novel's close, drowns herself, the words that conclude the book are "My name is gone" (229). Her final self-baptism has entirely wiped away her history and identity, ostensibly, as she imagines, providing a new birth, a new chapter for her both literally and figuratively. She has made incarnate the words of prayers that she overheard murmured behind her dead brother's door. The mourners collectively chant these lines drawn almost verbatim from Isaiah 43:2:

> Do not be afraid—I will save you.
> I have called you by name—you are mine.

---

[46] Jacqueline Rose, "From the Inside Out," rev. of Eimear McBride *The Lesser Bohemians, London Review of Books* 38:18 (September 22, 2016): 11–12, 11.

92 PRAYING

> When you pass through deep water [*sic*], I will be with you;
> your troubles will not overwhelm you.
> When you pass through fire, you will not be burned;
> The hard trials that come will not hurt you.
> For I am the Lord your God. (220)

Read in light of her suicide by drowning, these lines of prayer might suggest that its promised comforts are realized: that the girl will "pass through deep water" and as a result "hard trials that come will not hurt you." McBride contends that this final moment of the novel is transcendent, the suicide an act of authority that allows her protagonist to escape the suffering and oppression of her life and to name and thus claim herself.[47] That reading suggests that the prayer that suffuses the book, even as McBride demonstrates its constant failure, ultimately maintains its promise and potentiality for the girl. If the afterlife that these prayers, no matter how mechanical, seek to announce, address, and therefore create actually exists, then perhaps the girl seizes her own satisfying ending, choosing for herself a good death leading to a compensatory afterlife. As such, her self-baptism finds its place in a legacy of Irish writing in which women take on the authority of a Catholic priest, such as that seen when Maurya in J. M. Synge's *Riders to the Sea* (1904) scatters holy water over the corpse of her drowned son.

However, the reality of this young woman's death by suicide pushes against any redemptive reading of the conclusion. The suicide offers neat closure, leaving readers with little of the openness and ambiguity frequently associated with the modernist novel. While the novel's language is richly ambiguous, its plot is not. The modernist experiment, including the unmediated access to her consciousness, neither conceals the suffering she endures nor justifies the fate she meets. As such, the end of this novel resonates more with the naturalism of Kate Chopin's feminist classic *The Awakening* (1899), whose protagonist drowns herself to escape the suffering imposed by social conventions, than with Molly's internal monologue in *Ulysses*, which ends with its affirmative "Yes." Readers are left to wonder whether such bleak determinism, in which the only option for the girl seems an elective escape from the mortal world, stems from Catholic doctrine with its implacable condemnation of female transgression, or from a literary naturalism that insists on a world governed by heredity and environment.

The static produced by the novel's constant friction between prayer and modernism is underscored by the title of the final chapter, named after an early Yeats poem, "The Stolen Child." A ballad published in 1886, "The Stolen Child" recounts the pagan tale of unearthly Sidhe who lure a child from the mortal to the fairy

---

[47] "Interview with Eimear McBride," interview by David Collard, *The White Review* (May 2014), http://www.thewhitereview.org/feature/interview-with-eimear-mcbride/.

realm.[48] Each of the poem's first three stanzas chronicles the fairies' activities and concludes with a refrain whose final line insists, "For the world's more full of weeping than you can understand" (ll. 12, 27, 41). In the fourth and final stanza, when the child goes away with the fairies, the last line of the poem announces that he has now moved from a world "more full of weeping than he can understand" (ll. 53), but the stanza largely highlights the quotidian pleasures of the human world, with its soothing routines of lowing calves, singing kettles on the hob, and bobbing brown mice. Such a contradiction exposes the sinister nature of the fairies and their incomplete representation of human experience. "The Stolen Child" also provocatively represents water as an alluring means of escape, with fairies beckoning the child to come "To the waters and the wild/With a faery hand in hand" (ll. 10–11, 25–26, 39–40, 51–52). These supernatural figures appear to offer the child nourishing guidance and relief from suffering, but in fact they lure him to death by water. So distilled of its poetry, this poem—like McBride's novel—culminates in the tragic drowning of a susceptible young person.

Both Yeats and McBride, in their respective versions of "The Stolen Child," highlight the risks of reverence—defined as the gracious acceptance of hierarchical structures and relationships. As William Fitzgerald notes in his study of prayer as rhetoric and performance, "Reverence springs from apprehension, acceptance, and articulation of a state of fundamental dependence on beings conceived as both otherworldly and vital to one's very self."[49] But reverence can be displaced onto the wrong objects of worship, stimulate the wrong states of emotion, and inspire the wrong forms of devotion. In the fiction studied across this chapter, the repeated prayers of female protagonists directed to a disembodied power often underscore the failures of the real-life individuals and institutions that neglect or too avidly (and malignantly) attend to these women and their petitions. Reverence, a dependence on that which is "otherworldly" and "vital," too easily allows for confusions that enable the very real abuse of power over vulnerable subjects. O'Brien, Lavin, Donoghue, and McBride use prayer in part to capture the qualities that make an adherence to the beliefs and practices of institutional Catholicism in Ireland alluring, so alluring that individuals might elect to ignore, justify, or even succumb to the abuses it allows. By placing prayer in dialogue with literary modernism, they ask readers to look more closely and more critically at conventional and even revered patterns of language, behavior, and thought tied to religion that obscure female suffering, and by doing so, they demonstrate the possibilities for social critique still embedded in and waiting to be extracted from the stubborn mode.

---

[48] W. B. Yeats, "The Stolen Child," *W.B. Yeats: The Poems*, ed. Daniel Albright (London: Dent, 1990), 44–45.
[49] William Fitzgerald, *Spiritual Modalities: Prayer as Rhetoric and Performance* (University Park, PA: Penn State University Press, 2012), 135.

3

Daydreaming

(Edna O'Brien, Anne Enright, Deirdre Madden)

Irish women's contemporary fiction, as I have argued, is invested in making the private experiences of Irish women public for broad readerships; to gain accessibility without sacrificing complexity, they often use easily identifiable literary forms and contexts to represent the maneuverings of female consciousness and to depict the complicated nature of privacy for Irish women. Prayer represents one rhetorical form that, when it collides with modernism, vividly demonstrates the ongoing frictions between public and private in a culture powerfully influenced by Catholic beliefs and practices. This chapter focuses on depictions of reverie, or daydreaming, a highly subjective and formless psychological experience. Reverie has been well represented through modernist experiment, with Molly Bloom's soliloquy in the final chapter of James Joyce's *Ulysses* likely the most renowned example. But reveries shape the content and form of other modernist fiction from the fragmented prose signaling the daydreams of the young expatriate female narrator in Jean Rhys's short story "Mixing Cocktails" (1927) to the escapist fantasy of a happier future in Europe that captivates Helga Crane in Nella Larsen's *Quicksand* (1928) to the entwined interior monologues of Virginia Woolf's *The Waves* (1931). A diffuse mode of consciousness that permits unconstrained and associative thought, reverie as depicted in fiction provides a means of exposing aspects of female consciousness that are considered taboo and hidden from view—with Molly's considerations of sexual pleasure, marital infidelity, and menstruation again providing a paradigm.

Irish women writers have adopted and adapted modernist representations of female reverie, often tempering those experiments. By neatening and giving order to stream of consciousness, while maintaining its more recognizable features, these writers manifest one of the dominant characteristics of contemporary Irish writing in all genres: a deliberate engagement with past forms to depict current conditions. Familiar by now to readers, stream of consciousness is the literary technique in which a character's thoughts, feelings, and conscious reactions to events are represented as a continuous flow of impressions.[1] The character's perceptions and

---

[1] For an account of the history and complexities of this term, see Rebecca Bowler and Claire Drewery, "One Hundred Years of the Stream of Consciousness," *Literature Compass* 17:6 (June 2020), https://doi.org/10.1111/lic3.12570.

Modernism in Irish Women's Contemporary Writing. Paige Reynolds, Oxford University Press. © Paige Reynolds (2024). DOI: 10.1093/9780191990540.003.0004

meditations appear on the page rendered as if an extended soliloquy, one generally uninterrupted by conventional dialogue or objective description. A term first coined by William James in *The Principles of Psychology* (1890) to describe a theory of mind, stream of consciousness as a literary technique appears to grant readers immediate and unfettered access to the thoughts of a character, even as it challenges readers with its rejections of narrative sequence and grammatical conventions. It can make public the interior psychic world of characters, as well as unveil experiences that were repressed or silenced.

By making use of this and other precedents found in literary modernism, Irish women's contemporary fiction explores how the private experience of female reverie is shaped by the dramatic cultural and economic transformations characterizing the late twentieth and early twenty-first centuries. Edna O'Brien's novella *Night* (1972) invokes the stubborn mode to represent not only the transgressive sexuality of its female protagonist, but also her complicated relationship with labor and material culture. O'Brien deliberately nods to Molly Bloom in her depiction of female reverie, but she tightens and orders Joyce's stream of consciousness to represent the thoughts of her Irish narrator living in 1970s England. This technique not only calls attention to O'Brien's mastery of modernist form, but also exposes new liberties, erotic and otherwise, available to her narrator who daydreams in the throes of the sexual revolution. The interplay between reverie and history becomes even more apparent in two twenty-first-century novels set in the Republic during the Celtic Tiger economic boom. Anne Enright's *The Gathering* (2007) considers the aftershocks of late twentieth-century revelations of widespread childhood sexual abuse in Ireland, and Deirdre Madden's *Molly Fox's Birthday* (2008), the effects of the shattering violence of the Northern Irish Troubles. Both temper the experiments of modernist stream of consciousness with lyrical realism to demonstrate how changing contemporary conditions enable imaginative excess for Irish women, even as their characters bear the lingering burden of cultural biases against female reverie.

Modeling the narrative incoherence and ambiguity characteristic of modernist experiment, these depictions of reverie propose a new way of thinking about this mental state, one that draws attention to its capacity for fostering creative personal reflection on thorny public issues. In particular, these novels consider how domestic objects—those commonplace things that litter our everyday lives, which we frequently overlook—prompt modes of consciousness. For the daydreamer, the material culture of everyday life can become a site of political promise. More than simply commodities that distract or oppress, everyday objects invite a stillness and attention that might be reparative. These objects invite the female narrators to become lost in thought, to process their grief, and to parse the unresolved events of their younger years. Their daydreams reveal the important dialectic between the constraints of daily life, with its routines and material entrapments, and the freedom of unrestrained thoughts that inevitably arise each day in the midst of those

96   DAYDREAMING

activities and objects. The meditations provoked by things are not always comfort-able or satisfying. Instead, they frequently spark intellectual or affective responses that are troubling, even appalling—so appalling in fact, that each of the female narrators discussed here retreats from what the object reverie reveals to her. In these instances, the stubborn mode of modernism may seek less to posit solutions for the stubborn problems on view than to underscore their intractability.

Reverie, Objects, and Irish Modernism

Our current understanding of reverie—which remains both abstract and oblique, much like the practice itself—derives largely from eighteenth- and nineteenth-century concepts related to psychology, trance, and phantasmagoria, and therefore focuses largely on interiority and the individual.[2] Modernist experiment was and remains an apt tool for representing reverie, not least because it famously urged a shift in attention from the objects populating the outside world to interior human psychology. Critical work in modernist studies has persuasively demonstrated that this dichotomy is a false one by revealing that the attentive depictions of the material world understood to characterize realist fiction also appear throughout modernist writing.[3] Drawing from such antecedents, Irish women writers con-sider the complexities of the relationship between material objects, those concrete things in the world, and daydreams, the ineffable meanderings of consciousness. Their contemporary fiction confirms that reverie can be aimless and invisible, but it is not necessarily without purpose—and it can, like the dreams depicted in Surrealist art, reshape the aesthetic forms that seek to represent it.[4]

Irish modernism provides ample instances of reverie prompted by objects, examples that lay bare native attitudes toward the material world. In many of these texts, a material object initiates a reflective state that culminates in the production of creative work. For instance, W. B. Yeats identified an object as the inspiration for his poem "The Lake Isle of Innisfree" (1890): "[P]assing a shop window [in London] where there was a little ball kept dancing by a jet of water, I remembered waters about Sligo and was moved to a sudden emotion that shaped itself into

---

[2] Attempts to theorize reverie in literary criticism are generally embedded in studies of other states of mind, and are (perhaps necessarily) oblique and imprecise. Patricia Meyer Spacks usefully eluci-dates the historical relationship between boredom and imagination in *Boredom: The Literary History of a State of Mind* (Chicago: University of Chicago Press, 1995); Terry Castle traces how the daydream becomes pathologized in *The Female Thermometer: Eighteenth-Century Culture and the Invention of the Uncanny* (Oxford: Oxford University Press, 1995), 140–167; and John Plotz considers drifting attention in *Semi-Detached: The Aesthetics of Virtual Experience since Dickens* (Princeton: Princeton University Press, 2018).

[3] See, for instance, Douglas Mao, *Solid Objects: Modernism and the Test of Production* (Princeton: Princeton University Press, 1998).

[4] Walter Benjamin, "Surrealism," *Reflections: Essays, Aphorisms, Autobiographical Writing*, ed. Peter Demetz (New York: Harcourt Brace Jovanovich, 1978), 177–192.

'The Lake Isle of Innisfree.'"[5] Here, an expressly commodified object transports him from the commercial market in which it participates to the imagination, the past, and nature. In *Cathleen ni Houlihan* (1902), written by Augusta Gregory and Yeats, the young Irish hero Michael's reveries push him away from the material world, including new clothes and the rewards of a dowry, and toward the political self-sacrifice demanded by the 1798 Rising. In Synge's *The Playboy of the Western World* (1907), Christy's reveries about the pleasures of household objects in the shebeen partly inspire the budding poet's exodus from the corrupted community of Mayo. These "good" reveries elicted by objects push their male subjects, real and imagined, away from the corruptions of the material world and into the more vaunted realms of imagination, political struggle, and artistic freedom.

However, after the founding of the Free State in 1922, daydreams in Irish literature, particularly those expressly associated with the material, were more frequently represented as dangerous for both men and women, as a "bad" form of private excess that must be constrained by Foucauldian discipline. In Teresa Deevy's play *The King of Spain's Daughter* (1935), Annie's reveries of romance and freedom are quashed by her domineering father who consigns her to indentured factory work, and in Mary Lavin's novel *The House in Clewe Street* (1945), Gabriel's consistently bad judgment is associated with his propensity to daydream. In a similar vein, a 1968 short film commissioned by the Department of Posts and Telegraphs exhorts Irish citizens to resist reverie and open a Post Office Savings Account. In this film, entitled *Love and Money*, a young office worker played by Milo O'Shea passes the time by daydreaming about various schemes to "get rich quick," a series of elaborate fantasies portrayed in scenes to which the film audience is privy.[6] When his fiancée ends their relationship because he lacks savings, the young man is compelled to reject reverie in favor of industry so that he might obtain the rewards of a new home and a family. His smiling visage in the final shot confirms that the reality of Irish thrift trumps his Hollywood-inflected daydreams. In these instances, high and low, reverie was at odds with the industrious rural ideal celebrated by de Valera's Ireland, a bias neatly coupled with the frugal anti-materialism advanced by church and state.

Thus while reverie emerged as a crucial motif influencing the form and content of many influential twentieth-century texts, a deep and persistent ambivalence, and even suspicion, about the practice is manifest in experimental Irish literature. For Flann O'Brien's student in *At Swim-Two-Birds* (1939), daydreaming can be read as mere procrastination; for Elizabeth Bowen's Pepita in the short story "Mysterious Kôr" (1944), it represents a consoling if misguided retreat from wartime reality; for the eponymous protagonist of Samuel Beckett's *Krapp's Last*

---

[5] W. B. Yeats, *The Memoirs of W. B. Yeats*, ed. Denis Donoghue (New York: Scribner, 1972), 31.
[6] *For Love and Money*, dir. Ronald Liles, 1968, *Seoda: Treasures from the Irish Film Archive 1948–1970*. DVD. Irish Film Institute, 2009.

98 DAYDREAMING

Tape (1958), it codes as an instance of mental constipation. The residue of modernism's more general anxieties about reverie not only coats these works, but also more recent critical considerations of female reverie in Irish writing. For example, in Seamus Deane's account of "boredom" he represents female reverie as defined largely by its erotic content, while Gregory Dobbins's account of "idleness" suggests reverie is a practice unnecessary for satisfied wealthy or working Irish women.[7] But a look at Joyce's *Dubliners* (1914) suggests that female characters in Irish modernism were neither too busy working to daydream, nor focused wholly on sex in their reveries.

In "Eveline," the titular character—who "had to work hard both in the house and at business"—sits at home with her head propped against a window observing the outside world and recalling her "rather happy" childhood.[8] As Eveline peruses her domestic surroundings, "reviewing all its familiar objects which she had dusted once a week for so many years," she worries that if she elopes with her suitor Frank, "she would never see again those familiar objects from which she had never dreamed of being divided" (37). Her attachment to these objects seems less vexed than her attachment to her abusive and manipulative father, who also lives in the home. Despite their evident decay and disuse, these objects are comforting in their familiarity. And yet, as she observes a "yellowing photograph" hanging below a "broken harmonium" and "the coloured print of the promises made to Blessed Margaret Mary Alacoque," each a decaying object loosely tied to the consolations promised by art and religion, Eveline realizes that she does not recognize the priest depicted in the photograph.[9] Because it represents the fate of emigration (the priest lives in Melbourne now, her father casually tells visitors), the photograph triggers further ruminations about what she might lose if she leaves Dublin, what she might retain if she elects to stay. In this story, a domestic object spurs complex critical thinking, which can be accommodated in the time of a private reverie. But ultimately, the reverie in this story serves merely as an internal manifestation of Eveline's external paralysis, made evident at the story's conclusion by her inability to leave her home for a new life in Buenos Aires.

Dubliners again represents female reverie as an exercise culminating in the passive acceptance of restrictive social norms in "The Boarding House." The final

---

[7] Along with the "pursuit of a private, bodily pleasure," the "day-dream" is for Seamus Deane one means by which Joyce's bored female characters elude the regulatory and systemizing qualities of modern life in *Strange Country: Modernity and Nationhood in Irish Writing since 1790* (Oxford: Oxford University Press, 1997), 169. For Gregory Dobbins, Yeats can indulge productive reverie while Gregory is merely the patron who enables it, and his "lazy idling schemer" is "specifically gendered as male" because Irish women writers focused on "alternative female public spheres in which women enjoy a degree of agency and satisfaction in their work prohibited to them at large in an increasingly conservative Irish society" in *Lazy Idle Schemers: Irish Modernism and the Cultural Politics of Idleness* (Dublin: Field Day, 2010), 28.

[8] James Joyce, "Eveline," *Dubliners: Viking Critical Edition*, eds. Robert Scholes and A. Walton Litz (New York: Penguin, 1969), 36–41, 37, 36.

[9] Ibid., 37.

scene of this story depicts the reverie of Polly, the daughter of Mrs. Mooney who manages the eponymous property. In this moment, as Mrs. Mooney coerces the lodger Bob Doran into proposing to her daughter, Polly sits alone on a bed where she "regarded the pillows for a long time and the sight of them awakened in her mind secret amiable memories. She rested the nape of her neck against the cool iron bed-rail and fell into a revery."[10] That is, until her mother interrupts her daydream and calls her downstairs to speak with Mr. Doran, who now must propose to Polly as the socially mandated corrective to their previous sexual indiscretions. As the story ends, Polly is jerked away from the pleasures of her daydream by her mother's call, and the final line reads, "Then she remembered what she had been waiting for."[11] The brief moment of pleasure and imaginative freedom that Polly's reverie allows, her authority to focus electively on "secret amiable memories," is evacuated by the external call of real life, the harbinger of a future as a wife and mother over which she has little control.

For Eveline and Polly—both near nineteen years old, both working women—the reverie represents what Jonathan Crary has labeled a "counter form of attention." For Crary, the "daydream ... has always been a crucial but indeterminate part of the politics of everyday life," one that has the potential to challenge the imperatives of efficiency and productivity.[12] But while this subversive quality is hinted at in *Dubliners*, where these instances of female reverie suggestively remove the characters from the burdensome demands of modern life, this state is only temporary and ends for these young women in a predictable fate—as caretaker to an abusive father, or as wife to a resentful husband. In these stories, free indirect discourse draws further attention to the tension in the narrative between female authority and external constraints; it allows readers to feel that they have immediate access to the interior states of these women, when in fact, literary form reminds us that an anonymous narrator (and male author) choreographs and controls our access to their daydreams.

Night's Feminist Reverie

Joyce's representations in *Dubliners* of female reverie resonate with those found in the work of other modernists. As Bryony Randall recounts, modern thinkers ranging from Max Nordau to T. S. Eliot helped secure our understanding of daydreaming as a negative or even dangerous distraction. Many of those whom she studies, including William James and Henri Bergson, regard reverie as a form

---

[10] Joyce, "The Boarding House," *Dubliners*, 61–69, 68.

[11] Ibid., 69.

[12] Jonathan Crary, *Suspensions of Perception: Attention, Spectacle, and Modern Culture* (Cambridge, MA: MIT Press, 1999), 77.

100 DAYDREAMING

of dispersed attention, a practice that is passive and unproductive—and often gendered female. For Randall, however, the dispersed attention of the daydream instead offers "an alternative modernist temporality," one counter to the more familiar and disruptive shock commonly ascribed to this movement, an "everyday temporality which evades the quantifiable, the masculine and the public."[13] The fictional depiction of the meandering of consciousness has long been regarded as one way to resist aspects of modernity including the standardization and the relativity of time. Rejuvenated by Irish women writers, such familiar experiments demonstrate the possibilities that derive from imaginatively reviewing, and potentially recalibrating, obdurate problems under new historical conditions. There is a utopian quality to the modernist daydream: to step out of public time in such a way, an untimeliness highlighted through the revivification of a literary mode, is also to suggest the possibility of evading conventions that govern conduct. However, the continued invocation of a time-honored modernism showcases the obduracy of certain modes of representation and thus underscores how difficult it is to escape particular patterns of behavior or ways of thinking.

The final chapter of *Ulysses*—in which Molly Bloom's nighttime reverie is tracked through stream of consciousness, in eight long and almost entirely unpunctuated sentences—might be the paradigmatic modernist daydream. Though critics continue to debate the accuracy of Joyce's representation of female consciousness, "Penelope" does depict, through its experimental form, a reverie largely uninterrupted by the intrusion of daily responsibility (though not bodily imperatives) on its female protagonist, whose musings unfold in a private bedroom, uninterrupted by her sleeping husband. Molly is sequestered, virtually the entire day, in her bedroom, demonstrating the tension between the liberties of private consciousness and the constraints of the domestic interior—a trope that surfaces across representations of female reverie. But her reverie is not a full-stop retreat from real life. For example, externally ordered time interrupts her thoughts, as when a train whistle inaugurates the chapter's fourth sentence or when her monthly menses begins. Nor is the content of her daydream strictly personal. The understanding of Molly as laser-focused on sexual matters has held tight to this chapter since its publication, but her reverie touches on a range of vexing social problems, among them Catholic patriarchy, women in the workplace, military conflicts in India and southern Africa, Irish national politics, capital punishment, urban crime, religious and ethnic prejudice, and issues related to sexual welfare including birth control, pornography, and venereal disease. Many of these problems are merely noted, with Molly quickly diverting her attention back to personal matters, but her recognition of such challenges, as well as her outlandish imagined alternatives to them, might be understood as one early stimulus for the small,

[13] Bryony Randall, *Modernism, Daily Time and Everyday Life* (Cambridge: Cambridge University Press, 2007), 39, 40.

practical changes in her routines, including ones that may enable a meaningful reconciliation with her husband. In *Ulysses*, the innovative formal structures of modernism capture the surprising interior states that foster self-reflection and provoke real-world action, suggesting that the daydream is not simply a regressive retreat into bourgeois interiority.

Published a half-century after *Ulysses*, Edna O'Brien's *Night* (1972) may provide in its reworking of Molly's reverie the most explicit example of Joyce's modernism invoked by a contemporary Irish woman writer.[14] Over one evening in the early 1970s, the narrator Mary Hooligan delivers from the comforts of bed a rambling soliloquy, one that deliberately echoes "Penelope" in form and content. No longer married and parent to an adult son, Mary is an Irish immigrant temporarily house-sitting for her English employers. Plagued by insomnia, she reminisces across this sleepless night about her childhood in the fictional Irish town of Coose, her migration to Liverpool and London, her roles as wife and mother, and a string of lovers and jobs spun across her lifetime. Mary's detailed attention to her erotic history presupposes an audience schooled in new norms put in place by the sexual revolution and second-wave feminism. But it also hails readers familiar with modernism's rebellious intentions and desire to shock. The erotic content, which might invite the book to be dismissed as romantic fiction, is awarded intellectual gravitas through its association with modernism. As the promotional copy on a 1987 paperback edition trumpets, this "erotic reverie ... shows Edna O'Brien as one of our foremost heirs to modernism," and it plucks from a 1973 review asserting that "'some of the sexual passages here are worthy of Joyce.'"[15]

O'Brien's characteristic attention to female sexuality often has been paramount in popular and critical assessments of her work, but to be entirely distracted by the salacious content of *Night* is to misunderstand its broader appropriations and critique. The book was written amid the furor set off by Kate Millett's feminist classic *Sexual Politics* (1970), which tethered literary to political analysis. In her evaluation of male writers, including the modernists D. H. Lawrence and Henry Miller, Millet dissected misogynistic literary representations of female sexuality to expose the stubborn problem of masculine cultural authority. *Night* does similar work, adapting the experiments of canonical male modernists to display the limits of their representations of not only female sexuality, but also female consciousness. Much has been made of Joyce's influence on O'Brien's writing, and the resonance with his work throughout this novel is unmistakable.[16] Yet *Night* also demonstrates

---

[14] Other contemporary fiction that revisits and revises the character of Molly Bloom includes Judith Kitchen's *The House on Eccles Street* (2002), J. M. Coetzee's *Elizabeth Costello* (2003), and Maya Lang's *The Sixteenth of June* (2014). For a reading of Lang, see Leah Culligan Flack, *James Joyce and Classical Modernism* (London: Bloomsbury, 2020).

[15] Edna O'Brien, *Night* (New York: Farrar Straus Giroux, 1987). Subsequent references parenthetical.

[16] See Michael Patrick Gillespie, "Edna O'Brien and the Lives of James Joyce," *Wild Colonial Girl: Essays on Edna O'Brien*, eds. Lisa Colletta and Maureen O'Connor (Madison, WI: University of Wisconsin Press, 2006), 78–91, and Ellen McWilliams, "James Joyce and the Lives of Edna O'Brien,"

102 DAYDREAMING

the wider ambit of O'Brien's expertise in modernist writing. She described it as a "hallucinatory novel" written while she read Proust, a writer whose work reminded her that "our needs, our feelings, and our loves and our half loves are formed in our youth and that as adults we are retapping them in our relationships with men and women."[17] She also recalled, upon moving to London in 1960, attending a scholarly lecture on Hemingway in which the speaker "read out the first paragraph of *A Farewell to Arms* and I couldn't believe it—this totally uncluttered, precise, true prose, which was *also* very moving and lyrical."[18] In his reading of the novel as a response to the Troubles, Dan O'Brien cites her praise for "those who had written about war, especially Hemingway, Orwell and Auden" even as she noted that the Troubles were "a different war ... fought openly and in the shadows."[19] The admixture of influence in *Night* reveals O'Brien as not only an heir but also a critic of a masculine modernism—a point cemented by her dedication of the book, "For the lads." Although literally addressed to her sons, this might also be read as a cheeky nod to the male modernist writers with whom she engages in the novel.

The collision of an array of modernist forms—from Joyce, Proust, Hemingway, and Lawrence, among others—draws attention to the artifice of a male modernism, the limits and freedoms their innovations offer contemporary women writers as a means of personal expression. O'Brien plucks female reverie free from the hero's myth that structures and organizes *Ulysses*, but the legacies of a male literary tradition nonetheless intrude on this novel. Throughout, form calls out overtly or nods subtly to these influences. Mary provides a sweeping personal history, of the sort found in the ordered and expansive realist novel, but her thoughts and memories are associative and impressionistic. The novel skips from moment to moment across her life, and it conveys her thoughts through well-worn modernist tactics including stream of consciousness, unindicated temporal and spatial shifts, and short fragmented sentences filled with unconventional syntax and invented words. At the same time, O'Brien regularly modifies and neatens the form used to represent Molly Bloom's uninterrupted reverie: there are complete sentences, paragraph breaks, indicated dialogue, standard punctuation. For Mary, sexual conventions and personal relationships are easily revoked, but the rules governing literary form and standard language appear difficult to shed. Modernist influences, modernist form, and even modernist writers live beyond their moment in *Night*.

Modernist Afterlives in Irish Literature and Culture, ed. Paige Reynolds (London: Anthem Press, 2016), 49–60.

[17] Elgy Gillespie, "Our Edna—A Song of S.W.3," *Irish Times,* June 10, 1972, in *Conversations with Edna O'Brien*, ed. Alice Hughes Kersnowski (Jackson, MS: University Press of Mississippi, 2014), 13–17, 15, 16. On *Night* as an extension of modernist texts that use hysteria as a narrative technique, see Helen Thompson, "Hysterical Hooliganism: O'Brien, Freud, Joyce," *Wild Colonial Girl*, 31–57.

[18] Shusha Guppy, "Edna O'Brien, The Art of Fiction, No. 82," *The Paris Review* 92 (Summer 1984), https://www.theparisreview.org/interviews/2978/the-art-of-fiction-no-82-edna-obrien.

[19] Dan O'Brien, *Fine Meshwork: Philip Roth, Edna O'Brien, and Jewish-Irish Literature* (Syracuse: Syracuse University Press, 2020), 107.

Mary house-sits for "Jonathan and Tig," characters who bear the real-life nick-names of John Middleton Murry and Katherine Mansfield, though these writers died decades before her reverie unfolds.[20]

Night enacts its critique of twentieth-century constraints on Irish women by rendering its protagonist the culture's worst nightmare: a financially independent, sexually promiscuous woman who daydreams. Like Eveline and Polly in *Dubliners*, Mary is a working woman whose thoughts drift amid the economic, familial, and libidinal constraints that order her life. Unlike these characters, she is a middle-aged woman who can indulge her sexual freedoms at little cost. But Mary cannot shake free the cultural baggage that condemns the permissiveness of daydreams, as reverie celebrates the individual, imaginative pleasure, the wasting of time—all contrary to the industrious, self-sacrificing collectivity at the heart of Irish rural imagination.[21] Despite her many years in England, the anxieties about reverie that infiltrated Irish culture continually surface in Mary's soliloquy. Having settled into her position as a temporary house-sitter, she looks about the well-appointed English surroundings and wonders, "Maybe I should not have come here, maybe it has given me a taste for reverie. I should have gone as a dairymaid or a lady's companion, or even a gentleman's companion" (44–45). Here again, O'Brien offers readers an askew temporality, as Mary imagines herself in industrious occupations more fitted to a nineteenth-century novel than to her present-day reality. Throughout her reverie, Mary's language further reminds readers of the tensions between tradition and innovation. She employs anachronistic terms that allude to the outdated ideological inheritance that shapes her, or conversely she invents entirely new terms to capture what the vocabulary available to her in the present fails to describe.

The novel recapitulates the associative nature of female reverie that Joyce sought to depict, but it also underscores the fact that, even in her more contemporary moment, Mary remains subject to external forces, often dated ones, that impose themselves on her imagination and shape her daydreams. In England, Mary obtains her economic security through temporary employment, which ranges from barmaid to nude model, and a short-lived marriage, which ends when her husband accuses her of infidelity. She represents her precarity as adventure, and the novel invites us to regard her lack of professional control as matched by her sexual freedom, her economic penury compensated with romantic excess. As she reviews her life, she insists, "I've had better times, of course—the halcyon days, rings, ringlets, ashes of roses, shit, chantilly, high teas, drop scones, serge suits, binding attachments, all that" (3). The novel's experimental prose

---

[20] Thompson, 38.
[21] See Clair Wills, "Women, Domesticity and the Family: Recent Feminist Work in Irish Cultural Studies," *Cultural Studies* 15:1 (2001): 33–57.

104 DAYDREAMING

points, through its many inventories, to an imaginative world shaped by accumulation. This inflects even Mary's erotic history, which she describes as unfolding with "A motley crew, all shades, dimensions, breeds, ilks, national characteristics, inflammatingness, and penetratingness. Some randy, many conventional, one decrepit" (23).

Yet throughout the novel, objects give the lie to Mary's empowered narrative and the consolations of excess such lists suggest. For Mary, daydreams are pleasant exercises but ones that render her vulnerable. Recounting her early days in an English resting hall where she could indulge "another read or a daydream," she notes, "The only thing that mars the full bliss of it is that I am perpetually afraid that people are going to trip over me. I have the impression that there is some frangible inside me that's going to get dislodged and fall out if I am crashed into" (35). That this memory is recounted in the present tense demonstrates the immersive quality of reverie. And that Mary interprets her vulnerability in such vividly material terms—that her consciousness is like a fragile object that might topple if disturbed—reflects the novel's larger investment in material objects as way to understand and convey the amorphous and abstract content of such reveries.

Night early and often undermines any notion that modernism should be defined by its hostility toward the object-ridden world of the realist novel. In her depiction of objects, O'Brien grants authority to another predecessor, Elizabeth Bowen. Throughout Mary's extended reverie, objects play a familiar symbolic role. But the uncanny nature of the things in this novel derives in part from Gothic conventions, such as those James Wurtz identifies in the colonial modernism of Elizabeth Bowen's *The Last September* (1929). There, "exhausted chairs and sunburnt windows" convey the enervation of the Anglo-Irish inhabiting the Big House at the center of Bowen's novel, and "household objects take on the energy that the characters do not have."[22] For Mary, an Irish immigrant working in the former imperial capital, objects in the home take on similarly uncanny attributes in her imagination. This energy can stem from the animation awarded to sacred Catholic objects, as found in the "little altar" she makes in the home, peopled with "various statues and icons" (45); or it may reside in the deliberate confusion of subject and object, as with the "papier-maché lady, very gruesome but nice" (47) that Mary "covet[s]" (47) and that accompanies her at dinner.

In reverie, objects are imbued with autonomy and authority by the free play of Mary's imagination. As she prepares to depart the home, domestic goods prompt her exodus: she hears the mirrors, the ingots, the silver cockatoos, and the "beautiful brass Portuguese chandelier" urge her to "Begone, begone" (117). But often, rather than a productive tool to stimulate awareness of her conditions and generate new modes of critique, the objects in this novel—as manifest in

---

[22] James F. Wurtz, "Elizabeth Bowen, Modernism, and the Spectre of Anglo Ireland," *Estudios Irlandeses* 5 (2010): 119–128, 122.

her reveries—simply showcase the cultural limitations in place due to her gender and class status. Mary exists as an Irish domestic servant to English professionals, and her reveries necessarily unfurl across one sleepless night because that allows her the uninterrupted time necessary for such self-examination. If stream of consciousness seeks to expand the present moment, using form to present new modes of temporality, Mary's soliloquy exposes the strain actual female experience places on this modernist tactic. In the final line of the novel, Mary addresses the star of the morning, imploring, "let's live a little before the awful all-embracing dark enfolds ..." (117). Rather than the neat and assertive "Yes." that clinches Molly's reverie in *Ulysses*, the ellipsis at the conclusion of *Night* signals a lack of closure. It reflects the diffuse nature of her nighttime reverie, now ended by the start of the day whose practical necessities—where will she live, what work will she do—will demand Mary's full attention.

Even in a novel that regards the material world largely as a register of limitations for its female protagonist, objects still manifest in reverie the potential to expose hidden truths. They provide tangible traces of an otherwise invisible history. At the novel's end, Mary considers her impending displacement upon the imminent return of her employers. As she prepares to abandon the comforts of this home, damaged domestic objects left behind telegraph her personal travails. She catalogs "the breakages, the dining-room table, the patched sugar bowl, the ignoble graffiti, and the brandy snifters that so joyously got severed from their stems" (116). These objects, as we discover in her reveries, provide evidence of her dramatic break from her lover Moriarty. They make public the private experiences and thoughts of a domestic worker told by letter to "vamoose" (116) before the owners return home.[23] These battered objects, when observed or "read" by her employers, might extend and make visible the content of her private ruminations. But of course, they cannot convey the complete story to those who will encounter them and thus embody the same puzzlements as found in the narrative's blank spaces and discontinuous plot.

Using the modernist mode, O'Brien demonstrates where and how female reverie, even in the contemporary moment, is interrupted, shaped, or denied by the insistent demands of the outside world. By evoking modernist depictions of female reverie, and by making the anticipated sinuousness of the form repeatedly stall or fracture, O'Brien exposes where and how and why a characteristically male modernism fails to capture female interiority. She also highlights ongoing cultural anxieties about the allure and danger of unfettered female reverie. Weaving together sexual freedom and class consciousness, she renders contemporary female experience in tune with the earlier experiments of Lawrence, and

---

[23] Rebecca Pelan reads the destruction of objects as a sign of Mary rejecting the house and her "inheritance as an Irish woman" of "values of an entrenched rural culture." See Rebecca Pelan, "Edna O'Brien's 'Love Objects,'" *Wild Colonial Girl*, 58–77.

106   DAYDREAMING

she depicts immigration as characterized by a sense of rootlessness understood both as liberation and hazard like Rhys before her. Finally, Mary's detailed attention to the outside world and the objects that people it gives shape and meaning to the charged experiences she recounts, ranging from the appearance of her mother's ghost to her multiple ménages à trois. The residue of stream of consciousness in *Night* insists on the immersive and subjective nature of perception, and underscores the obdurate centrality of material culture and everyday domestic experience in the imagination of female characters.

Object Reveries in Celtic Tiger Fiction

Decades after Mary Hooligan's soliloquy, the twenty-first century in Ireland might appear to promise female characters more space and time to daydream, to indulge their reveries whenever and wherever they wish. The narrators of Anne Enright's *The Gathering* and Deirdre Madden's *Molly Fox's Birthday* are both university-educated women cushioned by their financial security from back-breaking labor. Veronica in *The Gathering* is a former journalist, whose career has taken a backseat to her domestic responsibilities as wife and mother, as well as the recent redecoration of her home in an affluent Dublin suburb. The unnamed narrator of *Molly Fox's Birthday*, unmarried and living in London, is a guest in Molly's well-appointed Dublin home. She is a successful playwright who has recently suffered her first failure and consequently grapples with writer's block. Neither woman is so consumed by the demands of practical labor that she cannot indulge, or even deliberately create time for, reverie. The central characters in these novels seemingly have the social and economic authority to invent or reshape, reject or embrace traditional domesticity. Both women have, as Woolf once implored, a room of their own.

As such, they benefit from transformative material changes in women's lives in Ireland. Across much of the twentieth century, domestic labor had been composed of demanding everyday tasks and routines: until the 1940s, half of Ireland's population heated water and cooked over an open fire, and had no sanitary facilities; until the 1950s, many homes did not have access to electricity; and throughout the 1960s, running water remained an anomaly for most rural households.[24] Women were granted more freedoms by certain social and material changes of the late twentieth century, including wider educational opportunities, birth control, and the women's movement, factors to which Evelyn Conlon attributes the profusion

---

[24] See Jenny Beale, "Maidens and Myths: Women in Rural Life," *Women in Ireland: Voices of Change* (Gill and Macmillan, 1986), 20–40; Caitriona Clear, *Social Change and Everyday Life in Ireland, 1850–1922* (Manchester: Manchester University Press, 2007); Mary Daly, "'Turn on the Tap': The State, Irish Women, and Running Water," *Women and Irish History*, eds. Maryann Valiulis and Mary O'Dowd (Dublin: Wolfhound Press, 1997), 206–219.

OBJECT REVERIES IN CELTIC TIGER FICTION 107

of women's writing in contemporary Ireland.[25] During the economic boom of the Celtic Tiger, more women joined the workforce, a change also attributable to employment equity standards set by the European Union. However, even today, women continue to bear the greater burden of childrearing and household labor, and their attention remains in demand. Nonetheless, a rising standard of living and increased purchasing power for many during these years may have enabled more, or at least different, space and time for reverie—as, no doubt, did the long commutes engendered by Ireland's new and notorious suburban sprawl.[26]

The Gathering and *Molly Fox's Birthday* outline varieties of privileged domesticity that now permit certain Irish women creativity and daydreaming. Crucially, the dreamers in these books are both writers. As with the "purported autobiography" of *Jane Eyre* deftly analyzed by Debra Gettelman, these novels draw attention to themselves as an aesthetic form that can ably represent the routine consciousness of reverie, the imaginative meandering that characterizes these women's lives.[27] Enright and Madden, as well as the female narrators whom they have created, transform, as Sigmund Freud a century before had urged, private daydreams into aesthetic objects to be consumed by broad publics, thereby keeping alive the activist energies of Irish women's modernism. In his 1907 lecture "Creative Writers and Day-Dreaming," Freud described the daydream as a compensation or substitute for real-life frustration, and he celebrated the capacity of (male) writers to transform the free play of their private daydreams into accessible public art.[28] That the reveries in these novels are documented by women writers, real and fictive, deliberately draws attention to the ethical necessity of representing female consciousness not simply to understand better individual human experience, but also to invite the public to share in these clandestine thoughts.

More particularly, these novels depict the workings of female consciousness in an Ireland suddenly flush with things, suggesting a new and potentially provocative relationship between material objects and reverie.[29] Gaston Bachelard has

---

[25] Ruth Carr, "Contemporary Irish Fiction," *The Field Day Anthology of Irish Writing: Irish Women's Writings and Traditions*, vol. 5, eds. Angela Bourke, et al. (New York: NYU Press, 2002), 1130–1138, 1131.

[26] For an overview of the economic conditions of these years, see John O'Hagan, "The Irish Economy 1973 to 2016," *The Cambridge History of Ireland 1880 to the Present*, vol. 4, ed. Thomas Bartlett (Cambridge: Cambridge University Press, 2018), 500–526. For an account of how the Tiger unevenly benefitted women, see Sinéad Kennedy, "Irish Women and the Celtic Tiger Economy," *The End of History: Critical Reflections on the Celtic Tiger*, eds. Colin Coulter and Steve Coleman (Manchester: Manchester University Press, 2003), 95–109.

[27] Debra Gettelman, "'Making Out' *Jane Eyre*," *ELH* 74:3 (Fall 2007): 557–581, 574.

[28] Sigmund Freud, "Creative Writers and Day-Dreaming" (1908), *The Standard Edition of the Complete Psychological Works of Sigmund Freud*, trans. and ed. James Strachey (London: Hogarth Press: The Institute of Psycho-Analysis, 1953–1974), vol. 9: 141–154.

[29] Toby Barnard has bemoaned the neglect of material culture studies in Ireland, attributing it to a shortage of relevant documentation, the scarcity of artifacts, and an "ideological resistance to the topic" fostered by colonialism and sustained poverty, and nurtured by religious and political ideologies. Toby Barnard, *A Guide to Sources for the History of Material Culture in Ireland, 1500–2000*, Maynooth Research Guides for Irish Local History 10 (Dublin: Four Courts Press, 2005), 16.

108 DAYDREAMING

identified the capacity of material objects to trigger reverie, a form of consciousness that he regards as among the highest states of mind, in part because of these objects' associations with childhood. These "object reveries" manifest when the individual isolates and contemplates an object, then subsequently imbues it with meaning. The "faithfulness to a familiar object" enables a form of fruitful intimacy between subject and object.[30] As Bachelard asserts, "The reverie dreamer's diffuse *cogito* receives from the objects of its reverie a tranquil confirmation of its existence."[31] Here, objects are awarded the beneficial ability to secure attention and evoke reverie, a critical and creative form of consciousness, and thus to consolidate and confirm reciprocal being. For other theorists, the relationship between objects and daydreams is vexed, particularly for women. In *Everyday Life in the Modern World*, Henri Lefebvre regards reverie as "an escape into make believe," a retreat from critical thinking that is inspired by the everyday, which "weighs heaviest on women."[32] In his assessment, everyday life and the commodities that clutter it prompt women to "close their eyes to their surroundings, to the bog into which they are sinking and simply ignore it."[33] Objects are delusional traps and reverie a pathetic coping mechanism that renders women "incapable of understanding" their relationship to "everyday life and modernity."[34]

The objects that populate everyday life—in Lefebvre's censorious account, "the things that matter" to women—provide for the narrators of *The Gathering* and *Molly Fox's Birthday* a useful inspiration for reverie, for becoming lost in thought. The nature of daydreams—their fantastic, even ridiculous, content and their capacity to offer temporary, if illusory, relief from overwhelming reality—means they are often devalued. But as with O'Brien's *Night*, these novels suggest that reverie might be a valuable component of critique, one that heightens awareness of our surroundings and forces us to attend with fresh eyes to familiar but perhaps unseen circumstances. It invites the consideration of outlandish possibilities, richly creative alternatives that otherwise would (and sometimes should) be constrained by reality and actual practice. By offering a mode of imaginative detachment from habit and distraction, reverie provides the women in these novels access

---

While true, Stephanie Rains has documented Dublin's vibrant consumer culture across the nineteenth and early twentieth centuries in *Commodity Culture and Social Class in Dublin 1850–1916* (Dublin: Irish Academic Press, 2010), and the influence of American consumerism on notions of early twentieth-century Irish womanhood is addressed in Gerardine Meaney, Mary O'Dowd, and Bernadette Whelan, *Reading the Irish Woman: Studies in Cultural Encounters and Exchange, 1714–1960* (Liverpool: Liverpool University Press, 2013), 171–195.

[30] Gaston Bachelard, *The Poetics of Reverie: Childhood, Language, and the Cosmos* (1960), trans. Daniel Russell (Boston: Beacon Press, 1969), 166.

[31] Ibid.

[32] Henri Lefebvre, *Everyday Life in the Modern World* (1968), trans. Sacha Rabinovitch (New Brunswick, NJ: Transaction Publishers, 1984), 73.

[33] Ibid.

[34] Ibid.

OBJECT REVERIES IN CELTIC TIGER FICTION   109

to the "slightly marginal position" vis-à-vis the everyday that Lefebvre allows male intellectuals.[35]

Modernist form in *The Gathering* and *Molly Fox's Birthday* helps to convey the vital but complicated role the object reverie plays in depictions of familial and social trauma. Written in the wake of revelations about widespread childhood sexual abuse in Ireland and the aftermath of the Troubles, these novels put on display female characters as they process the effects of these historical traumas. Like Ford Madox Ford's *The Good Soldier* (1915), both novels are impressionistic, and their non-linear narratives depict how individual consciousness moves between past and present. By mimicking this type of modernist non-linearity, both novels call into question the reliability of their female narrators, as well as suggesting more generally that memory, as managed by a single consciousness, is fickle and even fallacious. Enright has spoken of her interest in exploring the "connections" between realism and modernism in her fiction, explaining that modernism "is often concerned with a kind of ever-expanding present, a moment" and realism "is about continuity, about cause and effect."[36] Through the attention awarded to Veronica's daydreams, atemporal episodes that interrupt and arrest the narrative's forward trajectory, Enright foregrounds the formal tension between the modernist "moment" and realist "cause and effect." Veronica's reveries, particularly those centered on the past, are circuitous and subject to frequent revision, qualities Enright identifies as distinctly modernist. She contends, "the process of remembering and forgetting and undoing the forgetting and re-remembering and all of those, these are great, and also very modernist, questions."[37] In her representation of female consciousness, Madden is likewise concerned with memory and representing the distension of the present moment, a quality that explains her affinity for Proust, whom she has called "the great artist of time and memory."[38] The lack of action and meandering prose of *Molly Fox's Birthday* functions formally to expand time, a tactic that Madden inherits from not only Proust, but also Henry James and Woolf.[39]

Contrary to prior literary and theoretical accounts of female reverie, these contemporary novels hint that the interior state of the object reverie is not just a source of distraction and an escape from daily life, but may be a critical exercise necessary to engender meaningful cultural and political change. Written amid the Celtic

---

[35] Ibid., 74.

[36] Anne Enright, "An Interview with Anne Enright," *Anne Enright, Visions and Revisions: Irish Writers in Their Time*, eds. Claire Bracken and Susan Cahill (Dublin: Irish Academic Press, 2011), 13–32, 30.

[37] Ibid.

[38] Deirdre Madden, "Looking for Home: Time, Place, Memory," *Canadian Journal of Irish Studies* 26:27 (Fall 2000/Spring 2001): 25–33, 32.

[39] Carly J. Dunn, "The Novels of Deirdre Madden: Expanding the Canon of Irish Literature with Women's Fiction," PhD diss., Indiana University of Pennsylvania, 2014, 203. See also Margarita Estévez-Saá, "Deirdre Madden's Portraits of the Woman Artist in Fiction: Beyond Ireland and the Self," *Nordic Irish Studies* 10 (2011): 49–62.

110 DAYDREAMING

Tiger, these novels also consider the provocative role that material culture might play in such a process. Concerned with memory and identity, Enright and Madden focus on characters whose highly subjective recollections of the past intrude on their present-day reality, a practice made visible through their use of the stubborn mode of modernism. In these novels, the invocation of modernism urges a reconsideration of female reverie; both demand reverie be understood as more than simply passive retreat, as more than simply the futile imaginative reconstruction of necessarily inexact personal history. Retrospective reverie is personal and therapeutic, but it also can hold prospective imaginings of a social future.[40] A conscious engagement with the past, the modernist mode in these novels suggests, might change time to come.

Object Reveries in *The Gathering*

Winner of the 2007 Booker Prize, *The Gathering* has invited rich considerations of its depiction of memory, its engagement with the sex abuse scandals in Ireland, its interrogation of modernity, and its representation of mourning. It also offers a provocative study of the complexities of female reverie. In a sustained interior monologue, the protagonist Veronica Hegarty deliberately records her actions and thoughts following the death by suicide of her younger brother Liam. The novel puts on view her imaginative reconstruction of three generations of her family's past in her attempt "to bear witness to an uncertain event," the possible molestation of Liam as a child, "this thing that may not have taken place."[41] Veronica's heightened attention in her own writing to reverie suggests that literary form can ably represent the imaginative meandering that characterizes her daily life in the aftermath of Liam's death. It also reveals the role that form plays for her in stoking, as well as managing, unchecked or excessive reverie.

As documented in her first-person narrative, Veronica's reveries are triggered by the crisis of Liam's shocking death. They surface as she manages the practical tasks demanded of her by this loss: she announces his death to family members, identifies the corpse and chooses the coffin, organizes and attends the wake and funeral. Early on, as she leaves Dublin to claim her brother's body in Brighton, household imperatives like carpooling and preparing meals shift to her husband and children, and Veronica observes, "There is something wonderful about a death, how everything shuts down, and all the ways you thought you were vital are not even vaguely important" (27). In the throes of mourning her brother, she suffers from acute depression and dissociation. As a result, she retreats from her domestic life,

---

[40] This quality of reverie is also considered in Matthew Schultz, "Molly Bloom's Nostalgic Reverie: A Phenomenology of Modernist Longing," *Irish Studies Review* 26:4 (2018): 472–487, 476.

[41] Anne Enright, *The Gathering* (New York: Black Cat, 2007), 1. Future references parenthetical.

OBJECT REVERIES IN *THE GATHERING*   111

in particular from her relationship with her husband, and her familiar routines are disrupted, due in part to insomnia. In her current state of grief, Veronica manifests an obsessive and repetitive mental state that interferes with her capacity to function normally. Following Liam's death, she explains, "I stay up all night. I write, or I don't write. I walk the house" (36). Her evenings are spent in fanciful meditations interrupted by cleaning, drinking wine, and writing "endlessly" about her fantasies of how her grandmother Ada and her landlord Lamb Nugent first met (38). Trying to describe this unusual behavior, she writes, "There are long stretches of time when I don't know what I am doing, or what I have done—nothing mostly, but sometimes it would be nice to know what kind of nothing that was" (38). Veronica's imagination takes flight in the wake of this family trauma. Yet to the outside world, and even sometimes to herself, this imaginative labor looks like "nothing."

Awash in the new freedoms available to women in contemporary Ireland, Veronica nonetheless bears the burden of long-standing notions of female reverie as fruitless or even decadent. Trying to identify the origins of her daydreams, Veronica recalls the act of washing dishes as a child with Ada. During these visits to her grandmother's home, she would move seamlessly in reverie between past and present, truth and fiction. She could imagine, as she worked, the nature of her grandmother's orphaned childhood, the inevitable death of her own mother, and the future adventures she and Liam would share. Yet she recalls that Ada disliked such imaginative exercises: "There was something about imagining things, or even remembering them, that she found slightly distasteful—like gossip, only worse" (90). Despite this legacy, Veronica notes, "These days, of course, I do little else. And it is all her fault. Because if I look to where my imagining started, it was at Ada's sink, in Broadstone" (90). Here the features of passivity and excess that have historically characterized female reverie are embedded in Veronica's assessment of this habit as she blames Ada for the compulsive "imagining" that currently consumes her days. But her assessment suggests another characteristic of female reverie. For Veronica, reverie is hard, unsettling work and not without cost; it reveals heart-breaking truths, it lands her in dark places, it troubles her family life.

Veronica's anxiety about reverie is heightened further by her family history. She dreads any association with her mother, who as a younger woman suffered a series of psychological "breakdowns" (46) induced by her many pregnancies and her twelve children, and now in old age is a "vague person" (4) in the throes of dementia. Likewise, Veronica fears the contagion represented by Liam, whose interior state she imagines describing to her daughters as such: "there are little thoughts in your head that can grow until they eat your entire mind. Just tiny little thoughts—they are like a cancer, there is no telling what triggers the spread, or who will be struck, and why some get it and others are spared" (175). The consuming quality of "little thoughts" that feel unpredictable and pathological, even biological and potentially fatal like cancer, seem particularly threatening to Veronica, as she is

112   DAYDREAMING

consumed by her quest to understand the potential source of Liam's depression, his drinking, and his status as a *"messer"* (163). Veronica, steeped in narratives about the dangers of reverie and living amid family members whose interiority has bred only pain for themselves and others, has reason to fear her own meditative intemperance.

As Veronica attempts to reconstruct her family history, a diverse array of material objects evokes memories and triggers fantasies about the "uncertain event" she hopes to recall and communicate. Throughout the novel, everyday things elicit from her fantastic reveries that may or may not be true: a pink fingerstall on her grandmother's hand leads her to consider violence and suffering in her family, an old rent account book might reveal the origin of her brother's abuse, a restaurant's wet wipe links her to St. Veronica, who wiped the face of Christ on the way to Calvary. The novel insists that objects, rather than representing mere commodities that distract or oppress as Lefebvre suggests, demand a kind of stillness and attention that heightens awareness and improves comprehension. Everyday objects invite Veronica to become lost in thought, to process the grief stemming from Liam's death, to parse the events of her youth, and to evaluate the unsatisfying middle-age she has been living in "inverted commas" (181). Her object reveries, facilitated by the rich topos of the everyday, help her better comprehend her individual and historical conditions, though she is often dismayed by their revelations.

These material objects on occasion seem to promise Veronica a prophylactic from reverie and the dark places it might take her. They serve, for example, to distinguish her from her mother and Liam. She notes that Liam was notoriously careless with objects, which he would consistently "lose" or "steal" (126), and her mother, even when young, was constantly misplacing her purse, keys, and glasses, generating in her children a feeling of "collective guilt" about the loss of these items (3). In stark contrast, Veronica's relationship to things is thoughtful and deliberate, as evidenced in part by her careful and ongoing attention to material objects past and present. She recognizes that everyday things offer the promise of distraction, of comforting narratives, of effective self-presentation. As the novel begins, Veronica recalls pocketing a cuttlefish bone while walking on the beach with her daughters in order to privately "comfort my hand with the secret white arc of it" (1). Before we have any sense of the childhood sexual abuse she will describe in the middle of her narrative, Veronica conveys a desire to remake touch by musing about her consoling contact with an inanimate object, notably one that, as the skeleton of a former living creature, gives durable, concrete evidence of a life once lived. In such instances, material objects communicate clear messages and provide ontological security—a found cuttlefish bone offers comfort in grief, just as lost keys suggest a perilous carelessness to be avoided.

But even as objects provide the impetus for her reflective daydreams and offer a flash of consolation, the material world in reverie largely fails to grant Veronica the psychic security she seeks. For example, as she recollects time spent as a child at her grandparents' home with her siblings Liam and Kitty, a pink rubber bathing cap with yellow flowers provides the object around which her shifting adult memories of these visits circulate. Remembering "the delicious, fantastic pink bathing hat, with the floppy yellow flowers," she recalls eating the plastic flowers and having them appear the next day in her diaper (99). She then almost compulsively revises the memories caused by the bathing cap as she considers actual dates and contexts; she questions which sibling ate the cap, whether or not her grandfather found the flowers, if the cap was pulled over her head as a child, how it got there, if her grandmother removed it and comforted her. As an adult, Veronica wants to retrieve and handle the bath cap, as she had the cuttlefish bone. She writes, "Sometimes, in second-hand clothes shops, I look for objects like these, thinking that if I could hold the hat in my hands, if I could stretch it and smell it, then I would know which was which and who was who out of Kitty, and Liam, and me" (99–100).

This is one of many instances in which Veronica hopes that objects and her consideration of them will expose or secure facts—here, the truth of her identity, the boundaries separating her from her siblings—and one of many instances in which those objects refuse her. The "delicious" and "fantastic" nature of the object matters here, because it demonstrates her confusion between the object itself—the banal, mass-produced rubber bathing cap—and the incredible reveries it provokes. It also represents one of many times that Veronica's imagination confuses and conflates a material object with the human body. In her mind's eye, she sees "me, definitely, pulling the bathcap over my face. I lick the salty inside of it, until it seals me up ... Then I start to drown in the pink light" (99). She continues, imagining this incident as if a revised scene of birth, with the cap a womb from which she emerges and Ada as her mother: "Did this happen? The world hurting as the cap is pulled away; Ada, outside of me, shouting. Me being pushed into her meagre breast" (99). The cap inspires meditations on childhood, meditations Veronica can reshape through fantasy into positive experiences like being saved from certain death or being comforted by a nourishing maternal figure, even as this object and the reverie it inspires, refuse to clarify "which was which and who was who."

The refusal of reverie to reveal in imagination what is hidden in fact appears elsewhere in the novel. In another example, Veronica remembers in detail the marital bed of her grandparents, Charlie and Ada, as "a mahogany affair, with two swags of little flowers joining in a bow on the headboard" (57). The bed, according to Veronica, represents the site of Ada's newfound authority through marriage, the bed "is luxury to lie in and Ada has come into her estate: her own bed, with her own bottles and potions on the chest of drawers, and all her things, books and breakfast, about her" (58). In this imaginative account, Ada's marriage to Charlie grants her previously unavailable pleasures: physical conjugal pleasures, of course, but also the material rewards that attend the joining of households such as gifts and

114 DAYDREAMING

dowries. As well, those material rewards manifest the delights of female authority: "if the bed is a palace to her, then Charlie is her magnificent fat guest" (58). Veronica romanticizes the bedroom here, as well as the early relationship between her grandparents. Importantly, she filters her understanding of their history—which eludes her because it is private, as private as the acts that unfold in their bed— through the objects occupying their bedroom. These visible household objects allow her imagined access to their interiority. Like ruins, these things provide concrete evidence that allows Veronica to construct, through her daydreams, a plausible narrative about the past. Yet even though these objects offer evidence that might expose the truth of their relationship, the actual nature of Ada and Charlie's marriage remains cloistered.

Through such reveries, Veronica comes to understand the limitations of things: they cannot make legible her family history. She hopes, for example, that photographs, a packet of letters, and even the rent account books she finds in her mother's home will explain the relationship between Ada and her landlord Nugent; these in turn will help her to determine whether or not Nugent molested her brother. The rent books fail to provide this answer, though the ruminations prompted by the drab books confirm for her that discomfiting understanding that the Hegarty children "were manifestly *of little account*" (236). For all of the auspicious qualities of everyday objects, their promise to secure human connections and, like material evidence in a detective novel, to reveal what is hidden, these commonplace objects fail to do more than unnerve those who make time to ponder their status as things. This likely explains why, when considering her own new home in the present day, Veronica catalogs the domestic objects she has thoughtfully sourced and announces, "I spend my time looking at things and wishing them gone, clearing objects away. This is how I live my life" (37). Given the profligate reveries these objects stimulate, and their failure to reveal or secure the facts of history, this comes as little surprise.

Object Reveries and Childhood Sexual Abuse

Like other works of Irish women's contemporary fiction, *The Gathering* demonstrates the repercussions of external circumstance on female consciousness. In this instance, Veronica grapples with the exposure of a long history of widespread sexual abuse in Ireland and how these revelations require she revise her reading of her own childhood and that of her brother. When considering the distance that arose between her and Liam as teenagers, she notes, "Over the next twenty years, the world around us changed and I remembered Mr. Nugent. But I never would have made that shift on my own—if I hadn't been listening to the radio, and reading the paper, and hearing about what went on in schools and churches and in people's homes. It went on slap-bang in front of me and still I did not realise it" (172–173).

Here, Veronica demonstrates the power of retrospective reading, of seeing experiences from the past more accurately in light of the altered conditions of the present day. But even in this moment of awareness, her linguistic obfuscation suggests the difficulty of directly tackling "it"—the unfathomable, and here literally unnamable, horrors of childhood sexual abuse.

In the middle of the novel, Veronica announces that she intends "to make things clear" about Liam's abuse because "real events have real effects. In a way that unreal events do not. Or nearly real. Or whatever you call the events that play themselves out in my head" (223). Her dawning awareness of the suffering of Liam, and others like him, provoked not only by his suicide but also by the public scandals disclosing widespread childhood sexual abuse in Ireland, turns her—temporarily, as she grieves—from people to things, from public institutions to private reverie. Throughout the novel, her close attention to objects may be explained in part by "how tainted by trauma [her] relationship with the human body has become," a dilemma identified by Liam Harte in his study of unresolved trauma in the novel.[42] That is, Veronica turns to objects for relief from corrupted bodies. But her object reveries also suggest the political potential of imaginative retreat. The radical ambiguity of the daydream allows Veronica, in creative imagination, safely to confront potentially overwhelming risky subjects and disturbing possibilities. Though volatile, her object reveries are private and invisible: they have no inherent practical consequence and can therefore enable radical imaginative considerations of real-world issues. Female reverie is thus wrested from its long-standing representation as an entirely personal and vacuous experience to one that might promise some ultimate public benefit.

Sitting uneasily between waking rationality and sleeping dreams, reverie troubles and provokes Veronica throughout the novel. She is aware that her reveries are fanciful and fictive, that they are a tool that she uses to access and construct a narrative that may or may not be accurate. Yet the familiar objects that might anchor her thoughts and expose reality, that might reveal certitudes surrounding Liam's abuse, become in her reveries even more alien, confirming Giorgio Agamben's assertion that "the troubling alienation of the most familiar objects is the price paid by the melancholic to the powers that are custodians of the inaccessible."[43] Objects reveal themselves to be dangerously unpredictable, to conceal discomfiting truths as frequently and randomly as they expose them.

This ambiguous space between subject and object, dreaming and rational thought, allows Veronica tentatively to imagine, to manage, and eventually perhaps to accept sweeping, and often dark, realities about human nature. Throughout her daydreams, she is confronted by disturbing interrelations and overlaps between

---

[42] Liam Harte, "Mourning Remains Unresolved: Trauma and Survival in Anne Enright's *The Gathering*," *LIT: Literature Interpretation Theory* 21:2 (2010): 187–204, 198.

[43] Giorgio Agamben, *Stanzas: Word and Phantasm in Western Culture*, trans. Ronald Martinez (Minneapolis: University of Minnesota Press, 1993), 26.

116 DAYDREAMING

subject and object.[44] One evening, she sleepily and drunkenly considers from a window in her home the headrest of her parked Saab. Anthropomorphized, the car's headrest gives upsetting testament to "the possibility that people don't care about each other" (132). According to Veronica, this "slumped figure in the front seat"—again, the headrest—"talks ... quite bluntly, of patience and the ability to endure" and informs her of men that "what they want most in life is sport" (132). In this instance, the dance between subject and object allowed Veronica by the freedoms of reverie facilitates her deep consideration of personal concerns (her alienation from her husband Tom), as well as more general societal questions (male characteristics, the cultural obsession with sport) and larger human questions regarding patience, endurance, and compassion.

Such intuitions, inspired by objects and revealed in imagination, suggest the political potential of female reverie. Throughout the novel, as Veronica grapples with the cultural scourge of childhood sexual abuse that has destroyed her brother, her object reveries move from personal history to public life. On a later seemingly innocuous shopping trip to the posh department store Brown Thomas, she mourns, "there is nothing here I can not buy" (189). Her privileged class status, which allows her the time for reverie, also triggers middle-class guilt. Belying Lefebvre's concerns, female reverie and what he identifies as the "the things that matter" to women refuse to allow Veronica to renounce the social or the political. The reverie elicited by nine Brabantia storage jars on sale and intended for her kitchen directs her to the suffering of others, to "the starving people in Africa, with their bellies out and their eyes running with pus" (190). As with the car headrest, Veronica's bleak reveries in Brown Thomas move uncontrollably from the personal to the social and communal.

The provocative imaginative confusion of subject and object holds obvious, palpable risks in real life. To objectify and exchange human beings is to reduce them to the status of a less significant thing and thus to permit their abuse, a tactic Susan Cahill notes when she claims that *The Gathering* "shows the consequences of turning people into commodities ... [through abuse that] turns people into objects."[45] Objectification represents a particularly salient threat to Veronica, who mourns the sexual abuse of her younger brother. Yet Veronica regularly objectifies people throughout her reveries, suggesting that these private thought exercises transform this pernicious tactic into something positive for her. For instance, she sometimes in imagination objectifies her family as a means of con-

---

[44] In recent decades, a wealth of "thing theory" has argued that the long-standing divide separating subject and object, the human and the material, is neither neat nor secure. For examples of this critical approach in an Irish context, see *Irish Things: Special issue on Irish material culture, Éire-Ireland* 46: 1–2 (Spring/Summer 2011).

[45] Susan Cahill, *Irish Literature in the Celtic Tiger Years 1990–2008: Gender, Bodies, Memory* (London: Continuum, 2011), 183.

OBJECT REVERIES AND CHILDHOOD SEXUAL ABUSE   117

necting to them psychologically. When she recalls first meeting her husband and his then-partner, she describes him as an object for exchange and personal possession, declaring that "the moment I saw them I knew two things. The first was that he did not belong to her, and the second was that he belonged to me" (69). In the midst of another late-night reverie, she notes, "The girls are just a residue; a movie protruding from the mouth of the machine, a glitter lipstick beside the phone" (36). By indulging the language of objectification in these instances, announcing her custody of her husband and identifying the trace of her daughters' presence in the home, Veronica secures a feeling of human connection and affection.

Objectification in her reveries also allows her to approach cautiously the appalling memory of her brother's abuse. When she finally recollects the sight of Nugent abusing nine-year-old Liam, she describes "the peculiar growth at the end of Mr. Nugent's penis, the bridge of flesh between the man and boy" (144). Such an image seems to confirm her grandmother's assessment that "there is something immoral about the mind's eye" (91). But to reconstruct and comprehend this horrific and traumatic event—even as she asserts, "I know it is *true* that this happened" (144)—requires hypothetical objectification. In the mind's eye, the fantastic nature of reverie allows objectification to become a potentially healing gesture, even if in practice it is immoral and destructive. Nonetheless, after she envisions Liam's abuse, Veronica seeks a reprieve from the distress of imagination. To draw this reverie to a close, she begins licking and smelling herself, experiencing "The odd comforts of the flesh. Of being me" (146). Here, her own flesh confirms her separation from Liam and detaches the present from the past; it yanks her from reverie into reality, which is a consolation material objects repeatedly have refused to provide. This moment confirms for her that humans and objects, flesh and material, real and imagined are marked by valuable differences.

These fantastic reveries allow Veronica access to a more complex understanding of the realities of sexual abuse. She comes to understand the risks of objectification in practice, as evident when she asserts that "[w]hen Nugent saw a child he saw revenge" (236) for his own various disappointments and dissatisfactions. Here, the sentence structure and repetition of "saw" suggest that Veronica understands Nugent's different and pernicious equivalence of subject and object, of child and injurious outcome. She imagines that Nugent regarded Liam as an object circulating in "the whole tedious business of human exchange that a man has to go through in order to get what he might want" (236). Yet Veronica understands herself as susceptible to the impulses that drive Nugent's pederasty: she will "manhandle" (38) her daughters to elicit affection from them, she longs to touch Liam's young son Rowan for consolation (242). She too uses children as tools to sate her desires, even though these children manifest toward her the same indifference as objects. The clear divide between "good" mother and "bad" pederast reveals itself, in the language of her reveries, to be less secure than imagined. This alerts her, powerfully,

118   DAYDREAMING

to the fact that the flesh offers peculiar and particular comforts, ones that must be carefully policed.[46]

The Failure of Form

In the very first line of *The Gathering*, Veronica announces that she would "like to write down what happened in my grandmother's house the summer I was eight or nine, but I am not sure if it really did happen. I need to bear witness to an uncertain event" (1). Whether a material object or a literary genre, Veronica seeks a form, any form, that might contain, explain, and resolve for her the shifting memories surrounding this event. In her object reveries, she regularly confuses the operations and aims of material and literary forms, seeking through both a means to impose on her internal thoughts the security and surety she hopes might be guaranteed by a recognizable external world. For Veronica, form promises a fix, an antidote to the disruptive and daunting amorphousness of consciousness. Yet across her narrative, as she seeks to document and understand Nugent's sexual abuse of Liam as a child, these diverse literary forms fall short. Her reveries, stuffed with objects, refuse a consoling retreat into nature and imagination, or any of the warm nostalgia for childhood promised by Romantic poetry. Nor does she find herself in a crime novel: in reverie, material objects for Veronica are not distinct and evidentiary, but instead ambiguous and disquieting. The gruesome monster of the Gothic or horror novel, who appears in the guise of Nugent, can be identified but not vanquished, and the romance plot that Veronica tries to construct for Ada and Nugent comes to nothing.[47] The clarity of realism cannot adequately capture the atrocity of childhood sexual abuse, nor does a neat narrative resolution stem abuse or its effects in real life. Modernist ambiguity and obfuscation threaten to conceal the distinct and particular motivations, practices, and outcomes characterizing such abuse, and a commitment to modernist irresolution as a representative strategy might have a real human cost.

As witness and narrator, Veronica throughout seeks, with uneven success, to corral her drifting thoughts and pace her insights about the past though an engagement with material objects as well as literary form. Modernism, with its stream of consciousness representing a spontaneous flow of internal impressions and memories, marked by interruptions from the outside world, provides an especially

[46] For a psychoanalytically informed account of the eroticism characterizing parent-filial relationships in *The Gathering*, see Joseph Valente and Margot Gayle Backus, *The Child Sex Scandal and Modern Irish Literature: Writing the Unspeakable* (Bloomington: Indiana University Press, 2020), 196–231.

[47] On the romance narrative, see Keelan Harkin, "An Uncertain Event: The Politics of Reliability in Anne Enright's *The Gathering*," *Textual Practice* 35:1 (2021): 57–72.

apt means to depict her reveries, but its digressive associations threaten to lead her, too quickly and too intensely, to overwhelming epiphany. Thus when, in the middle of the novel, Veronica announces that she will reconstruct Nugent's sexual abuse of Liam, she prefaces her account by writing, "It is time to put an end to the shifting stories and the waking dreams. It is time to call an end to romance and just say what happened in Ada's house, the year that I was eight and Liam was barely nine" (142). Following this announcement, Veronica's habits of mind reveal themselves. Rather than dive into "what happened in Ada's house," Veronica stalls by offering a thorough register of the domestic things in her grandmother's front room where she imagines the abuse occurred: a yellowing white door, dusty pink wallpaper, a clapped-out sofa, two stiff wing-chairs, cushions, signed theater photographs in frames, a beige roller blind, lace curtains, a mirror over the mantel (142–143). The attention to material objects once more provides a temporary buffer between her and the revelations provoked by her reveries.

The provocative, and ultimately productive, failure of form reveals itself perhaps most vividly in the conclusion of *The Gathering*. Throughout the novel, Veronica has languished in the throes of marital, professional, and familial crises from which, thanks in large part to reverie, she has literally and figuratively retreated. Her narrative ends in Gatwick Airport and its hotel, where she temporarily has escaped her family and home. Once there, she imagines having another child and resolves to return to Dublin, but concludes, "And though it would be amazing to have another child, this is not what I want most as I stand in the queue in Gatwick airport with my eyes closed: a woman with no luggage, no sharp objects, and nothing I haven't packed myself. I just want to be less afraid. That's all" (260–261). She imagines that she returns home, entirely free of objects except for sparkly flip-flops as gifts for her daughters. As gifts, which anthropologists and cultural critics assure us secure relationships, material objects now safely embody and clearly communicate Veronica's desired interior affective state. Choosing to reject isolated and isolating reverie and to return to her family and its demands, she announces that she has "no luggage"—though she remains encumbered by "emotional baggage," the popular term for burdensome personal issues. This new child, she prospectively imagines, will help her shed the fears stirred by the ambiguities of the daydream.

This final daydream—one that projects a move into the consuming demands of new motherhood—sits uneasily next to the insights Veronica's other daydreams have elicited about the intransigent problems facing her society. On a personal level, at the novel's conclusion, Veronica identifies the source of Liam's suffering, which she intends to share with her family, and she plans to return home and reconcile with her husband and children. She will move out of the suspended time and isolation of the reverie. But on a broader social level, the cultural scourge of childhood sexual abuse remains unresolved—even as this sustained and systemic

120 DAYDREAMING

problem begs for the categorical solution often provided in the final pages of a crime novel.

Faced with this reality, *The Gathering* can hazard only a tentative conclusion, one both neat and messy, closed and open, realist and modernist. The promise of a new child suggests the tidy resolution of a domestic plot, and hints at the final chapter of *Ulysses*, in which Molly in reverie imagines resuming her sexual relationship with Bloom and thereby potentially having another child. This Joycean precedent invites readers to consider the final moments of *The Gathering* as a satisfying conclusion to a difficult and disorienting personal experience. Yet nothing in the novel has suggested that Veronica will be able to escape the concerns that dominate her thinking. Another tale of loss, disillusionment, and family life, Joyce's "The Dead," is more apposite to the novel's conclusion. As she prepares to buy her plane ticket home, Veronica closes her narrative by explaining her fear of flying: "you are up so high, in those things, and there is such a long way to fall. Then again, I have been falling for months. I have been falling into my own life, for months. And I am about to hit it now" (261). The snow that Gabriel Conroy observes and understands in the last lines of "The Dead" as "falling faintly through the universe and faintly falling, like the descent of their last end, upon all the living and the dead" is appropriated, corporealized, and personalized by Veronica.[48] Her final words acknowledge the alertness to mortality evident in Joyce's epiphany, but she imagines and invokes the metaphor of a plane crash, an unnatural modern disaster entirely out of her control, one from which she might suffer through no fault of her own. In her revised epiphany, imagined in the wake of child abuse, observers will see and necessarily confront the horrifying detritus of fallen bodies accidentally scattered and visible on the ground, rather than the beauty of a snow-covered vista that conceals the disconcerting objects beneath.

Like James's *The Turn of the Screw* (1898), *The Gathering* insists on a profusion of interpretation, on the fundamental inability to secure one accurate reading of the events that unfurl in the novel. Modernist doubt, playing out in the consciousness of an individual female narrator, is an operative theme in this twenty-first-century novel. But so too is the value of such imaginative insecurity. Object reverie, as an undirected mode of consciousness, a form of interiority that lacks laser focus or a deliberate end point, takes Veronica to surprising places. Through the object reverie, she learns that human projections onto things, while powerful and comforting, cannot ultimately conceal existential truths; a pink bathing cap does not make you any less alone, a rent book cannot expose your grandmother's romantic history, interior decorations will not make apparent the source of your brother's lethal depression. Nonetheless, Veronica—by looking over the precipice at this truth, even as she steps back from it—is tantalizingly close to the revolutionary "utopian" consciousness for which Lefebvre and other critics of

---

[48] James Joyce, "The Dead," *Dubliners*, 175–224, 224.

the everyday pine. *The Gathering* thus employs the modernist mode to draw attention to the moment situated between reverie and everyday practice, when attention shifts from private to public, and asks us to consider that precise moment as a critical site for thinking about political change and the potential eradication of horrific stubborn problems.

Object Reveries in *Molly Fox's Birthday*

For Deirdre Madden, the object provides a stimulus to memory, a material and visual trigger for a Proustian *memoire involontaire*, that like the famous madeleine elicits recollections of the past. In a 2001 lecture, Madden recalled a long forgotten glass bottle of oil from St. Anne's Shrine in Quebec that was kept in her mother's dressing table, and observed how this item prompted vivid, and object-ridden, memories that "led me straight back to my own childhood and to the very heart of my own imagination."[49] In this same lecture, she quoted a line from Proust's *Contre Sainte-Beuve* (1895–1900), translated by the modernist Sylvia Townsend Warner, that reads, "as soon as each hour of one's life has died, it embodies itself in some material object, as do the souls of the dead in certain folk stories, and hides there."[50] For Madden, whose representations of the contraction and expansion of time reflect those percolating through high modernism, the object has supernatural qualities, seen not least in its ability to invite individuals to recollect and memorialize the past.

Molly Fox's Birthday, like O'Brien's *Night*, explicitly nods to Joyce's *Ulysses*. The focus of the narrator's attention is a female performer named Molly, and the story unfurls in Dublin on a single day in June. Less overtly experimental than *Ulysses*, the psychological realism of this novel nonetheless embodies many characteristics of a Joycean modernism, most particularly in its representation of the complicated relationship between objects and daydreams. In her analysis of the "Ithaca" chapter in *Ulysses*, Vike Martina Plock has observed that "Bloom establishes connections to other individuals and to his surroundings by relying on objects" and thus extends the ambitions of modernists such as Woolf and Willa Cather to represent such objects as more than mere "markers of characters' social environment and materialist provision."[51] Madden's novel is an interior monologue, a more readily accessible and less dialogic form than the question-and-answer experiments of "Ithaca." But her perspective on objects resonates with

---

[49] Madden, "Looking for Home: Time, Place, Memory," 26. For an account of Madden as "a practitioner of realism and a critic of bourgeois materialism" (84), see Sylvie Mikowski, "Objects in Deirdre Madden's Artist Novels," *Deirdre Madden: New Critical Perspectives*, eds. Anne Fogarty and Marisol Morales-Ladrón (Manchester: Manchester University Press, 2022), 83–101.

[50] Ibid., 32.

[51] Vike Martina Plock, "'Object Lessons': Bloom and His Things," *James Joyce Quarterly* 49: 3–4 (Spring/Summer 2012): 557–572, 558.

122 DAYDREAMING

those of modernists who through experiment demonstrated how objects might enable human intimacy—even though the object reveries suffusing *Molly Fox's Birthday* ultimately confirm the inability of this practice to reveal satisfactorily the contours of human subjectivity and experience.

Like *The Gathering*, this novel moves between meditations on the past and events in the present. As a guest in Molly's Dublin home, the narrator-playwright goes about the mundane business of her day, including shopping, cleaning, and cooking, and amid this activity, her reveries—again, regularly provoked by objects—are consumed primarily by memories of her long friendships with Molly, who years before had starred in the narrator's first play, and with the art historian Andrew Forde, whom the narrator first met while they attended Trinity in the 1980s. Much of the novel is spent puzzling out the identities of those closest to her by pondering their relationship to the object world that surrounds them. Never physically present during this day, Molly's character is conveyed by the detailed catalog of her household objects. Her home, exhaustively described by the narrator, is filled with "stylish bric-a-brac, unusual but inexpensive things that she has picked up on her travels" (10); she has bookcases lined with special editions of plays in which she has performed; her hallway is a "small shrine to her career, to her success" (98) lined with posters, photographs of her performances, and awards (99); her kitchen is outfitted with "cheery" egg-cups (42) and the "correct" glasses for champagne (170).[52] The long descriptive passages about things in this book amount to a stoppage akin to reverie for the reader—the form of the novel demands that we too pause and attend to Molly's things, rather than to the forward propulsion of the narrative.

The narrator regards objects as materialized metaphors that might make public and concrete ineffable concepts like identity. Early on, she makes clear her admiration for those who can piece together from objects a coherent persona, as well as her skepticism about this strategy. She admits that the projection of self through such man-made objects "baffled and defeated me" (99–100). Instead, she represents her own identity as natural and durable. As she announces, "I have always believed that I know who I am, no small thing in the shifting dream that is contemporary life. I put this down to my background, my identity as solid as the mountainside on which I grew up" (58). This confidence may also be attributable to her lingering Catholicism. As she notes,

> We build our self out of what we think we remember, what we believe to be true about our life; and the possessions we gather around us are supposedly a part of this, that we are, to some extent, what we own. I have always been, and still

---

[52] Deirdre Madden, *Molly Fox's Birthday* (London: Faber & Faber, 2008). Future references parenthetical.

am, hugely resistant to these ideas, because, I think, they are so much at odds with the Catholic idea of the self with which I was raised. I still believe that there is something greater than all our delusions about ourselves, all our material bits and pieces, and that this is where the self resides. (37–38)

The narrator's announced commitment to land and religion as central to her character also suggests her ambivalence about a new and unsettling relationship between objects and identity in contemporary Ireland. As Toby Barnard establishes in his study of possessions in Stuart and Hanoverian Ireland, objects in Irish culture were long tethered to the binaries that divided colonial culture more generally, including those between English and Irish, Protestant and Catholic, colonizer and colonized.[53] He describes the performative function of objects in Ireland, their capacity to register publicly social status, and he reveals how possessions in the eighteenth-century exacerbated the divide between affluent Protestants and the Catholic majority in Ireland when there were fewer things due to poverty, an overwhelmingly rural economy, restrictive trade laws, protectionist economic policies, religious anti-materialism, and other factors.

Madden, like Enright, writes in a historical moment that troubled this longstanding relationship in Ireland between objects and identity, one characterized by a rabid and more democratic consumer culture fed by relatively cheap commodities sourced from across the globe and financial credit untethered to actual capital. This means that possessions, while signaling publicly an individual's affiliations, might more easily lie: the couple with an expensive Smeg refrigerator might be penniless or the person in the Aran sweater might be from Des Moines or Dubai. In this era, the Irish might not be who their possessions say they are, and so the attentiveness to commodities in the novel exacerbates the instability of the narrator's memories. Unlike the narrator, however, Molly appears to have little doubt about things as the bricks and mortar of identity. The domestic objects in her home are like props, symbolic objects calculated to convey to her audience the contours of her character. In particular, they embody her personal relationships. She places on display gifts, such as a small bowl made of olive wood given to her by Molly's brother Tom, that confirm, sustain and make concrete human connections, as well as postcards and invitations that similarly indicate her bond with others. These objects prompt further feelings of attachment from the three visitors to Molly's house on this day, who observe them in the actor's "little museum to her own success" (216). They elicit admiration from Molly's brother Fergus (157–158), adoration from Andrew (204), and awe from Molly's neighbor (216).

---

[53] Toby Barnard, *Making the Grand Figure: Lives and Possessions in Ireland, 1641–1770* (New Haven, CT: Yale University Press, 2004). See also Claudia Kinmonth, *Irish Country Furniture and Furnishings 1700–2000* (Cork: Cork University Press, 2020).

124   DAYDREAMING

The narrator's skepticism about the capacity of things to embody the self keeps her outside of this circuit of esteem.

Instead, she considers the treasured objects that people Molly's home and through them comes to understand that her friend's true identity eludes her. In the intimate space of Molly's bedroom, she ponders a series of unanswered questions: "What kind of woman has a saffron quilt on her bed? Wears a white linen dressing gown? Keeps beside her bed a stack of gardening books? Stores all her clothes in a shabby antique wardrobe, with a mirror built into its door? Who is she when she is in this room, alone and unobserved, and in what way does that differ from the person she is when she is in a restaurant with friends or in rehearsal or engaging with members of the public? Who, in short, is Molly Fox?" (8–9). Here, the questions of Joyce's "Ithaca," embedded in Madden's lyrical realism, showcase the interrogative and critical plenitude reverie allows but, because they go unanswered, demonstrate the limitations of this silent and solitary colloquium.

Woolf's Material Modernism

On this June day, the narrator's mental peregrinations often return to events from her past, most notably those tied to her friendships with Molly and Andrew. In the years since their graduation from Trinity, Andrew has become a renowned art historian whose documentary series on memorials is currently airing on television. The second episode on war memorials is televised this June evening, and as the narrator watches it, she reports: "he quoted Virginia Woolf's remark about how sometime around 1910 human nature changed ... Time and again he came back to this idea of the self, of what had brought about this change in perception (the development of psychology, the wars of the twentieth century, the rise of science and rationalism). The self we were left with after this was, according to Andrew, a much more nebulous and evanescent thing, more socially determined than would have been conceivable in the nineteenth century" (161). This citation neatly reflects one abiding theme of *Molly Fox's Birthday*, the endeavor to secure and understand the "idea of the self." But this nod to Woolf also invites further consideration of the object reverie rendered through the modernist mode, and what it might tell us about the creative labor of Irish women contemporary writers like the narrator.

Of the many object reveries found in modernist writing, perhaps the most renowned appears in Woolf's "Solid Objects" (1920), which depicts the capacity of objects not only to stimulate reverie, but also to dramatically disrupt daily life.[54]

---

[54] Virginia Woolf, "Solid Objects" (1920), *The Complete Shorter Fiction of Virginia Woolf*, ed. Susan Dick (New York: Harcourt Brace Jovanovich, 1985), 96–101. This story has become a touchstone for studies of the relationship between modernism and material objects, as well as an argument for Woolf's

In this short story, the protagonist John becomes mesmerized by a piece of green sea glass, as well as by other objects that he subsequently discovers and collects; they prompt in him fascination, wonder, and amazement. They also lead John to abandon his promising political career and to alienate his close friend Charles, who fails to grasp their all-consuming allure. The hazards posed in Woolf's story by objects, their ability to misdirect attention and to thwart action, haunt the narrator of *Molly Fox's Birthday*. Through the exercise of narrative control, she represents herself as someone largely able to tolerate the unsettling messages conveyed by objects to those who consider them closely in reverie. Reveries slow the pace of her day but, unlike those of Woolf's character John or even Veronica in *The Gathering*, they do not radically disrupt her patterns of behavior or disturb her personal relationships.

Nonetheless, the narrator remains burdened by the notion that the daydream is a wasteful distraction, unless it can produce a work of art or some other salubrious outcome. As she sits in Molly's garden early in the day, she notes, "The morning was moving along but I wasn't moving with it. I would have been happy to sit there for at least another hour just thinking about the past, but I knew that if I let more time slip away, I would regret it later" (42). In this moment, she regards "just thinking about the past" as wasteful distraction, and she tidies up to feel productive. She then determines to work in the study. The narrator, who suffers from writer's block, cannot recognize or embrace the merits of unfettered reverie. Such a response suggests that she fears that the object reverie will trigger the distraction that concerned Lefebvre, rather than produce the fruitful intimacy between self and other that Bachelard celebrates or that manifests in the creative work that Freud urges. On her way to the study, she pauses in Molly's sitting room and library, where she handles the books that the actor has purchased to commemorate her various roles on stage. Such a collection, according to Susan Stewart, must be considered as "infinite reverie" because it creates a new whole based on its new context, and "replaces origin with classification."[55] Molly's book collection thus provides another example of her careful self-fashioning; in this instance, her troubled youth is redacted from her origin story and replaced with confirmation of her more recent professional successes. But for the narrator, the plenitude of the collection prompts an anxiety of influence, as she fears that "It would have been easy to repeat things that had been successful, to slip into stale and formulaic writing" (54).

---

championing of slow aesthetic contemplation over bourgeois industriousness. In addition to Mao's *Solid Objects*, see Bill Brown, "The Secret Life of Things (Virginia Woolf)," *Other Things* (Chicago: University of Chicago Press, 2015), 49–78; Holly Henry, *Virginia Woolf and the Discourse of Science* (Cambridge: Cambridge University Press, 2003); Lorraine Sim, *Virginia Woolf: The Patterns of Everyday Experience* (Surrey: Ashgate, 2010), 47–53.

[55] Susan Stewart, *On Longing: Narratives of the Miniature, the Gigantic, the Souvenir, the Collection* (Durham, NC: Duke University Press, 1993), 152, 153.

126 DAYDREAMING

Among these books is the "erotic, dangerous-looking little volume" (47) of John Webster's seventeenth-century revenge tragedy *The Duchess of Malfi* purchased to mark Molly's performance of this coveted role. With this edition in her hands, the narrator falls into further reflection. Her attention turns to considerations of an early failed relationship and her work with the cast of her first play, *Summer with Lucy*, and she ponders why she now is recalling these "painful" memories of human disconnection and loss (52). She then notices a collection of Chekhov's short stories and "in spite of myself" lifts it out, opens the book, and soon notes, "I was on a jetty in Yalta" (52). She becomes engrossed in reading, an uncharacteristic act for which she apologizes: "Usually I am a most disciplined writer ... I do not procrastinate, I do not waste time" (52). The tactile here, as in *The Gathering*, offers the narrator temporary comfort and consolation, as the book in hand becomes a vehicle that moves her away from painful memories. But it also stokes her greatest anxiety, that she will be unable to write an original and successful new play. Having imbibed cultural anxieties about daydreaming and other forms of imaginative excess, the narrator fails to see the merits of aimless reading and regards it instead as mere stalling.

This moment offers a fascinating example of the complexities of female reverie, which can be misunderstood even by those whose contemporary professional and economic conditions more readily allow it. The narrator describes her work that day as "wool-gathering," a term that has come to mean idle daydreaming. But this phrase originally referred to the rote labor of pulling sheep wool from bushes or fences: the expression itself confuses productive work and purposeless thinking. She continues to report on her attempts to write, as she finds herself "staring out of the window into the back garden, reading over my notebooks, writing things down and then crossing them out again moments later" (52). But amid her seemingly ineffectual efforts to write, she lights on a provocative image from her past, a man she observed carrying a large hare on a Munich tram, an image that will provide the "the trigger" for her new play (53). As she revisits this image in memory, she contends that "by grasping imaginatively something" (54) about the man and the hare, she now might be able to write. But the outcome of this image, unlike the objects of Molly's actual books before her, cannot be "grasped"; it is, at this present moment, merely a kernel of inspiration that she hopes to see realized in the material form of a new script.

In Woolf's "Solid Objects," object reveries pull the daydreamer, John, entirely away from political labor, and they create an unbreachable rift between him and his close friend. Not so in *Molly Fox's Birthday*. Through its first-person soliloquy, the novel underscores in form and content the authority of its female narrator and reworks gendered assessments of the reverie such as those voiced by Bachelard and Lefebvre and represented in literary modernism. Madden employs the modernist mode to portray reverie as an anxiety-producing, but nonetheless necessary and manageable, stage in the narrator's creative process. Offering neither the array of formal experiments found in *Ulysses*, nor the shifting point of view found in Woolf, the narrator, even in the throes of this amorphous and seemingly unproductive state, remains at the helm of the narrative, corralling the drift of her thoughts and even signaling to readers the logics driving the seemingly random associations that appear among her reveries. Decades after the critique of male modernist writing embedded in the soliloquy of O'Brien's Mary Hooligan, Madden's narrator not only showcases the advances in autonomy and authorship for contemporary Irish women—the narrator is, after all, that rare figure, a critically and commercially successful female playwright—but also the messy internal process that enables such creative work.

Troubles Trauma and Ambivalent Objects

Like other depictions of female reverie found in Irish writing, *Molly Fox's Birthday* considers how contemporary conditions shape private consciousness. The novel is set in the aftermath of the Troubles, when the terms of the 1998 Belfast/Good Friday Agreement had helped secure a fragile peace in Northern Ireland after the three decades of devastating sectarian violence. Born in Co. Antrim, Madden has asserted that "the Troubles are almost always in [my work] in some way, at some level."[56] Unlike her novels *Hidden Symptoms* (1986) and *One by One in the Darkness* (1996), *Molly Fox's Birthday* largely shies away from a direct consideration of the Troubles. Nonetheless, amid her day in Dublin, the narrator recounts events from her own youth in Northern Ireland; she shares stories of Andrew and his family, also from Northern Ireland; and she describes various interactions with members of her family, who still reside there. Like Madden's *Authenticity* (2002) and *Time Present and Time Past* (2013), *Molly Fox's Birthday* is set in the Republic during the Celtic Tiger, seemingly at a remove both temporally and spatially from the violent events of the Troubles, but the novel reveals that its legacies still encroach on female consciousness.

In his study of *One by One in the Darkness*, Brian Cliff notes the "ambivalent qualities" of that novel, seen for example in Madden's sustained attention to the multiple after-effects of events rather than to the events themselves.[57] In his reading, Madden's ambivalence provides a riposte to the stark divides, literal and figurative, that characterize the sectarian thinking that sustained the Troubles. *Molly Fox's Birthday* projects a similar ambivalence in not only its content, but also its form. For example, the narrator's ambivalence about her romantic relationships

---

[56] Christina Patterson, interview with Deirdre Madden, *The Guardian*, June 14, 2013: 13.

[57] Brian Cliff, "Class and Multiplicity in *One by One in the Darkness*," *Deirdre Madden: New Critical Perspectives*, 66–79. See also Liam Harte and Michael Parker, "Refiguring Identities: Recent Northern Irish Fiction," *Contemporary Irish Fiction: Themes, Tropes, Theories*, eds. Liam Harte and Michael Parker (London: Palgrave Macmillan, 2000), 232–254.

128 DAYDREAMING

past and present intrudes on her present-day musings: without taking action, she ruminates on her former failed relationships, and she weighs a future relationship with Andrew but hesitates to initiate it. Such mixed feelings, as mentioned earlier, shape her understanding of the daydream, which is represented as both wasteful distraction and a productive creative exercise, and of material objects, which she contends can and cannot communicate hidden aspects of self. Thus it makes sense that ambivalence also reveals itself in Madden's use of form: is this the interior monologue of the realist novel that advances with the action of the day, or is this the associative stream of consciousness of the modernist novel that moves seamlessly between past and present? The answer is yes, both. These modes in dialogue underscore the novel's thematic considerations of overlapping contraries, as well as suggesting the importance of holding such contraries in mind.

Early in the evening of Molly's birthday, Andrew turns up unannounced at her door to surprise and celebrate the actor, unaware that instead the narrator is house-sitting. Like a character in an Ibsen play, Andrew's appearance disrupts the quotidian rhythms of the bourgeois home. With his arrival, objects become charged with disruptive potential on a broader scale. As these longtime friends chat in the garden, Andrew recalls his vexed relationship with his brother Billy, a paramilitary Loyalist killed in the Troubles. When describing how his brother's death inspired his documentary project on memorials, Andrew asks the narrator, "'Do you ever think about the energy there can be in things? Jewellery, or a piece of sliver or glass, for example. I think about it sometimes in the course of my work. There's the pure aesthetic of the thing, but sometimes you can't help being aware of something more, as if it still means what it meant to the person who used to own it'" (175–176). She responds to Andrew's question by telling him about mediums who claim to be able to describe a person in detail "simply by handling an object they had habitually used" (176). Rather than embrace the potential supernatural quality of things, she mediates her position by sharing the story of a clairvoyant. However, other instances in her monologue point to the narrator's awareness of the magical properties of things, a kind of mystery one might attribute in part to her Catholic background. The novel opens with a dream in which her grandmother gives her soft shoes and a thick green woolen blanket in which to wrap herself. These ordinary objects in her unconscious generate a real feeling of unconditional love that spills into her conscious waking life. The narrator also recognizes the theatrical superstitions associated with the peacock feather and respects, but does not share, Molly's intense fear of them. Both Andrew and the narrator accept, if only with the skepticism of rational modern subjects, the notion that material objects have an excess of meaning, a magical quality.

Such objects hold not only personal meaning, but also broader political relevance. Andrew tells the narrator the story of a ring once belonging to his brother Billy, which his father presented him after Billy's murder. Though Andrew disdains the gaudy ring, when he is almost killed in a random terrorist bombing in Paris, this ring comes to have particular importance to him. He explains, "'A lot of things came together that night. Billy's ring went from being something I didn't want to being something very precious to me ... I started to think about how people disappear, and then how they're forgotten or remembered; the things we make in their memory, the way we try to honour them'" (192–193). The shock of the bombing leads Andrew to award his dead brother's ring the status of a Freudian fetish, a super-charged object that, as the substitute for some loss, promises to ameliorate psychic trauma. In his work, he intends to translate the magical properties of his personal inheritance into a public memorial of communal loss, one that might offer connection with and consolation to his television audience. By transforming that familial trauma into a sweeping narrative for the public, he hopes to defuse the debilitating personal emotions associated with loss.

In this moment, Andrew's earlier reference to Woolf invites readers to tack away from "Solid Objects" and veer toward *Mrs. Dalloway* (1925). Written as Woolf read *Ulysses*, *Mrs. Dalloway* registers the after-effects of the First World War by tracking the affluent Clarissa Dalloway, and other characters, as they make their way through London on an ordinary June day in 1923. As Karen DeMeester notes, modernist form in this novel ably depicts post-war trauma: the fragmented, associative nature of stream of consciousness captures the disorientation and disordered thought of traumatized characters, while modernist repetition conveys how survivors experience past trauma as ever-present.[58] Like Clarissa Dalloway, the narrator of *Molly Fox's Birthday* has experienced political violence at a remove, but she nonetheless occupies a world still grappling with the diffuse consequences of wartime brutality and suffering. By filtering the narrative entirely through one perspective, Madden's novel puts on view how the narrator gives order and structure in her thinking to personal and historical trauma. We see her attempt to make meaning of these unfathomable events. The healing quality of narrative for victims of trauma is an accepted credo of psychoanalytic and trauma theory, but the form of this novel vividly demonstrates the tension between a neat, forward-moving narrative constructed by an individual in imagination, and the ease with which outside interruptions can disturb or disrupt this process.[59] As such, the ambivalent display of form reveals the diffuse and difficult work of recovery. The novel's recombination can carry forward the fragmented, repetitive, and isolating modernist legacies of the traumatic wartime past even as it also suggests, through

---

[58] Karen DeMeester, "Trauma and Recovery in Virginia Woolf's *Mrs. Dalloway*," *Modern Fiction Studies* 44:3 (Fall 1998): 649–673, 649.

[59] Stefanie Lehner notes that Madden's narrators often propel the narrative forward, despite the regular intrusion of the past as represented by memories that are often traumatic and represented as visual. See Lehner, "'Images ... at the absolute edge of memory': Memory and Temporality in *Hidden Symptoms*, *One by One in the Darkness*, and *Time Present and Time Past*," *Deirdre Madden: New Critical Perspectives*, 17–31.

130 DAYDREAMING

the steady evolution of a realist narrative, that characters might heal and move forward, albeit unsteadily and imperfectly, in a recognizable exterior world.

In this novel, the consequences of the Troubles echo among and spread across different individuals, objects, moments, affects, and media. Any particular violent incident in a given moment suffered by a specific individual such as Billy ripples out, accidentally or by design, to different audiences in different historical moments. But this diffusion, reflected in the shape of the reverie, threatens to dilute the suffering of the Troubles, and so for Andrew, the ring provides an external, concrete piece of material evidence that promises to distill and secure the power of that trauma and memorialize that loss. Rendering the ineffable consequences of trauma and loss into a concrete, public, documented artifact is, for Andrew, transformative. Not so for the narrator. She maintains her skepticism about objects and the messages they might convey, even as in private reverie she timidly acknowledges their fantastic potential. Although Andrew announces that his relationship to the vexatious ring, which he places on a table between him and the narrator, is now positive, she continues to see the ring as "a thing full of bad energy" (203).

The narrator seems deeply unnerved by the notion that things can replace people, that the slippage between subject and object might tip the balance and the subject will be lost. When she recalls first entering Andrew's campus room, she remembers seeing a line of his empty shoes and "... looking at them I was struck by the strange pathos of someone's possessions when the person themselves is absent" (39). Likewise, while cooking dinner, she glimpses Molly's kitchen tools and notes, "Looking at these things made me feel weirdly nervous, too close to Molly at a moment when I felt disconnected from her" (166). Even as the things in Molly's house elicit memories of friends, remind her of their personalities and histories, signal their shared professional experiences and give testament to the exchanged intimacies of their relationships, these mundane personal objects also serve as concrete registers of absence and loss, and remind her of the utter isolation of humans.

In his review of *Molly Fox's Birthday*, Joseph O'Connor contends, "this is in some ways a religious novel, in which existentialism is given short shrift by the narrator."[60] But in fact, the objects in the novel suggest that existentialism gets its due. The narrator understands that things have magical qualities and convey meaning, but she categorically refuses the notion that they are who we are. Things have their limits. In Molly's garden, there sits a decorative fiberglass cow, which Molly adores and the narrator loathes, and which stimulates in her "a sudden anger" and sends her "spiralling into some strange mental state that I only half understood but that I knew I needed to get out of fast" (166). Unlike Veronica in *The Gathering*, who falls like Alice in Wonderland into the abyss of the "strange mental state" prompted by

---

[60] Joseph O'Connor, "Getting in on the Act," *The Guardian*, August 29, 2008, https://www.theguardian.com/books/2008/aug/30/fiction.deirdremadden.

TROUBLES TRAUMA AND AMBIVALENT OBJECTS   131

things, the narrator of *Molly Fox's Birthday* regularly steps back from that uneasy reverie. The thing in this instance has sparked something she is not prepared to tackle. Most obviously, the material here reveals to her the gaps in understanding between even the closest of friends and family members, signaling to her the impossibility of true intimacy and understanding, even with the passage of time. Once again, an artful detachment leads her to step back from the brink of these disturbing messages.

This imaginative management of difficult feelings becomes even more vivid in a moment near the novel's close, a moment that demonstrates how once again a female protagonist finds herself in a reverie activated by a material object that places her perilously close to knowledge almost too much to bear. Near the close of the day, the narrator studies and winds Molly's treasured grandfather clock. She thinks,

> As I started to wind the clock first [one weight] ascended slowly and then the other. I thought of the day that was ending and how, as I rose, as I tried to work, as I walked the hot streets of the city and talked to Fergus, to Andrew, to the late-night caller, all that time these weights had been slowly descending. I thought of them being raised up and slowly falling all the days of our lives in other houses, other rooms: on the night Billy was shot, on the night I spent with Andrew, on the day Molly's mother left home, until it seemed to me that this dark, narrow wooden compartment held time itself. (218)

The mechanical parts of the clock trigger a meditation on time that, as in the conclusion of *The Gathering*, echoes the final paragraph of Joyce's "The Dead." In *Molly Fox's Birthday*, a similar sonorous rhythm echoes the protagonist's attention moving inward, as she observes the weights "slowly descending ... slowly falling all the days of our lives." Rather than the natural snow, whose fall reminds Gabriel of the shared inevitability of human mortality, these manufactured weights rivet Molly's attention and prompt her reverie. The predictable, repetitive movement of these weights, which are contained in the coffin-like "dark, narrow wooden compartment" of the clock, spans to link the disparate individuals, spaces, and events that people the narrator's past.

Molly unintentionally interrupts this reverie by phoning from the States, after which the narrator turns her attention once more to the garden. There, she sees a hedgehog intrigued by the discarded champagne cork she and Andrew had left on the ground. The final lines of the novel read, "The hedgehog stopped for a moment, sniffed it, tapped it with its foot, sniffed it again. Inscrutable, mysterious, it moved on once more and then disappeared into the shadows and was gone" (221). The mysteries of human consciousness, and the limits of intimacy as well as self-understanding, are embodied in this moment by an animal responding instinctively to a common household object—this is an object reverie that reveals

132   DAYDREAMING

nothing. Like Charles in "Solid Objects," the hedgehog simply walks away from this derelict found object, leaving no insights in its wake. Yet this final scene, by suggesting the symbolic currency of the cork, one similar to the snow whose complexity has captivated readers of "The Dead" for a century, asks us to regard this encounter between animal and object as another epiphany: one that grants insight into the inscrutability of consciousness and the behaviors provoked, even in a hedgehog, by the contemplation of a solid object.

Invisible Female Labor

Written in the decades encompassing Ireland's preparations to join the EEC through the rise of the Celtic Tiger, *Night*, *The Gathering*, and *Molly Fox's Birthday* all center on Irish women who must reckon with things in order to understand their place in a contemporary world increasingly suffused with material objects. All three novels, written in the first person, suggest that the "daydreaming" that Freud wholeheartedly celebrated for male writers in 1907 may contain particular dangers for contemporary Irish women artists attracted to the "things that matter" and trained to embrace the private sphere. In his early and influential formulation of "thing theory," Bill Brown contends that "Modernity artificially made an ontological distinction between inanimate objects and human subjects ... modernism's resistance to modernity is its effort to deny the distinctions between subjects and objects, people and things."[61] These narratives insist that relationship between "subject and object, people and things" is neither good nor bad: things may sunder and secure relationships, things rivet attention and cultivate distraction, things encourage passive acceptance and stoke active resistance. Here, the fictive depictions of interiority, which rely heavily on stream of consciousness, insist on the unsettling confusion and ambivalence invited by material objects.

These novels extend the legacy of modernism to explore female reverie in the contemporary moment, to pay tribute to the imaginative possibilities engendered by its privacy and permissiveness as well as to underscore how the daydream remains fettered by constraints imposed by the outside world. Strikingly, they often neaten and order the knottier aspects of modernism's familiar but still alienating formal experiments to elucidate the contours of female reverie. The intellectual and emotional labor that female reverie represents, the puzzling out of crucial questions related to stubborn problems, is labor invisible to others until it is made visible and interpretable. By rendering such complexities and contradictions though the modernist mode but in more accessible prose, O'Brien, Enright, and Madden each invite readers through literature to attend more closely to that which often is dismissed or flies under the radar—not only daydreaming, but

---

[61] Bill Brown, "Thing Theory," *Critical Inquiry* 28:1 (Autumn 2001): 1–22, 12.

also other aspects of female experience that might go unseen and unrecognized, from the labor that goes into constructing a self, to the sustained efforts necessary to maintain relationships, to the working-through of emotional burdens that are personally and, as these novels insist, socially significant.[62]

---

[62] On the varieties of work as represented by Irish women contemporary writers see Orlaith Darling, Liam Harrison, and Dearbhaile Houston, eds., Special issue on *Women Writing Work*, *Irish Studies Review* 31:1 (2023).

136 LOGGING OFF

O'Brien. Both of these models have proven durable, with the conscious withdrawal from the norms and habits of contemporary urban life posed as one antidote for stubborn problems.

The novels in this chapter use these tropes to provide counter-narratives to the utopian promise of the digital age, voicing concerns that insistent publicness might, by too readily exposing personal experience and too explicitly represent-ing interiority, too easily subject individuals to malignant surveillance, discipline, and misinformation. Logging off may seem an oddly conservative gesture, one that resurrects not only the mode of modernism but also its hoary, and frequently misogynistic, apprehensions about mass culture.[3] Or it might appear to dismiss the exhilarating feminist cyber-activism of the twenty-first century, interventions that echo the avant-garde energies of a century before.[4] But in fact, these writers center on logging off to insist that elective seclusion and solitude are worth safekeeping. Using modernist forms and themes drawn from the early twentieth-century, yet set in an era when Irish women have more public authority, *The Dancers Dancing* and *Pond* put on view examples of productive privacy, ones without hazard for their female protagonists, while *Only Ever Yours*, situated in the future, dramati-cally reminds readers of the fragility of such privacy under assault from the radical publicness encouraged, and even demanded by, new digital technologies.

Anodyne Privacy in *The Dancers Dancing*

The plot of Éilís Ní Dhuibhne's *The Dancers Dancing* unfolds before women's equality was "a concept known to women," tracking the summer of 1972 as thirteen-year-old Orla travels from her home in Dublin with friends to attend Irish-language college in Tubber, her father's hometown located in the Donegal Gaeltacht.[5] The novel depicts Irish life during the early years of Vatican II, center-ing on a pivotal moment prior to the rush of cultural changes that characterized the late twentieth century—before Ireland joined the European Economic Com-munity, before power sharing in Northern Ireland, before the advent of the Celtic Tiger, before two women had served successively as president of Ireland. The teens

---

[3] See Andreas Huyssen, *After the Great Divide: Modernism, Mass Culture, Postmodernism* (Bloom-ington: Indiana University Press, 1986), and Gerardine Meaney, Mary O'Dowd, and Bernadette Whelan, *Reading the Irish Woman: Studies in Cultural Encounter and Exchange, 1714–1960* (Liverpool: Liverpool University Press, 2013), 179–195.

[4] See Lisa Fitzpatrick, "Contemporary Feminist Protest in Ireland: #MeToo in Irish Theatre," *Irish University Review* 50:1 (May 2020): 82–93; Margaret Kelleher and Karen Wade, "Irish Literary Femi-nism and its Digital Archive(s)," *Technology in Irish Literature and Culture*, 235–252; Kim McFalone, "#IBelieveHer: Representations of Rape Culture in Northern Ireland's Media Surrounding the 2018 Ulster Rugby Rape Trial," *International Journal of Media and Cultural Politics* 17:3 (September 2021): 291–314.

[5] Éilís Ní Dhuibhne, *The Dancers Dancing* (Dublin: Blackstaff Press, 1999), 72. Subsequent refer-ences parenthetical.

escape a Dublin increasingly shaped by modernity, one peopled with working mothers, mass-produced goods, budding secularism, international travel, and a "half-caste" boarder lodging at Orla's home (95). The antidote for contemporary conditions offered to Orla and her friends, one supported by subventions from a Department of Education now protected by the Common Market, is recognizable from modern Irish literature: an escape to the rural west and the embrace of the Irish language which "restores to them dignity and elegance" (36). The novel nostalgically suggests that nature provides a curative for modern urban life, in part because it affords Orla a space for productive solitude.

In addition to this rural setting, the novel invokes literary forms from the modernist mode to depict Orla's development. Written largely in third-person indirect discourse, *The Dancers Dancing* is bookended by two chapters from different points of view. In between, fifty-nine chapters, ranging in length from a few short paragraphs to many pages, convey Orla's summer experiences, as well as those of her family, peers, and teachers. These chapters provide a composite of connected perceptions and experiences, using the properties of modernism—including contradictory narration, juxtaposition, multiple points of view, and unmarked leaps in time—to undermine the novel's easy progression and thwart any sense that Orla and her peers will be seamlessly integrated into the adult world by the novel's end. Nevertheless, Orla's development is depicted through a largely linear narrative, one unfurling according to clearly marked events on a calendar and places on a map: the trip from Dublin to Tubber, the introduction to camp, excursions to the beach, the weekly dances, her monthly menses. An omniscient narrator guides readers through this recognizable external reality, interspersing the novel with assertions such as "Nobody in Ireland likes a child who knows anything" (40). The recognizable aspects of the bildungsroman here are almost parental, benevolently governing the enigmatic modernism that represents the murkier aspects of adolescent experience.

If fiction by Irish women writers has consistently cautioned against the forced sequestration of women, this novel advocates a different and more productive relationship with solitude and seclusion enabled by the country's belated modernity. In the 1970s, the privacy Orla finds out west is anodyne, harmless as well as nourishing. In the confines of the Gaeltacht, she can begin to experiment with varieties of privacy that allow her to determine her own sense of self. From the start, she elects to keep secret her familial affiliation with Tubber and her facility with Irish, suggesting she has access to an elective privacy that enables self-development. Such confidentiality is difficult, but not impossible, for her to situate within the protective structures of family and camp that seek transparency. At Irish college, Headmaster Joe carefully organizes the students' time, though "of course there are intervals, interstices, crevices in the edifice he has constructed that he can't afford to know about. Creases of time, worn patches and tiny holes that in the beginning seem too insignificant to be worth thinking about, but which are gradually

138   LOGGING OFF

expanding as the summer wears on. Slowly his map is cracking, and through the cracks the insects start to creep" (79). In her study of the novel, Kelly McGovern astutely notes the "panoptical time" that structures adolescence across this narrative, but the blank spaces and cracks in this map also suggest there is no way to expose entirely the clandestine aspects of individual experience and subjectivity.[6]

The novel, set decades before widespread internet use, presciently identifies the allure of social media but situates Orla outside of its pleasures: "Some people—most people, especially if they are adult—love to feel the eyes of others on them. Reality is being perceived, condoned or condemned. But privacy is what Orla craves. The reality she is looking for is inside herself, hidden from all eyes" (81). Her most vivid experiments with privacy appear in a series of five chapters in which she retreats to the same deep stream, a burn the girls have been warned is dangerous and thus to be avoided. Titled "The burn scene one" through "The burn scene five," these progressively numbered chapters are interspersed among other descriptively titled chapters, flowing through the novel not unlike the stream they reference moves through the landscape. As Patricia Coughlan has observed, the burn provides an organizing symbol, an "out of bounds" site whose camouflaging natural features represent "Orla's interiority, specifically the mystery of her developing selfhood."[7] These "scene" chapters suggest the visual qualities of the short story: set at this same watercourse, each presents a snapshot of Orla's maturation, and when read together like the running frames of a film, they depict her development inching forward. But these chapters, with their freeze-frame returns to the burn, also interrupt the novel's overarching progressive narrative and as such help to convey the uneven nature of her personal growth.

At the burn, Orla experiences a series of epiphanies ranging among matters including her peer relationships and her attraction to a local boy. Her repeated visits to this site, which interrupt the collective routines of summer camp, underscore the privacy required for this thirteen-and-a-half-year-old girl to develop psychologically. In "The burn scene five," the final in this series of chapters, Orla skips class and seeks out the burn alone, where she discovers the liberations of solitude. Once there, she screams, "I can do anything I want to!" (234), then repeatedly yells aloud "Fuck" and other "taboo words" (234). These profanities are echoed back to her, and her voice becomes "louder and louder, clearer and clearer, as she gets used to it" (234). Here, she speaks out loud about sex in language shocking and straightforward, in adult terms she can articulate only in private. Exhausted by this exercise, she stumbles across "Half a dozen, a dozen, small round white skulls" (236) in the mushy ground near the burn, which she unearths with "curiosity"

---

[6] Kelly J. S. McGovern, "'No Right to Be a Child': Irish Girlhood and Queer Time in Éilís Ní Dhuibhne's *The Dancers Dancing*," *Éire-Ireland* 44:1–2 (Spring/Summer 2009): 242–264, 257.

[7] Patricia Coughlan, "Irish Literature and Feminism in Postmodernity," *Hungarian Journal of English and American Studies* 10:1–2 (2004): 175–202, 191.

rather than horror (236). Her familiarity with such buried skeletons might stem from histories of the Famine, as well as from reports of undocumented cases of infanticide, among other possible cultural traumas that go uncited here. She likely has happened on a *cillín*, an unconsecrated burial ground for unbaptized or still-born babies, and these exhumed infant skulls provide tangible evidence of the potentially injurious consequences of the sexual acts she announced in her soliloquy. Of note, the tonal flatness of this scene suggests that, without an audience, Orla can process this discovery without being prompted to respond histrionically.

The unearthed contents of the *cillín* demonstrate that privacy historically has been, for many Irish women and their children, dangerous and punitive. However, Orla's discovery alludes to reparative public exposure, which potentially might correct societal wrongdoing and heal trauma. Likewise, an oral interview with Orla's Auntie Annie, in which the aged woman's stories are recorded for posterity by teachers at the college, suggests a promising developmental turn not only for Orla but also for Irish culture more generally, as it unearths and exposes the hidden experiences of rural women. Early in the novel, when Orla arrives in Tubber, she pretends to be unfamiliar with the town despite having regularly visited her relatives there, a posture the residents accept. But her elderly Auntie Annie who lives there "is a different story" and "won't understand Orla's wish for privacy" (162). Because Tubber is small, Orla must hide from her aunt to remain anonymous, and her shame about that secrecy is projected onto the body of her elderly aunt, a "disaster" that threatens to compromise Orla's status in the eyes of her friends. Yet when her relationship with Auntie Annie is discovered late in the summer, there is no negative fallout among her peers, and "Orla feels something break inside her head, like the shell of an egg. Her big secret is disintegrating" (257). The warmth of Auntie Annie's embrace toward the end of the novel inspires Orla to imagine being home with her mother, where she will "tell her everything, everything good and everything bad that has happened during this holiday in the Gaeltacht" (258). Her reconciliation with her aunt, as well as the dispassionate revelation of their relationship, prompts in Orla an epiphany, a feeling of control and connectedness that inspires her to craft and make public her story of the summer.

The Dancers Dancing generously allows its adolescent protagonist to experiment safely with privacy, a privacy enabled by the eschewal of certain technologies. Orla's mother, distracted throughout the summer by her own personal and professional concerns, does not respond to her daughter's letters from camp. Even as this lack of communication triggers anxiety for Orla, her mother's silence demands she learn to tolerate isolation and difference in a culture that demands community and acquiescence. Formally, the temporal and narrative gaps between chapters allow Orla privacy: readers are not privy to what happens between the disjointed chapters, nor do we learn much about dramatic events in the narrative such as the collapse of Auntie Annie in a dark barn or the end of Orla's relationship with her first love Micheál. Even when the narrative shifts to first person in the final

140　LOGGING OFF

chapter, the adult Orla, looking back on her romantic past, elects for the privacy she learned at the burn, skipping over the intimate details of her various romantic relationships and her current family life. The abstraction and obliquity that pervaded women's writing in Ireland to represent how women were oppressed has become, by the late twentieth-century publication of this novel, a positive exercise in setting appropriate boundaries.

The Model of Mansfield

The Dancers Dancing evinces a nostalgia not only for the nourishing features of nature as depicted in Romantic poetry, but also for those found throughout modernist writing. It draws its title from the final line of Yeats's "Among School Children" (1928), which articulates private meditations on the past prompted by the poet's visit to a convent classroom, and it assertively reframes modernist tradition: the situatedness of Joyce now manifests in the Gaeltacht, the "mythical modernism" of Eliot surfaces in allusions to Celtic folklore and myth, the formal experiments resonate with those seen in Pádraic Ó Conaire's Irish-language fiction.[8] As critics have noted, the novel does not shy away from the narrative artifice associated with modernism and postmodernism.[9] In particular, its chapters hold tight to the potency of the modernist short story, with its brevity and foreshortening, as a means to communicate the intensity and instability inherent in adolescent development.

The importance of Irish writers to the development of the modernist short story is a commonplace. As seen in their influential critical and creative writings, Seán Ó Faoláin and Frank O'Connor regarded the Irish short story as a national and naturalist form.[10] Their assessments, however, stand at odds with those of Elizabeth Bowen in her introduction to *The Faber Book of Modern Stories* (1936). There, Bowen identified the impact of new media on literature, citing the affinities

---

[8] Angela Bourke has claimed Ó Conaire's *Deoraíocht* as "the earliest example of modernist fiction in Irish." See Bourke, "Legless in London: Pádraic Ó Conaire and Éamon a Búrc," *Éire-Ireland* 38:3–4 (2003): 54–67, 54. See also Louis de Paor, "Irish Language Modernisms," *The Cambridge Companion to Irish Modernism*, ed. Joe Cleary (Cambridge: Cambridge University Press, 2014), 161–173; and Brian Ó Conchubhair, "The Parallax of Irish-Language Modernism, 1900–1940," *The Oxford Handbook of Modern Irish Fiction*, ed. Liam Harte (Oxford: Oxford University Press, 2020), 167–184.

[9] See Susan Cahill, *Irish Literature in the Celtic Tiger Years 1990–2008: Gender, Bodies, Memory* (London: Continuum Books, 2011), 43–54; Heather Ingman, *Irish Women's Fiction: From Edgeworth to Enright* (Dublin: Irish Academic Press, 2013), 231; Giovanna Tallone, "Past, Present and Future: Patterns of Otherness in Éilís Ní Dhuibhne's Fiction," *Irish Literature: Feminist Perspectives*, eds. Patricia Coughlan and Tina O'Toole (Dublin: Carysfort Press, 2008), 167–184.

[10] See Adrian Hunter, *The Cambridge Introduction to the Short Story in English* (Cambridge: Cambridge University Press, 2007). For valuable overviews, see Elke D'hoker, *Irish Women Writers and the Modern Short Story* (Houndsmill Basingstoke: Palgrave Macmillan, 2016) and Heather Ingman, *A History of the Irish Short Story* (Cambridge: Cambridge University Press, 2009).

shared by cinema and the "young art" of the short story.[11] She also emphasized the significance of writers outside of Ireland, celebrating Chekhov in particular for having "opened up for the writer tracts of emotional landscape" in which subjectivity can "edit and rule experience and pull art, obliquely, in its way" (9). Here, she commends Katherine Mansfield's dissemination of his innovations, noting the "influence" of her English translations and adaptations, which allowed Chekhov to be "indirectly copied by writers who do not read, or intend to read, him at all" (10).[12] This is but one indication of Mansfield's potent influence. The indeterminacy characterizing her short stories, particularly those centered on female sexuality, courses through contemporary fiction by Irish women, with writers echoing her untrustworthy narrators, her muddled epiphanies, her open endings, her potent symbolism.

Ní Dhuibhne reworks Mansfield's modernism to represent the changing contours of female privacy. As merely one example, in her short story "Summer's Wreath" (2013), a work of historical fiction, Ní Dhuibhne explicitly demonstrates the ways in which Mansfield's modernism abets the depiction of generative female privacy enabled by retreat. Written in the first person, this short story is a fictionalized account of Mansfield's exile to Germany following an unplanned pregnancy. The narrative is set across six months in Bad Wörishofen, during which Mansfield began an affair with the Polish writer Floryan Sobieniowski, and it imagines the events that precipitated the publication of her first collection, *In a German Pension* (1911). While there, Mansfield is encouraged by Floryan to translate into English a little-known Chekhov story about a nurse who, driven mad by sleeplessness, strangles a baby. Without publicly citing the Russian author, she sends her adapted story "The-Child-Who-Was-Tired" to A. R. Orage's magazine *The New Age*, where it would be published in 1910. Modernism thus surfaces in the plot of "Summer's Wreath" through broadly recognizable aspects of Mansfield's actual biography, as well as through its themes and form. In this story, for example, Mansfield's forced exile is reframed as temporary and liberating, allowing her to experience sexual and intellectual freedoms unavailable at home, and her modernist impressionism is refashioned to convey the sensations evoked by these new freedoms.

In "Summer's Wreath," Ní Dhuibhne undermines tenacious critical biases not only by embracing Mansfield's modernism, but also by insisting that literary translation is creative invention and refusing the association of women's literary experiment with "aberrant" sexuality. In *The Lonely Voice* (1963), for example, O'Connor impugned Mansfield's sexuality, contemptuously citing her "homosexual experiences" and "sordid love affairs," and he labeled her reworking of established literary

---

[11] Elizabeth Bowen, "The Short Story," *The Faber Book of Modern Stories* (London: Faber, 1936), 7–19, 7. Subsequent references parenthetical.

[12] On their shared settler colonial aesthetics, see Rebecca Ruth Gould, "The Aesthetic Terrain of Settler Colonialism: Katherine Mansfield and Anton Chekhov's Natives," *Journal of Postcolonial Writing* 55:1 (2019): 48–65.

142   LOGGING OFF

form mere facsimile and trickery, announcing that she "palmed off on Orage a fla-
grant imitation of Chekhov's famous story about the little baby sitter who is so
tired that she smothers the crying baby."[13] Yet in the preface to her 1957 edited
collection of Mansfield's short stories, Bowen asserted, "Of love for experiment
for its own sake, Katherine Mansfield shows not a sign. Conscious artist, she carries none of the marks of the self-consciously 'experimental' writer. Nothing in her
approach to people or nature is revolutionary; her story-telling is, on its own plane,
not much less straightforward than Jane Austen's. She uses no literary shock tactics."[14] Bowen continued, "Born into the English traditions of prose narrative, she
neither revolted against these nor broke with them—simply, she passed beyond
them. And now tradition, extending, has followed her."[15] For O'Connor, Mansfield is a deviant copycat. For Bowen, as for Ní Dhuibhne, she is an exemplar of
those who use the stubborn mode.

More particularly, "Summer's Wreath" suggests how the modernist mode allows
for a different and corrective set of "emotional landscapes," to recall Bowen's
admiring phrase. Ní Dhuibhne employs Mansfield's modernist impressionism,
which was inspired by Chekhov's "suggestive ... impressionist" stories, not only
to tone down the punitive aspects of forced exile, but also to revise the anticipated
emotional intensities associated with female sexuality and reproduction found
across Irish literature.[16] While at this spa town, the fictional Mansfield finds her
pregnancy less a source of shame than freedom: she can now ride a bike without
risking her maidenhead, as her father once warned; she can enjoy sex with Floryan, who "knew many tricks, most of them new to me and quite good" (144);
she can openly confess her pregnancy to the Irish housekeeper Rosaleen, and
embark on a sexual relationship with her, finding herself "tickled ... but in a different way" (145). The invocation of Mansfield's abstractions and distortions also
revises instantiated notions of women's creative labor. When her story is accepted
by Orage, it seems Mansfield's professional ambitions will be realized. But after
reading her acceptance letter, she begins to imagine her unborn child eating her
stories, cradled as a book in green nasturtium leaves, with his enormous mouth
and shark teeth. She turns her desk to the wall, only to wake two days later and
find that "The baby was no longer there. In the nasturtiums. Or anywhere" (155).
The muted emotional response to her pregnancy and miscarriage stands in contrast to the more heightened unconscious one attached to her writing. As well, we
learn the protagonist's name only late in the story, from Orage's acceptance letter

[13] Frank O'Connor, The Lonely Voice: A Study of the Short Story (Brooklyn: Melville Press, 2004),
126–127, 130.
[14] Elizabeth Bowen, "Stories by Katherine Mansfield" (1957), Afterthought: Pieces about Writing
(London: Longman's, 1962), 53–74, 60.
[15] Ibid., 60–61.
[16] Éilís Ní Dhuibhne, "Summer's Wreath," Town and Country: New Irish Short Stories, ed. Kevin
Barry (London: Faber and Faber, 2013), 133–157, 148. Subsequent references parenthetical.

addressed to "Miss Mansfield" (153). This letter inaugurates her career and suggests that her professional achievement as a writer, rather than a given parental or marital surname, or even the potential role of mother, earns this character her distinctive identity.

On Not Drowning

The Dancers Dancing similarly uses the stubborn mode of modernism to represent a more constructive relationship with privacy and likewise reorients certain expected emotional intensities. Its illustratively (rather than sequentially) titled chapters capture loosely aligned subjective impressions, of the kind found in the short stories of Chekhov and Mansfield, which isolate and concentrate the experiences of summer camp as experienced by Orla and her peers. The predictable forward-moving trajectory that guides most of the book, as well as the authoritative narrative voice, provides a safe and recognizable structure in which the abstracted intensities of adolescence experience can unfurl. In this way, the novel provides an aesthetic alternative to the devastating realities of female adolescence in contemporary Ireland as exemplified by the cases of Ann Lovett or of Girl X, the fourteen-year-old Irish girl who sought an abortion in 1992 after being raped and impregnated by a friend's father.

The characters at the center of this novel remain safe, a provocative gesture in a tradition where nature is often dangerous, where water in particular is often fatal. Among the works discussed in this study alone, Kate O'Brien's *The Land of Spices* sees Anna's brother Charlie drown accidentally, Enright's *The Gathering* describes Veronica's brother Liam drowning himself, and McBride's *A Girl Is a Half-formed Thing* concludes when the girl drowns herself. Ní Dhuibhne refuses a similarly tragic narrative for her protagonist. There are drownings in *The Dancers Dancing*, but they occur off camera: a boy once drowned in the burn, and children from another camp are reported to have drowned in the ocean, but these events remain for Orla merely disturbing cautionary tales. The novel at all times resists directly imperiling Orla. Despite being set during the height of the Troubles, she knows of its political violence only through chattered implications (one of Orla's roommates from the North has a father imprisoned in Long Kesh) or mistaken interpretation (Orla confuses a loud noise for an IRA bomb) or the sight of a soldier entering their school bus at a checkpoint. The domestic struggles of her parents, her Irish father and English mother who are clawing their way into the Dublin middle classes, are at a literal remove. In Donegal, when Orla finds Aunt Annie collapsed in a barn, she runs away and abandons her infirm aunt, without consequence. Even the chapter titles hint at violence evaded or merely imagined: a chapter labeled "Blood" signals only the age-appropriate arrival of Orla's first menstruation; the subsequent chapter "The Workhouse" describes the infanticide of an unwanted

144 LOGGING OFF

child by its mother Nuala Crilly, but this is only a dream. And the novel ends with the adult Orla on a beach vacation, seemingly contentedly married with children, enjoying the ocean recreationally.

Nonetheless danger hovers on the margins, suggesting that privacy in this novel remains, for all of the female characters, simultaneously a help and a hazard. When a precocious student named Pauline sneaks into a clifftop cottage, she finds it inhabited by Killer Jack, an older teacher with whom she has flirted. This adolescent girl violates the domestic privacy of a grown man, and their flirtation turns monstrous, as the ominously nicknamed teacher grabs her t-shirt and looks at her with eyes that "glitter like Dracula's before a deadly bite" (199). In this chapter, "Pauline, numb with terror, awaits her fate," which ultimately turns out to be the offer of a glass of orangeade and a packet of crisps from a yawning and bored Killer Jack (199). As she recognizes, she "is not to be the hapless victim after all. She is not to be a mangled corpse, a girl child wronged. She is to be a nuisance. That is all" (199). The uneventfulness of this encounter is provocatively ambiguous. This moment recalls the legacy of monstrous sexuality and exploited young women found in Gothic novels like Bram Stoker's *Dracula* (1897) and Sheridan Le Fanu's *Carmilla* (1872), or in the expressionist film *Nosferatu* (1929). But it also evokes punishing memories of real-life Irish women marked as sexually transgressive and institutionalized by the church, or tarred during the Troubles for dating across sectarian lines. These literary and historical legacies, amplified by the dramatic propensities of Pauline's teenage imagination, create a heightened narrative perception at odds with the banal reality of Pauline's transgressive behavior and Killer Jack's lackluster response.

Using such modes in concert, the novel puts forward an anodyne version of female adolescent development in Ireland, one in which the girls are approximate to but never directly harmed by serious trauma. Progressing slowly and deliberately, the narrative refuses the faster-paced rhythms of the modern, urban Dublin that Orla calls home. It also repudiates the intensities of extraordinary adolescent crisis. Determined by the calendar of the summer camp, the narrative moves inexorably forward, driven not by events, but instead by predictable timetables and sensation. Such a strategy led one reviewer of *The Dancers Dancing* to bemoan, "The pace is sluggish, and the characters, introduced in initially engaging portraits, develop no further as the book progresses. Such obstructions to narrative flow and realized characters blunt the power of Dhuibhne's [sic] occasionally lovely prose."[17] Yet the novel's slow pace makes sense when understood, at least in part, as a reworking of Mansfield. In his study of colonial boredom, Saikat Majumdar has described Mansfield's fiction as characterized by "narrative entropy" and "aesthetic unfulfillment," seeing her as a writer on the margins of empire who rarely

---

[17] "Dancer's Dancing," *Publisher's Weekly*, February 1, 2000, https://www.publishersweekly.com/978-0-85640-650-8.

literalizes the "trauma and violence lurking within colonial and indigenous land-scapes."[18] The same can be said for Ní Dhuibhne. In Declan Kiberd's postscript to *The Dancers Dancing*, he cites Gertrude Stein and Yeats as influences on the novel, and he concludes that the "subtlety of this marvellous *Bildungsroman* lies in its refusal of any sense of a grand narrative. There is no major catastrophe, because everything happens elsewhere, further up the coast, in Derry, or back in the past."[19] That is, of course, true. But as the novel itself might insist, this claim is also "Half false" (3). There is a grand narrative here, but it is not one based in national or personal trauma. It is based instead on the largely predictable and mostly healthy process of adolescent female development for a middle-class Dublin teenager, an experience rarely depicted in Irish fiction as of 1999.

Necessary Privacy in *Pond*

The possibilities made available to women through elective and anodyne privacy also characterize the resuscitated experiments of Claire-Louise Bennett's debut novel *Pond*, first published by The Stinging Fly Press in 2015. Described both as a fragmented novel and as twenty linked short stories, *Pond* is an elliptical first-person narrative delivered by an unnamed female protagonist temporarily living in a rented thatched cottage in rural Ireland, a location she (inaccurately) situates in a larger global framework as "the most westerly part of Europe."[20] In titled chapters of varied lengths, some containing only a few sentences, the narrator ponders the world around her and muses on personal concerns ranging from romantic relationships to her unfinished dissertation. The novel is yet another provocative rewriting of the modernist bildungsroman, that oft-studied genre that charts the development of a young protagonist into adulthood. Like *The Dancers Dancing*, it stages a realm in which privacy is not dangerous for its female charac-ter, but instead a constitutive element of self-realization. Taking a cue from Irish modernism, the novel situates its female protagonist in the rustic west, electively secluded from the pressures of modern, urban life. Set after the fall of the Celtic Tiger, *Pond* suggests a more fruitful version of solitude for recessionary Ireland, where neoliberal discourses of individualism infect daily life, austerity measures undermine collectivity, and meritocratic fantasies suggest there is only one winner.

The modernist mode suffuses Bennett's writing. She is author of *Fish Out of Water* (2020), an essay that considers the portraiture of American artist Dorothea

---

[18] Saikat Majumdar, *Prose of the World: Modernism and the Banality of Empire* (New York: Columbia University Press, 2013), 75, 79.

[19] See Declan Kiberd, "Reading *The Dancers Dancing*," in Ní Dhuibhne, *The Dancers Dancing*, 293–296, 296.

[20] Claire-Louise Bennett, *Pond* (Dublin: Stinging Fly Press, 2015), 74. Subsequent references parenthetical.

146 LOGGING OFF

Tanning, whose paintings were threaded with Surrealism well after the twentieth-century heyday of that movement, and her second novel *Checkout 19* (2021) mentions a multitude of modernist writers and books, with E. M. Forster's *A Room with a View* (1908) playing a central role in the imagination of its female narrator. Critics have name-checked Joyce and Beckett as reference points for *Pond*'s experiments; however, Bennett has refused modernism as an instrument to understand the book, claiming, "I do like modernist writing, yes, but I don't know if it's been an influence."[21] There are, nonetheless, obvious resonances between *Pond* and the modernism that preceded it. The opening chapter, entitled "Voyage in the Dark," is named for Jean Rhys's 1934 feminist critique of colonialism and patriarchy, and Bennett's use of stream of consciousness, attending closely to one woman's perceptions of the natural and domestic world, inevitably invites comparisons to works by Virginia Woolf and Dorothy Richardson, as well as chiming with other modernist representations of female interiority discussed in this study. *Pond*'s close, sustained consideration of everyday objects, and its deliberately poetic language, have invited reviewers aptly to associate it with Wallace Stevens's "plain sense of things" as well as the poetry of e e cummings.[22] Here again the admixture of literary modes might make plain a critique: the crowding of material objects in Bennett's narrative is reminiscent of the Edwardian novels Woolf criticized in "Mr Bennett and Mrs Brown" (1924) for their obsession with the external material world, even as the surfeit of associative detail untethered from narrative progression, a strategy drawn from modernism, reframes the logics of acquisition and accumulation that characterized the Celtic Tiger years by destabilizing any promise that consumer capitalism might render daily life easier, faster, or more secure.

The recent and radical transformations wrought by digital technologies simmer through *Pond*, which might seem an odd claim given the few overt references to their devices and forms. This apparent "ghosting" of the digital world is one way to refuse its ubiquity and authority, but the modernist mode offers another means of resistance. Bennett's deployment of forms and themes drawn from the literary past repudiates the fast-paced rhythms and present-focused nature of contemporary life in the digital age, as well as undermines the facile reading and perceptive practices that the internet cultivates. References to "online platforms" (75) and texting appear in the book, but they are rarely considered closely, and that most familiar of internet genres—the cat meme—is rendered as something not of the web:

---

[21] Susanne Stich, "Claire-Louise Bennett: Modes of Solitude, Embodiment and Mystery," *The Honest Ulsterman*, June 2015, http://humag.co/features/claire-louise-bennett.

[22] For the cummings reference, see Sarah Gilmartin, "*Pond* by Claire-Louise Bennett Review," *Irish Times*, May 2, 2015, https://www.irishtimes.com/culture/books/pond-by-claire-louise-bennett-review-a-rewarding-voyage-into-the-interior-1.2196696; for the Stevens reference, see Andrew Gallix, "*Pond* by Claire-Louise Bennett Review," *The Guardian*, November 18, 2015, https://www.theguardian.com/books/2015/nov/18/pond-claire-louise-bennett-review.

"I hate coming across photographic records of putatively outlandish cat behavior and I hate hearing about cats" (132).

Nevertheless, *Pond* exposes the unavoidable contradictions that the digital world poses for understandings of female privacy and authority in the twenty-first century. In "Morning, Noon, & Night," the second chapter, the narrator recalls a torrid sexual affair she has in London with a postgraduate "bloke" with whom she corresponds over email (11). As she notes, "We wrote each other hundreds of lustful emails, and by that I mean graphic and obscene," but she expunges the "almost two thousand emails" when they end the relationship (12). The protagonist mourns the forfeiture, not of her lover's affection, but of her early linguistic experiment. She feels the loss of "using language in a way I'd not used it before, to transcribe such an intimate area of my being that I'd never before attempted to linguistically lay bare" (12). This account celebrates the protagonist's writerly experiments abetted by a new form, the email, as well as revealing her cavalier relationship to privacy in the digital age. Her emails document, disclose, and disburse intimate experiences, making visible erotic encounters formerly concealed by necessity or punished as recompense, and she claims the authority not only to document but also to expunge them. However, though it goes unmentioned, hovering over her memory of this erasure is the fact that the records of this personal exchange, the "hundreds of lustful emails" (12), likely remain in the hands of others, possibly kept by her lover or archived by some invasive multinational technology company. Such a threat to her privacy goes unmentioned, either because she is unaware of, or unperturbed by, the possibility of such exposure.

With its concentration on interiority, *Pond* poses a pointed alternative to the heightened publicness of the everyday fostered by social media, in which individuals flood digital platforms with reports and images of their vacations, their daily meals, their fashion choices. Here, privacy and secrecy produce no devastating personal and social consequences for the narrator, as they did for actual victims of abuse in Ireland, or for characters depicted by other contemporary Irish women writers. In Irish fiction, the namelessness of protagonists often suggests that society has neglected, or failed to see and protect, these marginalized characters. In *Pond*, however, a sense of liberation accompanies the protagonist's anonymity. Not knowing the history of where she lives, the unnamed narrator relishes the fact that "All the names mean nothing to you, and your name means nothing to them" (79).

Another register of Bennett's critique of digital life, and how it reshapes female interiority, rests in the surprising affective contours of this narrative. In pursuit of viewers and clicks and advertising revenue, contemporary media culture seeks to make an event out of the mundane, to manufacture crises. Bennett resists this strategy, as well as demonstrating how our imagination has been structured by such logics, by an unquenchable thirst for the constant feed of blatantly dramatic content. In "Morning, 1908," for example, the protagonist encounters an unfamiliar hooded man in the woods, and her mind leaps to imagining his assault of her,

148 LOGGING OFF

but in fact, "Nothing happened of course. I stood at a gate and a young man passed by. That was all" (101). Like the characters of *The Dancers Dancing*, she remains unharmed by physical threat. Primed by suspenseful narratives and hyperbolic news stories, as well as by the actual vulnerability of being a woman alone, the narrator visualizes a dramatic climax for her walk, but that anticipation, which is laden with expectations of catastrophe, is thwarted. The chapter ends not with her reaching out to others on her smartphone or checking online reports for news of possible assailants, but instead with her perusing a book of photographs by Clarence H. White, the early twentieth-century American photographer known for his impressionistic photographs of the quotidian and the rustic—her retreat into this published book a riposte to the consolations promised by new technologies that permit immediate access to the outside world with the touch of a screen or a vocal command to a virtual-assistant speaker.

Despite having studied as an actor, Bennett throughout deliberately refuses to snag attention with heightened rhetoric or dramatic events. This is a provocative gesture for a writer living in a contemporary Ireland reeling from the persistent exposure of shocking abuses and scandals. Irish fiction is rife with experimental novels about lives pocked with ruinous trauma including sexual abuse and death by suicide, as well as with threatened and actual deep personal loss. Yet *Pond* holds no such shocking upheavals. The narrator does feel terror, as she announces in "Words Escape Me," but it is free-floating and the source never named (128). Or it is purely imagined and psychologically managed. In the penultimate chapter "Lady of the House," for example, she imagines a "monster," "the creature beneath the water" (129), but resolves, "It wouldn't be a big deal—the monster's coming up from beneath wouldn't be a big show" (130). The protagonist refuses the horror-movie bubbling beneath this tale set in a sparsely populated rural area, as well as the Gothic psychological drama of a proto-modernist feminist narrative like Charlotte Perkins Gilman's "The Yellow Wallpaper" (1892), even as another chapter "The Gloves Are Off" describes the narrator's deciding to paint the walls of her home yellow.

Nonetheless, cautionary tales abound. For example, her management of negative affect, the self-talk that quells the protagonist's ambient fear, risks diffusing the collective injuries of the past, and the lessons those might teach in the present, when they are transmuted into personal anxiety. In "Control Knobs," the narrator worries over the broken knobs on her outdated cooker and recalls the "history of starvation which did in fact take many hundreds of lives hereabouts and beyond" even as she counters "the exact spot where I live is pleasant overall" (74). She imaginatively addresses the South African manufacturer of the damaged cooker, identified from her research online, noting, "I mention the famine, Salton, not in order to establish any sort of sociohistorical affinity, which would be a very crass contrivance indeed, but simply because my mind is currently more susceptible to images of hunger than it has ever been" (74). Pivoting from the unspoken history of colonial violence and food insecurity that haunts South Africa, she turns closer to home and recalls having read that "as many as two thousand stricken bodies were pulled out of ditches and piled onto carts then wheeled down the hill to the pit at the churchyard below" (75). Her mind then travels from famine trauma to her unsuccessful quest for replacement parts: these material objects are as elusive as the unmarked graves of those who died from hunger in nineteenth-century Ireland. Seemingly attributed to frustrated internet shopping, the temporary feeling of "loss" elicited in this moment is tidily conflated with "indifference" (76). The distracted forgetfulness of the internet has redirected her consciousness and muted her emotions, even as the inescapable global legacies of colonial oppression, human suffering, and buried trauma weave themselves throughout this introspective account of her relationship with a worn-out household appliance.

So while *Pond* does not report any significant immediate trauma suffered by its female narrator, an autonomous adult who seeks and appreciates the satisfactions of the privacy she has chosen, the novel suggests her consciousness is marked by ambient fear. Her fears can be denied or dismissed, and she can distract herself from distress with internet browsing or other diversions, but they resurface in moments of slow solitude. In certain chapters, she details her inchoate apprehensions, ones often heightened because of her isolation and seclusion. In the aforementioned "Words Escape Me," she provides a sustained account of unidentifiable sounds in her cottage that elicit from her an "overall sensation [that] was quite calamitous" (126). In this chapter, she shares her detailed and reasoned internal dialogue in the midst of this distress, an attempt to quash the panic triggered by these sounds (128). The source of the noise is never identified, and it becomes clear that her anxiety is both abstract and free-floating. As she ponders these feelings, "I wasn't much keen on the idea that I had been terrified for years, but it seemed possible" (128). The story ends with her announcing the oblique, but nonetheless interpretable and recognizable, source of her fear, one discovered by her "sinking words into the pages" of her "notebook": it is a fear of death, one that finds her "far beneath the ground at last" (128). The stubborn reality of encroaching mortality, of the inevitable end to her story, provides one potent explanation for the use of modernist experiments that stall the pace of the narrative.

Slow Modernism and the List

Pond repackages a motif familiar not only from Thoreau's *Walden* (1854), that manifesto of self-reliance also set by a pond, but also from Irish revivalism, in which the pastoral promises a haven from the contagions of modern life. The organizing metaphor of the book is a natural body of water that is small, discrete, and contained, one even more placid than a burn, and the situatedness of the rural Irish setting provides a counter to the internet's placeless deracination.

150 LOGGING OFF

The narrator appears through retreat to resist technology's domination of everyday life—nothing here, such as those knobs of the oven that she considers for a full chapter, is progressive and efficient. The laborers she encounters are ratcatchers and Irish-speaking thatchers, both evincing an appreciation for deliberate, anti-modern work. More particularly, Bennett invokes the modernist mode to depict and consider the experience of time for its Irish female character. Working amid new technologies of mass communication, travel, and production, modernists endeavored to depict the altered temporality that arose with modernity's rapid acceleration of time, whether in the sculptures of the Italian Futurist Umberto Boccioni or in the fifty-year span and pacing of Proust's seven-volume *In Search of Lost Time* (1913–1927). Published roughly a century after the height of high modernism, in the wake of the crash of the Celtic Tiger, and amid the powerful economic and cultural influence of the internet in Ireland and abroad, *Pond* captures the changed contours of temporality in the twenty-first century and aggressively resists their imperatives.

Writing in the throes of fast capital, twenty-four-hour news cycles, and the patter of the internet, Bennett uses form in *Pond* to slow things down: the recursive prose and unfocused plot undermine any notions of progress, both personal and societal, as well as impede the pace of textual consumption.[23] Unlike *The Dancers Dancing*, *Pond* largely refuses any narrative arc. To paraphrase Vivian Mercier's notorious 1956 review of Beckett's *Waiting for Godot*, *Pond* is a collection in which nothing happens, twenty times. As one example, despite the book's recursion to the protagonist's erotic life, it refuses to represent desire as something kinetic that moves forward and demands release. Bennett's meandering style and the puttering of her protagonist seem an overt challenge to the accelerated time of the present enabled by communication technologies and the media. Readers are left to pluck among associative links, among them the protagonist's interests in nature, writing, and sex, and objects both domestic and professional.

Modernist difficulty long has been understood as one riposte to the cultural ascension of easily consumed mass culture, and *Pond* invokes that logic to challenge readers. It mounts an old-fashioned critique of new problems generated or exacerbated by the internet, among them the temptations of reading quickly and impulsively, gathering masses of new information, producing easy summary, promoting manufactured drama as "clickbait" for revenue, and championing media-concocted communities over the intimacies of shared time and space. The slow attentiveness represented in, as well as demanded by, *Pond* is a practice that runs counter to the intensified use of the internet, which truncates attention and undermines concentration. And like prayer or reverie, it might enable space for more capacious critical reflection in our contemporary moment—one that

---

[23] For a slow reading of *Pond*, see Brian Dillon, "Gusto Notwithstanding," *Suppose a Sentence* (New York: New York Review of Books, 2020), 207–216.

reimagines and potentially reinvigorates the activism that informed Irish women's early twentieth-century modernism. As Lutz Koepnick contends in his account of "slow modernism": "Slowness asks viewers, listeners, and readers to hesitate, not in order to step out of history, but to enable the possibility of simultaneously looking left and right, forward and backward, up and down; slowness diverts directional movement so as to reveal the different stories, durations, movements, and speeds that energize the present, including this present's notions of discontinuity and rupture, of promise and loss."[24] This "slowness" in *Pond* exposes the nature of the narrator's consciousness and reveals how it has been inflected by her awareness and consequent refusal of the connected, hyper-publicness of the digital age. It refutes, as Bennett observes in *Checkout 19*, a world in which "Convenience replaces ritual, devices replace daydreaming, spotlights replace shade, and the discord between one's inner world and the immediate surroundings goes through the roof."[25]

Pond speaks to a moment in which practices such as slow food, slow parenting, and mindfulness have been suggested as counteragents to the breakneck pace of contemporary life, and it engenders a reading experience that resists the notion of arrival, one common trait shared by Irish women's fiction using the stubborn mode. Such "slowness" means that the protagonist is sometimes bored and stalled, without the easy distractions of her time. In their studies of modernism, Alison Pease attributes boredom in modernist writing to female desire unfulfilled, and Saikat Majumdar cites its source as the unfulfilled desire of the colonial subject to be in the center of empire and action.[26] Fulfillment does not seem, in *Pond*, to be an objective. Indeed, Bennett deliberately thwarts fulfillment with her formal strategies. Repetition, which for many Irish women writers has been a stylistic device employed to depict the threat of a dark history repeating itself, seems here largely meditative and creative, a device used to convey female experience characterized by routine and banality, rather than interruption and crisis. Likewise, her indifference to narrative progress, to the impulse to prod stillness into motion merely for the sake of motion, underscores the interpretive possibilities that might stem from narrative suspension. Other features similarly might be interpreted as retorts to contemporary life: the protagonist's thoughtful self-examination counters the pernicious self-interest of the neoliberal subject; the stasis that informs the book's plot and characterization refuses economic models that champion without question the merits of growth and progress; her sustained attention to the familiar urges contemplation rather than the constant acquisition of new information valued by the media age.

---

[24] Lutz Koepnick, *On Slowness: Toward an Aesthetic of the Contemporary* (New York: Columbia University Press, 2014), 45.

[25] Claire-Louise Bennett, *Checkout 19* (London: Jonathan Cape, 2021), 84.

[26] Allison Pease, *Modernism, Feminism, and the Culture of Boredom* (Cambridge: Cambridge University Press, 2012), and Majumdar, *Prose of the World*.

152 LOGGING OFF

Looking at *Pond* in tandem with the work of Gertrude Stein elucidates further Bennett's refusal of the expectations of narrative and of a world buzzing with posts, tweets, and feeds. Here again, the productive tension between modernism and the contemporary reveals itself. The logics of slow time and privacy work together in the novel's form, most vividly in the lists that appear throughout. Rather than a "to do" list seeking an end result or a top-ten list demonstrating preferences, the protagonist's lists are accumulations. In discussing her writing process, Bennett recalled, "Some of my earlier writing consisted of long lists of what was on the bedroom floor, for example. Cheese, a diary, a knife, a tampon, stones, a cup, a Shirley Bassey record, a half bottle of gin. And so on. It amazes me that out of all the things in the world it is those things that have come together in this particular place at this specific time. They assemble and then they depart, like orbiting planets."[27] Making meaning in process rather than planning, the method Stein described in *Composition as Explanation* (1925–1926), is evident here in the description of this list's objective record of random objects on the floor. Yet in the linguistic freeze-frame of this list, Bennett reveals herself to be a young woman, self-observant, a drinker, writer, and maybe even dangerous. The objects carry the weight of characterization, of who she is at the moment she records them.

As Hugh Kenner and Liesl Olson have demonstrated, lists are central to Joyce's *Ulysses*, so once more it could be argued Joyce's modernism emerges in fiction by an Irish woman writer.[28] However, the lists in *Pond* resonate even more saliently with those found in *Tender Buttons*, Stein's 1914 prose poems. Divided into "Objects," "Food," and "Rooms"—the same ordinary topics that consume *Pond*'s protagonist—*Tender Buttons* is likewise repetitive and paratactic. Extracted from the poems, Stein's titles provide a list of things found in many homes including "A Carafe That Is a Blind Glass," "A Substance in a Cushion," "A Box," "A Piece of Coffee." The content of these prose poems is filled with seemingly random lists, which point to quotidian objects and actions. Even as readers recognize the words on the page, these inventories refuse transparent access to the particularities of the distinctive private world from which they are drawn. For both Stein and Bennett, lists ultimately resist fixed meaning and confirm, in an aesthetically pleasing way, the inability of readers to know fully a character or predict confidently how events will unfold.

Ironically, for all of the objects, food, and spaces (both domestic and natural) listed in *Pond*, the narrator claims in the collection's penultimate story, "Lady of the House," that "I don't have much enthusiasm for inventorial reflection" (138). She then knowingly violates this claim by cataloging the characteristics of Martin's

---

[27] Emma Nuttall, "Claire-Louise Bennett on debut collection, *Pond*," *The Skinny*, November 20, 2015, http://www.theskinny.co.uk/books/features/claire-louise-bennett-pond-fitzcarraldo-stinging-fly.

[28] Hugh Kenner, *Ulysses* (Baltimore: Johns Hopkins University Press, 1987); Liesl Olson, *Modernism and the Ordinary* (New York: Oxford University Press, 2009).

SLOW MODERNISM AND THE LIST   153

Hill, one setting of her childhood: "The lake, the river, the ruined castle, the shrubs, the tall trees, the dismal clouds, the pissed upon reeds, the rowers and their boats, the monster, the house nearby, the children, their mother, the garage, the garden tools, the drying clods, the hallway, the stairs, the doors, the keyholes, the bed, the underneath, the terror, the cold floor, the ankle-straps, the perpetuating dust" (139). The same surprising menace that appears in Bennett's list via the knife, which might be simply a harmless tool to slice cheese, appears here. This feeling of peril is exacerbated in the lines that follow, where repetition stalls the trajectory of the plot:

> ... I think my brother's ball must have rolled down it you see, there must have been something anyway that lured him to that side of the hill because you wouldn't normally go that side ever—it was very steep you see, and overgrown—steep, uneven, and overgrown. Orange. Blue. Orange. Blue. Orange. And then he was alright for the first few steps, then he couldn't keep pace—he lost control and he fell actually. Fell all the way down to the bottom of Martin's Hill. All on his own with me just looking, and there was the proof I suppose that I was older at last. (139)

Just as her brother loses control and falls down the hill, so too does the protagonist find herself trapped in a predictable narrative arc, moving from the rising action of chasing the ball, to the climax of the fall, to resolution at the bottom of Martin's Hill. This natural progression, with its clear and inevitable outcome thanks to gravity, provides the narrator "proof I suppose that I was older at last." Although seeking to slow, suspend, and even undermine ready interpretation, the list collides with the advancing narrative here, and in doing so sheds light on character. The narrator describes her "radical immaturity—characterised by a persistent lack of ambition" (138), but this anecdote of her brother's fall and her reluctant awareness of her own maturity, which appears almost at the end of the novel, insists on the forward march of time, even as she admits, "I hated feeling that actually" (139).

Even swathed in modernist difficulty, the list might appear an attempt to lock down and transmit meaning, to document the mysteries of self through a surfeit of detail. At one point, the narrator expresses skepticism that language can represent interiority at all, asserting, "I'm not sure it can be made external you see. I think it has to stay where it is; simmering in the elastic gloom betwixt my flickering organs" (31). She understands that her self-containment unnerves others and observes, "no one can know what trip is going on and on in anyone else's mind and so, for that reason solely perhaps, the way I go about my business, such as it is, can be very confusing, bewildering, unaccountable—even, actually, offensive sometimes" (140). She then recounts once meeting a colleague at a hotel conservatory, where the list again creates trouble as he conveys to her "an unflattering compendium of controvertible opinions pertaining to my character and outlook—an apocryphal

154 LOGGING OFF

catalogue of puerile anecdotes" (140). She finds this attempt to itemize and articulate her private self "very off-putting" and "very disturbing actually" (140), until
she parses the encounter with a friend "a few times" and "felt sure enough of myself
not to give two hoots about it any more" (140).

Pond demonstrates that the modernist mode is not without didactic undertones
in the meritocratic age where selfhood is communicated through achievements,
ones now frequently documented online. As Bennett has asserted, "You reach an
age when you must make plans and then you immediately have to dedicate yourself lastingly to firming up those plans; from that age onwards most of what you do
every day is bound up with this enterprise. It is imperative that you achieve regularly, and thereby establish yourself strongly and neatly in the minds of others. And,
soon, what other people think undermines and redirects many of your percipient
impulses and cherished and private occupations."[29] In "Lady of the House," and in
fact throughout the entirety of *Pond*, the narrator displays the potential and pitfalls
of lists, of repetitions, of forward-moving plot—the narrative tricks that propel
a story and neatly convey character or meaning. She also refuses the clarifying
details that might be revealed through interior monologue, perhaps as a riposte to
the oversharing encouraged by the internet. And while *Pond* evinces the dialogic
qualities found in other accounts of female interiority throughout Irish women's
contemporary fiction, it refuses readers the effortless apprehensions made available by the internet. For example, the chapters are rife with the apostrophe "you,"
who might be a romantic partner but might also be a variety of other characters
who range across the narrative, or even perhaps the reader. The elective privacy
provided by such obfuscation is crucial; as Bennett has asserted, "In solitude you
don't need to make an impression on the world, so the world has some opportunity
to make an impression on you."[30]

Coming and Not Coming of Age

The stubborn mode also surfaces in *Pond*'s complicated relationship with the
modernist bildungsroman. As Gregory Castle notes, the classical bildungsroman
of self-formation morphs with the advent of early twentieth-century modernism
and begins to attend to the "dynamism and expressive capacity of inner life,"
as seen not only in Forster's *A Room with a View*, but also in novels by Woolf,
Richardson, H. D., and Bowen.[31] Each of these, he argues, refracts and reframes

[29] Claire-Louise Bennett, "Claire-Louise Bennett on Writing *Pond*," *Irish Times*, May 26, 2015,
https://www.irishtimes.com/culture/books/claire-louise-bennett-on-writing-pond-1.2226535.
[30] Ibid.
[31] Gregory Castle, "The Modernist Bildungsroman," *A History of the Bildungsroman*, ed. Sarah Graham (Cambridge: Cambridge University Press, 2019), 143–173, 145. See also Gregory Castle, *Reading
the Modernist Bildungsroman* (Gainesville: University of Florida Press, 2006).

the bildungsroman to feature "female protagonists whose desire for the aesthetic life is grounded not in a heroic posture towards art but in a revolutionary way of understanding and acting on (and in) the sensible world" (146). Castle's essay usefully identifies not only the centrality of the aesthetic appreciation of everyday life for protagonists of the modernist bildungsroman, but also a pattern of female protagonists who fail, or willfully refuse, to meet societal expectations. The echoes of these strategies in *Pond* are likely self-evident, even from this brief study, as are the ways that Bennett seeks to reframe these modernist strategies for the contemporary moment. Situated somewhere in between bildungsroman and anti-bildungsroman, her novel conveys through the organization of its chapters the arrested development apparent in the protagonist's repeated announcement of her immaturity, the lack of overt character development, and the use of formal tactics including lists or repetitions. In the chapters, few narratives seamlessly march forward, and most undermine the discourse of achievement. Further, the narrator never obtains or accomplishes anything big or small—a successful relationship or career, a clean house or neat garden—that might register as tangible evidence of her "adulting," the millennial neologism for behaviors associated with mature, responsible adulthood.

The Dancers Dancing trots Orla through the paces of development, offering a forward-moving narrative rich with moments that point to her psychological and physical growth. Although fragmented in form, the novel's final first-person chapter introduces Orla's adult retrospective, one that demonstrates she has found her place in the traditional role of wife and mother. *Pond* resists that developmental structure: it begins with a chapter set in the narrator's childhood and concludes with a chapter dumping readers back in her childhood, suggesting that there is no real escape from, or advance beyond, those seminal moments. This tactic may be a reflection of contemporary economic conditions that go unmentioned in the book but that have extended adolescence for a generation of young adults in the twenty-first century, individuals who live amid precarious economic circumstances that stall their career ambitions, trap them in early debt, return them home to live with their parents, and halt any plans for a traditional mature future of home ownership, marriage, or children. But the structure of the bildungsroman that arches over this book, like the list burrowed within it, represents a familiar form that might safely contain and express its young female protagonist's imaginative and personal risk-taking, explored in privacy and privately, that does not culminate in probable tragedy. As Bennett herself has noted, "You almost need structure to be protected, not only from everything else, but also from yourself."[32]

In *Pond*, the young adult protagonist is self-possessed, if sometimes wobbly in feeling or confidence, and the meandering of her observations made visible suggests a recalcitrance to the current systems that organize contemporary life and

---

[32] Stich, http://humag.co/features/claire-louise-bennett.

156 LOGGING OFF

the historical systems that haunt it. The temporary nature of retreat, and the fact that the narrator must move now that her landlady has placed all three cottages on the real estate market, invite us to regard the narrator's ruminations at the pond as the function of a temporary exile from real life, as a short-term opportunity for close self-reflection, something that will allow her to move forward—beyond her failed relationships, her thwarted academic career. *Pond* is thus in tune with aspects of the late modernist bildungsroman studied by Jed Esty, which represent youth as "unseasonable" and tied to "the uncertain future of a colonial world system" and in which, as seen in the writing of women like Rhys and Bowen, "long histories of colonial dispossession inform the failed processes of self-possession" of female characters.[33] Yet through Bennett's contemporary writing runs an artery of female self-possession. This novel is highly self-conscious, reminding readers that it is constructed by a protagonist skeptical of writerly modes that direct events and manipulate interpretation. As the narrator asserts, "the pressure exerted by so much emphatic character exposition and plotted human endeavor becomes stifling" (66–67). Despite its aggressively anti-developmental qualities, at the center of this recessionary narrative sits, stalled though sometimes she may be, a self-assured female protagonist who is highly alert to the imperatives of development, canny both in her resistance and acquiescence to the cultural scripts provided her. While marking the changing contours of female development in the twenty-first century, Bennett's embrace of the modernist mode exposes palpable new freedoms available to Irish women, suggesting the cultural changes that have fostered the capacity for her narrator's assertions. In the highly networked and digitally mediated present, the modernist mode reminds readers of the merits of an individualism that is not strictly characterized by "uncertainty, fragmentation, and isolation, with alienation represented as a marker of subjective experience in neoliberalism" of the Celtic Tiger period nor by the "conversation, exchange, and address in post-Celtic Tiger feminist literatures," the qualities Claire Bracken astutely identifies in Irish women's contemporary writing.[34] This protagonist, as her interior monologue reveals, can be alone but not lonely, connected but not networked, quiet but not silenced.

In *Pond*, fragmentation can enable generative juxtaposition, the list can promise abundant possibility, paralysis can be reframed as valuable and even necessary stillness. Nonetheless, Bennett admits the stubborn problems that plague her protagonist. For example, of the works in this study that might be categorized as coming-of-age novels, few stage for readers a young female protagonist whose imagined ambitions for a better future are realized: *The Land of Spices* does not follow Anna to university, *Hood* does not depict Pen's coming out to her mother.

---

[33] Jed Esty, *Unseasonable Youth: Modernism, Colonialism, and the Fiction of Development* (Oxford: Oxford University Press, 2012), 25, 32.

[34] Claire Bracken, "The Feminist Contemporary: The Contradictions of Critique," *The New Irish Studies*, ed. Paige Reynolds (Cambridge: Cambridge University Press, 2020), 144–160, 144.

The rare depictions of ambition realized are distressing, as when the alienated protagonist of *A Girl is a Half-formed Thing* dies by suicide, or cheerily formulaic, as when the protagonists of *Beautiful World, Where Are You* find themselves in committed heterosexual relationships. These two extremes—one alienated and bleak, the other connected and customary—underscore the limited outcomes that Irish literature can imagine for its female characters, and suggest the difficulty of finding satisfying alternatives that deviate from patterns previously established. By depicting the stasis that characterizes the inner life of her protagonist, and trapping her between two chapters that return to her childhood, even as she sits comfortably with how suspended time can nourish her inner life outside of the expected temporalities of achievement embraced or refused by the bildungsroman tradition, Bennett puts on display one of many problems that continue to afflict women in the present day. The globalized digital world may now present users with a vast array of alternative possibilities, but the stasis that characterizes *Pond* underscores the ongoing challenges of imagining and enacting a future outside the obdurate paradigms of traditional Irish womanhood.

Forbidden Privacy in *Only Ever Yours*

The Dancers Dancing and *Pond* represent further examples of the frequency and ingenuity with which the modernist mode is engaged and reworked in Irish women's contemporary fiction. Whether pulled from Joyce or Mansfield or Stein, a recalibrated modernism allows these writers to showcase the pleasures and perils of privacy, and to draw notice to the slow time necessitated by an increasing technological and public world for women. In her novel *Only Ever Yours*, Louise O'Neill takes modernist form and critique one step further by invoking the dystopian futurism of late modernist classics such as Aldous Huxley's *Brave New World* (1932) and George Orwell's *1984* (1949) to underscore the ongoing threats to women from patriarchal institutions and practices. *Only Ever Yours* suggests that the sequestration and shaming of Irish women so vividly cataloged across the past century continues apace, not only in the contemporary moment, but also into the future.

In her survey of Irish women's fiction between 1922–1960, Gerardine Meaney notes that popular genre fiction often proposed "fantasy resolutions to dilemmas which, in retrospect, we know to have been intractable," a tactic "perhaps best exemplified in the persistence of Gothic and supernatural fiction, where generic convention offered both vehicle and camouflage for social criticism."[35] *Only Ever*

---

[35] See Gerardine Meaney, "Fiction, 1922–1960," *A History of Modern Irish Women's Literature*, eds. Heather Ingman and Clíona Ó Gallchoir (Cambridge: Cambridge University Press, 2018), 187–203, 191.

158 LOGGING OFF

Yours highlights the complex relationship between modernism and popular culture, as well as between literary fiction and genre fiction, evident in many works of contemporary Irish women's writing.[36] The novel is laden with the expected features of mass market fiction targeted to a broad audience. Like another bestselling dystopian YA work from the era, Suzanne Collins's trilogy *The Hunger Games* (2008–2010), it provides readers a female protagonist living in a postapocalyptic world divided into districts, one ruled by a powerful elite and rife with inequity, where rebellion is managed in part through technology and state messaging. Unlike *The Dancers Dancing* or *Pond*, this novel provides neither a digressive plotline nor other experimental features intended to slow the process of reading and interpretation. But the bleak conclusion, as well as an insistent attention to the issue of female privacy, refuses the escapism and satisfying resolution often promised by genre fiction. Despite formal affinities with easily digested commercial fiction, the novel's pessimistic representation of female privacy connects it to a modernist tradition that challenged readers to question social norms and consider the knottiest aspects of female experience, even in a future moment when women are clones produced by and for men.

In their novels, Ní Dhuibhne and Bennett resurrect the modernist trope of rural retreat, recommending this practice as one means of access to nourishing female privacy, but O'Neill can prescribe no such curative. In *Only Ever Yours*, privacy is entirely unavailable to women, who are subject to, as well as the product of, neoteric technologies controlled by men. Set in the near future, *Only Ever Yours* is told from the first-person perspective of freida [sic], a sixteen-year-old student at the School, an institution that prepares young women cloned to serve as "companions" (spouses), "concubines" (sexual partners), or "chastities" (the disdained celibate woman who administrate the School). The novel invites us to see the narrative hinging on the troubled relationship of freida and her friend isabel, but its energies rest elsewhere—most obviously in O'Neill's depiction of how the dynamics of contemporary social media and similar technologies, when rendered extreme and situated in a not entirely impossible future, malform female experience.

Despite its dark premise and its troubling depictions of emotional and physical abuse, *Only Ever Yours* has been aggressively (and successfully) marketed as a young adult novel. And in fact, Patrick Sproull has proclaimed O'Neill "the best YA fiction writer alive today," citing encomiums from authors including Jeannette Winterson and Marian Keyes.[37] This novel is, in some ways, a derivation of

---

[36] For an overview of the mutual interdependence of modernism and mass culture, of experimental fiction and genre fiction, see Elana Gomel, "'Rotting Time': Genre Fiction and the Avant-Garde," *The Routledge Companion to Experimental Literature*, eds. Joe Bray, Alison Gibbons, and Brian McHale (London: Routledge, 2014), 393–406.

[37] Patrick Sproull, "Louise O'Neill," *The Guardian*, September 2, 2015, https://www.theguardian.com/childrens-books-site/2015/sep/02/louise-oneill-asking-for-it-interview. For an account of the

FORBIDDEN PRIVACY IN *ONLY EVER YOURS* 159

Margaret Atwood's *The Handmaid's Tale* (1985), or Kazuo Ishiguro's *Never Let Me Go* (2005), but one directed to the common reader. This may explain its invocation of more blatant modernist tactics: the novel uses unconventional punctuation to underscore the powerlessness of the girls, keeping their names in lowercase, and its narrative pastiche results largely from an infusion of text messages and blog posts, frequently rendered in italics. The plot is ordered in a linear manner, with many chapters marked by the approaching date of the Ceremony, the pageant event in which the boys select a companion from among the girls and the remaining girls are assigned a role as concubine or chastity. But the narrative is interrupted by pages filled with bold, large-print excerpts from the *Audio Guide to the Rules for Proper female Behavior* authored by the Original Father who led the earliest Zones. Likewise, repetitions—such as those evident in prayer—course through the novel, including a mantra reminding the students that "I am a good girl." By identifying these formal tactics as registers of a persistent modernism, it becomes clear that this mode now is not only legible in popular commercial literature, but also seamlessly integrated into new media.

The fact that *Only Ever Yours* employs a canned version of modernism, one that seems both forced and fatigued, might reflect the fact that the mode is now weaker than when individualism was a presupposed right with inherent value.[38] In this future, neoliberal privatization has run amok: for women of all ages, the family has been replaced by the institution, the individual melded into a social aggregate, female consciousness supplanted by an instrumentalized body. Irish women remain cloistered—not in the home or convent, but in institutions that manage them with pharmaceuticals and monitor their every move through technology. Adolescent development is programmed, organized through Messages sent to all girls, reiterating the appearance-centric and competitive messages identified decades ago in Naomi Wolf's *The Beauty Myth* (1990), which critiqued the harm done to women by unrealistic images of beauty proffered by advertising and media. A computerized Personal Stylist Program (PSP), along with VoiceCommand, helps girls in the School choose among outfits from Fashion TV, and monitors their weight with a "voice [that] fills the room."[39] Administered doses of SleepSound and collagen, among other medications, ensure the girls look fresh and well rested, while Messages endlessly assert, "*I am pretty. I am a good girl. I always do as I am told*" (9). The temporary distraction granted by streamed episodes of *The Americas-Zone's Next Top Concubine* or the nostalgic Nature

---

critical interventions made possible by such work see Jennifer Mooney, *Feminist Discourse in Irish Literature: Gender and Power in Louise O'Neill's Young Adult Fiction* (London: Routledge, 2023).

[38] See Kelly Rich, "'Look in the Gutter': Infrastructural Interiority in *Never Let Me Go*," *Modern Fiction Studies* 61:4 (Winter 2015): 631–651.

[39] Louise O'Neill, *Only Ever Yours* (New York: Quercus, 2014), 11. Subsequent references parenthetical.

160 LOGGING OFF

Channel series *Destruction*, which depicts earth before the climate was devastated, are among the panaceas available in this world.

Little about this novel's representation of social media and its pernicious influence on women and female collectivity is subtle. In its opening pages, freida cannot sleep so she grabs her "ePad" and updates her "MyFace" status, seeking to connect with other girls. Distraction is the constant threat, the tool used to thwart any psychological development or complexity among the girls. *The Dancers Dancing* celebrates the promise of slow time and a retreat into nature in the panoptical world of a summer camp, and *Pond* likewise advocates their benefits for its adrift protagonist. *Only Ever Yours* allows its female characters neither. The girls exist in a world of "mirrored ceiling[s]" (3), relentless pinging messages from peers and School authorities, routinized eating and medication, constant photographs and public rankings of physical beauty, and repeated warnings not to "dawdle" (40). The media inscribes patriarchal authority, as the Father delivers a Public Address that opens with flashing images of the highly ranked girls and his voice roaring "ROOM FOR IMPROVEMENT" (37).

For Ní Dhuibhne and Bennett, nature provided one sanctuary that constructively enabled in their female protagonists a measure of self-understanding. In *Only Ever Yours*, the planet has been environmentally devastated due to rising sea levels, and its reduced population has been divided into Zones (the Euro-Zone, the Chindia-Zone, the Americas-Zone), managed and wired to produce women who serve powerful men. When the girls escape to the manufactured garden to play a secret game of "spin the bottle," they rank each other "face-to-face" (83). This intimate encounter makes them nervous because such invasive comparisons typically happen only "in private, protected behind the anonymity of our computers" (83). In *The Dancers Dancing*, Orla can escape alone to the burn and scream the word "Fuck." There, she can privately perform her adult self—cosseted by nature, she transgresses without repercussion from any authorities. In this scene from *Only Ever Yours*, the girls are overheard cursing by a furious chastity-ruth, who interrupts their secret meeting and punishes them. Their use of the "F-word" (88) invites not a feeling of private emancipation but the experience of shaming and public punishment. The only genuinely private space in the novel is freida's unconscious, in one instance triggered by the maternal touch of her friend isabel when they are alone in her room, after which freida dreams of "fields of lavender, of boys and of mothers. I dream of things I know nothing about" (121).

The protagonists of *The Dancers Dancing* and *Pond* are both temporarily removed from their daily routines and habitats: Orla spends summer at Irish-language camp in Donegal, the unnamed protagonist of *Pond* retreats to an isolated rural enclave. These young women, on the cusp of different stages of adulthood, develop thanks to their withdrawal from the normal rhythms of their everyday lives. More particularly, both seek solace from small bodies of water: Orla discovers her voice at the burn, the protagonist of Bennett's novel at the pond.

The burn and the pond, like the baths enjoyed by Ní Dhuibhne's fictive Katherine Mansfield, provide a stark contrast to the awesome power of the ocean. In our digital present, these different but still insular bodies of water might be read as symbols that speak to a desire to log off, to find privacy and autonomy in a local setting. In contrast, oceans symbolize a natural means of global connectedness that, in the era of climate change, literally threaten engulfment and loss. As Orla and *Pond*'s protagonist isolate themselves from their long-standing affiliations and habits—their peers, their families, their daily routines—the small bodies of water with which they identify grant them a symbol of measured connectedness with nature and the self, one without the anxieties associated with formless, seemingly infinite oceans.

In *Only Ever Yours*, there are no oceans, rivers, streams, or ponds—and no authentic natural retreat for its protagonist. Instead, freida wanders through man-made gardens that replicate the natural world that has been destroyed. Melting icecaps and rising seas have drowned low-lying countries and their populations; those who survived joined the Noah Project, in which survivors were housed in self-contained Zones rid of "anything that would weigh us down," such as animals and organized religion (49). As freida walks along the cloisters, postered with pre-lapsarian images of the Grand Canyon or the Taj Mahal and carpeted with synthetic grass and trees, she imagines the world outside, "Rotted away, decaying like female babies in the uterus. Decomposing from the inside out" (49). This simile stems from the history of the Zones, in which unwanted infant girls were tossed into "girl Graves" until Genetic Engineers were forced to create "the new women, the eves" (50–51). This novel lacks the situatedness that characterizes so much Irish writing; little here suggests an Irish setting, except perhaps these "girl Graves." Like the buried infant bones that Orla discovers at the burn in *The Dancers Dancing*, or the real-life bones unearthed in Tuam, the bodies of dead babies and the shame of childbirth in *Only Ever Yours* endure as a vivid Irish historical legacy, the gruesome register of a stubborn societal problem.

Privacy and Sexual Futures

The temporal and spatial gaps and obfuscations that allowed the female protagonists of *The Dancers Dancing* and *Pond* nourishing moments of privacy are nowhere to be found in the Euro-Zone. Everything in this world is monitored and public—there are no private secrets, only public facts. The girls are open about their medication dosages, their physical attributes from hair and eye color cataloged and available online, their rankings made public every week. Each day, freida must step into an "empty booth, sliding the door shut behind me," but only so that her photo can be taken and "uploaded instantly to the School website for the Euro-Zone Inheritants to judge, determining my opening rank for the year"

162   LOGGING OFF

(13). The first chapter ends with freida thinking after the photograph is taken, "I'm left in the darkness. I should leave, but just for a moment I want to stay in here. I want to hide, fold into the shadows and become invisible so no one can *look* at me anymore" (13), a fantasy of solitude and seclusion. However, the next and final line of the chapter reads, "I hope the foto was perfect" (13), revealing that these practices have insidiously undermined freida's nascent desire to go unseen and unjudged.

In the novel, the only privacy available is associated with the Inheritants, the boys from the main Zone who will choose among the School's eligible girls. When the boys are revealed over video to the girls, they swoon over the highest ranked Inheritant, named Darwin Goldsmith. In their first face-to-face encounter, Darwin tells freida he finds her intriguing because "You don't give much away, do you?" (187) Despite being male, Darwin also suffers from hypervisibility due to his exalted social status and the small size of Euro-Zone. With him, however, freida obtains her first moment of sanctioned privacy during "Heavenly Seventy," a dystopian version of the game "Seven Minutes of Heaven" in which couples are locked in a dark closet to prompt intimacy. A private room, ironically covered in mirrors, is the lone space in which freida and Darwin are alone and can share an honest exchange. Yet freida cannot tolerate the intimacy of these encounters, and she divulges to another student a confidence Darwin shares; she discloses the secret history of "aberrants," two girls who fell in love and were caught engaged in adultery and executed, and her revelation alienates Darwin and destroys their relationship (285). This violation of trust reflects a typical theme in YA depictions of female friendship and loyalty, but that customary subject is dramatically heightened by this novel's dystopian contexts: the rampant lack of privacy demonstrates the heightened importance of secrets for women, as well as exposing that they fundamentally misunderstand how private communication works. Secrets are the currency that might buy freida fellowship unbolstered by good feeling among the female students, rather than a form of fruitful intimacy between man and woman.

As the Ceremony approaches, freida notes, "We eves in final year were designed on the same day. We were hatched together and we have lived as we will die, our bones touching. Yet it has only been these last few days that I have felt like I am suffocating with our togetherness" (309). At the Ceremony, rejected by Darwin and the other boys, freida is consigned to becoming a chastity and in response feels "nothing" (366). When criticized by the Father at the Ceremony, she feels nothing again, with her emotions muted by drugs, fear, and a learned incapacity for self-analysis and expression. In crisis, she is only aware of what she "should" (377) feel. Her life as a chastity resembles that of a nun, one characterized by routine and a commitment to ideals like selflessness, devotion, and humility. Her head is shaved, her "useless womb" (395) removed, her self rendered "empty" (395). In a short chapter of repetitive recitations, akin to prayer, the logics of the patriarchal

Euro-Zone and the patriarchal Catholic Church fuse, as both elicit prayers to the "Father" and share the ideal of female sacrifice and abnegation.

Her gestures toward more fully realized female interiority, it seems, are largely to blame for freida's fate—a fact revealed when chastity-ruth confronts her, observing "how prone to flights of fancy you are. I've been trying to crush it out of you for years, haven't I?" (396) At the novel's end, freida is consigned to the Underground, where she will provide a specimen to be studied by the Engineers, one of many nude female bodies wired to machines and "marinating in clear containers" (404). This horrific outcome holds appeal for her as, once drugged, she understands that she will "feel nothing, forever" (404). The burn provided a site for self-realization in *The Dancers Dancing*, and *Pond* poses its titular pool of water as a venue for self-exploration. But *Only Ever Yours* ends with freida embalmed in unnatural liquids that keep her useful but not sentient, that simultaneously and entirely expose and isolate her. The knowledge associated with freida is not self-knowledge. Instead, her body provides the scientific matter from which the male Engineers can draw in order to improve future students—to alter their hard-wiring so that future women have even less capacity for autonomy and self-awareness than freida.

A New Media Age

The experiments of modernism during the early twentieth century have been understood as one response to the radical transformations, both social and personal, engendered by technologies including the telegraph and telephone, radio and film. In his account of "the first media age," David Trotter examined British fiction and poetry written between 1927 and 1939 to demonstrate how the telephone, radio, and cinema screenings synchronized the consumption of cultural products and generated unexpected means of collectivity among individuals who were, for the first time, linked by these new media forms. Literature, he argues, became suffused with representations of these technologies and the "behavior virtual interactions made possible" as it altered everyday life.[40] For Trotter, these changes helped to facilitate social activism and were largely constructive. Today, contemporary writing similarly depicts the pervasive presence of digital platforms and suggests their benefits: they can foster collectivity and connectivity, expose toxic behaviors and institutions, and help to normalize behaviors and attitudes once wrongly censured. But as recent history demonstrates, these technologies also can undermine attention and encourage addiction, circulate dangerous misinformation, flatten experiment with their algorithms, compromise security, and abet pernicious standards of appearance and behavior, among other problems.

---

[40] David Trotter, *Literature in the First Media Age: Britain between the Wars* (Cambridge: Harvard University Press, 2013), 1.

164 LOGGING OFF

The novels studied here use the modernist mode to consider the past, present, and future of female privacy in a "new media age" dominated by digital technologies.[41] *The Dancers Dancing* and *Pond* foreground the benefits of female privacy, a right increasingly made available to Irish women, but *Only Ever Yours* reminds readers that such freedoms must be vigorously defended: the erosion of privacy, O'Neill dramatically demonstrates, undermines female development and potentially could wipe out women as a natural biological category. Employing modernism's many resources, these writers regard new digital technologies with the same distrust Irish women writers across nearly a century have focused on more long-standing external forces, including religious practice and domestic routine. Today, the menace is not the jazz that troubled Theodor Adorno or the mechanized eroticism depicted in Eliot's *The Waste Land*, but instead the perils the digital world represents to productive modes of female privacy. These writers' considerations of logging off, published during an early stage of our swiftly evolving digital era, employ modernism as a bulwark against the threats posed by a mass culture embodied by the internet. Their fiction offers a premonition of sorts, a guidebook to the benefits of logging off, the consequences of logging on. Amid what might seem to be the entirely original socio-cultural problems generated by digital technologies, the current of the modernism running through all three novels reminds readers that the threats to the productive exercise of imaginative and critical thinking abetted by solitude are age old, even as they take new forms.

---

[41] See also Orlaith Darling, "'It Was Our Great Generational Decision': Capitalism, the Internet, and Depersonalization in Some Millennial Irish Women's Writing," *Critique: Studies in Contemporary Fiction* 62:5 (2021): 538–551.

5

Reading

(Sally Rooney, Anna Burns)

For roughly a century, Irish women writers who employed the more conventional features of literary modes in their fiction often found their work ignored, dismissed, or maligned for merely recapitulating exhausted aesthetics. Yet such modes were vividly apparent in two high-profile novels published in 2018, Sally Rooney's *Normal People* and Anna Burns's *Milkman*. Both deploy the textbook strategies of realism and modernism to showcase the effects of contemporary life in Ireland and Northern Ireland on the consciousness of their female protagonists. Written in the omniscient third-person, *Normal People* follows the romantic and sexual relationship of two young adults, Marianne and Connell, from their final year of secondary school in 2011 through their time as university students at Trinity College Dublin. *Milkman* traces, through a first-person narrative voiced in retrospect, the travails of an unnamed eighteen-year-old Northern Irish woman amid the Troubles as she is stalked by an older republican paramilitary dubbed "Milkman." These two novels were commercially successful and garnered widespread critical praise, evident not least when both were long-listed for the 2018 Booker Prize, with *Milkman* ultimately winning the award. Their achievements suggest that in the second decade of the twenty-first century, Irish women writers no longer represent the neglected periphery of Anglophone literature but now occupy its bullseye.

Normal People and *Milkman* share the critical and commercial benefits of appearing in a moment when the use of stubborn literary modes is recognized, welcomed, and understood. The overt deployment of realism and modernism in these novels confirms that Irish women writers continue to see the value in resurrecting and reworking familiar modes to showcase the hidden complexities of female subjectivity. What is striking, given the shared success of these two novels in the same calendar year, is that both evince such a dramatic commitment to this tactic as a potential corrective for intractable problems, particularly those related to female privacy. Their female protagonists command public attention, but often the wrong kind of attention—they are harassed, or shamed, or hypersexualized. By calling notice to their status as texts to be parsed through the analysis of time-honored literary modes, these novels ask from readers a different type of attention to these characters, one that can be realized through close reading. The practice of close reading, which came of age roughly in tandem with the development of modernism as a critical concept, necessarily reveals the work

---

Modernism in Irish Women's Contemporary Writing. Paige Reynolds, Oxford University Press. © Paige Reynolds (2024).
DOI: 10.1093/9780191990540.003.0006

166 READING

such forms can continue to do in representing Irish women's experience by insisting on, in the words of Rachel Sagner Buurma and Laura Heffernan, "an attention to attention—including a sense of how, and to what, and with whom we bestow it."[1]

Like praying and daydreaming and logging off, reading suggestively offers the female characters at the center of these two novels a practice that fosters privacy and can elicit productive insights. In both, reading is imagined by these young women as a withdrawal from the troubled and troubling world that surrounds them. Contemptuous of her secondary school classmates, Marianne from *Normal People* "spends her lunchtimes alone reading novels," a strategy developed partially in response to her vexed family and school life.[2] Middle sister in *Milkman* reads while walking as a means of mental and physical retreat from the personal and political crises that surround her, with the caveat that "I did not like twentieth-century books because I did not like the twentieth century."[3] But such behavior is also a provocation. The act of reading books confuses people and distinguishes these young women from the surrounding community, pulling further unwanted attention to them.

Set in dialogue, these novels offer a fruitful test case for our understanding of the historical resistance to Irish women's writing as too easy (too realist, too popular) or too hard (too modernist, too marginal). *Normal People* seems an easy read: its form accessible, its themes customary, its language unpretentious. *Milkman* seems a difficult read: its form challenging, its setting alienating, its idioms deliberately obscure. Yet as I argue below, the shopworn literary modes on which these novels rely serves to complicate such perspectives. In her study of "Romantic Difficulty," Anahid Nersessian writes that "Difficult art is hard to understand and it is hard to tolerate. It is hard to understand because it is often embedded in obscure or minoritarian idioms, at a remove from better-established habits of aesthetic judgment."[4] As Nersessian considers the overt challenges presented by rebarbative contemporary performance art, as well as the less obvious ones posed by William Wordsworth's poetry, it becomes clear that even difficulty can be difficult, lurking in texts that seem easy to access. *Normal People* and *Milkman* are both difficult books that encourage different types of misapprehension. They encourage readers to rehearse interpretive tactics that allow them better to push through mechanisms seeking to stall or stem the identification and interpretation of stubborn problems. As a result, we are invited to see these problems in a fresh way, thanks in part to the repeated practice of resistance and persistence elicited by the stubborn mode.

---

[1] Rachel Sagner Buurma and Laura Heffernan, "Poetry Explication: The Making of a Method," *Modernism and Close Reading*, ed. David James (Oxford: Oxford University Press, 2020), 69–85, 85.
[2] Sally Rooney, *Normal People* (London: Faber and Faber, 2018), 2. Future references parenthetical.
[3] Anna Burns, *Milkman* (London: Faber and Faber, 2018), 5. Future references parenthetical.
[4] Anahid Nersessian, "Romantic Difficulty," *New Literary History* 40:4 (Autumn 2018): 451–466, 458.

Normal People's Realism

Out of the gate, Sally Rooney has been understood as an author who fuses different forms and genres drawn from long-standing literary traditions. One among many who see stubborn modes at play in Rooney's fiction, Gloria Fisk identifies in *Normal People* influences from Jane Austen to Henry James and asserts, "The effect is less old-with-a-veneer-of-the-new than old and new at once, all the way through. That is Sally Rooney's brand."[5] No longer the excuse to deride an Irish woman writer as merely a copycat and dismiss her innovations, "old and new at once" now provides a launching pad for critical analyses, as well as a savvy marketing tool. Coming roughly a century after the heyday of modernism, Rooney's enthusiastic reception also suggests that the tactical deployment of easily recognized literary devices can reinvigorate their avant-garde energies, their capacity to seize notice and challenge norms. As Claire Jarvis observes of Rooney's pastiche of realism and modernism, "Sally Rooney is doing something new. And, I find her uncomfortably familiar."[6] That endeavor to engage and unsettle readers simultaneously with a representation of present-day circumstance through seemingly superannuated forms is one hallmark of Irish women's writing across nearly a century.

In *Normal People*, Rooney deploys these stubborn modes to represent female experience and subjectivity in post-Celtic-Tiger Ireland. She has described her years as a university student "grappling with the modernists and 19th-century novels," and pronounced her fiction "basically nineteenth-century novels dressed up in contemporary clothes."[7] The clear-cut structure of the novel's chronological plot and the accessibility of its unadorned prose have meant a ready and wide audience for the book, one that has embraced in particular its candid representation of human sexuality. Writers such as Mary Lavin, Edna O'Brien, and Eimear McBride employ modernist obfuscation to represent the impenetrable complexities of human sexuality, but Rooney appears to do the opposite. She represents in user-friendly prose the romantic lives of her characters to suggest that desire, even when clearly depicted and candidly discussed, remains largely inscrutable and its outcomes often arbitrary. In a historical moment when vivid and detailed sexual

---

[5] Gloria Fisk, "What Are Feelings for?," "Reading Sally Rooney," ed. Gloria Fisk, *Post45*, June 15, 2020, http://post45.org/2020/06/what-are-feelings-for/.

[6] Claire Jarvis, "Contemporary Clothing: Is Sally Rooney a Millennial Novelist or a Nineteenth-Century One?," *Slate*, April 22, 2019, https://slate.com/culture/2019/04/sally-rooney-normal-people-austen-james-lawrence.html.

[7] Claire Armitstead, "Sally Rooney: I Don't Respond to Authority Very Well," interview with Sally Rooney, *The Guardian*, December 2, 2018, https://www.theguardian.com/books/2018/dec/02/sally-rooney-interview-dont-respond-authority-normal-people. Lauren Collins, "Sally Rooney Gets in Your Head," *The New Yorker*, January 7, 2019, https://www.newyorker.com/magazine/2019/01/07/sally-rooney-gets-in-your-head. On *Normal People* and realism see Jane Hu, "Race and Romantic Realism," *Post45*, June 15, 2020, http://post45.org/2020/06/race-and-romantic-realism/, and Jarvis, "Contemporary Clothing."

168 READING

content is merely a computer click away, *Normal People*, despite its seeming clarity and predictable narrative structure, often insists on the murky and capricious nature of human desire, and this strategy is advanced further by its consistent use of vague, mundane diction. As Connell observes amid one of their early trysts, "he understood why people did insane things for sexual reasons then. In fact he understood a lot of things about the adult world that had previously seemed mysterious. But why Marianne?" (25)

In the endeavor to reflect the contours of this relationship, *Normal People* holds tight to realism. This is perhaps most obvious in the novel's use of the marriage plot, the device found throughout realist fiction, in which two characters overcome a series of obstacles ultimately to wed. Since its debut in the eighteenth-century novel, the marriage plot has remained impressively durable in the face of dramatic social changes, surfacing for example in Troubles-era "love across the barricades" novels, which depict individuals from opposite sides of the sectarian divide whose romantic relationship offers hope for a broader political reconciliation.[8] Traditionally, the marriage plot posits courtship and marriage as a corrective for class stratification, as in the exemplar of Austen's *Pride and Prejudice*, and *Normal People*, which stresses the disjunction between Connell's working-class background and Marianne's affluence, neatly fits that model. Yet at the end of this novel, there is no promise of marriage, nor any clear understanding for a shared future, between the two main characters. Instead, Rooney leaves readers with an indefinite resolution, rather than the comforting narrative closure often provided by romantic fiction.

Although Anne Enright has claimed that "there is no hint of modernism" in *Normal People*, the novel's stripped-down prose points to the precedent of Ernest Hemingway, who like Rooney received immediate public acclaim for his writing.[9] Moreover, critics have suggested that Rooney's attention to sexual violence and debasement corresponds with that found in the fiction of D. H. Lawrence and Elizabeth Bowen.[10] Yet perhaps the most telling instance of modernism revivified emerges in the novel's open ending. By the conclusion, set in 2015, Marianne and Connell have settled into a relationship. However, Connell has been accepted to an MFA program at a university in New York and seems likely to move away in order to pursue a degree in creative writing, while Marianne stays behind in Ireland. Rather than the tidy resolution of the marriage plot, the novel leaves readers with

---

[8] For examinations of the "love across the barricades" plot as privatizing and eroticizing social and political problems, see Joe Cleary, "Domestic Troubles: Tragedy and the Northern Ireland Conflict," *South Atlantic Quarterly* 98:3 (1999): 501–537; Stefanie Lehner, "Nation: Reconciliation and the Politics of Friendship in Post-Troubles Literature," *The New Irish Studies*, ed. Paige Reynolds (Cambridge: Cambridge University Press, 2020), 47–62; Stephanie Schwerter, "Transgressing Boundaries: Belfast and the 'Romance-Across-the-Divide,'" *Estudios Irlandeses* 2 (2007): 173–182.

[9] Anne Enright, "It's Time for a Sharp Inhale, People," *Irish Times*, September 1, 2018, https://www.irishtimes.com/culture/books/it-is-time-for-a-sharp-inhale-people-sally-rooney-s-normal-people-is-superb-1.3608184.

[10] See Matthew Hart, "Wet Newspaper" and Claire Jarvis, "The Sweet Stuff" in *Post45*, June 15, 2020, https://post45.org/sections/contemporaries/reading-sally-rooney/.

an open ending resembling that found in Joyce's bildungsroman *A Portrait of the Artist as a Young Man* (1916). In this, as well as through its focus on university students roaming the streets of Dublin, *Normal People* gives testament, once again, to how pervasively and powerfully Joyce's modernism continues to shape Irish women's fiction. The omniscient third-person narrator of *Normal People* toggles between the point of view of Marianne and Connell, like the twinned bildungsromane of Kate O'Brien's *The Land of Spices*, another novel that self-consciously reworks the conclusion of *Portrait*. However, while O'Brien's open ending suggests that the young student Anna will break away from the inhibitions imposed by the conservative logics of her rural, Catholic background, Rooney offers no such promise for her female protagonist.

In fact, the conclusion of *Normal People* underscores limitations familiar from the modernist moment, limitations that continue to constrain Marianne in the present day. In *Portrait*, Stephen Dedalus intends to escape entirely the constricting "nets" of Irish "nationality, language, religion" for the life of an artist in Paris.[11] In Rooney's novel, Connell slips neatly into Stephen's place, preparing to take the same path plotted roughly a century earlier for Joyce's "artist as a young man." Modernism thus provides the extra-novelistic context for a richer reading of Connell's aims and his potential—even as this allusion suggests his exodus will culminate in failed ambitions and his reluctant return home to Ireland, as it did for Stephen. At the same time, this contemporary novel's conclusion reminds readers through its very familiarity about the limitations of modernism's legacies for Irish women. Marianne, who is also "a very gifted writer" (204) according to one lover, has no such tradition available to her. Her words close the novel: "You should go, she says. I'll always be here. You know that" (273). She elects to stay put in Ireland. Admittedly, this decision to separate geographically seems less absolute in the contemporary moment: international travel is within their means and digital communication has proven for Marianne and Connell, at times, even more suturing than their erotic attraction and shared history. But Marianne's resolution nonetheless seems strikingly old fashioned. In the final sentences of the novel, with no clear path before her, she seems to default to the loyal and transparent feminine ideal that has long populated Irish nationalist discourse. Despite the promised liberties of post-feminism, enhanced gender equity, and more expansive sexual norms, among other freedoms available to young women in the twenty-first century, Marianne might be Eveline, Molly, or any of Joyce's female characters who remain trapped at home, their imagination and actions largely determined by choices others have made.

Marianne's passive receptivity in this final moment tracks with Rooney's representations of female consciousness throughout the novel. Despite a seeming

---

[11] James Joyce, *A Portrait of the Artist as a Young Man*, ed. Seamus Deane (New York: Penguin Classics, 2003), 220.

formal commitment to the revelations of character provided through indirect discourse, the novel presents Marianne as someone who remains largely a mystery. The makings of a rich and complicated female psyche are named in the plot: her father died when she was thirteen; she maintains a troubled relationship with her mother and brother; she is uniquely unpopular in high school; she repeatedly chooses domineering romantic partners. But the narrative provides little detailed access to the workings of her consciousness, largely refusing the assumptive interiority of realist writers such as George Eliot or Gustave Flaubert. Her motivations and desires remain at two extremes, clearly articulated or entirely oblique, and the scope and scale of the likely complexity of her emotional responses and personal choices largely go unexplored.

Such a vague representation of Marianne's consciousness is sustained throughout *Normal People*, and it suggests a starker and perhaps more problematic issue for female subjectivity amid the heightened publicness of the twenty-first century, a time when graphic content and vivid pictures flow easily, and blogs and Instagram posts convey the intimacies of personal identity. From the start, despite being understood as "smart" by her peers, Marianne perceives herself as having "a face like a piece of technology, and her two eyes are cursors blinking" (9). She understands herself as all surface, merely a vessel for content. Without the rich context of the realist novel's indirect discourse, or the insights provided by stream of consciousness or other techniques of modernist interior monologue, her self-understanding remains unavailable to the reader, and perhaps to herself as a character. Here, the friction between realism and modernism emphasizes constraints that even today hinder the interior lives of Irish women, constraints characteristic of, but not exclusive to, recessionary Ireland.[12] The vagueness of Marianne's interiority might also suggest that this is what female subjectivity looks like in the digital present, with Rooney refusing the clarity promised by realism as well as the depth exposed by modernism in her depiction of individual consciousness.

However, like Stephen Dedalus before her, Marianne does appear to have an epiphany, one tied to publicness. Her struggles in the novel seem tied largely to the secret nature of her relationship with Connell, a point confirmed by the novel's conclusion. After years of back and forth in their relationship, Marianne and Connell celebrate New Year's together at the local pub in their hometown of Carricklea. There, Connell makes public their relationship when he kisses Marianne in front of their former school friends, a moment in which "She could feel, like a physical pressure on her skin, that the others were watching them" (268). Marianne, who had been traumatized by the covert nature of their relationship in high school, and had withdrawn from school when Connell declined to ask her as his date to

---

[12] See María Amor Barros-Del Río, "Sally Rooney's *Normal People*: The Millennial Novel of Formation in Recessionary Ireland," *Irish Studies Review* 30:2 (2022): 176–192.

the Debs, is now consoled by the fact that Connell elects, roughly four years later, to bring together their private and public lives. This quotidian gesture signals for Marianne the transfer and display of their private romantic experience to a public space. Following this open authorization of her desires, she can endorse Connell's tentative plan to leave Ireland, asserting to herself, "They've done a lot of good for each other. Really, she thinks, really. People can really change one another" (273).

The novel makes Marianne's ambitions to be available to Connell clear throughout, but any understanding of her other motivations remains obscure, and her future is unclear. Though their kiss in the pub suggests for Marianne a moment of epiphany, the repetition of "Really ... really ... really" merely indicates the fragility of her confidence rather than conveying the intensity of any sudden Joycean epiphany. In this scene, Marianne stands in place literally, imaginatively, and rhetorically. Rather than a tool for subversion, as in the hands of modernists like Stein or Beckett, or contemporary Irish writers like Donoghue, Madden, or Ní Dhuibhne, linguistic repetition here conveys the bounds of Marianne's imagination. Her stasis draws attention to the ongoing deficiency of agency and authority for women, even in this starkly contemporary novel. Like many of the female characters in this study, Marianne's vexed relationship to her interiority is shaped by circumstance. Throughout the novel, she is hyper-public, the object of close scrutiny by her family and her peers, despite her practiced attempts to render herself less visible. As she recalls,

> She spent much of her childhood and adolescence planning elaborate schemes to remove herself from family conflict: staying completely silent, keeping her face and body expressionless and immobile, wordlessly leaving the room and making her way to her bedroom, closing the door quietly behind her. Locking herself in the toilet. Leaving the house for an indefinite number of hours and sitting in the school carpark by herself. None of these strategies had ever proven successful. (201)

Such sequestration and psychic suppression mean that, even near the close of the novel, years later, Marianne understands herself in a moment of intimacy with Connell as "an abyss that he can reach into, an empty space for him to fill" (242). The formal impediments put in place by Rooney often reflect psychic constraints imposed by forces beyond Marianne's control, including a history of familial abuse, and thus help to explain her stunted self-awareness, even amid the supposed freedoms of twenty-first-century Ireland. She cannot successfully secure the elective and anodyne privacy, the stillness and stability, necessary to develop fully realized selfhood.

If we read such obliquity in characterization as strategic, and tied to the redeployment of literary modes, Marianne's motivations become more interesting. That is, the novel invokes realism to showcase the limits of what we, as an audience

172 READING

of readers, can know about the private lives of Rooney's two characters, particularly her female protagonist. We can witness the rough contours of Marianne's decisions, but not the complex psychological workings that might explain her contradictory and often unfathomable choices. Marianne herself cannot sufficiently embrace and parse the messy complexities of her own interiority. And that inadequacy is performed by the novel's commitment to realism. Realism's attention to the outside world amid a cultural moment profoundly attuned to two-dimensional surfaces and punchy narratives of the self—the type of self-representation embodied in this historical moment by the Facebook posting or the Instagram story—vividly displays Marianne's incapacity to identify and assess what unfolds in her consciousness. Such constraints as evidenced in *Normal People* may explain why modernism has become such a powerful tool for other Irish women writers.

Milkman's Modernism

Normal People skims the surface of its female protagonist's motivations and perceptions, but this is adamantly not the case in *Milkman*, a novel that engages modernism to put on detailed display the psychological maneuvers of its unnamed female protagonist. The novel trains its laser focus on middle sister's negotiation of privacy amid deeply challenging circumstances, a concern disclosed through her dense and formally complicated interior monologue. In the novel, set in Northern Ireland during the Troubles, the adult narrator—the self-dubbed "middle sister"—reviews the events of a traumatic year from her past in which, among other travails, she is stalked by an older paramilitary republican called Milkman. Modernist form here, as it has in Irish women's fiction for nearly a century, fleshes out and exposes persistent social problems: intractable political violence, the brutal divisions of sectarianism, the difficulties of family relationships, the suffering of vulnerable subjects, the manipulation of language to obscure truth. O'Brien's *Night*, McBride's *A Girl Is a Half-formed Thing*, Bennett's *Pond*—these are among the novels examined in this study that similarly concentrate on female interiority and aggressively poach modernist tactics to produce narratives that are challenging to read as well as to interpret. Through its invocation of modernist difficulties, *Milkman* likewise suggests that the interpretive roadblocks placed by this mode might stoke a practice of deep reading and attention that moves beyond the words on the page and into the contemporary "real world."

Since its publication, critics have noted the many challenges posed by *Milkman*, either celebrating or condemning the novel for its perceived difficulty.[13] The historical setting invites a feeling of incompetence, displaying the bounds of

---

[13] For sample praise of its difficulties, see A. N. Devers, "Anna Burns' Booker-winning 'Milkman' Isn't a Difficult Read; It's a Triumph," *Los Angeles Times*, January 4, 2019, https://www.latimes.com/books/la-ca-jc-anna-burns-milkman-review-20190104-story.html. For a rebuke of its difficulties, see

what most readers understand about Northern Ireland and the complexities of the Troubles—its history, its geography, its alliances. But the novel's form also insists on what we do not or cannot understand about more common or typical issues including rocky adolescent friendships, dangerous streets, frustrating romantic relationships, familial conflict. The novel documents shocking instances of political violence, and its complex prose is immersive and unrelenting. Throughout, details and observations are piled together, and there are few natural breaks signaled by sentences and paragraphs within each of the seven chapters. As a result, the pacing of the narrative risks burying the most harrowing details in a rush of knotty prose, a risk heightened by its lack of tonal complexity. It also requires the constant and attentive parsing of details and associations specific to the Troubles and unfamiliar to many readers. Such difficulties entice even an educated and invested reader to skip over details, to put the book down, to surface read. These potentially alienating tactics deliberately require that readers slowly and thoroughly read and re-read middle sister's narrative, that we award her the discerning and empathetic attention that her community in the novel refuses.

Milkman is difficult in part because it documents difficult experiences. The repetition of one word, Milkman, throughout middle sister's interior monologue might be the most overt and crucial example of this tactic. Now an adult, the narrator recapitulates her deeply distressing experiences with political and sexual violence decades prior, when she was eighteen years old. Even years later, the loose associations between and among the various people, places, and events that she depicts from her youth are interrupted, insistently and insidiously, by the appearance of the word Milkman (or milkman, before this is revealed to be his proper name). While his physical presence is infrequent in the novel, and he never actually touches middle sister, his name nevertheless intrudes throughout the entire narrative to signal the disruptive and disturbing quality of his stalking. And of course, his authority in shaping her story is most evident in the title splashed across the dust jacket; to discuss this account of a young woman's victimization necessarily means that we must cite the name of her harasser.

Across the novel, then, form follows function. With citizens under constant surveillance by state and community, the Troubles required a language ridden with euphemisms and silences to hide or protect clarifying details that might invite acts of violence or containment. Middle sister speaks from the historical vantage of peace and reconciliation in Northern Ireland, and yet she continues to withhold revealing details. Few of the characters are identified by a proper name, the prose is laden with pronouns lacking clear antecedents, and the precise setting of the

---

Dwight Garner, "'Milkman' Slogs through Political and Cultural Tensions in Northern Ireland," *New York Times*, December 3, 2018, https://www.nytimes.com/2018/12/03/books/review-milkman-anna-burns-man-booker-prize-winner.html.

174   READING

novel goes unspecified, though close reading suggests 1970s Belfast.[14] The trauma of the Troubles, and the rhetorical habits it generated, continue to inflect and infect her language. Across her narrative, arcane and euphemistic terms like "renouncers" (for republican militants) or "beyond the pales" (for those whose behavior has been deemed odd or transgressive) suggest the obduracy not only of outdated words and phrases, but also of archaic ways of thinking. Throughout, such obfuscations reflect the particularities of twentieth-century political conditions, as well as conveying the limited understandings of its late adolescent protagonist, a tactic seen in the stories of childhood from Joyce's *Dubliners*. Yet middle sister is fluent in her culture, and knowingly navigates dangerous objects, spaces, and experiences such as "the van, the ten-minute area, the war-time bomb which had brought up dead da and his depressions with ma attacking him for his depressions" (101).

Modernist form conveys not only Milkman's harassment of middle sister and the community's problematically accommodating response to his menacing behavior, but also underscores the subtler, unseen psychological effects of such actions on this young woman. Middle sister's first-person narrative is sustained and associative, flecked with instances of stream of consciousness as well as reported dialogue, and reveals her intermingled impressions of past experiences. The cascade of prose—the long sentences, the extended lists, the paragraphs that run for pages—captures the intensity of adolescent experience as well as her breathless fear of being stalked. While the narrative makes clear such threats are widespread, the immersive quality of her interior monologue urgently calls attention to middle sister and her individual experience. *Milkman* makes vivid the psychic costs of the Troubles particular to women and in doing so pushes against the seemingly intractable masculinity that has long characterized nationalist thinking. Critics have noted the uniform tone of *Normal People* and the flat affect of its characters, citing this as one sign of the novel's attention to surface rather than depth. These traits, which are sometimes explained as characteristic of millennial ennui, mean that the register of Rooney's novel remains roughly the same throughout. *Milkman* has a similarly consistent register, but one that signals its narrator's attempt to manage the intensities of her young adulthood amid violent religious and ethnic conflict.

Early in the novel, for instance, the narrator recapitulates an argument with her mother in which she denies her mother's accusations that she is having an affair with Milkman. Burrowed in the pages of middle sister's reconstruction of this dispute are details from her father's deathbed, when he confessed, "I was raped many times as a boy" (55). Her father's announcement of this abuse is merely a subset of the more vivid and sustained detailing of her mother's lack of trust and the quarrel which proved to mother and daughter that "in truth it was that we

---

[14] For an exemplary close reading see Clare Hutton, "The Moment and Technique of *Milkman*," *Essays in Criticism* 69:3 (July 2019): 349–371.

had no faith in each other" (56). The father's childhood abuse is shocking, but its mention is terse as well as nestled amid a less recognized and understood type of abuse—the emotional cruelty and sustained trauma that stems from her mother's knee-jerk acceptance of the misperceptions of the community, when she chooses public rumor over the private truth shared by her vulnerable daughter. The scope and scale of this encounter with her mother demonstrate the unexpected impact of this maternal failure on the narrator, one represented as more significant than her discovery of the shocking physical violence perpetuated on her father as a child. Here, the narrative mimics that found in Virginia Woolf's modernism, where in a novel like *To the Lighthouse* (1927), an externally significant event like Mrs. Ramsey's death is awarded only a few sentences, while a personally crucial dinner party consumes almost an entire chapter. *Milkman* similarly distorts the scale of events to reflect the psyche of its narrator by magnifying events that seem objectively less consequential, but that are enormously significant to this young character whose subjectivity we are invited to witness and even share.

The equivalent tone of this long passage recalling her adolescent conflict with her mother, and the associative drift linking the two distinct events it describes, signal their unexpected similarities: each a maltreatment suffered by a child and perpetuated by an adult, both triggering lifelong injurious consequences. This moment in the novel is the formal manifestation of the stubborn problem of abuse, underscoring its presence in different historical moments for different children in different forms. There are so many types of abuse and suffering cataloged in this novel that, like the list that flattens by serializing, the entire novel becomes an oppressive register of the psychic, sexual, physical, intellectual, and ideological injuries that characterize life during the Troubles. This same tactic plays out on the sentence level as seen in the opening page's inventory of euphemisms for a woman's vagina—"my quainte, my tail, my contry, my box, my jar, my contrariness, my monosyllable" (1)—hurled at the narrator starting at age twelve by her much older "first brother-in-law." Here, a preteen girl is sexualized by a grown man as an exercise of power, and this list of corrupted terms, in its excess, accentuates the perceived intensity of his verbal attacks. This type of battering linguistic assault, the deluge of detail and language, is the operating system of this novel.

Despite the overt invocation of modernist technique across the novel, such meticulously illustrated moments might remind readers of realist fiction. *Milkman* provides a teleological novel of formation stuffed with everyday details seeking to portray a recognizable external world. Using a narrative device as familiar to readers as the names Pip and David Copperfield, the novel is written from the point of view of a narrator who constructs in retrospect the story of her youth. The interior monologue is ridden with knowing insights and altered assessments, which she can provide due to her distanced adult perspective. Only in looking backward, as she recalls the moment she first heard of Milkman's death, can she identify "how much I'd been closed down, how much I'd been thwarted into a carefully

176   READING

constructed nothingness by that man. Also by the community, by the very mental atmosphere, that minutiae of invasion" (303). The very nature of a monologue suggests that middle sister alone, both as teenager and adult, must grapple with the incredible events before her and sort their meaning. The weight of those events and her epiphanies are registered in the burdensome quality of the dense prose, displaying to the reader the difficulties of such experiences and the uneven assessment of their consequences in the private world of consciousness. If, as Patricia Malone asserts in her astute reading of trauma in the novel, the narrative is marked by "a phenomenology of *jamais vu* ... this paramnesiac state in which the present appears to be detached from the past despite being both bound to and dictated by that past," the modernist mode here helps to remind readers of the past as a determining factor not only in the novel's particular form and concerns, but also more generally in a longer and less situated history marked by female trauma.[15]

Like other works of Irish women's contemporary fiction, the novel explores the carefully cultivated privacy enacted by its female protagonist through the esteemed tradition of interior monologue. For the narrator, living amid the Troubles, such overt and nuanced attention to self as demonstrated through form is a radically countercultural gesture, an attempted refusal not only of her culture's ubiquitous surveillance, but also of the totalizing perspectives with which she grew up. According to middle sister, communal absolutes were second nature in the polarized political climate in which she came of age, a collective imaginative habit through which individual distinctions were subsumed in the hostile contest between the broad categories of "'us' or 'them'" (2). Such logics predictably apply to gender in her republican culture, where women are regarded by men not "as a person but instead as some cipher, some valueless nobody whose sole objective is to reflect back onto them the glory of themselves" (133). But even in more personal and intimate settings, such as the family or local community, it remains difficult to distinguish the narrator. In her birth order, middle sister is embedded amid ten other siblings, a surfeit that leads her father to describe any one of his children simply as son or daughter, and her siblings to call each other brother or sister (55).

This practice of reducing individuals to types has a profoundly adverse effect on the capacity for self-understanding and representation. But such clouding is a cultural habit, a quality of family and communal life, a political and personal necessity. In *Normal People*, Marianne draws attention due to nonthreatening factors like her elevated class status or her mildly eccentric and oppositional teen behavior. In *Milkman*, where the political stakes are more overt and intense, middle sister first draws public notice because she reads while walking, an utterly benign behavior that the community regards as aberrant because of its performance of her inattention and isolation. For the female protagonists of novels such

---

[15] Patricia Malone, "Measures of Obliviousness and Disarming Obliqueness in Anna Burns' *Milkman*," *Textual Practice* 36:7 (2021): 1–32, 13.

as *The Dancers Dancing* and *Pond*, young women who live in the Republic, such elective privacy is represented as a necessary and constructive strategy, a choice made to encourage maturity and healthy independence. But for middle sister, such an exercise of autonomy only helps to draw the unwanted interest of Milkman, and thus garners her even greater public notice. Such attention during the Troubles in Northern Ireland can be toxic or even lethal, as for those coming to notice of the psychologically disturbed "tablets girl" who secretly and selectively poisons members of the community, or for the local feminist activists who are threatened for holding consciousness-raising meetings.

To be seen is to court danger and to suffer. Provoked by external circumstance, privacy in *Milkman* is represented as a vigilantly constructed shield, a defensive response to the threats invited by a too-public Irish woman. For middle sister, after being singled out by Milkman for grooming, the deliberate crafting of an oblique and unreadable public self becomes an even more overt strategy for survival. In yet another instance of the novel's structure reflecting its themes, she explains her camouflage in a passage that is buried in the middle of the novel: "I minimalised, withheld, subverted thinking, dropped all interaction surplus to requirement ... Just me, downplayed. Just me, devoid. Just me, uncommingled" (174–175). She hopes this strategy will render her less interesting to the local gossips who have mistakenly presumed she is in a romantic relationship with Milkman. If Marianne in *Normal People* understands herself as a blank computer screen, middle sister imagines that if she can present herself "as a textbook, some kind of log table—as in correct, but not really right either," she might be "free, safe" from community notice, if not from that of Milkman (176). Yet even as she claims and describes such strategies, they repeatedly fail her. Despite them, she is terrorized by Milkman, emotionally betrayed by her family and friends, cultivated by the "local paramilitary groupies," poisoned by tablets girl, and beaten by a local man called "Somebody McSomebody." By her own admission, these strategies ultimately serve only to erase her "inner world" (178). Her retrospective narrative represents an endeavor to recoup and make visible her interiority. Written in the past tense, and filled with questions that review and assess her past experiences, the narrative suggests that middle sister no longer understands her trauma as ever-present. Nonetheless, Milkman's harassment remains the event that orders her consciousness, and in fact her narrative opens by noting the "day the milkman died" (1). The legacy of his abuse also reveals itself in the knotty prose that is difficult to parse. Rich with detail and insight, but formally abstruse, middle sister's story, even twenty years later, is visible but not too visible. Its form provides further evidence of the lingering effects of what she understands to be the menacing consequences of being seen in her culture.

In retrospect, under new historical conditions, and with the heightened confidence of an adult narrator, she can alert readers to the remedial logics of the cultural practices and individual responses to them that she identifies. She regards

178 READING

such carefully calibrated self-fashioning as a pathology not personal, but endemic to her community. As she notes, "Just as most people here chose not to say what they meant in order to protect themselves, they could also, at certain moments when they knew their mind was being read, learn to present their topmost mental level to those who were reading it whilst in the undergrowth of their consciousness, inform themselves privately of what their true thinking was about" (36–37). This practice contaminates even her most intimate relationships. As she asserts of her relationship with her mother, "the less I gave, the less she could get in" (45). Later, while talking to her "longest friend from primary school," she announces, "I was continuing not to reveal anything which was now a full-time, batting away process with me" (195). She notes, "I needed my silence, my unaccommodation, to shield me from pawing and from molestation by questions ... This was my one bit of power in this disempowering world" (205). Here, she reaffirms her commitment to elective privacy, but she represents any outside interest as molestation. Although Milkman never abuses her physically, his psychological predation has infected how she perceives the world and the metaphorical language she uses to describe her experience of it.

As an adult, middle sister's detailed retrospective account of her predation is informed by the changed conditions of her now contemporary moment, by the relative safety awarded by efforts toward peace and reconciliation in Northern Ireland, and by the public exposure and punishment of harassment and sexual abuse in the wake of the #MeToo movement.[16] As a complement to these activist movements, *Milkman* suggests the necessary tasks that remain: the repeated parsing of the complexities of individual consciousness and experience, as well as of the social and cultural systems and habits that enable and sustain such abuse. These are daunting, but the novel through its formal challenges suggests necessary analytical and interpretive skills that might move us closer to repair. Burns employs the modernist mode to make it difficult for readers to see the various emotional and psychic abuses that middle sister suffers, just as they are difficult to detect in real life.

At one point in *Normal People*, amid one of their separations, Marianne tells Connell, "There are worse things than getting beaten up" (126). *Milkman* is an entire novel spinning out this claim. It concludes with a string of seemingly neat

---

[16] The chair of judges for the 2018 Booker Prize, Kwame Anthony Appiah, commended *Milkman* for providing "a deep and subtle and morally and intellectually challenging picture of what #MeToo is about." See Alison Flood and Claire Armitstead, "Anna Burns Wins Man Booker Prize for 'incredibly original' *Milkman*," *The Guardian*, October 16, 2018, https://www.theguardian.com/books/2018/oct/16/anna-burns-wins-man-booker-prize-for-incredibly-original-milkman. For examples of the many assessments of *Milkman* that directly note the context of #MeToo, see Rosa Inocencio Smith, "How to Tell an Open Secret," *The Atlantic*, January 16, 2019, https://www.theatlantic.com/entertainment/archive/2019/01/three-novels-metoo-era/580369/; and Parul Sehgal, "#MeToo is All Too Real. But to Better Understand It, Turn to Fiction," *New York Times*, May 1, 2019, https://www.nytimes.com/2019/05/01/books/novels-me-too-movement.html.

resolutions for middle sister: Milkman has been killed, the community has punished Somebody McSomebody for assaulting her, her family relationships have begun to settle. In the final pages, middle sister also reinitiates the routine of running with her well-meaning third brother-in-law, whose serious crossness about her experiences reassures her that "People in this place did give a fuck" (346). But this conclusion is less resolved than it appears, as this encounter exposes the lack of nuanced understanding that enables the violence suffered by middle sister. To even a sympathetic individual like third brother-in-law, "Rape was rape. It was also black eyes. It was guns in breasts. Hands, fists, weapons, feet, used by male people, deliberately or accidentally-on-purpose against female people" (346). Despite the fact that he is the lone character who accepts with certainty that she is not involved with Milkman, she notes, "Not seeing mental wreckage then, seemed one of his downsides" (347).

And so middle sister in this novel documents the "mental wreckage" of such gendered violence, injuries less visible as well as entirely invisible, in her unceasing rush of details and a consistently associative narrative. She reveals herself to be someone who can revisit instances of trauma from her past without denying, erasing, or blindly repeating them. But this is not simply a personal exercise. By making public through the modernist mode the private experience of "the predations upon me by the community and by Milkman" (347), the narrative reignites the activist impulses of Irish women's early modernism. As well, within the diegesis, middle sister productively changes the course of action. When third brother-in-law expresses a desire to punish Somebody McSomebody further, she stops him. As she does, she looks to the sky and notes the "softening" of the light and "for a moment, just a moment, I almost nearly laughed" (348). This final line not only signals her personal satisfaction following this intervention, but also conveys through its repetitions the tentative hope that such a discrete interpersonal act might help to solve larger societal problems. Though fragile, the joy almost expressed in this conclusion suggests a genuine revision of the pernicious logics documented across the novel, as middle sister recounts and records a small and local, but nonetheless still meaningful, solution for a stubborn problem.

Reading, Risk, and the Open Ending

The open ending found in both *Normal People* and *Milkman* is a structural device in which the plot culminates in an ambiguous conclusion, leaving the reader without resolution and pointing to an unknown future. As such, it can provide an intellectual as well as an ethical challenge for readers, one that potentially moves attention from the private act of reading to public activism. In 2015, Richard Lea mused on the trend of "open endings" in contemporary fiction, citing as one pertinent example the short stories in *Young Skins* (2013) by the Irish writer Colin

180 READING

Barrett. Lea notes that the rush of recent short stories "full of open narratives" offers "nothing new in a lesson that can be traced back to the 'uncontestable father of the modern short story,' Anton Chekhov."[17] With its precedents located in the Russian psychological realism and early twentieth-century modernism that suffuse Irish women's contemporary writing, the open ending aptly represents not only the complexity of the ongoing issues faced by the characters in *Normal People* and *Milkman*, but also those that confront the readers of these novels. The open ending offers the stability of a familiar narrative structure, which can underscore through literary form the obduracy of problematic social and political forms, and dishearteningly indicates that the problems described by those venerable forms—familial failures, political violence, sexual harassment, economic inequities—will drag out beyond the last page.

In this way, as Lea suggests in his assessment of the open ending in contemporary fiction, there is "nothing new" here. However, the open ending grants a sense of unrestricted possibility to the young protagonists of *Normal People* and *Milkman*, hinting at the role they might play in solving such problems. The trick, these novels propose, is to develop not only the interpretive skills to identify and interpret these problems, but also the capacity to tolerate doubt and uncertainty. Both Marianne and middle sister encounter mind-bending personal and social challenges, quandaries that apparently can be neither fully understood nor entirely resolved, but that nonetheless require slow and deep consideration. This is a salient lesson for the present moment. In the digital age, when the proper search term promises to locate a solution for every dilemma, these novels insist on ambiguity and the unknown. Both highlight the complex and ongoing nature of stubborn problems and place the burden of any desired resolution on the reader, in a world outside of the book.

The vast popularity of *Normal People* may derive in part from its open ending, which encourages readers to interpret the novel as popular romance, the distracting but entertaining little sister of literary realism: who knows, perhaps Marianne and Connell will find each other in the future, their established pattern of romantic reconciliation akin to that which pulls public interest when celebrities, or even high school sweethearts, reconcile decades after separating. But the open ending of *Normal People* offers more than simply an invitation to imagine *Normal People 2*, a second season of the successful 2020 television miniseries based on the novel. While Rooney's novel evinces little commitment to the formal difficulties of modernism, it nonetheless holds tight to the movement's characteristic ambiguities, in structure if not in style, with its unresolved conclusion. In a 2019 conversation with the American novelist Ben Lerner, Rooney suggested that a formal commitment

---

[17] Richard Lea, "An Unexpected Ending for Literary Progress," *The Guardian*, February 6, 2015, https://www.theguardian.com/books/booksblog/2015/feb/06/an-unexpected-ending-for-literary-progress.

to "open-endedness" means "not wanting to resolve the contradictions, leaving a space to be challenged or to risk something."[18] Yet as they discussed the "individualistic tendency" of the novel, Rooney questioned whether "the novel is completely capable of accommodating radical politics." When Lerner repeatedly pressed for her opinion on this matter, she deferred and then finally responded, "I don't know." In this exchange, Rooney herself performs the uncertainties inherent in the open ending, dodging the question and thus giving voice to the intransigence of a concern that has dogged Irish women artists since their initial engagement with modernist practices a century ago: can form be political?

But the better question might be: can reading be political? And even more particularly, can reading about female subjectivity in a novel by an Irish woman writer make any real difference in the world? Can being alert to a literary mode and its interventions actually help us to see and solve stubborn problems? Reflecting the ambiguity of the open ending, the answer to this question might be: maybe. Both *Normal People* and *Milkman* are popular books in the hands of many readers. They have won numerous awards, been reviewed in high-profile venues, perched on bestseller lists, been selected as "Editors' Picks" on Amazon. The commercial triumphs of Rooney's novels are renowned, with her publisher announcing that her first two novels have sold roughly three million copies in all formats, and with bookstores across the United Kingdom opening for sales early on the day her third novel *Beautiful World, Where Are You* (2021) was released, a practice tied to the Harry Potter phenomenon.[19] But Burns also has experienced remarkable commercial success. As Clare Hutton points out, *Milkman* sold over 540,000 copies in the year following its publication and acquired a "deal for simplified Chinese rights believed to be the biggest single deal ever done for an author not previously published in China."[20]

Historically, such popularity provided one justification for excluding Irish women's fiction from the canon, even as it remains a fact that the market necessarily enables and abets any intervention a novel might make. But while copies of these books might be purchased with enthusiasm, perhaps merely as an accessory conveying cultural capital, for them to sustain or enact the activist energies of the Irish women's modernism as I claim they do, readers must make their way through them and sit patiently with their complexities. Those analytical skills must be taught and honed, and these novels suggest the ongoing value of humanistic skills such as close reading in the contemporary moment. Both propose that the

---

[18] "Ben Lerner and Sally Rooney in Conversation," *Theaters of Speech*, FSG Works in Progress, October 11, 2019, https://fsgworkinprogress.com/2019/10/11/theaters-of-speech/.

[19] John Meagher, "The Sally Rooney Industry: Beautiful Sales, Where Are You," *Irish Independent*, September 4, 2021, https://www.independent.ie/entertainment/books/the-sally-rooney-industry-beautiful-sales-where-are-you-40815128.html.

[20] Clare Hutton, "Why Anna Burns' *Milkman* Is Such a Phenomenon," July 31, 2019, OUPblog, https://blog.oup.com/2019/07/why-anna-burns-milkman-is-such-a-phenomenon/.

182 READING

scrupulous study of literature is crucial in this process, realized or not, for their female protagonists in the understanding of self and other. Both characters manifest the capacity to sit patiently with themselves and their circumstance, but in vastly different ways: Marianne remains in Ireland because she lacks the ability to imagine and enact a different resolution for herself and her relationship, while middle sister elects to dwell on the story of her past trauma in order to understand her past and seek to mend its injuries.

The psychological and emotional development of these young adults is explained in part by their relationship to reading, which often occurs in educational settings. The act of reading in *Normal People* is not only a means of securing personal privacy for Marianne, of creating a shield from the invasions of the social world, but also a tool for conveying publicly her private self in a way that draws additional attention, sometimes wanted. In secondary school, the fact that Marianne reads *Swann's Way* in the cafeteria suggests to Connell that "She's not leading the same kind of life as other people" (26). As a result, "He wants to understand how her mind works" (26). The novel intimates such reading may have helped Marianne develop unique interrogative skills that face outward. Connell notes that she asks him direct questions that demonstrate her "forensic attentiveness to his silences" (26), while he tries to understand Marianne by writing privately about her in "run-on sentences with too many dependent clauses, sometimes connected with breathless semicolons, as if he wants to re-create a precise copy of Marianne in print, as if he can preserve her completely for future review. Then he turns a new page in the notebook so he doesn't have to look at what he's done" (27).

As the novel moves forward, Rooney's representation of casual reading becomes one explanation for Marianne's shallow subjectivity: she is never seen to settle with her reading, to puzzle out the complexities conveyed in language, to use them as tools to understand better her surrounding conditions. Both Connell and Marianne are avid readers; as secondary school students, recognized as among the brightest in their class, they announce their familiarity with complex texts like *The Communist Manifesto* or James Baldwin's *The Fire Next Time*, and both go on to study literature at Trinity College Dublin. But once at university, Marianne is only seen reading the labels on yogurt pots and dried apple packets in the grocery (111, 113), or emails and texts from Connell and other friends (162), even as she is understood as opinionated and informed on political issues (173). Her shallow reading is further evident when her university friend Joanna suggests "books and articles, which Marianne reads or half-reads or reads summaries of" (87). Later, Marianne will "scroll" the posts on Facebook about Rob, a former secondary school acquaintance who dies by suicide, and award them her first considered reading as depicted in the novel. Done across evenings following his funeral, this endeavor of reading and rereading triggers in Marianne confusion, signaled by the list of unanswered questions these posts elicit from her, as well as stimulating an anger that she can neither understand nor explain to herself. In

READING, RISK, AND THE OPEN ENDING   183

retrospect, discussing Rob later with Connell, she is similarly dismissive: "Thinking about it now, she can't understand why it bothered her" (232), a moment that culminates in her unanswerable question about this dead young man, "Who were you?" (233). While this question underscores the limits of understanding the hidden nature or motivations of others, it also intimates that there is little fully realized self-awareness prompted by this online reading, no sense that this moment enables for Marianne some type of enhanced understanding of others. She reads, feels confused and upset by this existential question, moves on.

These Facebook posts unsettle arguments such as those made by T. S. Eliot or Theodor Adorno asserting that aesthetic form necessarily must be difficult to reflect the difficult conditions of modern life.[21] That is, these posts invite from Marianne the same unanswerable questions about human nature provoked by complex modernist texts. The issue here is less about the capacity of form, literary or otherwise, to elicit sophisticated thought than about Marianne's inability to sit with the difficulties and ambiguities generated by any reading. Her limitation suggests that the aptitude for meaningful textual interrogation invited by literature and honed in the classroom is fragile and might slip away, particularly when the texts before a reader are largely food labels and emails.

Even so, reading has informed Marianne's sense of herself, as revealed in the rare glimpses of her consciousness as depicted through the modernist mode. This becomes most evident when, once again, a female protagonist in contemporary fiction by an Irish woman writer harkens to the final paragraph of Joyce's "The Dead." Roughly in the middle of the novel, Marianne elects to leave her Swedish lover Lukas after he photographs her nude and bound, and announces that he loves her. As she departs, she wonders, "Could he really do the gruesome things he does to her and believe at the same time that he's acting out of love? Is the world such an evil place, that love should be indistinguishable from the basest and most abusive forms of violence? Outside her breath rises in a fine mist and the snow keeps falling, like a ceaseless repetition of the same infinitesimally small mistake" (205). Here, the ambiguity that characterizes the open ending reveals itself, at a much earlier point in the novel, through another series of unanswerable questions posed by Marianne. Her questions stand in contrast to the observational statements marking Gabriel's epiphany in the last paragraph of "The Dead," despite the shared mention of falling snow. But this moment also nods to the famous closing line of F. Scott Fitzgerald's *The Great Gatsby*, which reads, "So we beat on, boats against the current, borne back ceaselessly into the past."[22] This dual modernist allusion merges Joyce's epiphanic understanding that we can never fully grasp the subjectivity of another with Fitzgerald's awareness that particular national and economic

---

[21] See Theodor Adorno, *Essays on Music*, ed. Richard Leppert, trans. Susan H. Gillespie (Berkeley: University of California Press, 2002), and T. S. Eliot, *The Use of Poetry and the Use of Criticism* (London: Faber and Faber, 1933). Future references parenthetical.

[22] F. Scott Fitzgerald, *The Great Gatsby* (New York: Scribner, 1925), 180.

184 READING

conditions trap subjects in outdated myths, such as the American Dream, that thwart self-understanding. These are stubborn problems of the first order, ones that Marianne can identify by mimicking the concerns as well as the language of these modernist classics, but problems, as the question marks suggest, she cannot or will not parse.

The possibilities and limitations of this episode for Marianne are made even more explicit by the fact that the next chapter shifts attention to Connell and opens with his initiating psychological counseling. In the reports of his therapy sessions, we are made privy to his interrogations of self, seen less in the verbalized dialogue shared with "Gillian, the person assigned by the university to listen to his problems for money" (213) than through his interior monologue circulating around these discussions. This chapter culminates at a literary reading, which Connell finds pretentious, and concludes with his own epiphany mediated explicitly by literature and the act of reading. Upon first arriving at Trinity, Connell had sensed the mysteries of self that might be illuminated by reading, a process he regards as simultaneously pleasurable and baffling. As he reads Austen's *Emma*, he observes that he enters "a state of strange emotional agitation," the result of "getting wrapped up in the drama of novels like that": "It feels intellectually unserious to concern himself with fictional people marrying one another. But there it is: literature moves him" (71). His assessment of reading is not all that dissimilar from his account of his initial sexual attraction to Marianne, in that both are enjoyable but potentially compromising, their complexities noted but scarcely interrogated. As a university student, Connell seems to develop a more fully realized relationship with literature and reading. In secondary school, literature had represented a form of cultural capital that might help him secure his desires, sexual or social. But when he arrives at Trinity, he wonders "why all their classroom discussions were so abstract and lacking in textual detail, and eventually he realized that most people were not actually doing the reading" (71). His bookish intelligence at university has more currency than it did in secondary school, though he uses it judiciously: "He likes when someone is struggling to remember the name of a book or an author, and he can provide it for them readily, not showing off, just remembering it" (102–103), though he might as readily be "quiet at parties, stubbornly quiet even, and not interested in showing off how many books he has read" (92).

By the novel's close, because of his work in the classroom and a measure of therapy, in tandem with psychotropic medication, Connell's take on literature appears somewhat altered. The final paragraph of the chapter in which he begins therapy opens with a tinge of skepticism about books and reading, with his awareness that "a lot of the literary people in college see books primarily as a way of appearing cultured ... literature fetishized for its ability to take educated people on false emotional journeys ... they liked to read about" (228). Books, he understands, are "status symbols" (228) that are produced to make money, an activity in which even the most talented writer is complicit. He observes, "Literature, in the way it appeared at these public readings, had no potential as a form of resistance to anything. Still, Connell went home that night and read over some notes he had been making for a new story, and he felt the old beat of pleasure inside his body, like watching a perfect goal, like the rustling movement of light through leaves, a phrase of music from the window of a passing car. Life offers up these moments of joy despite everything" (228). This moment is an outlandish demonstration of Joyce's free indirect discourse, of the "Uncle Charles Principle" in *Dubliners* described by Hugh Kenner in which the narrative is influenced by the language and features of a particular character.[23] It also references Stephen's decision in *A Portrait of the Artist as a Young Man*, inspired by an epiphany at the beach as he observed the "bird girl," to become an artist. Connell's move inward to his writing from the public world, and the labor of crafting his own "new story," stimulates in him a pleasure similar to that triggered by his earlier reading of Austen. Understood as tainted by commerce, books nonetheless promise him good feeling, satisfying labor, and represent however fallaciously a mode of production at odds with the marketplace, an old modernist fantasy. Connell sees literature in the public sphere, understood here as a personal performance calculated to sell books and accrue approbation for the author, as having "no potential as a form of resistance to anything," even as the "joy" tied to his creative labor reflects an emotional tenor akin to that of Molly Bloom's final "Yes," a harbinger of future possibilities generated by private self-examination.

Through their relationships to literature and reading, Marianne and Connell suggest the untapped possibilities inherent in the sustained critical analysis of the imaginative worlds represented in books. But *Normal People*, in characterization and plot, as well as in form, underscores certain deficiencies as its characters attempt to transfer the tactics of close reading to the analysis of their own thorny conditions. In this novel, Connell is not just Marianne's lover, but her foil. Marianne seems stuck, staying put in a traditional role dictated in part by Irish literature and culture, while Connell appears better able to shake off any paralysis. He follows a different cultural script, and he also reads attentively and risks psychological therapy. The counseling office has obvious shortcomings but may provide him, in some ways, the most satisfying classroom at Trinity. In contrast, Rooney demonstrates through her depictions of reading how Marianne consistently pulls away from the painful work of interrogating difficult personal issues, how she employs her knowledge largely as a conversational gambit, as a sociable "form of resistance" with little significant value for her or others. What is remarkable about the book is how it deploys literary modes to expose such limitations. Rooney seems to offer readers a realist "what you see is what you get" in the structure and style of this novel, but it becomes clear in her quiet use of modernism, evident only through persistent close reading and a familiarity with literary history, that she identifies

[23] Hugh Kenner, *Joyce's Voices* (Berkeley: University of California Press, 1978), 15–38.

186   READING

the issues that explain why Marianne, so smart and so readerly, is nonetheless so limited in her self-understanding.

Reading Sunsets: Pedagogy and the Stubborn Problem

In their accounts of books and reading, *Normal People* and *Milkman* demonstrate how contemporary authors artfully render less ordinary not only contemporary conditions, but also the everyday experiences that readers assume they recognize and understand. These works represent long-standing and complex social problems, among them sexual harassment, emotional abuse, issues of consent, and crises generated by class or political difference. Such problems are rife and entrenched, as evidenced by the disheartening assortment of ongoing personal and institutional failures depicted in fiction by Irish women writers across almost a century. To reframe such stubborn problems, *Normal People* and *Milkman* differently invoke literary modes, but both leave their conclusions unresolved. In doing so, they provide valuable lessons in the open ending, inviting readers to assess the challenges of living with ambiguity and sitting comfortably with the unknown. *Milkman* displays modernism's particular aptitude in this contemporary project by representing the open ending as not simply a formal strategy, but a lived practice—a willingness to indulge and tolerate ambiguity, to sit patiently with not knowing.

As in *Normal People*, reading in *Milkman* informs how a young female protagonist understands her lived experience. Initially, by her own admission, reading seems to provide middle sister merely an escape, an immersive distraction that captures the past but cannot promise any real or immediate effect on her crisis-ridden present. In the face of real-world problems, she notes that her response was to "keep the lid on, buy old books, read old books, seriously consider those scrolls and clay tablets. That was me then, age eighteen" (115). So when she encounters Milkman, she asserts that she had no idea how to contend with him, and she finds herself paralyzed by her "confused, panicked thoughts, not my usual nineteenth-century, safe-and-sound literary thoughts" (115). And yet, as she acknowledges in her retrospective assessment of this encounter, she was able to read closely the disturbing real-life situation before her, noting the array of threats and possibilities "underlined by this milkman in the subsoil of our conversation" (115). Books have provided her transferable analytical skills that, while they cannot themselves eradicate her abuse and suffering, nonetheless represent apparatus that enable not only self-protection, but also self-awareness. Such critical reading of herself and others allows her to avoid the traps set by the "old-time storybooks" (122) her mother warns her against, fictional narratives suggesting to middle sister that she can tame the romantic hero her mother fears middle sister fallaciously imagines Milkman to be.

READING SUNSETS: PEDAGOGY AND THE STUBBORN PROBLEM   187

Books shape the way that middle sister reads the world; they foster her complex thinking. She references the chivalric romance of *Ivanhoe*, "nineteenth-century books" (5), and Gogol's "The Overcoat" (20). She explains "in a state of high excitement" to her "maybe-boyfriend" the contents of "*The Brothers Karamazov, Tristram Shandy, Vanity Fair or Madame Bovary*" (17). She parses her own experiences through the literary tropes she encounters in such books. For example, she understands her psychic distress as similar to that of the "sickly, misanthropic Reeve" of *The Canterbury Tales*, and she perceives her upset in terms of Gothic horror, with her house "banging and retorting and causing discordance— all to berate me, to warn me, to call attention to the threat that already I knew was surrounding me" (184). Despite her protestations otherwise, modernist and contemporary literature also have a role to play in her perceptions. After she is poisoned by tablets girl, middle sister has "a nightmare of Proust, in which he turned out to be some reprehensible contemporary Nineteen-Seventies writer passing himself off as a turn-of-the-century writer, which apparently was why he was being sued in court in the dream by, I think, me" (231). In addition to this unwanted intrusion of modernism and the contemporary into her psyche, her intellectually precocious "wee sisters" are drawn to modernist books, regularly demanding that middle sister read them aloud. Their tastes, even before they are ten years old, run to Hardy, Kafka, and Conrad—a reading list from which middle sister retreats by turning to "*Some Considerations on the Causes of Roman Greatness and Decadence* which, published in 1734, was pretty much, I reckoned, how all books should be" (276–277). But the title of this book, which she reads in Northern Ireland amid the late stage of English imperialism, suggests that mere chronology does not render certain books obsolete and therefore safely irrelevant.

This attention to middle sister's reading, to her consideration of the texts and subtexts of literature and life, becomes a valuable means of exploring the varieties of attention that middle sister herself experiences amid the Troubles. The problem of not being fully and accurately "seen" rests at the heart of this novel, a point exemplified in its focus on sunsets. The conclusion of *Milkman* unfolds "in the early evening light" (348), and the cover of the novel, chosen by Burns, is a photograph of twilight on Belfast Lough. Twilight is the liminal moment between light and dark when the sun sits below the horizon and its illuminating rays are refracted and therefore less clarifying: the sky's blue shade explodes into an array of different colors that meld together, and it becomes harder to see things clearly. It is a rich symbol for the ambiguity and diffusiveness that renders the novel challenging to read. In the third chapter, middle sister reports on two of her early considerations of sunset. The first occurs at the beach with her "maybe-boyfriend" and the second in her evening French language class. Middle sister notes that on "both occasions," in the classroom and at the beach, the colors of the sky were "blending and mixing, sliding and extending, new colours arriving, all colours combining, colours going on forever" (77). This is one of many instances in which things

188   READING

that appear to be opposites are revealed instead to be adjacent or intersecting. Notably, the narrator is introduced to "the shock of the sky, the subversiveness of a sunset" (77) by characters who embody seeming contraries: maybe-boyfriend is involved in relationships both straight and gay, the teacher speaks both French and English. In these sunset scenes, the novel clearly proclaims its commitment to the ethical necessity of learning to sit with difficulty and the discomfort generated by ambiguity.[24]

But it is the classroom that teaches middle sister the value of sitting with ambiguity as well as embracing repetition as a means for effectively learning new lessons. Middle sister recalls one evening class when the teacher reads a literary passage from a French novel in which the sky is not described as blue. One student protests that the author is "complicating things with fancy footwork when all he need say is that the sky is blue" (69). In response, the teacher demands that the students look outside at the actual sunset, urging them to note the array of colors in the sky. Such evident complexity unnerves middle sister and her classmates. Faced with her students' protestations against the multifarious colors of the sky, the French teacher announces playfully, "Don't worry ... Your unease, even your temporary unhingement, dear students, in the face of this sunset is encouraging. It can only mean progress. It can only mean enlightenment" (77). Insisting they look at the vibrant sunset through the classroom window, she introduces her recalcitrant pupils to the idea that language holds excess meaning. Further, she suggests that such nuance might beneficially apply to real-life thinking outside of the classroom. Laughing with satisfied pleasure, the teacher chides those who resist figuration. Ambiguity is uncomfortable, a fact that middle sister comes to understand intellectually as well as viscerally.

As the teacher insists, to achieve even small changes, "*Attempts and repeated attempts ... That's the way to do it*" (101). Rereading and revising are, as this command placed in italics suggests, the tools necessary to hone one's ability to tolerate, assess, and move through difficulties; they enable one to claim and articulate individual experience. Middle sister notes that she "enjoyed" the class, identifying in the moment the pleasures of critical thinking, and regards the lesson retrospectively as "valuable" "to people who were not only not into metaphors, but not into admitting to what patently was there" (100–101). As a teenager, she frets about such repetition, imagining her future and fearing, "What if all chapters stayed the same or even, as time went on, got worse?" (101). Yet as an adult, her retelling of her trauma demonstrates the constructive potential of repetition. Although the associative narrative with its consistent tone merely repeats the already experienced events of her youth, it nonetheless displays the "progress" and "enlightenment"

---

[24] For an insightful reading of how "fluid" characters in the novel trouble the political logic of binaries that defined the Troubles, see Siân White, "A 'Hair-Trigger Society' and the Woman Who Felt Something in Anna Burns's *Milkman*," *Genre* 54:1 (April 2021): 111–137.

that the French teacher promised derived from *"repeated attempts."* With this rereading of her past, middle sister can "years after" filter her late adolescent perceptions amid "what is now the era of psychological enlightenment" (37) in which "moods" (85) are now understood as depression, and bad feeling openly diagnosed as "shame" (53). Repetition brings the narrative to an open ending that offers not a total resolution of the stubborn problems middle sister diagnoses, but evidences a small advance for her and for her third brother-in-law, which corroborates the classroom lesson provided by her French teacher.

In her generative reading of pleasure in *Milkman*, Caroline Magennis contends, "reading alone only goes so far in the novel. Trauma is experienced primarily through strong bodily sensations, and it is only by reclaiming the body that any sort of small freedom is possible."[25] But *Milkman* insists upon the therapeutic importance of the interrogative skills of rereading and revision, as we see when middle sister returns to her teenage experience from an adult perspective, and displays the analytical, emotional, and even aesthetic benefits generated by such intellectual persistence. The flashes of pleasure visible across the narrative, evident not least in middle sister's dark humor, chime with those identified by Virginia Woolf in her musings on childhood from "A Sketch of the Past" (1939), where she describes having learned not to fear, but instead to welcome, "sudden shocks" because they encourage retrospection, award revelations, enable writing, and abet recovery.[26] As Woolf explained of her recovered memories, "It is only by putting it into words that I make it whole; this wholeness means that it has lost its power to hurt me; it gives me, perhaps because by doing so I take away the pain, a great delight to put the severed parts together. Perhaps this is the strongest pleasure known to me" (72). Middle sister likewise associates the intellectual and creative exercise of chronicling her traumatic stories with a more muted but nonetheless real pleasure, one reflecting the measured satisfaction that derives from grappling with and then articulating her struggles.

But again, such lessons are difficult to see. With its modal challenges, middle sister's narrative demands significant intellectual and imaginative labor, as well as patience and tolerance. These are not corrective practices to be required only of those aligned with malignant institutions or organizations, or of bad actors such as Milkman or Somebody McSomebody. To begin to solve systemic problems requires the type of work that even third-brother-in-law, despite his best intentions, cannot do because he does not yet have the capacity to read closely and deeply, to understand figuration. These are skills that must be learned, that should be taught broadly. In the twenty-first-century, when digital media summarizes and encapsulates even the densest material for fast and easy reading, and politics

---

[25] Caroline Magennis, *Northern Irish Writing after the Troubles: Intimacies, Affects, Pleasures* (London: Bloomsbury, 2021), 157–158.

[26] Virginia Woolf, "A Sketch of the Past," *Moments of Being: A Collection of Autobiographical Writing*, ed. Jeanne Schulkind (New York: Harcourt, 1985), 61–160, 72.

190 READING

are marked by increasingly entrenched opposing factions, contemporary fiction's "complicating things with fancy footwork" offers not only aesthetic rewards, but ethical and practical ones as well.

One clear message to be drawn from middle sister's experience is an old-fashioned one about the enduring value of the study of literature. Amid the violence, the classroom provides her not only temporary escape, but also another model and means of "living otherwise" (112) akin to her practice of reading or third-brother-in-law's exercise routine. She regards her French class as a low-stakes space in which to rehearse social and political modalities different than those found outside its parameters: "Observing the niceties therefore, not the antipathies, was crucial to coexistence and an example of that would be our French class, a mixed class, where it was okay to run down France, say, or more to the point, French metaphorical writers, but where absolutely it was not okay, not for one second, in respect of the proprieties, to demand someone declare themselves or make reference to their view or to your view at all" (112). To participate in this class, which defuses and distances the vexed concept of difference by mediating it through "foreign" literature, temporarily changes their focal point and demands from all students the weekly exercise of tolerance and self-control.

The lessons offered by the humanities classroom, and the new habits of attention it stimulates, are not without cost—a difficult lesson middle sister comes to understand when she discovers maybe-boyfriend in a romantic tryst with his male friend "chef." The ambiguity and ambivalence of her "maybe-category" relationship, she now realizes, is not a safe place to settle but instead a different way of being "done to death" (294). As observed, "The truth was dawning on me of how terrifying it was not to be numb, but to be aware, to have facts, retain facts, be present, be adult" (294). But such "dawning" awareness is also not without reward, for herself and for others. When middle sister and her "third sister" (the sister married to her running partner) endeavor to warn the "wee sisters" against their predatory "first brother-in-law," middle sister initially describes the misdirection that first brother-in-law might use to harass them. But she does so without saying explicitly that he will harass them, warning the girls, "if he tries to lure you in on the pretext of anything—science, art, literature, linguistics, social anthropology, mathematics, politics, chemistry, the intestinal tract, unusual euphemisms, double-entry bookingkeeping, the three divisions of the psyche, the Hebrew alphabet, Russian Nihilism, Asian cattle, twelfth-century Chinese porcelain, the Japanese unit—" (212). Baffled, the wee sisters cannot grasp the message their older sibling tries to convey. So third sister states the matter outright, clearly announcing that if he mentions such topics, "It'll be something abusive, sexually invasive, a violating, creepy thing, always a verbal thing, but on second thoughts, never you mind. You three are too young to know of that yet" (212). The girls receive from third sister a direct warning, with the previous intimations about the behavior of first brother-in-law revised and repeated in clear and direct prose, the subtext now made explicit. This small alteration in her habits of communication elicits from third sister, within the same sentence, an immediate and misguided retreat. In fact, none of the three sisters is "too young" for this warning. Yet even in light of her disclaimer, third sister's pointed and lucid communication represents an unusual moment in the novel—the accurate and clear-cut public articulation of a difficult private matter, one which seeks to stem an ongoing problem.

Such a gesture requires in this moment a diversion from the obfuscating modernist experiment the novel suggests is necessary to reflect and refract the abuse suffered, a point made by Jacqueline Rose, who has commended Eimear McBride for giving voice to the interwoven nature of sex and violence, deeming her "the writer of sexual abuse, now recognised as one of the hallmarks of the new century."[27] For Rose, "Modernist writing, famously difficult, is the appropriate form for that crisis. Most simply, it brings to an end the illusion that either language or the world can be made safe."[28] But there is another necessary step in this process. Readers must work their way through formally imposed difficulties in order to identify and enact the interventions proposed, implicitly or explicitly, in such works. The corrective attempted by third sister in *Milkman* exemplifies the type of small and local change in practice that might help to nudge a culture beyond stubborn problems, including sexual abuse, that have historically plagued its members—but it also exposes its challenges.

"no potential as a form of resistance to anything"

We, as literary critics, can discuss endlessly what literary modes do, what might be the possibilities inherent in forms, but both *Normal People* and *Milkman* powerfully demonstrate the mandatory labor required of readers and teachers to realize the ethical potential of such modes. In *Normal People*, a highly educated twenty-first-century Irish woman finds herself, despite her privileges, trapped in a larger cultural narrative of traditional womanhood. It is not clear Marianne can identify, let alone parse, her circumstances either personal or political due in part, the novel suggests, to her inability to take full advantage of any resource that might inspire and instruct her interrogations of literature or self. That labor demands risk, a risk Marianne does not take. She ends the novel at home in Ireland, not only staying put geographically but also mired in the weary tropes of good womanhood that have long defined Irish religious and political narratives. In *Milkman*, middle sister, crafting her narrative in retrospect, patiently stays put with her difficult personal history, examining closely in retrospect herself, her family, and her culture, using

---

[27] Jacqueline Rose, "From the Inside Out," rev. of Eimear McBride, *The Lesser Bohemians*, *The London Review of Books* 38:18 (September 22, 2016): 11–12.

[28] Ibid.

192 READING

the knowledge acquired from those lessons to recalibrate her actions and thoughts going forward. However, Burns's novel does not offer a triumphant celebration of literary close reading, or posit the full command of literary form, as some quick fix for systemic social problems. Instead, the book's celebration of the difficulties and rewards of the analytical attention to and exercise of stubborn forms offers a more modest, but crucially important lesson for readers. The practice of critical reading allows middle sister to relieve, slightly and perhaps temporarily, the burdensome weight of stubborn problems, including how to prevent childhood abuse for wee sisters, how to stem homophobia in her assessment of the relationship between maybe-boyfriend and chef, how to refuse the shame of mental health struggles suffered by her father, and how to reconcile and even support the sexual desires of her middle-aged mother, among other small but valuable correctives she initiates or embraces in the novel. In each of these cases, middle sister's own difficulties, her willingness to sit uncomfortably with them and the ambivalences that surround them, provide her the means to gently nudge the immediate world around her into a less pernicious place.

In both novels, the use of stubborn modes abets this project by reminding readers of the long history of literature, with its many and multifarious accounts of similar issues, and the obduracy of the problems they represent. They skew the world that the characters think they know and, in so doing, productively elicit from them a heightened awareness of their choices, behaviors, and place in a larger historical as well as imaginative framework. What the characters do with that information, as seen in these two novels, can differ widely. But even in this variability, readers can see the possibilities highly familiar literary modes continue to offer for the unsettling of stubborn problems. Crucially, these novels, like others in this study, draw attention to the demands of analysis and activism. *Normal People* is an easy, enjoyable read—but its characters are limited, perhaps by design, and as a result, they evince little of the insight that suggests the interventions they might make going forward. *Milkman* is a difficult book, enjoyable in as much as the reader commits to the hard work of reading and rereading, as the French teacher advocated.

As Eliot asserted in "The Use of Poetry and the Use of Criticism" (1933), one foundational text of high modernism, "modern poetry is supposed to be difficult" (150). For Eliot, these difficulties might stem from the poet's need to express himself in "an obscure way," the sheer "novelty" of a new form, or the reader's expectations from "having been told, or having suggested to himself, that the poem is going to prove difficult" (150). Thus, the "ordinary reader … is apt to be thrown into a state of consternation very unfavourable to poetic receptivity," one that thwarts "a state of sensitivity" with "the desire to be clever and to look very hard for something, he doesn't know what—or else by the desire not be taken in. There is such a thing as stage fright, but what such readers have is pit or gallery fright" (150–151). Readers in the wake of high modernism, those in the pricey as well as the cheap seats, have a more complicated relationship to difficulty. Such anticipated modernist "consternation" can serve an important ethical purpose by demanding they look more closely at female experience. Perversely, *Normal People* may require more of its readers, who have to work hard to understand the analytical payoff of two characters who are unable to read and assess either themselves or the contours of their romantic relationship, let alone the dynamics of the world that surrounds them. Though the prose is difficult, *Milkman* does a great deal of the analytical labor for its readers by delving deeply, even relentlessly, into the interior life of its female protagonist. Read in tandem, these two novels offer another twist on the common understanding of realism and modernism that has informed the critical assessments of both. The highly accessible realist form of *Normal People*, ironically, ultimately may exhibit more of the obscurantism and difficulty associated with *Milkman*'s modernism.

Coda: Recalibrating

(Mike McCormack)

Each of the novels and short stories by Irish women writers studied in *The Stubborn Mode* has documented what unfolds when the amorphous nature of individual consciousness bumps up against external ordering structures in the public world. In their depictions of interiority, these texts explore how female characters embrace, reject, and rework the ritual of prayer, the fixity of material objects, the intrusive networks of the digital world, and the ordered narrative of the book. The ritual of prayer promises consolation, transcendence, and community, but it can fail to provide supplicants comfort and salvation. The imaginative permissiveness of the daydream allows for productively unfettered considerations of real-world problems, but it appears nearly impossible to realize those insights in the practice of daily life. Digital technologies can make public social ills and thereby encourage collective intervention, but they also threaten to squelch independent thought and behaviors. And reading, the conscious attention to literature, can enable better critical thinking for characters, but it also offers a seductive escape from troubling realities. These writers use modernism, a familiar but still challenging literary mode, to encourage readers to think anew about fictional representations of female interiority in the throes of rapidly changing contemporary conditions. Set among imperatives of church, market, state, school, and family, these intimate, but at the same time political, negotiations between individual and society suggest the possibilities inherent in acts of imagination in a tradition often dominated by powerful institutions and hierarchies. Whether grappling with forces as old as a Christian god or as new as the internet, these writers harness the forms, themes, and histories of high modernism to reinvent a fictional interiority that might recapture, and thus advocate for, the private world as a valuable space in which to resist and even untangle stubborn problems. Yet each of these exercises—praying, daydreaming, logging off, reading—demonstrates the substantive challenge of translating personal insights into meaningful public action.

I end this book with a study of Mike McCormack's *Solar Bones* not to grant a male writer and his male protagonist the last word, but instead to demonstrate what horizons open when we consider contemporary fiction through a recalibrated tradition that foregrounds women's modernist experiment. In this novel, published in 2016, McCormack renders old-fashioned notions of womanhood through an old-fashioned modernist aesthetic, but he tweaks them to demonstrate

---

Modernism in Irish Women's Contemporary Writing. Paige Reynolds, Oxford University Press. © Paige Reynolds (2024).
DOI: 10.1093/9780191990540.003.0007

slight but meaningful alterations in the understanding of Irish women across the past century, as well as to underscore the ways in which those perceptions remain stalled. With its meticulous depiction of individual consciousness, the novel is in tune formally as well as thematically with the representations of female interiority studied throughout this book, using the stubborn mode of modernism to expose the interplay between public and private, order and chaos, form and formlessness characterizing contemporary experience.

Solar Bones records the interior monologue of its middle-aged protagonist, the engineer Marcus Conway, as he reviews meaningful events from his life after his death from an unexpected heart attack. Written as a single flowing sentence, one rarely punctuated, the novel appears on the page almost like poetry, with lines broken and ordered for emphasis or clarity, with regular repetitions of words or phrases securing meaning and underscoring themes. In this novel, Marcus prays: set on All Souls' Day, a day of prayer and remembrance for the souls of the departed, the plot commences with the ringing of the Angelus that accompanies the Catholic devotional prayer commemorating the Incarnation, and the text itself is suffused with actual prayers, both accurately reproduced or creatively reworked by Marcus. Marcus daydreams: in the review of his past, he recalls reveries provoked by objects, often broken objects such as a dismantled tractor engine from his youth or a damaged wind turbine, that elicit from him meaningful personal and political insights. Marcus "logs off": he is a citizen of a digital world, one who lives by his own admission "in a world awash in electronic imagery" and Skype-calls his emigrant son, but who finds that the internet triggers in him apocalyptic visions.[1] And Marcus reads: a former seminarian, he is an avid consumer of national and local news, one who deploys his critical reading skills to review and assess events past and present.

Solar Bones provides yet another vivid example of modernism revived and reworked in well-received contemporary Irish fiction, a fact noted by reviewers and literary critics, as well as by the author himself.[2] With its close attention to one character's internal response to contemporary external circumstances, this novel is in tune with many of the works studied here. McCormack likewise cleaves to the early experiments of modernism, regarding them as unsurpassed for their capacity to depict individual human subjectivity, and similarly appears dedicated to the

---

[1] Mike McCormack, *Solar Bones* (Dublin: Tramp Press, 2016), 41, 74. Future references parenthetical.

[2] See for example Stephanie Boland, "Bedad He Revives: Why *Solar Bones* Is a Resurrection for Irish Modernism," *The New Statesman*, July 4, 2016, https://www.newstatesman.com/culture/books/2016/07/bedad-he-revives-why-solar-bones-resurrection-irish-modernism; Claire Connolly, "Watery Modernism? Mike McCormack's *Solar Bones* and W. B. Yeats's *John Sherman*," *The Edinburgh Companion to Irish Modernism*, eds. Maud Ellmann, Siân White, and Vicki Mahaffey (Edinburgh: Edinburgh University Press, 2021), 452–469; Liam Harrison, "Mike McCormack's Style of Post-Mortem Modernism," *Textual Practice* (2022): 1–29, https://doi.org/10.1080/0950236X.2022.2111709; Joanna Jarząb-Napierała, "Retromodernism: New 'Structure of Feeling' in Mike McCormack's *Solar Bones*," *New Hibernia Review* 23:3 (Autumn 2019): 55–68.

196 CODA: RECALIBRATING

proposition that we must continue to decipher what it means to have an inner life. Formally, Marcus's sustained interior monologue bears obvious likeness to the "Penelope" chapter of *Ulysses*, but with respect to its treatment of women, its thematics tell us even more about Joyce's influence. Despite his alignment with aspects of female interiority as rendered by Irish women writers, Marcus resembles many of Joyce's male characters, who often respond to the challenges posed by the obscurity of female subjectivity by reducing women to flat and familiar types. This is, for Marcus, a habit of mind that continues into the afterlife. For example, when his wife Mairead falls violently ill from bacterial poisoning after drinking contaminated water, a traumatic personal incident that is the direct result of failed civic infrastructure, he observes her suffering but struggles to fathom her plight and its place in the larger political system. To manage his anxiety, he translates "the flesh and blood figure of Mairead" into an "allegorical figure in an altarpiece" (120). He imaginatively renders his ailing wife an aesthetic object and a religious symbol, a moment that demonstrates how the objectification of women, their iconicity, is used to manage overwhelming personal and social problems. As Orlaith Darling rightly asserts, "The women of *Solar Bones* are variously smote down by male-created crises and attempt to challenge and subvert patriarchally engineered infrastructures and systems; ultimately, however, they are doomed to symbolic and representational roles in a male-centric society."[3] This pattern, the stubborn mode reveals, is not a new one: Marcus might be yet another refashioning of the similarly well-intentioned but perceptively limited Gabriel Conroy, who surreptitiously observes his wife Gretta and understands her "as if she were a symbol of something."[4]

In his fiction, Joyce often represented women as ciphers, and the limitations of his male characters are frequently revealed through their inability to recognize the complex interior lives of women. *Solar Bones* makes its own intervention into the lineage of modernism by taking those limitations and making them a central concern, showing us how Marcus struggles and fails to understand fully Mairead and their daughter Agnes. My particular interest in the novel stems from how McCormack demonstrates, through his representation of male consciousness, what happens when these masculinist inclinations encounter the public interventions of Irish women artists. In this novel, Marcus's adult daughter Agnes bears the social potential of Irish modernism. She is described as a visual artist whose work makes "a sustained attempt to marry the vatic gaze of a hallowed tradition with a technique which strove to find some way out of the redundancy it was so often accused of in a world awash with electronic imagery" (40–41). In her art, she

---

[3] Orlaith Darling, "'[The] Immediate Heft of Bodily and Civic Catastrophe': The Body (Politic) in Crisis in Mike McCormack's *Solar Bones*," *Irish Studies Review* 29:3 (June 2021): 334–347, 335.

[4] James Joyce, "The Dead," *Dubliners: Viking Critical Edition*, eds. Robert Scholes and A. Walton Litz (New York: Penguin, 1969), 175–224, 210.

CODA: RECALIBRATING 197

appropriates the "redundant" tactics of fragmentation, flow, pastiche, and association, the very ones used to capture Marcus's interior monologue, and makes them insistently public. In her first solo exhibition, "The O Negative Diaries," Agnes juxtaposes textual fragments of news stories drawn from provincial papers detailing local crimes with "contextualising pieces and direct quotes from court transcripts in which voices of victims and the accused, plaintiff and defendant, sang clear off the walls"—all written in "a surge of red script flowing across the gallery, ceiling to floor" and penned with her own blood (43). Her flowing public narrative resembles stream of consciousness, prompting Marcus as a reader to observe, "it was quite something to stand there and have your gaze drawn across the walls, swept along in the full surge of the piece while resisting the temptation to rest and decipher one case or another, wanting instead to experience the full flow and wash of the entire piece, my gaze swept on in the relentless, surging indictment of the whole thing" (43). Her exhibit manifests the immersive qualities of modernist interiority, but the content comes from public record and is visible to all in the gallery.

Following in the modernist tradition, Agnes has crafted an exhibit calculated to "épater les bourgeoisie," a strategy that works as intended on Marcus. Unsettled and infuriated by the exhibit, by the sight of his daughter's blood as well as by her uncompromising exposure of rural crime, he exits the gallery and "examined once again what I had seen of the installation itself and more specifically try to fathom the shock I had in its presence, why had I felt so deeply about it all, why had I taken it so personally and, most bafflingly of all, how a man of my age could be so overcome by his own feelings ... I did not appreciate one little bit, sifting through feelings that grated and twisted within me, trying to give them their proper place" (46). In the hands of Agnes, a young female artist, modernism and the history it evokes expose his limits of perception and interpretation. He turns inward, taking the work personally and seeing himself as its inspiration, rather than engaging with her broader intent and the exhibit's wider reception. His vexed response to the installation suggests that Marcus suffers from an imaginative hangover, the effect of centuries of Irish history marked by efforts to curtail the public authority of women, and this inheritance shapes his relationship with his daughter in the present. At dinner later that night with Agnes and Mairead, Marcus announces that he has taken offense not at the display of blood and the "mutilation" (51) her exhibit represents, a concern Agnes laughingly dismisses, but at the "mixture of finger pointing and sanctimony in the whole piece, your righteous standpoint over the material" (51). Her self-injury is of less concern to him than her assertion of perspectival authority.

Throughout, *Solar Bones* is highly alert to the devices, literal and figurative, that order and structure Marcus's interior life—not least the genealogy he describes as the "line traceable to the gloomy prehistory in which a tenacious clan of farmers and fishermen kept their grip on a small patch of land ... men with bellies and short tempers" (9). Agnes's exhibit troubles her father's elemental and anxious

198   CODA: RECALIBRATING

understanding of form as necessarily cohesive, coherent, and patriarchal. As it does for many of the female characters throughout this monograph, interior monologue exposes how forms test Marcus's confidence in their promise to keep order, and their instability often reveals itself in quotidian experiences, "those daily/rites, rhythms and rituals/upholding the world like solar bones" (76). Agnes in her public art has literally broken things: she excises juridical and journalistic content, she "jab[s]" (51) her body to extract blood, she fragments and destroys narrative. Her rebarbative installation stands in dramatic contrast to the sinuous single sentence that captures Marcus's interior monologue, a story told to himself, by himself. By his own admittance, her experiment provokes in him new ways of thinking, new ways of feeling, "some new sensitivity to shock and fear" that he experiences as deeply unsettling and fears will be "corrosive," an evocative term suggesting damage and destruction (55). The intensity of Marcus's emotional response to "The O Negative Diaries" clouds his critical response to Agnes's work. This anxiety might stem from his dawning awareness that representational authority is slipping from his hands into those of a younger generation, one in which women might take the lead.

Solar Bones offers a glimpse of how the reception of Irish women's modernism plays out in the twenty-first century. For instance, despite Marcus's strong personal discomfort with his daughter's work, the present century reveals itself seemingly better able to accommodate the woman artist. In the aftermath of her exhibition, Agnes becomes something of a minor celebrity whose work is appreciated, promoted, and interpreted by the popular press, where it is covered in a "favourable print review in a Sunday broadsheet," which she notes "picked up on her theme of the body as a rhetorical field, a fitting conjunction for a time when the city itself was in the national news for reasons to do with the sovereignty and integrity of the body within a democracy" (184). Agnes successfully appropriates the hackneyed but tenacious symbols of womanhood that sustain her culture in order to advocate social change. She understands that because of the exhibit "people are anxious to see me as some sort of Jeanne d'Arc or someone like that, someone bent on self-sacrifice, the exemplary sufferer who's supposed to stand against I don't know what" (185). Taking her cue from the logics of Irish women's modernism, Agnes next stages a live performance that embraces the feminine symbols through which she has been read and spins them into public activism. In the wake of the exhibit, she participates in a carnivalesque spectacle intended to draw attention to the water crisis that led to the bacterial poisoning of her mother and other members of the community. At the close of a parade, the crowd convenes to discover Agnes standing nude on the roof of a municipal building. With "everyone teetering on the edge of some climactic gesture that would clinch the whole spectacle into a coherent act of political protest" (200), Agnes deliberately plummets five stories from the roof into a hidden air cushion from which she arises, "as a kind of Venus on the half-shell from beneath the blue projected waves of the lake that rippled across her body" (201). Reading women through such tropes has proven a stubborn problem, but Marcus's ready invocation of the goddess Venus as a "kind of" simile for Agnes also tentatively acknowledges the impact of her intervention.

Additional lessons are made available by analyzing this moment through the stubborn mode of modernism. Agnes—who is still, by her own admission, puzzling out the message in her art—has assumed the mantle of authority bestowed on her by the feminine avant-garde, picking up the performative legacy put in place a century before by Maud Gonne, Augusta Gregory, Alice Milligan, Constance Markievicz, and a host of others who embraced and refigured such symbols to help conceptualize an independent, forward-thinking Ireland. These women, who largely came from the educated upper and middle classes, were motivated to produce experimental art, performances, and institutions that might inspire in their audiences newfound ways of thinking, as well as stimulate actual change in the real world. They were alert to the historical avant-gardes unfurling across Europe during the late nineteenth and early twentieth centuries and recognized a place for themselves in these practices.[5] Agnes's revivification of modernist spectacle, now directed against the Irish state rather than against the English colonizer, suggests its new contours in the contemporary moment. Further, when read in the context of a tradition of Irish women's modernism, made visible in contemporary fiction, Agnes's public performance provides a valuable and even hopeful signal for future possibilities. Such possibilities surface in other novels addressed in this study. In *The Land of Spices*, for example, Anna Murphy recites poetry soon after she arrives as the youngest boarder at *La Compagnie de la Saint Famille*, a performance that helps to draw the nourishing attention and mentorship of Helen Archer. Anna's performance becomes the engine for her advancement, one prompt for the rigorous, if sometimes flawed, education that culminates in her ability at the novel's conclusion to escape the restrictive confines of her conservative rural background. In *Milkman*, published decades later, the "wee sisters" represent a pointed counter to the heightened, cloistered interiority of their older "middle sister." The wee sisters, described as precocious consumers of modernist writing, are outlandishly performative, adopting the choreography and costumes of the "International Couple"— the competitive ballroom dancers who have left the neighborhood for global televised fame, and who offer the girls a non-sectarian and even queer model of "living otherwise" (25). These live performances, reenacted on the local streets by the wee sisters, gesture outside of Northern Ireland as well as backward in time to the public theatricality of Irish women's modernism at the cusp of the twentieth century.

---

[5] Despite Terry Eagleton's claim that "in Ireland, there is little or no avant-garde," women's activities during these decades reveal a consistent, dynamic, and ambitious agenda that meshes with, and sometimes precedes, the anti-institutional imperatives of the historical avant-garde found elsewhere across the globe. See Terry Eagleton, *Heathcliff and the Great Hunger: Studies in Irish Culture* (London: Verso, 1995), 299. For comparative context, see Lucy Delap, *The Feminist Avant-Garde: Transatlantic Encounters of the Early Twentieth Century* (Cambridge: Cambridge University Press, 2009).

200   CODA: RECALIBRATING

Through his focus on Agnes, a contemporary artist working in the tradition of the historical avant-garde, Marcus vividly exposes the ongoing refusal of Irish women employing the movement's aesthetics to remain autonomous, to stand apart from culture and society. Read in light of a more capacious and thus more accurate history of Irish modernism, *Solar Bones* also demonstrates a trajectory of slow and steady intervention by women artists over nearly a century. Today, Irish women artists engage the modernist mode not simply to confront a society they regard as archaic, but also to interrogate what appears a more settled, prosperous, and socially progressive Ireland, one whose conditions, while not without profound flaws, can often appear a more forward-thinking alternative to retrenchments seen elsewhere across the globe. Yet Marcus's interior monologue exposes aspects of the stubborn problems that continue to plague the reception of women's experiments. As Deirdre Flynn notes, Agnes's interventions "help Marcus connect the dots" and understand the important role that bodies play in political movements, their capacity to startle the public into action, but they also underscore his status as a consumer, someone who watches and reads, someone who "fails to turn his anger into action."[6] Not only does *Solar Bones* demonstrate the demands that modernism as a stubborn mode places on its readers, it also exposes the slow and incremental interpretation that mode encourages. Marcus must learn to sit with the discomfort of the difficult text, one that poses challenges in form as well as content. Initially, he cannot acknowledge the crises that Agnes represents in her art or abide the feelings that her work triggers in him, but over time, he comes to recognize the puzzling complexities of his daughter and her vision. He must learn to tolerate, if not embrace, her cultural authority and professional success. His struggles, captured in his interior monologue, make visible that difficult intellectual and psychological work, the type of psychic labor frequently documented in fiction by Irish women writing in the wake of modernism.

The reception of *Solar Bones* offers a valuable lesson in the small but decisive changes evident in the literary field of twenty-first-century Ireland, ones that acknowledge the authority and influence of Irish women writers and suggest that the genealogy presented here can be, and will be, internalized into our understanding of contemporary Irish literature. When *Solar Bones* won the 2016 Goldsmiths Prize for experimental writing, an award for which it was nominated alongside Eimear McBride's *The Lesser Bohemians* and Anakana Schofield's *Martin John*, McCormack insisted on the crucial role played by women in the novel's success, describing the prize in part as "payback" to his agent Marianne Gunn O'Connor and to his publisher, the independent Tramp Press founded by Lisa Coen and

---

[6] Deirdre Flynn, "Holding on to 'Rites, Rhythms and Rituals': Mike McCormack's Homage to Small Town Irish Life and Death," *Representations of Loss in Irish Literature*, eds. Deirdre Flynn and Eugene O'Brien (London: Palgrave Macmillan, 2016), 37–52, 50.

Sarah Davis-Goff.[7] While he has been unabashed in acknowledging the influence of his modernist predecessors Joyce, Beckett, and Flann O'Brien, McCormack has also noted that "The generation behind me seem to be much more open to the idea of experiment," citing McBride in particular for helping contemporary writers reconcile with the legacy of Joyce's modernism: "She made no bones about the fact that she was influenced by Joyce. And you never, ever hear Irish writers saying that, because Joyce seemed to be more a luring, disabling presence in many ways. She saw him properly, as an enabling presence, and she ran with it."[8] McCormack's acknowledgment here of the experimentalism characteristic of contemporary Irish writing and its modernist sources, including not only Joyce but also McBride, signals something new in Irish letters. He gives voice to an altered relationship with the "anxiety of influence" elicited by modernism and identifies a woman writer as the spur for this transformation. By citing the inspiration of younger writers in the "generation behind me," he confirms that an accurate understanding of Irish literary tradition sometimes requires reading outside the conventional bounds of diachronic influence. His public stance, like the depiction of Agnes in the novel, offers a valuable example of how women's invocations of the modernist mode have reshaped contemporary Irish fiction, in this instance by changing the stubborn problem of Joyce's "disabling presence" into "an enabling presence."

There is much to celebrate about the current recognition awarded to many Irish women writers. But I will end here with a caution. Throughout the past century Irish women writers have faced a seemingly implacable triple-bind: if they are too vividly Irish, they are parochial; if they are too modernist, they are derivative; if they are too commercially appealing, they are apolitical or incorrectly political. Today, those binds seemed loosened, and their fiction increasingly has been celebrated, both critically and commercially, across the globe. Problem solved, it appears. But if the history of the stubborn mode teaches us little else, it is that such advancements for women writers are vulnerable, and that to sustain them, we must remain vigilant, remembering the history that preceded this "sudden" success. The logics for dismissing women's writing are highly familiar, but still potent. Today, for example, Sally Rooney's fictional portraits of millennial life have been denigrated by certain critics due to her class and racial privilege and her seemingly shallow Marxist politics.[9] But how different is this from the mid-twentieth

---

[7] Tom Morgan, "*Solar Bones* by Mike McCormack Wins the Goldsmiths Prize 2016," November 9, 2016, Goldsmiths University of London, https://www.gold.ac.uk/news/goldsmiths-prize-2016/.

[8] Justine Jordan, "Mike McCormack: 'On my fifth book I'm a debutante,'" *The Guardian*, June 24, 2017, https://www.theguardian.com/books/2017/jun/24/mike-mccormack-soundtrack-novel-death-metal-novel-solar-bones.

[9] See for example Melanie Schwartz, "How Should a Millennial Be?," *The New York Review of Books*, April 18, 2019, https://www.nybooks.com/articles/2019/04/18/sally-rooney-how-should-millennial-be/, and Jessie Tu, "Surely There Are Better Literary Heroes for Our Generation than Sally Rooney?," *Sydney Morning Herald*, August 21, 2021, https://www.smh.com.au/culture/tv-and-radio/surely-there-are-better-literary-heroes-for-our-generation-than-sally-rooney-20210817-p58jfp.html.

202   CODA: RECALIBRATING

century side-lining of Bowen as an "'aristocratic'" author of "peculiarly dated and blinkered" short stories?[10] Such critical chatter, for women writers, often has palpable and long-term negative consequences. Tracking the use of the modernist mode reminds us that any forward movement in the appreciation and recognition of women's writing, in Ireland and elsewhere, often has been characterized by backlash and relapse, a pattern that underscores the ongoing importance of the familiar project of women's literary history.[11] By closely examining a neglected literary tradition, *The Stubborn Mode* seeks to address one stubborn problem by sharpening our understanding of the force of women's writing across decades, as well as rescuing that writing from any reinvented form of marginalization.

The stubborn mode, which has surfaced across almost a full century of Irish women's writing, encourages us to think hard about the work these writers believe that literary modernism has done in the past and might do in the future. Its long history helps us to see that the "method wars" seeking to revitalize and reimagine critical reading and interpretation have always been in play, that close reading's insistent attention to the "words on the page" has evolved from its exclusionary roots and remains a valuable tool for instructing readers how better to attend to the world around us, that "presentism" and "relatability" are not cheap pedagogical tricks but tactics that can engage younger readers and demonstrate to them how literary imaginations have tackled difficult challenges across time and space. Though such lessons are not limited to a study of the modernist mode, it is my hope that the exercise of close reading Irish women's writing modeled in this book, which provides the impetus as well as the foundation for the larger sociocultural issues of this study, demonstrates why literary study matters deeply.

But the question remains, as we see with Agnes's creative work in *Solar Bones*, how do we realize the social potential of modernism in the quest to solve stubborn problems? Anne Mulhall has made a compelling argument that any notion that academic interventions can engender transformative political or cultural change is hubristic, unless academics work in tandem with social movements.[12] In closing, I would propose a middle space between the street and the novel, between external activism and internal cogitation—the classroom. Situated between the

---

[10] Elke D'hoker, "Bowen, *The Bell*, and the Late-Modernist Short Story," *Irish University Review* 51:1 (2021): 72–84, 73.

[11] See Devoney Looser, "Why I'm Still Writing Women's Literary History," *The Critical Pulse: Thirty-Six Credos by Contemporary Critics*, eds. Jeffery J. Williams and Heather Steffen (New York: Columbia University Press, 2012), 217–225. Examples calling out such patterns in the Irish literary field include Margaret Kelleher, "Long Gaze Back: We Need to Keep Our Eye on Our Contemporary Women Writers," *Irish Times*, April 12, 2018, https://www.irishtimes.com/culture/books/long-gaze-back-we-need-to-keep-an-eye-on-our-contemporary-women-writers-1.3458268; and Mary O'Donnell, "A Prosaic Lack of Women in *The Cambridge Companion to Irish Poets*," *Irish Times*, January 8, 2018, https://www.irishtimes.com/culture/books/a-prosaic-lack-of-women-in-the-cambridge-companion-to-irish-poets-1.3336413.

[12] Anne Mulhall, "The Ends of Irish Studies: On Whiteness, Academia, and Activism," *Irish University Review* 50:1 (May 2020): 94–111.

public arena and the private reading chair, the classroom can foster certain crucial recalibrations that might solve, or at the very least help to minimize, stubborn problems. Modernism cannot do anything on its own; it has to be read, analyzed, and enacted by readers, and those readers often need help parsing its formal challenges and knotty history. The rapid-fire pace of contemporary life can easily erase any command of the past, and the relentless emergence of new crises can threaten to undermine the persistence and resistance needed to solve any problem. As scholars working with students, we can teach budding citizens the invaluable skills of deep and slow critical thinking about the past in a moment overwhelmed with immediate, pithy distractions. The classroom, as Melatu Uche Okorie demonstrates in her story "Under the Awning" (2018), is no utopia; it can be riven with biases that demand notice and correction.[13] Yet our pedagogy abets the interrogation of difficult topics, which in turn threatens to unsettle long-standing privileges that benefit the few rather than the many. The efficacy of the humanities classroom in this exercise might be most visible in the current efforts to undermine the labor that sustains it, as documented by Deirdre Flynn and Sophie Corser, with these professional challenges, as Emilie Pine illustrates, often exacerbated for female academics.[14]

Today, the humanities classroom continues to provide one privileged, and admittedly old-fashioned, space to explore collectively how fiction imaginatively seeks to untangle stubborn problems.[15] It is no accident that so many of the texts analyzed here either set crucial scenes in the classroom or depict characters who are eager readers nostalgic for their schooldays. They show us that reading literature can stimulate self-awareness as well as social change. They also reveal that reading is considered dangerous, a point driven home by the dystopian future represented in Louise O'Neill's *Only Ever Yours*, where the female characters are illiterate and their access to books controlled by men. I have fashioned this study, with its reminders of how limitations placed on women have played out across the past century, and with its insistence on the important public role served by fiction, to highlight the importance of the modernist mode in Irish women's writing. I also hope immodestly that in its provocations, its intention to raise as many questions as it answers, *The Stubborn Mode* encourages future scholarship and classroom discussions to interrogate further the problems examined here and help, finally, to solve them.

[13] Melatu Uche Okorie, "Under the Awning," *This Hostel Life* (Dublin: Skein Press, 2018), 25–41.
[14] Deirdre Flynn, "On Being Precarious," *Irish University Review* 50:1 (May 2020): 51–54; Sophie Corser, "Reading Work with Claire-Louise Bennett and Doireann Ní Ghríofa," *Irish Studies Review* 31:1 (2023):1–18; Emilie Pine, "This Is Not on the Exam," *Notes to Self* (Dublin: Tramp Press, 2018), 157–181.
[15] On teaching modernist form, see Erin Kay Penner, "Making No Apologies for Difficulty: Putting Modernist Form at the Center of Classroom Discussions," *Journal of Modernist Literature* 37:2 (Winter 2014): 1–19. On the integration of the pedagogical, literary, and scholarly, see Rachel Sagner Buurma and Laura Heffernan, *The Teaching Archive: A New History for Literary Study* (Chicago: University of Chicago Press, 2021).

References

Adorno, Theodor. *Essays on Music*, edited by Richard Leppert, translated by Susan H. Gillespie. Berkeley: University of California Press, 2002.

Agamben, Giorgio. *Stanzas: Word and Phantasm in Western Culture*, translated by Ronald Martinez. Minneapolis: University of Minnesota Press, 1993.

Ahmed, Sara. *The Promise of Happiness*. Durham, NC: Duke University Press, 2010.

Akker, Robin van den, Alison Gibbons, and Timotheus Vermeulen, eds. *Metamodernism: Historicity, Affect, and Depth after Postmodernism*. London: Rowman and Littlefield International, Ltd., 2017.

Allen, Nicholas. *Modernism, Ireland, and the Civil War*. Cambridge: Cambridge University Press, 2009.

Armitstead, Claire. "Sally Rooney: I Don't Respond to Authority Very Well," interview with Sally Rooney, *The Guardian*, December 2, 2018. https://www.theguardian.com/books/2018/dec/02/sally-rooney-interview-dont-respond-authority-normal-people.

Arrington, Lauren. *Revolutionary Lives: Constance and Casimir Markievicz*. Princeton: Princeton University Press, 2016.

Asad, Talal. *Formations of the Secular: Christianity, Islam, Modernism*. Stanford: Stanford University Press, 2003.

Attridge, Derek. *J. M. Coetzee and the Ethics of Reading*. Chicago: University of Chicago Press, 2004.

Attridge, Derek. "Foreword." In *Joycean Legacies*, edited by Martha Carpentier, vii–xx. London: Palgrave Macmillan, 2015.

Attridge, Derek. "Modernism, Formal Innovation, and Affect in Some Contemporary Novels." In *Affect and Literature*, edited by Alex Houen, 249–266. Cambridge: Cambridge University Press, 2020.

Auge, Andrew J. *A Chastened Communion: Modern Irish Poetry and Catholicism*. Syracuse, NY: Syracuse University Press, 2013.

Ayo, Denise A. "Mary Colum, Modernism, and Mass Media: An Irish-Inflected Transatlantic Print Culture." In *Journal of Modern Literature* 35:4 (Summer 2012): 107–129.

Bachelard, Gaston. *The Poetics of Reverie: Childhood, Language, and the Cosmos*, translated by Daniel Russell. Boston: Beacon Press, 1969.

Backus, Margot Gayle. *The Gothic Family Romance: Heterosexuality, Child Sacrifice, and the Anglo-Irish Colonial Order*. Durham, NC: Duke University Press, 1999.

Backus, Margot Gayle and Joseph Valente. "*The Land of Spices*, the Enigmatic Signifier, and the Stylistic Invention of Lesbian (In)Visibility." In *Irish University Review* 43:1 (May 2013): 55–73.

Baker, Houston. *Modernism and the Harlem Renaissance*. Chicago: University of Chicago Press, 1987.

Barnard, Toby. *Making the Grand Figure: Lives and Possessions in Ireland, 1641–1770*. New Haven, CT: Yale University Press, 2004.

Barnard, Toby. *A Guide to Sources for the History of Material Culture in Ireland, 1500–2000*. Maynooth Research Guides for Irish Local History 10. Dublin: Four Courts Press, 2005.

Barros-Del Río, María Amor. "Sally Rooney's *Normal People*: The Millennial Novel of Formation in Recessionary Ireland." In *Irish Studies Review* 30:2 (2022): 176–192.

Battersby, Doug. *Troubling Late Modernism: Ethics, Feeling, and the Novel Form*. Oxford: Oxford University Press, 2022.

Bazarnik, Katarzyna. "A Half-Formed Thing, a Fully Formed Style: Repetition in Eimear McBride's *A Girl Is a Half-Formed Thing*." In *Studia Litteraria Universitatis Iagellonicae Cracoviensis* 13:2 (2018): 77–88.

Beale, Jenny. *Women in Ireland: Voices of Change*. Dublin: Gill and Macmillan, 1986.

"Ben Lerner and Sally Rooney in Conversation." *Theaters of Speech*, FSG Works in Progress, October 11, 2019. https://fsgworkinprogress.com/2019/10/11/theaters-of-speech/.

REFERENCES 205

Benjamin, Walter. "Surrealism." In *Reflections: Essays, Aphorisms, Autobiographical Writing*, edited by Peter Demetz, 177–192. New York: Harcourt Brace Jovanovich, 1978.

Bennett, Claire-Louise. "Claire-Louise Bennett on Writing *Pond*." In *The Irish Times*, May 26, 2015. https://www.irishtimes.com/culture/books/claire-louise-bennett-on-writing-pond-1.2226535.

Bennett, Claire-Louise. *Pond*. Dublin: Stinging Fly Press, 2015.

Bennett, Claire-Louise. *Checkout 19*. London: Jonathan Cape, 2021.

Binckes, Faith and Kathryn Laing. "A Forgotten Franco-Irish Literary Network: Hannah Lynch, Arvède Barine, and Salon Culture of Fin-de-Siècle Paris." In *Études Irlandaises* 36:2 (2011): 157–171.

Bluemel, Kristin, ed. *Intermodernism: Literary Culture in Mid-Twentieth-Century Britain*. Edinburgh: Edinburgh University Press, 2009.

Boland, Eavan. "James Joyce: The Mystery of Influence." In *Transcultural Joyce*, edited by Karen Lawrence, 11–20. Cambridge: Cambridge University Press, 1998.

Boland, Stephanie. "Bedad He Revives: Why *Solar Bones* Is a Resurrection for Irish Modernism." In *The New Statesman*, July 4, 2016. https://www.newstatesman.com/culture/books/2016/07/bedad-he-revives-why-solar-bones-resurrection-irish-modernism.

Bourke, Angela. "Legless in London: Pádraic Ó Conaire and Éamon a Búrc." In *Éire-Ireland* 38:3, 4 (2003): 54–67.

Bowen, Elizabeth, ed. *The Faber Book of Modern Stories*. London: Faber, 1936.

Bowen, Elizabeth. "Notes on Writing a Novel." In *Orion: A Miscellany 2*, edited by Rosamond Lehmann, C. Day Lewis, Denys Kilham Roberts, 18–29. London: Nicholson and Watson, 1945.

Bowen, Elizabeth. *Afterthought: Pieces about Writing*. London: Longman's, 1962.

Bowen, Elizabeth. *The Collected Stories of Elizabeth Bowen*. New York: Ecco Press, 1989.

Bowen, Elizabeth. *People, Places, Things: Essays*, edited by Allen Hepburn. Edinburgh: Edinburgh University Press, 2008.

Bowen, Zack. *Mary Lavin*. Lewisburg, PA: Bucknell University Press, 1975.

Bowler, Rebecca and Claire Drewery. Introduction. "One Hundred Years of the Stream of Consciousness." In *Literature Compass* 17:6 (June 2020): 1–10. https://doi-org.holycross.idm.oclc.org/10.1111/lic3.12570

Boxall, Peter. *Twenty-First-Century Fiction: A Critical Introduction*. Cambridge: Cambridge University Press, 2013.

Boyd, Ernest. *Ireland's Literary Renaissance*. New York: John Lane, 1916.

Bracken, Claire. "The Feminist Contemporary: The Contradictions of Critique." In *The New Irish Studies*, edited by Paige Reynolds, 144–160. Cambridge: Cambridge University Press, 2020.

Bracken, Claire and Tara Harney-Mahajan, eds. Special Issue "A Continuum of Irish Women's Writing: Reflections on the Post-Celtic Tiger Era." *LIT: Literature Interpretation Theory* 28:1 (January 2017).

Brady, Deirdre. *Literary Coteries and the Irish Women Writers' Club (1933–1958)*. Liverpool: Liverpool University Press, 2021.

Brannigan, John. "Explaining Ourselves: Hannah Berman, Jewish Nationalism and Irish Modernism." In *Irish Modernisms: Gaps, Conjectures, Possibilities*, edited by Paul Fagan, John Greaney, and Tamara Radak, 15–29. London: Bloomsbury, 2021.

Breen, Mary. "Something Understood?: Kate O'Brien and *The Land of Spices*." In *Ordinary People Dancing: Essays on Kate O'Brien*, edited by Eibhear Walshe, 167–190. Cork: Cork University Press, 1993.

Bronstein, Michaela. *Out of Context: The Uses of Modernist Fiction*. Oxford: Oxford University Press, 2018.

Brooks, Peter. *The Melodramatic Imagination: Balzac, Henry James, Melodrama, and the Mode of Excess*. New Haven: Yale University Press, 1976.

Brown, Bill. "Thing Theory." In *Critical Inquiry* 28:1 (Autumn 2001): 1–22.

Brown, Bill. "The Secret Life of Things (Virginia Woolf)." In *Other Things*, 49–78. Chicago: University of Chicago Press, 2015.

Buckley, Sarah-Anne and Caroline McGregor. "Interrogating Institutionalisation and Child Welfare: The Irish Case, 1939–1991." In *European Journal of Social Work* 22:6 (2019): 1062–1072.

Burns, Anna. *Milkman*. London: Faber and Faber, 2018.

206 REFERENCES

Buurma, Rachel Sagner and Laura Heffernan. "Poetry Explication: The Making of a Method." In *Modernism and Close Reading*, edited by David James, 69–85. Oxford: Oxford University Press, 2020.

Buurma, Rachel Sagner and Laura Heffernan. *The Teaching Archive: A New History for Literary Study*. Chicago: University of Chicago Press, 2021.

Cahill, Susan. *Irish Literature in the Celtic Tiger Years 1990–2008: Gender, Bodies, Memory*. London: Continuum, 2011.

Cahill, Susan. "My Abortion Was Not Remotely Traumatic." In *The Irish Times*, February 21, 2016. http://www.irishtimes.com/life-and-style/people/susan-cahill-my-abortion-was-not-remotely-traumatic-i-have-no-regrets-1.2542740.

Cahill, Susan. "A Girl Is a Half-formed Thing?: Girlhood, Trauma, and Resistance in Post-Tiger Irish Literature." In *LIT: Literature Interpretation Theory* 28:2 (2017): 153–171.

Cahill, Susan. "Post-Millennial Irish Fiction." In *The Oxford Handbook of Modern Irish Fiction*, edited by Liam Harte, 603–619. Oxford: Oxford University Press, 2020.

Caldwell, June. "Interview with June Caldwell," interview by Catherine Dunne, May 24, 2017. https://www.catherinedunneauthor.com/june-caldwell-room-little-darker-interview/.

Caldwell, June. *Room Little Darker*. Dublin: New Island Books, 2017.

Caneda-Cabrera, M. Teresa, ed. *Telling Truths: Evelyn Conlon and the Task of Writing*. Oxford: Peter Lang, 2023.

Caputo, John D. *The Prayers and Tears of Jacques Derrida: Religion without Religion*. Bloomington: Indiana University Press, 1997.

Carpentier, Martha C., ed. *Joycean Legacies*. London: Palgrave Macmillan, 2015.

Carr, Ruth. "Contemporary Irish Fiction." In *The Field Day Anthology of Irish Writing: Irish Women's Writings and Tradition*, vol. 5, edited by Angela Bourke, et al., 1130–1138. New York: NYU Press, 2002.

Carty, Ciaran. "Éilís Ní Dhuibhne: A Compelling Voice in Anyone's Language." In *The Irish Times*, April 27, 2016. https://www.irishtimes.com/culture/books/eilis-ni-dhuibhne-a-compelling-voice-in-anyone-s-language-1.2624994.

Casanova, Pascale. *The World Republic of Letters*, translated by Malcolm B. DeBevoise. Cambridge: Harvard University Press, 2005.

Castle, Gregory. *Reading the Modernist Bildungsroman*. Gainesville: University of Florida Press, 2006.

Castle, Gregory. "The Modernist Bildungsroman." In *A History of the Bildungsroman*, edited by Sarah Graham, 143–173. Cambridge: Cambridge University Press, 2019.

Castle, Terry. *The Female Thermometer: Eighteenth-Century Culture and the Invention of the Uncanny*. Oxford: Oxford University Press, 1995.

Central Statistics Office (Ireland). *This Is Ireland: Highlights from Census 2011*. Dublin: Stationery Office, 2012. https://www.cso.ie/en/media/csoie/census/documents/census2011pdr/Census_2011_Highlights_Part_1_web_72dpi.pdf.

Central Statistics Office (Ireland). "Internet Coverage and Usage in Ireland 2022." December 21, 2022. https://www.cso.ie/en/releasesandpublications/ep/p-isshict/internetcoverageandusageinireland2022/.

Church, Richard. "Realism and Poetry." In *John O'London's Weekly*, June 2, 1944: 93, ML/6/24.

Clare, David. "Reflections on Classic Gate Plays by Mary Manning, Christine Longford, and Maura Laverty." In *Irish Archives: Journal of the Irish Society for Archives* 25 (2018): 28–34.

Clear, Caitríona. *Social Change and Everyday Life in Ireland, 1850–1922*. Manchester: Manchester University Press, 2007.

Cleary, Joe. "Domestic Troubles: Tragedy and the Northern Ireland Conflict." In *South Atlantic Quarterly* 98:3 (1999): 501–537.

Cleary, Joe. "European, American, and Imperial Conjunctures." In *The Cambridge Companion to Irish Modernism*, edited by Joe Cleary, 35–50. Cambridge: Cambridge University Press, 2014.

Cleary, Joe. "Introduction." In *The Cambridge Companion to Irish Modernism*, edited by Joe Cleary, 1–18. Cambridge: Cambridge University Press, 2014.

REFERENCES 207

Cliff, Brian. "Class and Multiplicity in *One by One in the Darkness*." In *Deirdre Madden: New Critical Perspectives*, edited by Anne Fogarty and Marisol Morales-Ladrón, 66–79. Manchester: Manchester University Press, 2022.

Collins, Lauren. "Sally Rooney Gets in Your Head." In *The New Yorker*, January 7, 2019. https://www.newyorker.com/magazine/2019/01/07/sally-rooney-gets-in-your-head.

Collins, Lucy. "Poetry, 1920–1970." In *A History of Modern Irish Women's Literature*, edited by Heather Ingman and Clíona Ó Gallchoir, 167–186. Cambridge: Cambridge University Press, 2018.

Colum, Mary. *Life and the Dream*. New York: Doubleday, 1947.

Conlon, Evelyn. *Telling: New and Selected Stories*. Belfast: Blackstaff Press, 2000, 45–57.

Conlon, Evelyn. "Interview with Evelyn Conlon," interview by Caitriona Moloney. In *Irish Women Writers Speak Out: Voices from the Field*, edited by Caitriona Moloney and Helen Thompson, 17–29. Syracuse: Syracuse University Press, 2003.

Connolly, Claire. "Watery Modernism? Mike McCormack's *Solar Bones* and W. B. Yeats's *John Sherman*." In *The Edinburgh Companion to Irish Modernism*, edited by Maud Ellmann, Siân White, and Vicki Mahaffey, 452–469. Edinburgh: Edinburgh University Press, 2021.

Conradi, Peter J. *Iris Murdoch: A Life*. New York: Norton, 2001.

Constitution of Ireland. *Bunreacht Na hÉireann*. Dublin: Oifig an tSoláthair, 1937.

Corkery, Daniel. *Synge and Anglo-Irish Literature: A Study*. Cork: Cork University Press, 1931.

Corry, John. "About New York: An Irish View of City's Charms." In *New York Times (1923–Current file)*, January 10, 1975. ProQuest Historical Newspapers: *The New York Times*: 25.

Coughlan, Patricia. "Irish Literature and Feminism in Postmodernity." In *Hungarian Journal of English and American Studies* 10:1, 2 (2004): 175–202.

Corser, Sophie. "Reading Work with Claire-Louise Bennett and Doireann Ní Ghríofa." In *Irish Studies Review* 31:1 (2023): 1–18.

Cousins, James and Margaret Cousins. *We Two Together*. Madras: Ganesh & Co., 1950.

Crary, Jonathan. *Suspensions of Perception: Attention, Spectacle, and Modern Culture*. Cambridge, MA: MIT Press, 1999.

Crispin, Jessa. "*Normal People* Is Little More Than a Gutless Soap Opera for Millennials." In *The Guardian*, May 5, 2020. https://www.theguardian.com/commentisfree/2020/may/05/sally-rooney-normal-people-hulu-bbc-soap-opera.

Cronin, Michael G. *Impure Thoughts: Sexuality, Catholicism, and Literature in Twentieth-Century Ireland*. Manchester: Manchester University Press, 2012.

"Dancer's Dancing." In *Publisher's Weekly*, February 1, 2000. https://www.publishersweekly.com/978-0-85640-650-8.

D'Arcy, Michael and Mathias Nilges, eds. *The Contemporaneity of Modernism: Literature, Media, Culture*. New York: Routledge, 2016.

D'hoker, Elke. *Irish Women Writers and the Modern Short Story*. London: Palgrave Macmillan, 2016.

D'hoker, Elke. "Bowen, *The Bell*, and the Late-Modernist Short Story." In *Irish University Review* 51:1 (2021): 72–84.

D'hoker, Elke. "A Forgotten Irish Modernist: Ethel Colburn Mayne." In *Irish Modernisms: Gaps, Conjectures, Possibilities*, edited by Paul Fagan, John Greaney, and Tamara Radak, 29–42. London: Bloomsbury, 2021.

Dalsimer, Adele. *Kate O'Brien: A Critical Study*. Boston: Twayne, 1990.

Daly, Mary. "'Turn on the Tap': The State, Irish Women, and Running Water." In *Women and Irish History*, edited by Maryann Valiulis and Mary O'Dowd, 206–219. Dublin: Wolfhound Press, 1997.

Daly, Selena. "Mary Swanzy (1882–1978): A Futurist Painter from Ireland." In *International Yearbook of Futurism Studies* 5, edited by Günter Berghaus, 70–86. Berlin: de Gruyter, 2015.

Dango, Michael. *Crisis Style: The Aesthetics of Repair*. Palo Alto: Stanford University Press, 2021.

Darling, Orlaith. "'It Was Our Great Generational Decision': Capitalism, the Internet, and Depersonalization in Some Millennial Irish Women's Writing." In *Critique: Studies in Contemporary Fiction* 62:5 (2021): 538–551.

Darling, Orlaith. "'[The] Immediate Heft of Bodily and Civic Catastrophe': The Body (Politic) in Crisis in Mike McCormack's *Solar Bones*." In *Irish Studies Review* 29:3 (June 2021): 334–347.

208   REFERENCES

Darling, Orlaith, Liam Harrison, and Dearbhaile Houston, eds. Special Issue on Women Writing Work. *Irish Studies Review* 31:1 (2023).

Darling, Orlaith and Dearbhaile Houston, eds. Special Issue on Twenty-First-Century Irish Women's Writing. *Alluvium* 9:1 (Winter 2021).

Davis, Alex. "'Wilds to Alter, Forms to Build': The Writings of Sheila Wingfield." In *Irish University Review* 31:2 (2001): 334–352.

Deane, Seamus. *Celtic Revivals: Essays in Modern Irish Literature, 1880–1980.* London: Faber & Faber, 1985.

Deane, Seamus. *Strange Country: Modernity and Nationhood in Irish Writing since 1790.* Oxford: Oxford University Press, 1997.

Delap, Lucy. *The Feminist Avant-Garde: Transatlantic Encounters of the Early Twentieth Century.* Cambridge: Cambridge University Press, 2009.

DeMeester, Karen. "Trauma and Recovery in Virginia Woolf's *Mrs. Dalloway.*" In *Modern Fiction Studies* 44:3 (Fall 1998): 649–73.

De Paor, Louis. "Irish Language Modernisms." In *The Cambridge Companion to Irish Modernism,* edited by Joe Cleary, 161–173. Cambridge: Cambridge University Press, 2014.

De Valera, Éamon. "The Ireland That We Dreamed Of" (1943). In *Speeches and Statements by Eamon de Valera, 1917–1973,* edited by Maurice Moynihan, 466–469. New York: St. Martin's Press, 1980.

Devers, A. N. "Anna Burns' Booker-winning 'Milkman' Isn't a Difficult Read; It's a Triumph." In *The Los Angeles Times,* January 4, 2019. https://www.latimes.com/books/la-ca-jc-anna-burns-milkman-review-20190104-story.html.

Dillon, Brian. *Suppose a Sentence.* New York: New York Review of Books, 2020.

Dinnen, Zara. *The Digital Banal: New Media and American Literature and Culture.* New York: Columbia University Press, 2018.

Dobbins, Gregory. *Lazy Idle Schemers: Irish Modernism and the Cultural Politics of Idleness.* Dublin: Field Day, 2010.

Donnelly, James S. "Opposing the 'Modern World': The Cult of the Virgin Mary in Ireland, 1965-85." *Éire-Ireland* 40:1 (2005): 183–245.

Donoghue, Emma. *Hood.* New York: Harper Perennial, 2011.

Dougherty, Jane Elizabeth. "'Never Tear the Linnet from the Leaf': The Feminist Intertextuality of Edna O'Brien's *Down by the River.*" In *Frontiers: A Journal of Women Studies* 31:3 (2010): 77–102.

Dougherty, Jane Elizabeth. "Edna O'Brien and the Politics of Belatedness." In *The Oxford Handbook of Modern Irish Fiction,* edited by Liam Harte, 289–304. Oxford: Oxford University Press, 2020.

Dunn, Carly J. "The Novels of Deirdre Madden: Expanding the Canon of Irish Literature with Women's Fiction." PhD dissertation from Indiana University of Pennsylvania, 2014.

Eagleton, Terry. *Heathcliff and the Great Hunger: Studies in Irish Culture.* London: Verso, 1995.

Eliot, T. S. *The Use of Poetry and the Use of Criticism.* London: Faber and Faber, 1933.

Eliot, T. S. "*Ulysses,* Order, and Myth (1923)." In *Selected Prose of T. S. Eliot,* edited by Frank Kermode, 175–178. New York: Harcourt, Brace & Co., 1975.

Ellmann, Richard. *James Joyce.* Oxford: Oxford University Press, 1982.

Enright, Anne. *The Gathering.* New York: Black Cat, 2007.

Enright, Anne. "An Interview with Anne Enright." *Anne Enright, Visions and Revisions: Irish Writers in Their Time,* edited by Claire Bracken and Susan Cahill, 13–32. Dublin: Irish Academic Press, 2011.

Enright, Anne. "It's Time for a Sharp Inhale, People." In *The Irish Times,* September 1, 2018. https://www.irishtimes.com/culture/books/it-is-time-for-a-sharp-inhale-people-sally-rooney-s-normal-people-is-superb-1.3608184.

Enright, Anne. "Call Yourself George: Gender Representation in the Irish Literary Landscape." In *No Authority: Writings from the Laureateship,* 73–87. Dublin: University College Dublin Press, 2019.

Estévez-Saá, Margarita. "Deirdre Madden's Portraits of the Woman Artist in Fiction: Beyond Ireland and the Self." In *Nordic Irish Studies* 10 (2011): 49–62.

Esty, Jed. *Unseasonable Youth: Modernism, Colonialism, and the Fiction of Development.* Oxford: Oxford University Press, 2012.

Esty, Jed and Colleen Lye. "Peripheral Realisms Now." In *Modern Language Quarterly* 73:3 (September 2012): 269–288.

REFERENCES 209

Fagan, Paul, John Greaney, and Tamara Radak, eds. *Irish Modernisms: Gaps, Conjectures, Possibilities.* London: Bloomsbury, 2021.

Fahey, Tony. "Catholicism and Industrial Society in Ireland." In *Proceedings of the British Academy* 79 (1992): 241–263.

Falci, Eric and Paige Reynolds, eds. *Irish Literature in Transition, 1980–2020,* vol. 6, series editors Claire Connolly and Marjorie Howes. Cambridge: Cambridge University Press, 2020.

Ferriter, Diarmaid. *The Transformation of Ireland, 1900–2000.* London: Profile Books, 2004.

Ferriter, Diarmaid. *Occasions of Sin: Sex and Society in Modern Ireland.* London: Profile Books, 2009.

Fisk, Gloria. "'What Are Feelings for?'" In "Reading Sally Rooney," ed. Gloria Fisk, *Post45,* June 15, 2020. http://post45.org/2020/06/what-are-feelings-for/.

Fitzgerald, F. Scott. *The Great Gatsby.* New York: Scribner, 1925.

Fitzgerald, William. *Spiritual Modalities: Prayer as Rhetoric and Performance.* University Park, PA: Penn State University Press, 2012.

Fitzpatrick, Lisa. "Contemporary Feminist Protest in Ireland: #MeToo in Irish Theatre." In *Irish University Review* 50:1 (May 2020): 82–93.

Flack, Leah Culligan. *James Joyce and Classical Modernism.* London: Bloomsbury, 2020.

Flood, Alison and Claire Armitstead. "Anna Burns Wins Man Booker Prize for 'incredibly original' *Milkman.*" In *The Guardian,* October 16, 2018. https://www.theguardian.com/books/2018/oct/16/anna-burns-wins-man-booker-prize-for-incredibly-original-milkman.

Flynn, Deirdre. "Holding on to 'Rites, Rhythms and Rituals': Mike McCormack's Homage to Small Town Irish Life and Death." In *Representations of Loss in Irish Literature,* edited by Deirdre Flynn and Eugene O'Brien, 37–52. London: Palgrave Macmillan, 2016.

Flynn, Deirdre. "On Being Precarious." In *Irish University Review* 50:1 (May 2020): 51–54.

Flynn, Deirdre and Ciara L. Murphy, eds. *Austerity and Irish Women's Writing and Culture, 1980–2020.* London: Routledge, 2022.

Fogarty, Anne. "Discontinuities: *Tales from Bective Bridge* and the Modernist Short Story Tradition." In *Mary Lavin,* edited by Elke D'hoker, 49–64. Newbridge: Irish Academic Press, 2013.

Fogarty, Anne. "Women and Modernism." In *The Cambridge Companion to Irish Modernism,* edited by Joe Cleary, 147–160. Cambridge: Cambridge University Press, 2014.

Fogarty, Anne. "'It was like a baby crying': Representations of the Child in Contemporary Irish Fiction." In *Journal of Irish Studies* 30 (October 2015): 13–26.

Fogarty, Anne. "'A World of Hotels and Gaols': Women Novelists and the Space of Irish Modernism, 1930–1932." In *Modernist Afterlives in Irish Literature and Culture,* edited by Paige Reynolds, 11–22. London: Anthem Press, 2016.

Foster, John Wilson. "The Irish Renaissance, 1890–1940: Prose in English." In *The Cambridge History of Irish Literature,* edited by Margaret Kelleher and Philip O'Leary, vol. 2: 113–180. Cambridge: Cambridge University Press, 2006.

Foster, R. F. *Vivid Faces: The Revolutionary Generation in Ireland, 1890–1923.* London: Penguin Press, 2015.

Freud, Sigmund. "Creative Writers and Day-Dreaming" (1908). In *The Standard Edition of the Complete Psychological Works of Sigmund Freud,* translated and edited by James Strachey, 141–154. London: Hogarth Press: The Institute of Psycho-Analysis, 1953–74.

Gallagher, Conor. "Publications on Abortion Coming Off Banned Books List." In *The Irish Times,* July 19, 2019. https://www.irishtimes.com/news/health/publications-on-abortion-coming-off-banned-books-list-1.3960794.

Gallix, Andrew. "*Pond* by Claire-Louise Bennett Review." In *The Guardian,* November 18, 2015. https://www.theguardian.com/books/2015/nov/18/pond-claire-louise-bennett-review.

Garner, Dwight. "'Milkman' Slogs Through Political and Cultural Tensions in Northern Ireland." In *The New York Times,* December 3, 2018. https://www.nytimes.com/2018/12/03/books/review-milkman-anna-burns-man-booker-prize-winner.html.

Gettelman, Debra. "'Making Out' *Jane Eyre.*" In *ELH* 74:3 (Fall 2007): 557–581.

Gillespie, Elgy. "Our Edna – A Song of S.W.3." In *The Irish Times,* June 10, 1972, in *Conversations with Edna O'Brien,* edited by Alice Hughes Kersnowski, 13–17. Jackson, MS: University Press of Mississippi, 2014.

210 REFERENCES

Gillespie, Michael Patrick. "Edna O'Brien and the Lives of James Joyce." In *Wild Colonial Girl: Essays on Edna O'Brien*, edited by Lisa Colletta and Maureen O'Connor, 78–91. Madison, WI: University of Wisconsin Press, 2006.

Gilligan, Ruth. "Eimear McBride's Ireland: A Case for Periodisation and the Dangers of Marketing Modernism." In *English Studies* 99:7 (2018): 775–792.

Gilmartin, Sarah. "*Pond* by Claire-Louise Bennett Review." In *The Irish Times*, May 2, 2015. https://www.irishtimes.com/culture/books/pond-by-claire-louise-bennett-review-a-rewarding-voyage-into-the-interior-1.2196696.

Gledhill, Christine and Linda Williams, eds. *Melodrama Unbound: Across History, Media, and National Cultures*. New York: Columbia University Press, 2018.

Gomel, Elana. "'Rotting Time': Genre Fiction and the Avant-Garde." In *The Routledge Companion to Experimental Literature*, edited by Joe Bray, Alison Gibbons, and Brian McHale, 393–406. London: Routledge, 2014.

Gould, Rebecca Ruth. "The Aesthetic Terrain of Settler Colonialism: Katherine Mansfield and Anton Chekhov's Natives." In *Journal of Postcolonial Writing* 55:1 (2019): 48–65.

Gray, Katherine Martin. "The Attic LIPs: Feminist Pamphleteering for the New Ireland." In *Border Crossings: Irish Women Writers and National Identity*, edited by Kathryn Kirkpatrick, 269–298. Tuscaloosa: University of Alabama Press, 2000.

Guppy, Shusha. "Edna O'Brien, The Art of Fiction: 82." In *The Paris Review* 92 (Summer 1984). https://www.theparisreview.org/interviews/2978/the-art-of-fiction-no-82-edna-obrien.

Hadley, Elaine. *Melodramatic Tactics: Theatricalized Dissent in the English Marketplace, 1800–1885*. Stanford: Stanford University Press, 1995.

Hand, Derek. *A History of the Irish Novel*. Cambridge: Cambridge University Press, 2011.

Harkin, Keelan. "An Uncertain Event: The Politics of Reliability in Anne Enright's *The Gathering*." In *Textual Practice* 35:1 (2021): 57–72.

Harrison, Liam. "Mike McCormack's Style of Post-Mortem Modernism." In *Textual Practice* (2022): 1–29. https://doi.org/10.1080/0950236X.2022.2111709.

Hart, Matthew. "Wet Newspaper." In "Reading Sally Rooney," ed. Gloria Fisk, *Post45*, June 15, 2020. https://post45.org/sections/contemporaries/reading-sally-rooney/.

Harte, Liam. "Mourning Remains Unresolved: Trauma and Survival in Anne Enright's *The Gathering*." In *LIT: Literature Interpretation Theory* 21:2 (2010): 187–204.

Harte, Liam. *Reading the Contemporary Irish Novel, 1987–2007*. Chichester: Wiley-Blackwell, 2014.

Harte, Liam and Michael Parker. "Refiguring Identities: Recent Northern Irish Fiction." *Contemporary Irish Fiction: Themes, Tropes, Theories*, edited by Liam Harte and Michael Parker, 232–254. Basingstoke: Macmillan, 2000.

Harvey, Alison. "Irish Aestheticism in Fin-de-Siècle Women's Writing: Art, Realism, and the Nation." In *Modernism/modernity* 21:3 (September 2014): 805–826.

Haycock, David. "Edna O'Brien Talks to David Haycock about Her New Novel, *A Pagan Place* (1970)." In *Conversations with Edna O'Brien*, edited by Alice Hughes Kersnowski, 8–12. Jackson, MS: University Press of Mississippi, 2014.

Hayes, Katy. "Women's Writes." In *The Sunday Times*, September 6, 2015. https://www.thetimes.co.uk/article/womens-writes-znb8gnn9czb.

Hayot, Eric. "Critical Distance and the Crisis in Criticism (2007)." *Erichayot.org* (blog), November 11, 2013. http://erichayot.org/uncategorized/critical-distance-and-the-crisis-in-criticism-2007/.

Henry, Holly. *Virginia Woolf and the Discourse of Science*. Cambridge: Cambridge University Press, 2003.

Herbert, George. "Prayer (I)." In *The Complete English Poems*, edited by John Tobin, 45–46. London: Penguin Books, 1991.

Hill, Myrtle and Margaret Ward. "Conflicting Rights: The Struggle for Female Citizenship in Northern Ireland." In *Women and Citizenship in Britain and Ireland in the Twentieth Century*, edited by Esther Breitenbach and Pat Thane, 113–138. London: Continuum, 2010.

Hobson, Suzanne. *Angels of Modernism: Religion, Culture, Aesthetics 1910–1960*. London: Palgrave Macmillan, 2011.

REFERENCES   211

Hu, Jane. "Race and Romantic Realism." In "Reading Sally Rooney," ed. Gloria Fisk, *Post45*, June 15, 2020. https://post45.org/2020/06/race-and-romantic-realism/.

Humble, Nicola. *The Feminine Middlebrow Novel, 1920s–1950s: Class, Domesticity, and Bohemianism.* Oxford: Oxford University Press, 2001.

Hunter, Adrian. *The Cambridge Introduction to the Short Story in English.* Cambridge: Cambridge University Press, 2007.

Hutton, Clare. "The Moment and Technique of *Milkman*." In *Essays in Criticism* 69:3 (July 2019): 349–371.

Hutton, Clare. "Why Anna Burns' *Milkman* Is Such a Phenomenon." OUPblog, July 31, 2019. https://blog.oup.com/2019/07/why-anna-burns-milkman-is-such-a-phenomenon/.

Huyssen, Andreas. *After the Great Divide: Modernism, Mass Culture, Postmodernism.* Bloomington: Indiana UP, 1986.

Inglis, Tom. *Moral Monopoly: The Rise and Fall of the Catholic Church in Modern Ireland.* Dublin: University College Dublin Press, 1998.

Ingman, Heather. *A History of the Irish Short Story.* Cambridge: Cambridge University Press, 2009.

Ingman, Heather. *Irish Women's Fiction: From Edgeworth to Enright.* Dublin: Irish Academic Press, 2013.

Irish Women's Writing Network (1880–1920). https://irishwomenswritingnetwork.com/.

James, David, ed., *The Legacies of Modernism: Historicising Postwar and Contemporary Fiction.* Cambridge: Cambridge University Press, 2012.

James, David. *Modernist Futures: Innovation and Inheritance in the Contemporary Novel.* Cambridge: Cambridge University Press, 2012.

James, David. "Introduction." In *Modernism and Close Reading*, edited by David James, 1–18. Oxford: Oxford University Press, 2020.

James, David and Urmila Seshagiri. "Metamodernism: Narratives of Continuity and Revolution." In *PMLA* 129:1 (2014): 87–100.

James, William. *The Varieties of Religious Experience: A Study in Human Nature.* New York: Modern Library, 1902.

Jameson, Fredric. *The Political Unconscious: Narrative as a Socially Symbolic Act.* Ithaca: Cornell University Press, 1981.

Jameson, Fredric. "Magical Narratives: Romance as Genre." In *New Literary History* 7:1 (Autumn 1975): 135–163.

Jarrett, Kylie. "Digital Ireland: Leprechaun Economics, Silicon Docks, and Crisis." In *Routledge International Handbook of Irish Studies*, edited by Renée Fox, Mike Cronin, and Brian Ó Conchubhair, 188–198. London: Routledge, 2021.

Jarvis, Claire. "Contemporary Clothing: Is Sally Rooney a Millennial Novelist or a Nineteenth-Century One?" In *Slate*, April 22, 2019. https://slate.com/culture/2019/04/sally-rooney-normal-people-austen-james-lawrence.html.

Jarvis, Claire. "The Sweet Stuff." In "Reading Sally Rooney," ed. Gloria Fisk, *Post45*, June 15, 2020. https://post45.org/sections/contemporaries/reading-sally-rooney/.

Jarząb-Napierała, Joanna. "Retromodernism: New 'Structure of Feeling' in Mike McCormack's *Solar Bones*." In *New Hibernia Review* 23:3 (Autumn 2019): 55–68.

Jordan, Justine. "Mike McCormack: 'On my fifth book I'm a debutante.'" In *The Guardian*, June 24, 2017. https://www.theguardian.com/books/2017/jun/24/mike-mccormack-soundtrack-novel-death-metal-novel-solar-bones.

Joyce, James. *Dubliners: Viking Critical Edition*, edited by Robert Scholes and A. Walton Litz. New York: Penguin, 1969.

Joyce, James. *Ulysses.* New York: Vintage, 1986.

Joyce, James. *A Portrait of the Artist as a Young Man*, edited by Seamus Deane. New York: Penguin Classics, 2003.

Joyce, Simon. "Impressionism, Naturalism, Symbolism: Trajectories of Anglo-Irish Fiction at the Fin-de-Siècle." In *Modernism/modernity* 21:3 (September 2014): 787–803.

Katz, Tamar. *Impressionist Subjects: Gender, Interiority, and Modernist Fiction in England.* Champaign: University of Illinois Press, 2000.

212 REFERENCES

Keane, Damien. *Ireland and the Problem of Information: Irish Writing, Radio, Late Modernist Communication*. University Park, PA: The Pennsylvania State University Press, 2014.

Kearney, Richard. *Transitions: Narratives in Modern Irish Culture*. Manchester: Manchester University Press, 1988.

Kellaway, Kate. "Eimear McBride: Writing is Painful—but It's the Closest You Can Get to Joy." In *The Observer*, August 28, 2016. https://www.theguardian.com/books/2016/aug/28/eimer-mcbride-interview-lesser-bohemians-writing-never-stops-being-painful.

Kelleher, Margaret. "Long Gaze Back: We Need to Keep Our Eye on Our Contemporary Women Writers." In *The Irish Times*, April 12, 2018. https://www.irishtimes.com/culture/books/long-gaze-back-we-need-to-keep-an-eye-on-our-contemporary-women-writers-1.3458268.

Kelleher, Margaret and Karen Wade. "Irish Literary Feminism and its Digital Archive(s)." In *Technology in Irish Literature and Culture*, edited by Margaret Kelleher and James O'Sullivan, 235–252. Cambridge: Cambridge University Press, 2022.

Kelly, Aaron. *Twentieth-Century Irish Literature: A Reader's Guide to Essential Criticism*. London: Palgrave Macmillan, 2008.

Kelly, Maeve. *Orange Horses*. Dublin: Tramp Press, 2016.

Kennedy, Sinéad. "Irish Women and the Celtic Tiger Economy." In *The End of History: Critical Reflections on the Celtic Tiger*, edited by Colin Coulter and Steve Coleman, 95–109. Manchester: Manchester University Press, 2003.

Kenner, Hugh. *Ulysses*. Baltimore: Johns Hopkins University Press, 1987.

Kenner, Hugh. *Joyce's Voices*. Berkeley: University of California Press, 1978.

Kenny, Eva. "Christmas Story, a New Story by Eva Kenny." In *The Irish Times*, December 27, 2022. https://www.irishtimes.com/culture/books/2022/12/27/christmas-story-a-new-story-by-eva-kenny/.

Keown, Edwina. "New Horizons: Irish Aviation, Lemass and Deferred Anglo-Irish Modernism in Elizabeth Bowen's *A World of Love*." In *Irish Modernism: Origins, Contexts, Publics*, edited by Edwina Keown and Carol Taaffe, 217–236. Oxford: Lang, 2010.

Kiberd, Declan. *Irish Classics*. Cambridge, MA: Harvard University Press, 2001.

Kiberd, Declan. "Reading *The Dancers Dancing*." In Éilís Ní Dhuibhne, *The Dancers Dancing*, 293–296. Dublin: Blackstaff Press, 1999.

Kinmonth, Claudia. *Irish Country Furniture and Furnishings 1700–2000*. Cork: Cork University Press, 2020.

Kirsch, Adam. *The Global Novel: Writing the World in the 21st Century*. Columbia: Columbia University Press, 2016.

Knepper, Wendy and Sharae Deckard. "Towards a Radical World Literature: Experimental Writing in a Globalizing World." In *ariel: A Review of International English Literature* 47:1, 2 (2016): 1–25.

Koepnick, Lutz. *On Slowness: Toward an Aesthetic of the Contemporary*. New York: Columbia University Press, 2014.

Kornbluh, Anna. *The Order of Forms: Realism, Formalism, and Social Space*. Chicago: University of Chicago Press, 2019.

Kramnick, Jonathan and Anahid Nersessian. "Form and Explanation." In *Critical Inquiry* 43 (Spring 2017): 650–669.

Lavin, Mary. "Interview with Mary Lavin," interview by Tom A. Gullason, November 3, 1967, ML/5/3 dft. C, 31.

Lavin, Mary. *The Stories of Mary Lavin*, vols. 1–3, London: Constable, 1974.

Lea, Richard. "An Unexpected Ending for Literary Progress." In *The Guardian*, February 6, 2015. https://www.theguardian.com/books/booksblog/2015/feb/06/an-unexpected-ending-for-literary-progress.

Lefebvre, Henri. *Everyday Life in the Modern World*, translated by Sacha Rabinovitch. New Brunswick, NJ: Transaction Publishers, 1984.

Lehner, Stefanie. "Nation: Reconciliation and the Politics of Friendship in Post-Troubles Literature." In *The New Irish Studies*, edited by Paige Reynolds, 47–62. Cambridge: Cambridge University Press, 2020.

REFERENCES 213

Lehner, Stefanie. "'Images ... at the absolute edge of memory': Memory and Temporality in *Hidden Symptoms, One by One in the Darkness, and Time Present and Time Past.*" In *Deirdre Madden: New Critical Perspectives*, edited by Anne Fogarty and Marisol Morales-Ladrón, 17–31. Manchester: Manchester University Press, 2022.

Letts, W. M. *The Rough Way.* Milwaukee: The Young Churchman Co., 1912.

Levine, Caroline. *Forms: Whole, Rhythm, Hierarchy, Network.* Princeton: Princeton University Press, 2015.

Lewis, Cara. *Dynamic Form: How Intermediality Made Modernism.* Ithaca, NY: Cornell University Press, 2020.

Lewis, Pericles. *Religious Experience and the Modernist Novel.* Cambridge: Cambridge University Press, 2010.

Liles, Ronald, dir. *For Love and Money.* (1968) In *Seoda: Treasures from the Irish Film Archive 1948–1970.* DVD. Irish Film Institute, 2009.

Looser, Devoney. "Why I'm Still Writing Women's Literary History." In *The Critical Pulse: Thirty-Six Credos by Contemporary Critics*, edited by Jeffrey Williams and Heather H. Steffen, 217–225. New York: Columbia University Press, 2012.

Lynch, Claire. *Cyber Ireland: Text, Image, Culture.* London: Palgrave Macmillan, 2014.

Lynch, Claire. "Consoling Machines in Contemporary Fiction." In *Technology in Irish Literature and Culture*, edited by Margaret Kelleher and James O'Sullivan, 253–266. Cambridge: Cambridge University Press, 2022.

Madden, Deirdre. "Looking for Home: Time, Place, Memory." In *Canadian Journal of Irish Studies* 26:27 (Fall 2000/Spring 2001): 25–33.

Madden, Deirdre. *Molly Fox's Birthday.* London: Faber & Faber, 2008.

Madden, Deirdre. "Interview with Deirdre Madden," interview by Christina Patterson, in *The Guardian*, June 14, 2013: 13.

Magennis, Caroline. *Northern Irish Writing after the Troubles: Intimacies, Affects, Pleasures.* London: Bloomsbury, 2021.

Maher, Eamon. "Love, Loss of Faith, and Kate O'Brien." In *Doctrine and Life* 49:2 (February 1999): 87–97.

Majumdar, Saikat. *Prose of the World: Modernism and the Banality of Empire.* New York: Columbia University Press, 2013.

Malone, Patricia. "Measures of Obliviousness and Disarming Obliqueness in Anna Burns' *Milkman.*" In *Textual Practice* 36:7 (2021): 1–32.

Mao, Douglas. *Solid Objects: Modernism and the Test of Production.* Princeton: Princeton University Press, 1998.

Mao, Douglas, ed. *The New Modernist Studies.* Cambridge: Cambridge University Press, 2021.

Mao, Douglas and Rebecca L. Walkowitz. "The New Modernist Studies." In *PMLA* 123:3 (2008): 737–748.

Marcus, David and Terence Smith, eds. *Irish Writing: The Magazine of Contemporary Irish Literature*, vols. 1–37 (1946–1957).

Marcus, Laura. "The Legacies of Modernism." In *The Cambridge Companion to the Modernist Novel*, edited by Morag Shiach, 82–98. Cambridge: Cambridge University Press, 2007.

Martin, Theodore. *Contemporary Drift: Genre, Historicism, and the Problem of the Present.* New York: Columbia University Press, 2017.

Matz, Jesse. *Literary Impressionism and Modernist Aesthetics.* Cambridge: Cambridge University Press, 2001.

Matz, Jesse. *Lasting Impressions: The Legacies of Impressionism in Contemporary Culture.* New York: Columbia University Press, 2017.

McBride, Eimear. "Interview with Eimear McBride," interview by David Collard. In *The White Review*, May 2014. http://www.thewhitereview.org/feature/interview-with-eimear-mcbride/.

McBride, Eimear. "My Hero: Eimear McBride on James Joyce." In *The Guardian*, June 6, 2014. https://www.theguardian.com/books/2014/jun/06/my-hero-eimear-mcbride-james-joyce.

McBride, Eimear. *A Girl Is a Half-formed Thing.* New York: Hogarth, 2015.

214 REFERENCES

McBride, Eimear. "Joyce, Joy, and Enjoying *Ulysses* Still." In *The Irish Times*, December 17, 2022. https://www.irishtimes.com/culture/books/2022/12/17/eimear-mcbride-joyce-joy-and-enjoying-ulysses-still/.

McCoole, Sinéad. *No Ordinary Women: Irish Female Activists in the Revolutionary Years, 1900–1923.* Dublin: O'Brien Press, 2003.

McCormack, Mike. *Solar Bones.* Dublin: Tramp Press, 2016.

McCormick, Kathleen. "Reproducing Molly Bloom: A Revisionist History of the Reception of 'Penelope,' 1922–1970." In *Molly Blooms: A Polylogue on "Penelope" and Cultural Studies,* edited by Richard Pearce, 17–39. Madison: University of Wisconsin Press, 1994.

McCormick, Leanne. *Regulating Sexuality: Women in Twentieth-Century Northern Ireland.* Manchester: Manchester University Press, 2009.

McCrea, Barry. "The Novel in Ireland and the Language Question: Joyce's Complex Legacy." In *Logos: A Journal of Modern Society and Culture* (2022). https://logosjournal.com/2022/the-novel-in-ireland-and-the-language-question-joyces-complex-legacy/.

McDiarmid, Lucy. *The Irish Art of Controversy.* Ithaca: Cornell University Press, 2005.

McDonald, Rónán. "The Irish Revival and Modernism." In *The Cambridge Companion to Irish Modernism,* edited by Joe Cleary, 51–62. Cambridge: Cambridge University Press, 2014.

McEvoy, Tara. "How a New Wave of Irish Women Writers Are Making Their Mark." In *Vogue,* March 2, 2019. https://www.vogue.co.uk/article/irish-female-writers-sally-rooney-anna-burns-emilie-pine.

McFalone, Kim. "#IBelieveHer: Representations of Rape Culture in Northern Ireland's Media Surrounding the 2018 Ulster Rugby Rape Trial." In *International Journal of Media and Cultural Politics* 17:3 (September 2021): 291–314.

McGlynn, Mary M. *Broken Irelands: Literary Form in Post-Crash Irish Fiction.* Syracuse: Syracuse University Press, 2022.

McGovern, Kelly J. S. "'No Right to Be a Child': Irish Girlhood and Queer Time in Éilís Ní Dhuibhne's *The Dancers Dancing.*" In *Éire-Ireland* 44:1, 2 (Spring/Summer 2009): 242–264.

McHale, Brian and Len Platt, eds. *The Cambridge History of Postmodern Literature.* Cambridge: Cambridge University Press, 2016.

McMinn, Joseph. "Versions of Banville: Versions of Modernism." In *Contemporary Irish Fiction: Themes, Tropes, Theories,* edited by Liam Harte and Michael Parker, 79–99. London: Palgrave Macmillan, 2000.

McWilliams, Ellen. "James Joyce and the Lives of Edna O'Brien." In *Modernist Afterlives in Irish Literature and Culture,* edited by Paige Reynolds, 49–60. London: Anthem Press, 2016.

Meagher, John. "The Sally Rooney Industry: Beautiful Sales, Where Are You?" In *Irish Independent,* September 4, 2021. https://www.independent.ie/entertainment/books/the-sally-rooney-industry-beautiful-sales-where-are-you-40815128.html.

Meaney, Gerardine. *Gender, Ireland, and Cultural Change: Race, Sex, and Nation.* London: Routledge, 2010.

Meaney, Gerardine. "Fiction, 1922–1960." In *A History of Modern Irish Women's Literature,* edited by Heather Ingman and Clíona Ó Gallchoir, 187–203. Cambridge: Cambridge University Press, 2018.

Meaney, Gerardine. "A Disruptive Modernist: Kate O'Brien and Irish Women's Writing." In *A History of Irish Modernism,* edited by Gregory Castle and Patrick Bixby, 276–291. Cambridge: Cambridge University Press, 2019.

Meaney, Gerardine, Mary O'Dowd, and Bernadette Whelan. *Reading the Irish Woman: Studies in Cultural Encounter and Exchange, 1714–1960.* Liverpool: Liverpool University Press, 2013.

Mehegan, David. "For This Writer, Identity Is Subject to Change." In *The Boston Globe* February 27, 2008. http://archive.boston.com/ae/books/articles/2008/02/27/for_this_writer_identity_is_subject_to_change/?page=2.

Mentxaka, Aintzane Leggareta. *Kate O'Brien and the Fiction of Identity: Sex, Art, and Politics in* Mary Lavelle *and Other Writings.* Jefferson, NC: McFarland and Co., 2011.

Mentxaka, Aintzane Leggareta. "Kate O'Brien and Virginia Woolf: Common Ground." In *Irish University Review* 48:1 (2018): 127–142.

REFERENCES 215

Micir, Melanie and Aarthi Vadde. "Obliterature: Toward an Amateur Criticism." In *Modernism/modernity* 25:3 (2018): 517–549.

Mickalites, Carey. *Contemporary Fiction, Celebrity Culture, and the Market for Modernism: Fictions of Celebrity.* London: Bloomsbury, 2022.

Mikowski, Sylvie. "Objects in Deirdre Madden's Artist Novels." In *Deirdre Madden: New Critical Perspectives*, edited by Anne Fogarty and Marisol Morales-Ladrón, 83–101. Manchester: Manchester University Press, 2022.

Mildenberg, Ariane. "'Hooks' and 'Anchors': Cézanne, the Lived Perspective, and Modernist Doubt." In *Understanding Merleau-Ponty, Understanding Modernism*, edited by Ariane Mildenberg, 59–72. London: Bloomsbury, 2018.

Miller, Brook. "The Impersonal Personal: Value, Voice, and Agency in Elizabeth Bowen's Literary and Social Criticism." In *Modern Fiction Studies* 53:2 (Summer 2007): 351–369.

Miller, Tyrus. *Late Modernism: Politics, Fiction and the Arts Between the World Wars.* Berkeley: University of California Press, 1999.

Moloney, Caitriona and Helen Thompson, eds. *Irish Women Writers Speak Out: Voices from the Field.* Syracuse: Syracuse University Press, 2003.

Mooney, Jennifer. *Feminist Discourse in Irish Literature: Gender and Power in Louise O'Neill's Young Adult Fiction.* London: Routledge, 2022.

Mooney, Sinéad. "Unstable Compounds: Bowen's Beckettian Affinities." In *Elizabeth Bowen: New Critical Perspectives*, edited by Susan Osborn, 13–33. Cork: Cork University Press, 2009.

Morgan, Tom. "*Solar Bones* by Mike McCormack Wins the Goldsmiths Prize 2016." Goldsmiths University of London, November 9, 2016. https://www.gold.ac.uk/news/goldsmiths-prize-2016/.

Morris, Catherine. *Alice Milligan and the Irish Cultural Revival.* Dublin: Four Courts Press, 2012.

Mulhall, Anne. "'The Well-Known, Old, but Still Unbeaten Track': Women Poets and Irish Periodical Culture in the Mid-Twentieth Century." In *Irish University Review* 42:1 (2012): 32–52.

Mulhall, Anne. "The Ends of Irish Studies: On Whiteness, Academia, and Activism." In *Irish University Review* 50:1 (May 2020): 94–111.

Mulrooney, Jonathan. "Stephen Dedalus and the Politics of Confession." In *Studies in the Novel* 33:2 (Summer 2001): 160–179.

Murdoch, Iris. "The Sublime and the Good" (1959). In *Existentialists and Mystics: Writings on Philosophy and Literature*, edited by Peter Conradi, 205–220. London: Chatto, 1997.

Murphy, James H. "Fiction, 1845–1900." In *A History of Modern Irish Women's Literature*, edited by Heather Ingman and Clíona Ó Gallchoir, 96–113. Cambridge: Cambridge University Press, 2018.

Murphy, Neil. *Irish Fiction and Postmodern Doubt: An Analysis of the Epistemological Crisis in Modern Irish Fiction.* Lewiston: Edward Mellen Press, 2004.

Murray, Simone. "The Cuala Press: Women, Publishing, and the Conflicted Genealogies of 'Feminist Publishing.'" In *Women's Studies International Forum* 27:5 (2004): 489–506.

Murray, Tony. "Writing Irish Nurses in Britain." *A History of Irish Working-Class Writing*, edited by Michael Pierse, 195–208. Cambridge: Cambridge University Press, 2017.

Nersessian, Anahid. "What Is the New Redistribution?" In *PMLA* 132:5 (2017): 1220–1225.

Nersessian, Anahid. "Romantic Difficulty." In *New Literary History* 40:4 (Autumn 2018): 451–466.

Nersessian, Anahid. *The Calamity Form: On Poetry and Social Life.* Chicago: University of Chicago Press, 2020.

Ní Dhuibhne, Éilís. *The Dancers Dancing.* Dublin: Blackstaff Press, 1999.

Ní Dhuibhne, Éilís. "Summer's Wreath." In *Town and Country: New Irish Short Stories*, edited by Kevin Barry, 133–157. London: Faber and Faber, 2013.

Ní Dhuibhne, Éilís. "Introduction." *Look! It's a Woman Writer!: Irish Literary Feminisms 1970–2020*, edited by Éilís Ní Dhuibhne, 13–33. Dublin: Arlen House, 2021.

Nolan, Emer. "Modernism and the Irish Revival." In *The Cambridge Companion to Modern Irish Culture*, edited by Joe Cleary and Claire Connolly, 157–172. Cambridge: Cambridge University Press, 2005.

Nolan, Emer. *Catholic Emancipations: Irish Fiction from Thomas Moore to James Joyce.* Syracuse: Syracuse University Press, 2007.

North, Michael. *What Is the Present?* Princeton, NJ: Princeton University Press, 2018.

216 REFERENCES

Nutall, Emma. "Claire-Louise Bennett on Debut Collection, *Pond*." In *The Skinny*, November 20, 2015. https://www.theskinny.co.uk/books/features/claire-louise-bennett-pond-fitzcarraldo-stinging-fly.

O'Brien, Dan. *Fine Meshwork: Philip Roth, Edna O'Brien, and Jewish-Irish Literature*. Syracuse: Syracuse University Press, 2020.

O'Brien, Edna. *Night*. New York: Farrar Straus Giroux, 1987.

O'Brien, Edna. *The Love Object: Selected Stories*. New York: Little, Brown and Company, 2015.

O'Brien, Edna. "How James Joyce's Anna Livia Plurabelle Shook the Literary World." In *The Guardian*, October 1, 1969. https://www.theguardian.com/books/2017/jan/27/edna-obrien-how-james-joyces-anna-livia-plurabelle-shook-the-literary-world.

O'Brien, George. *The Irish Novel: 1960–2010*. Cork: Cork University Press, 2012.

O'Brien, Kate. *Without My Cloak*. London: Virago Press, 1987.

O'Brien, Kate. *The Land of Spices*. London: Virago Press, 2014.

O'Brien, Kate. "Ireland and Avant-Gardisme," typescript, 12 pp., Kate O'Brien Papers (P12/157).

O'Brien, Kate. "James Joyce and *Ulysses*." 1 October 1969, typescript of speech given at Canterbury College of Art (Box 4, Folder 6D).

Ó Conchubhair, Brian. "The Parallax of Irish-Language Modernism, 1900–1940." In *The Oxford Handbook of Modern Irish Fiction*, edited by Liam Harte, 167–184. Oxford: Oxford University Press, 2020.

O'Connor, Elizabeth Foley. "Kate O'Brien, James Joyce, and the 'Lonely Genius.'" In *Joycean Legacies*, edited by Martha Carpentier, 11–32. London: Palgrave Macmillan, 2015.

O'Connor, Frank. "Introduction to *A Portrait of the Artist as a Young Man*." In *A Frank O'Connor Reader*, edited by Michael Steinman, 341–345. Syracuse: Syracuse University Press, 1994.

O'Connor, Frank. *The Lonely Voice: A Study of the Short Story*. Brooklyn: Melville Press, 2004.

O'Connor, Joseph. "Getting in on the Act." In *The Guardian*, August 29, 2008. https://www.theguardian.com/books/2008/aug/30/fiction.deirdremadden.

O'Connor, Maureen. *Edna O'Brien and the Art of Fiction*. Lewisburg, PA: Bucknell University Press, 2021.

Ó Donghaile, Deaglán and Gerry Smyth. "Remapping Irish Modernism." In *Irish Studies Review* 26:3 (2018): 297–303.

O'Donnell, Mary. "A Prosaic Lack of Women in *The Cambridge Companion to Irish Poets*." In *The Irish Times*, January 8, 2018. https://www.irishtimes.com/culture/books/a-prosaic-lack-of-women-in-the-cambridge-companion-to-irish-poets-1.3336413.

Ó Faoláin, Seán. *Vive Moi!* London: Sinclair Stevenson, 1993.

O'Hagan, John. "The Irish Economy 1973 to 2016." In *The Cambridge History of Ireland 1880 to the Present*, vol. 4, edited by Thomas Bartlett, 500–526. Cambridge: Cambridge University Press, 2018.

O'Neill, Louise. *Only Ever Yours*. New York: Quercus, 2014.

O'Toole, Tina. *The Irish New Woman*. London: Palgrave Macmillan, 2013.

O'Toole, Tina. "George Egerton's Translocational Subjects." In *Modernism/modernity* 21:3 (September 2014): 827–842.

O'Toole, Tina. "New Woman Writers." In *A History of Modern Irish Women's Literature*, edited by Heather Ingman and Clíona Ó Gallchoir, 114–130. Cambridge: Cambridge University Press, 2018.

O'Toole, Tina and Anna Teekell, eds. Special Issue on Elizabeth Bowen. *Irish University Review* 51:1 (2021).

Okorie, Melatu Uche. "Under the Awning." In *This Hostel Life*, 25–41. Dublin: Skein Press, 2018.

Olson, Liesl. *Modernism and the Ordinary*. New York: Oxford University Press, 2009.

Osborn, Susan. "'How to measure this unaccountable darkness between the trees': The Strange Relation of Style and Meaning in *The Last September*." In *Elizabeth Bowen: New Critical Perspectives*, edited by Susan Osborn, 34–60. Cork: Cork University Press, 2009.

Pašeta, Senia. *Irish Nationalist Women, 1900–1918*. Cambridge: Cambridge University Press, 2013.

Pašeta, Senia. "Peace and Protest in Ireland: Women's Activism in Ireland, 1918–1937." In *Diplomacy and Statecraft* 31:4 (2020): 673–696.

Patten, Eve. "Women and Fiction, 1985–1990." In *Krino, 1986–1996: An Anthology of Modern Irish Writing*, edited by Gerald Dawe and Jonathan Williams, 8–16. Dublin: Gill and Macmillan, 1996.

REFERENCES 217

Patten, Eve. "Contemporary Irish Fiction." In *The Cambridge Companion to the Irish Novel*, edited by John Wilson Foster, 259–275. Cambridge: Cambridge University Press, 2006.

Pearson, Nels. *Irish Cosmopolitanism: Location and Dislocation in James Joyce, Elizabeth Bowen, and Samuel Beckett*. Gainesville: University Press of Florida, 2015.

Pease, Allison. *Modernism, Feminism, and the Culture of Boredom*. Cambridge: Cambridge University Press, 2012.

Pelan, Rebecca. *Two Irelands: Literary Feminisms North and South*. Syracuse: Syracuse University Press, 2005.

Pelan, Rebecca. "Edna O'Brien's 'Love Objects.'" In *Wild Colonial Girl: Essays on Edna O'Brien*, edited by Lisa Colletta and Maureen O'Connor, 58–77. Madison: University of Wisconsin Press, 2006.

Penner, Erin Kay. "Making No Apologies for Difficulty: Putting Modernist Form at the Center of Classroom Discussions." In *Journal of Modernist Literature* 37:2 (Winter 2014): 1–19.

Pine, Emilie. *The Politics of Irish Memory: Performing Remembrance in Contemporary Irish Culture*. London: Palgrave Macmillan, 2011.

Pine, Emilie. *Notes to Self*. Dublin: Tramp Press, 2018.

Pine, Emilie, Susan Leavy, Mark Keane, Maeve Casserly, and Tom Lane. "Modes of Witnessing and Ireland's Institutional History." In *Irish Literature in Transition, 1980–2020*, vol. 6, edited by Eric Falci and Paige Reynolds, 278–294. Cambridge: Cambridge University Press, 2020.

Plock, Vike Martina. "'Object Lessons': Bloom and His Things." In *James Joyce Quarterly* 49:3, 4 (Spring/Summer 2012): 557–572.

Plotz, John. *Semi-Detached: The Aesthetics of Virtual Experience since Dickens*. Princeton: Princeton University Press, 2018.

Potts, Donna. "Irish Poetry and the Modernist Canon: A Reappraisal of the Poetry of Katharine Tynan." In *Border Crossings: Irish Women Writers and Nationalism*, edited by Kathryn Kirkpatrick, 79–99. Tuscaloosa: University of Alabama Press, 2000.

Potts, Donna. *Contemporary Irish Writing and Environmentalism: The Wearing of the Deep Green*. London: Palgrave Macmillan, 2018.

Quigley, Mark. "Re-imagining Realism in Post-Independence Irish Writing." In *Irish Literature in Transition, 1880–1940*, vol. 4, edited by Marjorie Elizabeth Howes, 265–284. Cambridge: Cambridge University Press, 2020.

Rains, Stephanie. *Commodity Culture and Social Class in Dublin 1850–1916*. Dublin: Irish Academic Press, 2010.

Randall, Bryony. *Modernism, Daily Time, and Everyday Life*. Cambridge: Cambridge University Press, 2007.

Regan, Stephen. "Note on the Text and Reception." George Moore, *Esther Waters*, edited by Stephen Regan, xxxii–xxxix. Oxford: Oxford University Press, 2012.

Reynolds, Paige. *Modernism, Drama, and the Audience for Irish Spectacle*. Cambridge: Cambridge University Press, 2007.

Reynolds, Paige. "Colleen Modernism: Modernism's Afterlife in Irish Women's Writing." In *Éire-Ireland* 44:3, 4 (Fall/Winter 2009): 94–117.

Reynolds, Paige, ed. "Irish Things": Special Issue on Irish Material Culture. *Éire-Ireland* 46:1, 2 (Spring/Summer 2011).

Reynolds, Paige. "Trauma, Intimacy, and Modernist Form." In *Breac: A Digital Journal of Irish Studies* (September 2014). http://breac.nd.edu/articles/trauma-intimacy-and-modernist-form/.

Reynolds, Paige, ed. *Modernist Afterlives in Irish Literature and Culture*. London: Anthem Press, 2016.

Reynolds, Paige, ed. Special Issue on Kate O'Brien. *Irish University Review* 48:1 (Spring/Summer 2018).

Reynolds, Paige. "Prose, Drama, and Poetry, 1891–1920." In *A History of Modern Irish Women's Literature*, edited by Heather Ingman and Clíona Ó Gallchoir, 131–148. Cambridge: Cambridge University Press, 2018.

Reynolds, Paige. "Bird Girls: Modernism and Sexual Ethics in Contemporary Irish Fiction." In *Modernism and Close Reading*, edited by David James, 173–190. Oxford: Oxford University Press, 2020.

Reynolds, Paige, ed. *The New Irish Studies*. Cambridge: Cambridge University Press, 2020.

218 REFERENCES

Reynolds, Paige. "An Ordinary Revival: Yeats and Irish Women Novelists." In *The Irish Revival: A Complex Vision*, edited by Marjorie Howes and Joseph Valente, 126–148. Syracuse: Syracuse University Press, 2023.

Rich, Kelly. "'Look in the Gutter': Infrastructural Interiority in *Never Let Me Go.*" In *Modern Fiction Studies* 61:4 (Winter 2015): 631–651.

Richardson, Dorothy. *Pilgrimage 1.* New York: Popular Library, 1976.

Robinson, Richard. *John McGahern and Modernism.* London: Bloomsbury, 2016.

Roche, Anthony. "Re-working 'The Workhouse Ward': McDonagh, Beckett, Gregory." In *Irish University Review* 34:1 (Spring/Summer, 2004): 171–184.

Rooney, Sally. *Normal People.* London: Faber and Faber, 2018.

Rooney, Sally. *Beautiful World, Where Are You.* New York: Farrar, Straus and Giroux, 2021.

Rooney, Sally. "Misreading *Ulysses.*" In *The Paris Review*, December 7, 2022. https://www.theparisreview.org/blog/2022/12/07/misreading-ulysses/.

Rose, Jacqueline. "From the Inside Out." In *The London Review of Books* 38:18 (September 22, 2016): 11–12.

Rustin, Susanna. "Eimear McBride: I Wanted to Give the Reader a Very Different Experience." In *The Guardian*, May 16, 2014. https://www.theguardian.com/books/2014/may/16/eimear-mcbride-girl-is-a-half-formed-thing-interview.

Schultz, Matthew. "Molly Bloom's Nostalgic Reverie: A Phenomenology of Modernist Longing." In *Irish Studies Review* 26:4 (2018): 472–487.

Schwartz, Alexandra. "A New Kind of Adultery Novel." In *The New Yorker*, July 24, 2017. https://www.newyorker.com/magazine/2017/07/31/a-new-kind-of-adultery-novel.

Schwartz, Melanie. "How Should a Millennial Be?" In *The New York Review of Books*, April 18, 2019. https://www.nybooks.com/articles/2019/04/18/sally-rooney-how-should-millennial-be/.

Schwerter, Stephanie. "Transgressing Boundaries: Belfast and the 'Romance-Across-the-Divide.'" In *Estudios Irlandeses* 2 (2007): 173–182.

Sehgal, Parul. "#MeToo is All Too Real. But to Better Understand It, Turn to Fiction." In *The New York Times*, May 1, 2019. https://www.nytimes.com/2019/05/01/books/novels-me-too-movement.html.

Seiler, Claire. *Midcentury Suspension: Literature and Feeling in the Wake of World War II.* New York: Columbia University Press, 2020.

Sell, Aran Ward. "Half-Formed Modernism: Eimear McBride's *A Girl Is a Half-Formed Thing.*" In *Hungarian Journal of English and American Studies* 25:2 (June 2020): 393–413.

Sherman, David. "Woolf's Secular Imaginary." In *Modernism/modernity* 23:4 (2016): 711–731.

Sherratt-Bado, Dawn Miranda. "*The New Yorker*'s Edna O'Brien Profile is Sexist and Cold-Hearted." In *The Irish Times*, October 16, 2019. https://www.irishtimes.com/culture/books/the-new-yorker-s-edna-o-brien-profile-is-sexist-and-cold-hearted-1.4051169.

Shovlin, Frank. *The Irish Literary Periodical: 1923–1958.* Oxford: Oxford University Press, 2003.

Shovlin, Frank. "The Struggle for Form: Seán Ó Faoláin's Autobiographies." In *The Yearbook of English Studies* 35 (2005): 161–170.

Sim, Lorraine. *Virginia Woolf: The Patterns of Everyday Experience.* Surrey: Ashgate, 2010.

Sisson, Elaine. "Experimentalism and the Irish Stage: Theatre and German Expressionism in the 1920s." In *Ireland, Design, and Visual Culture: Negotiating Modernity, 1922–1992*, edited by Linda King and Elaine Sisson, 39–58. Cork: Cork University Press, 2011.

Smethurst, James. *The New Red Negro: The Literary Left and African American Poetry, 1930–1946.* New York: Oxford University Press, 1999.

Smith, James. *Ireland's Magdalen Laundries and the Nation's Architecture of Containment.* South Bend, IN: University of Notre Dame Press, 2007.

Smith, Rosa Inocencio. "How to Tell an Open Secret." In *The Atlantic*, January 16, 2019. https://www.theatlantic.com/entertainment/archive/2019/01/three-novels-metoo-era/580369/.

Spacks, Patricia Meyer. *Boredom: The Literary History of a State of Mind.* Chicago: University of Chicago Press, 1995.

Specia, Megan. "Report Gives Glimpse into Horrors of Ireland's Mother and Baby Homes." In *The New York Times*, January 12, 2021. https://www.nytimes.com/2021/01/12/world/europe/ireland-mother-baby-home-report.html.

REFERENCES   219

Sproull, Patrick. "Louise O'Neill." In *The Guardian*, September 2, 2015. https://www.theguardian.com/childrens-books-site/2015/sep/02/louise-oneill-asking-for-it-interview.

Standlee, Whitney. *'Power to Observe': Irish Women Novelists in Britain, 1890–1916.* Oxford: Peter Lang, 2015.

Stephens, Robert and Sylvia Stephens. "Interview with Robert and Sylvia Stephens," interview by Mary Lavin, ML/5/6 dft. Q&A.

Stewart, Susan. *On Longing: Narratives of the Miniature, the Gigantic, the Souvenir, the Collection.* Durham, N. C.: Duke University Press, 1993.

Stich, Susanne. "Claire-Louise Bennett: Modes of Solitude, Embodiment and Mystery." In *The Honest Ulsterman*, June 2015. http://humag.co/features/claire-louise-bennett.

Storey, Michael L. *Representing the Troubles in Irish Short Fiction.* Washington, D.C.: The Catholic University of America Press, 2004.

Sullivan, Moynagh. "'I Am Not Yet Delivered of the Past': The Poetry of Blanaid Salkeld." In *Irish University Review* 33:1 (Spring/Summer 2003): 182–200.

Tallone, Giovanna. "Past, Present and Future: Patterns of Otherness in Éilís Ní Dhuibhne's Fiction." In *Irish Literature: Feminist Perspectives*, edited by Patricia Coughlan and Tina O'Toole, 167–184. Dublin: Carysfort Press, 2008.

Taylor, Charles. *A Secular Age.* Cambridge: Harvard University Press, 2007.

Teekell, Anna. *Emergency Writing: Irish Literature, Neutrality, and the Second World War.* Evanston, IL: Northwestern University Press, 2018.

Thersites (Thomas Woods), "Private Views," *The Irish Times (1921–Current File);* July 31, 1954; ProQuest Historical Newspapers: *The Irish Times* and *The Weekly Irish Times*: 6.

Thompson, Helen. "Hysterical Hooliganism: O'Brien, Freud, Joyce." In *Wild Colonial Girl: Essays on Edna O'Brien*, edited by Lisa Colletta and Maureen O'Connor, 31–57. Madison, WI: University of Wisconsin Press, 2006.

Tighe-Mooney, Sharon. "'Nun, Married, Old Maid': Kate O'Brien's Fiction, Women, and Irish Catholicism." PhD Thesis, Maynooth University, Ireland, October 2009.

Tramp Press. "Twitter / @TrampPress: Anne Enright: 'since the crash a lot has been disrupted. There's a resurgent modernism in writers like Eimear McBride and @emollientfibs,'" March 8, 2015, 11:23 a.m.

Trotter, David. *Literature in the First Media Age: Britain between the Wars.* Cambridge: Harvard University Press, 2013.

Tu, Jessie. "Surely There Are Better Literary Heroes for Our Generation than Sally Rooney?" In *Sydney Morning Herald*, August 21, 2021. https://www.smh.com.au/culture/tv-and-radio/surely-there-are-better-literary-heroes-for-our-generation-than-sally-rooney-20210817-p58jfp.html.

Valente, Joseph and Margot Gayle Backus. *The Child Sex Scandal and Modern Irish Literature: Writing the Unspeakable.* Bloomington: Indiana University Press, 2020.

Valiulis, Maryann Gialanella. *The Making of Inequality: Women, Power, and Gender Ideology in the Irish Free State, 1922–1937.* Dublin: Four Courts Press, 2019.

Walkowitz, Rebecca. *Born Translated: The Contemporary Novel in an Age of World Literature.* New York: Columbia University Press, 2015.

Walsh, Keri. "Elizabeth Bowen, Surrealist." In *Éire-Ireland* 42:3, 4 (Fall/Winter 2007): 126–147.

Walshe, Eibhear. *Kate O'Brien: A Writing Life.* Dublin: Irish Academic Press, 2006.

Ward, Margaret. *Unmanageable Revolutionaries: Women and Irish Nationalism.* London: Pluto Press, 1995.

Watt, Stephen. *Beckett and Contemporary Irish Writing.* Cambridge: Cambridge University Press, 2012.

White, Frances. "'Despite Herself': The Resisted Influence of Virginia Woolf on Iris Murdoch's Fiction." In *Iris Murdoch Connected: Critical Essays on Her Fiction and Philosophy*, edited by Mark Luprecht, 3–28. Knoxville: University of Tennessee Press, 2014.

White, Siân. "Spatial Politics/Poetics, Late Modernism, and Elizabeth Bowen's *The Last September*." In *Genre: Forms of Discourse and Culture* 49:1 (2016): 27–50.

White, Siân. "A 'Hair-Trigger Society' and the Woman Who Felt Something in Anna Burns's *Milkman*." In *Genre: Forms of Discourse and Culture* 54:1 (April 2021): 111–137.

220 REFERENCES

White, Siân. "'Stories Are a Different Kind of True': Gender and Narrative Agency in Contemporary Irish Women's Fiction." In *The Edinburgh Companion to Irish Modernism*, edited by Maud Ellmann, Siân White, and Vicki Mahaffey, 351–367. Edinburgh: Edinburgh University Press, 2021.

Williams, Linda. *Playing the Race Card: Melodramas of Black and White from Uncle Tom to O. J. Simpson*. Princeton: Princeton University Press, 2001.

Wills, Clair. "Edna O'Brien and Eimear McBride." In *Irish Literature in Transition, 1980–2020*, vol. 6, edited by Eric Falci and Paige Reynolds, 295–303. Cambridge: Cambridge University Press, 2020.

Wills, Clair. "Women, Domesticity and the Family: Recent Feminist Work in Irish Cultural Studies." In *Cultural Studies* 15:1 (2001): 33–57.

Wills, Clair. *That Neutral Island: A Cultural History of Ireland during the Second World War*. Cambridge: Belknap Press, 2007.

Wills, Clair. *The Best Are Leaving: Emigration and Post-War Irish Culture*. Cambridge: Cambridge University Press, 2015.

Wills, Clair. *Lovers and Strangers: An Immigrant History of Post-War Britain*. London: Allen Lane, 2017.

Winston, Diane. "Irish Catholics Continue to Flee the Church." In *Global Post*, March 26, 2013. https://www.pri.org/stories/2013-03-26/irish-catholics-continue-flee-church.

Woolf, Virginia. *Death of the Moth and Other Essays*. New York: Harcourt, Brace & Co., 1942.

Woolf, Virginia. "A Sketch of the Past." In *Moments of Being: A Collection of Autobiographical Writing*, edited by Jeanne Schulkind, 61–160. New York: Harcourt, 1985.

Woolf, Virginia. *The Complete Shorter Fiction of Virginia Woolf*, edited by Susan Dick. New York: Harcourt Brace Jovanovich, 1985.

Workman, Simon. "A Life of One's Own." In Maeve Kelly, *Orange Horses*, v–xx. Dublin: Tramp Press, 2017.

Wurtz, James F. "Elizabeth Bowen, Modernism, and the Spectre of Anglo Ireland." In *Estudios Irlandeses* 5 (2010): 119–128.

Yeats, W. B. *The Memoirs of W. B. Yeats*, edited by Denis Donoghue. New York: Scribner, 1972.

Yeats, W. B. *W. B. Yeats: The Poems*, edited by Daniel Albright. London: Dent, 1990.

Zaleski, Philip and Carol Zaleski. *Prayer: A History*. Boston: Houghton Mifflin, 2005.

Zarzosa, Agustin. "Melodrama and the Modes of the World." In *Discourse* 32:2 (Spring 2010): 236–255.

Zumhagen-Yekplé, Karen. *A Different Order of Difficulty: Literature after Wittgenstein*. Chicago: University of Chicago Press, 2020.

Index

For the benefit of digital users, indexed terms that span two pages (e.g., 52–53) may, on occasion, appear on only one of those pages.

abortion 45 n.39, 53–54
  Caldwell's "SOMAT" 25, 54–57
  Eliot's *The Waste Land* 46
  Girl X 143
Adorno, Theodor 164, 183
Agamben, Giorgio 115
Ahmed, Sara 18–19
Appiah, Kwame Anthony 178 n.16
Asad, Talal 64–65
Attridge, Derek 44, 52–53, 54–55
Atwood, Margaret, *The Handmaid's Tale*
  158–159
Auden, W. H. 101–102
Auge, Andrew 70–71
Austen, Jane 71, 141–142, 167
  Emma 184–185
  Pride and Prejudice 168

Bachelard, Gaston 107–108, 125, 126–127
Backus, Margot 69
Baker, Houston 21
Banville, John 42–43
Barlow, Jane 7–8
Barnard, Tony 107–108 n.29, 123
Barnes, Djuna 28
Barrett, Colin, *Young Skins* 179–180
Battersby, Doug 51–52 n.53
Baume, Sara, *Spill Simmer Falter Wither* 3–4
Beckett, Mary 29–30
Beckett, Samuel 5, 9–11, 13–14, 16–17, 171
  complicated women 42
  Dreams of Fair to Middling Women 59–60
  influence on Bennett 145–146
  influence on McCormack 200–201
  Krapp's Last Tape 97–98
  Lavin on 71
  McBride on 81–82
  O'Brien (Kate) on 62
  O'Brien's *The Land of Spices* comparison
    70–71
  prayer 59–60
  self-questioning 42–43
  Waiting for Godot 150

Belfast/Good Friday Agreement 24–25, 127
Bennett, Claire-Louise
  Checkout 19 145–146, 150–151
  Fish Out of Water 145–146
  Joyce refused as an influence 49–50
  Pond 3–4, 26, 135–136, 145–158, 160–162,
    163–164, 172, 176–177
Bergson, Henri 99–100
bildungsroman 154–157
  Bennett's *Pond* 145, 154–157
  Joyce's *A Portrait of the Artist as a Young Man*
    168–169
  Ní Dhuibhne's *The Dancers Dancing* 137,
    144–145
  O'Brien's *The Land of Spices* 65
Binchy, Maeve, *Light a Penny Candle* 54
Blake, William
  "The Chimney Sweeper" 70
  "The Shepherd" 70
  Songs of Experience 70
  Songs of Innocence 70
Blundell, Mary Elizabeth 7–8
Boccioni, Umberto 149–150
Boland, Eavan 48–49
  "Mise Éire" 17–18
Bourke, Angela 140 n.8
Bowen, Elizabeth 4–5, 8–9, 13–14, 29–30, 39–40,
  46, 135–136, 154–156, 201–202
  "The Demon Lover" 35–36
  "Hand in Glove" 35–36
  The Heat of the Day 35–36
  "James Joyce" 48–49
  The Last September 35–36, 104
  "Mainie Jellett" 35
  "Mysterious Kôr" 97–98
  Rooney comparison 168–169
  "The Short Story" 140–141
  "Stories by Katherine Mansfield" 141–143
  "Summer Night" 25, 30–31, 36–38, 53–54
Bowen, Zack 73
Boxall, Peter 27–28
Bracken, Claire 54, 155–156
Brady, Catherine 38–39 n.24

222 INDEX

Brontë, Charlotte, *Jane Eyre* 107
Brophy, Brigid, *In Transit: An Heroi-Cyclic Novel*
    13–14
Brown, Bill 132
Burns, Anna 4–5
    Milkman 26, 165–166, 172–182, 186–193, 199
Buurma, Rachel Sagner 165–166

Cahill, Susan 44, 53–54, 116–117
Caldwell, June 4–5
    Room Little Darker 54–55 n.61
    "SOMAT" 25, 30–31, 54–57
Caldwell, Lucy 38–39 n.24
    Multitudes 51–52
Carr, Marina 38–39 n.24
    The Mai 17–18
Casanova, Pascale 9–10
Casey, Eamon 82
Castle, Gregory 154–155
Castle, Terry 96 n.2
Cather, Willa 38–39 n.24, 121–122
Catholic Church
    abortion 56–57
    abuses 53, 60–61, 80–81, 82, 89
    anti-materialism 97
    Donoghue's *Hood* 77–80
    femininity 12
    Fifth Amendment of the Constitution Act 77
    Joyce's writing 51–52
        Ulysses 100–101
    Lavin's writing 72, 74, 76
        "The Living" 72–73
        "The Nun's Mother" 74–75
        "Sunday Brings Sunday" 75–76
    Madden's *Molly Fox's Birthday* 122–123, 128
    McBride's *A Girl Is a Half-formed Thing* 80,
        81–86, 87–93
    McCormack's *Solar Bones* 195
    O'Brien's *Night* (Edna) 104
    O'Brien's writing (Kate) 62–63, 70–71
        The Land of Spices 60–61, 63–71, 168–169
    O'Neill's *Only Ever Yours* 162–163
    repression of women 25–26, 27–28, 72
    Rooney's *Beautiful World, Where Are You*
        51–52
    see also prayer
celebrities 19–20
Celtic Tiger 12–13, 22, 54, 136–137
    Bennett's *Pond* 145–146, 149–150, 155–156
    Enright's *The Gathering* 25–26, 95, 106–121,
        122, 132
    Madden's *Molly Fox's Birthday* 25–26, 95,
        106–110, 127, 132

Ní Dhuibhne's *Fox, Swallow, Scarecrow* 38–39
    n.24
    O'Brien's *Night* (Edna) 132
    Rooney's *Normal People* 167–168
censorship 44–45, 72
Chekhov, Anton 38, 38–39 n.24, 38–39, 126,
    140–143
    influence on Lavin 71
    open ending 179–180
    Three Sisters 38–39 n.24
Chopin, Kate, *The Awakening* 92
Cleary, Joe 9–10 n.23, 13–14
Cleary, Michael 82
Cliff, Brian 127–128
close reading 20–24, 27, 155, 165–166, 181–182,
    194, 202–203
    Burns's *Milkman* 165–166, 172–174, 186–193
    McCormack's *Solar Bones* 195
    Rooney's *Normal People* 165–166, 182–186,
        191–193
Coen, Lisa 200–201
Coetzee, J. M. 52–53
    Elizabeth Costello 101 n.14
Collins, Suzanne, *The Hunger Games* 157–158
Colum, Mary 29, 48–49
Colum, Padraic 48–49
Conlon, Evelyn 4–5, 106–107
    "Furthermore, Susan" 45–46 n.40
    "Susan—Did You Hear . . ." 45–46 n.40
    "Taking Scarlet as a Real Colour or And Also,
        Susan . . ." 25, 30–31, 45–49, 53–54
Conrad, Joseph 36–37
    Heart of Darkness 42–43
Corkery, Daniel 33–34
Corless, Catherine 17–18
Costello, Mary, *The River Capture* 48–49
Coughlan, Patricia 138
Corser, Sophie 202–203
Coyle, Kathleen, *A Flock of Birds* 13–14
Crary, Jonathan 99
Crispin, Jessa 19–20
Cullen, Paul 65–66
cummings, e e 145–146

Darling, Orlaith 195–196
Davis-Goff, Sarah 200–201
daydreaming *see* object reverie
de Valera, Éamon 12, 33, 97
de Waal, Kit 21
Deane, Seamus 50–51, 97–98
Deckard, Sharae 14
Deevy, Teresa, *The King of Spain's Daughter* 97
DeMeester, Karen 129–130
Devlin, Denis 70–71

digital technology 26, 27–28, 43–44, 134, 194
    Bennett's *Pond* 135–136, 145–158, 160–162,
        163–164
    and close reading 189–190
    injustices revealed and scrutinized 56
    McCormack's *Solar Bones* 195
    Ní Dhuibhne's *The Dancers Dancing* 135–140,
        143–145, 147–148, 150, 155, 157–158,
        160–162, 163–164
    O'Neill's *Only Ever Yours* 135–136, 157–164
    Rooney's *Beautiful World, Where Are You*
        11–12
Dimbo, Ifedinma 21
Dinnen, Zara 134 n.2
Dobbins, Gregory 97–98
domestic roles 31–32, 34
Donoghue, Emma 4–5, 171
    Hood 25–26, 60–62, 77–80, 93, 156–157
    Room 19–20
Dostoevsky, Fyodor 38–39 n.24
Dunham, Lena 19–20
Duras, Marguerite 38–39 n.24

Eagleton, Terry 199 n.5
Edgeworth, Maria, *Castle Rackrent* 6–7
Egerton, George 13–14
Eliot, George 169–170
Eliot, T. S. 16–17, 25, 29, 30–31, 99–100
    aesthetic form 183
    Kelly's "Morning at My Window" 40–41, 42
    "The Metaphysical Poets" 64
    "Morning at the Window" 40–41, 56–57
    and Ní Dhuibhne's *The Dancers Dancing* 140
    prayer 59–60
    Prufrock and Other Observations 41
    "*Ulysses*, Order, and Myth" 16
    "The Use of Poetry and the Use of Criticism"
        192–193
    The Waste Land 1, 46, 164
Enright, Anne 3–4, 40
    The Gathering 25–26, 95–96, 106–121, 122,
        123–124, 126, 130–131, 132–133,
        143–144
    on Joyce 48–49
    on Rooney's *Normal People* 168–169
epiphany 48–49
    Burns's *Milkman* 175–176
    Donoghue's *Hood* 79–80
    Enright's *The Gathering* 118–119, 120
    Joyce's writing
        Dubliners 2–3, 183–184
        A Portrait of the Artist as a Young Man
            170–171, 184–185
        Ulysses 48, 120

Lavin's *Tales from Bective Bridge* 74
Madden's *Molly Fox's Birthday* 131–132
Mansfield's writing 140–141
McBride's *A Girl Is a Half-formed Thing* 87
Ní Dhuibhne's *The Dancers Dancing* 138–139
O'Brien's *The Land of Spices* 68, 70–71
Rooney's *Normal People* 170–171, 184
Ernaux, Annie 15–16
Esty, Jed 9–10, 155–156

Fahey, Tony 72
Faulkner, William 38, 59–60
Fianna Fáil 12
Fired! Irish Women Poets and the Canon 19–20
Fisk, Gloria 167
Fitzgerald, F. Scott, *The Great Gatsby* 183–184
Fitzgerald, William 93
Flaubert, Gustave 169–170
Flynn, Deirdre 200, 202–203
Fogarty, Anne 35, 74
Ford, Ford Madox, *The Good Soldier* 109
Forster, E. M. 71
    A Room with a View 145–146, 154–155
Foucault, Michel, *Discipline and Punish* 18–19
Francis, M. E. 7–8
Frawley, Oona, *New Dubliners* 48–49
Freud, Sigmund 107, 125, 132

Galley Beggar 16–17
genre fiction 157–158, 167
Gettelman, Debra 107
Gilbert, Lady (Rosa Mulholland) 7–8
    Cousin Sara: A Story of Arts and Crafts 8
Gilligan, Ruth 51–52 n.53
Gilman, Charlotte Perkins, "The Yellow
        Wallpaper" 148
Ginzburg, Natalia 15–16
Girl X 143
Gogol, Nikolai 38–39
Gonne, Maud 5–6, 199
Good Friday/Belfast Agreement 24–25, 127
Gothic 144, 157–158
    Bowen's writing 35–36
    Burns's *Milkman* 187
    Enright's *The Gathering* 118
    Gilman's "The Yellow Wallpaper" 148
    O'Brien's *The Land of Spices* 69
    O'Brien's *Night* 104
Grand, Sarah 8
Gray, Eileen 13–14
Gregory, Lady Augusta 5–6, 62, 96–97, 199
Gray, Katherine Martin 42
Guinness, May 13–14

224 INDEX

Hall, Radclyffe, *The Well of Loneliness* 44–45
Harney-Mahajan, Tara 54
Harte, Liam 115
Hayot, Eric 27–28
Heffernan, Laura 165–166
Hemingway, Ernest 1, 16–17, 30, 101–103
  Bowen on 38
  A Farewell to Arms 101–102
  Rooney comparison 168–169
Herbert, George, "Prayer (1)" 64, 69
Homer, *Odyssey* 16
Hurston, Zora Neale 59–60
Hutton, Clare 181
Huxley, Aldous, *Brave New World* 157
Hyde, Douglas 62

Ibsen, Henrik 62, 128
impressionism
  Bowen's "Summer Night" 36–37
  Chekhov's writing 142–143
  Enright's *The Gathering* 109
  Lavin's "Sunday Brings Sunday" 76
  Madden's *Molly Fox's Birthday* 109
  Moore's writing 40
  O'Brien's *Night* 102–103
  Rooney's *Beautiful World, Where Are You* 1
  White's photography 147–148
Inglis, Tom 65–66
Irish Times 29–30, 53–54, 54–55 n.61
Irish Writing 29–30
Ishiguro, Kazuo, *Never Let Me Go* 158–159

James, David 14–15
James, Henry 29–30, 33, 36–37, 109, 167
  The Turn of the Screw 120–121
James, William 33, 99–100
  prayer 59–60
  The Principles of Psychology 94–95
  The Varieties of Religious Experience 59–60
Jameson, Fredric 17, 34
Jarvis, Claire 167
Jellett, Mainie, "An Approach to Painting" 35
Joyce, James 5, 6–7, 9–11, 13–14, 16–17, 25,
    135–136, 157
  afterlife 48–53
  and Caldwell's "SOMAT" 30–31, 56–57
  "The Dead" 1–2, 51–52, 120, 131–132,
    183–184
  on Dublin 22
  Dubliners 1–3, 51–52, 97–100, 103–104,
    173–174, 184–185
    McCormack's *Solar Bones* comparison
    195–196

  Rooney's *Normal People* comparison
    183–185
  Finnegans Wake 12, 27–28, 48–49, 81–82
  influence
    on Bennett 145–146
    on Lavin 48–49
    on Madden 48–49
    on McBride 49–50, 52, 200–201
    on McCormack 200–201
    on Ní Dhuibhne 48–49, 140
    on O'Brien, Edna 48–51, 101–103
    on O'Brien, Kate 48–49, 62, 64–65
    on Rooney 51–52, 168–169
  "Ivy Day in the Committee Room" 48–49
  Lavin on 71
  and McCormack's *Solar Bones* 26–27
  Murdoch's reading of 38–39 n.24
  A Portrait of the Artist as a Young Man
    48–49, 51–52, 59–60, 62, 79, 168–169,
    170–171, 184–185
  prayer 59–60, 84–85
  reverie 94, 95, 97–101, 102–105, 120, 121–122,
    131
  self-questioning 42–43
  Ulysses 16, 19–20, 25–26, 30, 46, 48–51,
    52, 56–57, 62, 85, 86–87, 92, 94, 95,
    100–101, 102–103, 104–105, 120,
    121–122, 131
    and Enright's *The Gathering* 131
    lists 152
    and Madden's *Molly Fox's Birthday*
    121–122, 124, 126–127, 131
    and McCormack's *Solar Bones* 195–196
    and O'Brien's *The Ante-Room* 62
    and Rooney's *Normal People* comparison
    183–185
  women
    as ciphers 196–197
    complicated 42

Katz, Tamar 33
Kearney, Richard 42–43
Kelly, Maeve 4–5, 46
  "Morning at My Window" 25, 30–31, 40–42,
    53–54
Kenner, Hugh 152, 184–185
Kenny, Eva, "Christmas Story" 51–52
Keyes, Marian 158–159
  The Break 54
Kiberd, Declan 62, 144–145
Kitchen, Judith, *The House on Eccles Street* 101
  n.14
Knepper, Wendy 14
Koepnick, Lutz 150–151

INDEX 225

Lally, Caitriona, *Eggshells* 3–4
Lang, Maya, *The Sixteenth of June* 101 n.14
Larsen, Nella, *Quicksand* 94
late modernism 8–9, 13–14, 35–36, 155–156, 157
Late Show, The 19–20
Laverty, Maura 44–45 n.37
Lavin, Mary 4–5, 10–11, 25–26, 29–30, 38–39
    n.24, 60–62, 71–72, 87, 93, 167–168
  "The Green Grave and the Black Grave" 71
  "A Happy Death" 73
  The House in Clewe Street 97
  Joyce's influence 48–49
  "The Living" 72–73
  "Miss Holland" 71
  "The Nun's Mother" 74–75
  "Sarah" 46–47
  "Sunday Brings Sunday" 75–76, 89–90
  Tales from Bective Bridge 74
Lawless, Emily 7–8
  Grania 8
Lawrence, D. H. 101–103, 105–106, 168–169
Lea, Richard 179–180
Leavis, F. R. 33–34
Leavis, Q. D. 33–34
Le Fanu, Sheridan, *Camilla* 144
Lefebvre, Henri 107–109, 112, 116, 120–121,
    125, 126–127
Lehner, Stefanie 129–130 n.59
Lemass, Seán 39–40
Lermontov, Mikhail 38–39
Lerner, Ben 180–181
Letts, W. M. 7–8
  The Rough Way 8
Levine, Caroline 22, 61–62
Liberties Press 16–17
logging off *see* digital technology
Love and Money (dir. Ronald Liles, 1968) 97
Lovett, Ann 84–85, 143
Lye, Colleen 9–10
Lynch, Claire 134

McManus, L. (Charlotte Elizabeth) 7–8
Madden, Deirdre 4–5, 171
  Authenticity 127
  Hidden Symptoms 127
  Joyce's influence 48–49
  "Looking for Home: Time, Place, Memory"
    121
  Molly Fox's Birthday 25–26, 95–96, 106–110,
    121–133
  One by One in the Darkness 127–128
  Time Present and Time Past 127
Magdalene Laundries 18–19
Magennis, Caroline 189

Majumdar, Saikat 144–145, 151
Malone, Patricia 175–176
Manning, Mary 48–49
Mansfield, Katherine 16–17, 56–57, 140–143,
    157, 160–161
  "The-Child-Who-Was-Tired" 141–143
  In a German Pension 141
  influence on Lavin 71
  on Moore's *Esther Waters* 40
  and Ní Dhuibhne's *The Dancers Dancing*
    144–145
  and O'Brien's *Night* 102–103
Marcus, David 29
Markievicz, Constance 199
Martin, Diarmuid 82
Martin, Micheál 17–18
Martin, Theodore 27–28
Masterson, Graham, *How to Drive Your Man
    Wild in Bed* 44–45
Matz, Jesse 36–37
McBride, Eimear 167–168
  A Girl Is a Half-formed Thing 3–4, 19–20,
    25–26, 52, 60–62, 80–86, 87–93,
    143–144, 156–157, 172
  Joyce's influence 49–50, 52, 200–201
  The Lesser Bohemians 91, 200–201
McCormack, Mike, *Solar Bones* 26–27, 194–201,
    202–203
McCrea, Barry 49–50 n.48
McEvoy, Tara 3–4
McGahern, John 42–43, 70–71
McGovern, Kelly 137–138
Meade, L. T. 7–8
Meaney, Gerardine 107–108 n.29, 157–158
Mercier, Vivian 150
#MeToo movement 43–44, 178
Micir, Melanie 58
Mickalites, Carey 51–52 n.53
Miller, Henry 30–31, 47, 48, 101–102
  Tropic of Cancer 47
  Tropic of Capricorn 47
Millett, Kate, *Sexual Politics* 101–102
Milligan, Alice 199
mode 3–4, 17–18
Moore, George 13–14
  A Drama in Muslin 40
  Esther Waters 40
Morris, Thomas, *Dubliners 100* 48–49
Morrissy, Mary, *Penelope Unbound* 48–49
Mother and Baby Homes 17–19
Mulhall, Anne 202–203
Mulholland, Rosa 7–8
  Cousin Sara: A Story of Arts and Crafts 8

226 INDEX

Murdoch, Iris 34–35, 38–39 n.24
Murry, John Middleton 102–103

Nersessian, Anahid 166
New Age, The 141
New Yorker, The 51–52, 72
Ní Aonghusa, Cláir 38–39 n.24
Ní Dhuibhne, Éilís 4–5, 171
    The Dancers Dancing 26, 135–140, 143–145,
        147–148, 150, 155, 157–158, 160–162,
        163–164, 176–177
    Fox, Swallow, Scarecrow 38–39 n.24
    Joyce's influence 48–49, 140
    "Summer's Wreath" 141–143
Nordau, Max 99–100
North, Michael 27–28
Nosferatu (dir. F. W. Murnau) 144

O'Brien, Dan 101–102
O'Brien, Edna 30, 38–39 n.24, 70–71, 167–168
    Casualties of Peace 30
    The Country Girls 44–45 n.37
    Down by the River 30
    House of Splendid Isolation 30
    James Joyce 48–49
    Joyce's influence 48–51, 101–103
    Night 25–26, 30, 95–96, 101–106, 108–109,
        121–122, 126–127, 132–133, 172
    "A Scandalous Woman" 17–18
    Wild Decembers 30
O'Brien, Flann 13–14, 200–201
    At Swim-Two-Birds 12, 97–98
O'Brien, Kate 4–5, 29–30, 38–39 n.24, 62,
        135–136
    The Ante-Room 62–63
    "Ireland and Avant-Gardisme" 62
    Joyce's influence 48–49, 62, 64–65
    The Land of Spices 25–26, 44–45 n.37,
        60–62, 63–71, 76, 143–144, 156–157,
        168–169, 199
    Lavin comparison 71, 72
    Pray for the Wanderer 62–63
    Without My Cloak 62–63
Ó Cadhain, Máirtín 13–14, 38–39
O'Casey, Seán 13–14, 62
Ó Conaire, Pádraic 140
    Deoraíocht 140 n.8
O'Connor, Frank 27–28, 38–39, 140–141
    The Lonely Voice 141–142
O'Connor, Joseph 130–131
O'Connor, Marianne Gunn 200–201
O'Connor, Nuala, *Nora: A Love Story of Nora
        and James Joyce* 48–49
O'Dowd, Mary 107–108 n.29

Ó Faoláin, Seán 6–7, 38–39, 70–71, 140–141
O'Neill, Louise 4–5
    Only Ever Yours 26, 203
O'Riordan, Kate 38–39 n.24
object reverie 25–26, 27–28, 94–95, 96–98,
        99–101, 134, 150–151, 194
    Enright's *The Gathering* 95–96, 106–121,
        123–124, 126, 130–131, 132–133
    Joyce's *Dubliners* 97–100, 103–104
    Madden's *Molly Fox's Birthday* 95–96,
        106–110, 121–133
    McCormack's *Solar Bones* 195
    O'Brien's *Night* 95–96, 101–106, 108–109,
        121–122, 126–127, 132–133
Okorie, Melatu Uche 21
    "Under the Awning" 202–203
Olson, Liesl 152
One in Four 80–81
open ending 179–181
    Burns's *Milkman* 179–181, 186, 188–189
    Donoghue's *Hood* 79–80
    Lavin's writing 74
    Mansfield's writing 140–141
    Rooney's *Normal People* 168–169, 179–181,
        183–184
Orage, A. R. 141–143
Orwell, George 101–102
    1984 157
Ostrovsky, Alexander 38–39

Parker, Sarah Jessica 19–20
Parnell, Anna 8
Pease, Alison 151
pedagogy 28, 186–191, 202–203
Pelan, Rebecca 105 n.23
periodicity 8–9
Pine, Emilie 202–203
Pisemsky, Aleksey 38–39
Plock, Vike Martina 121–122
Plotz, John 96 n.2
Porter, Katherine Anne 71
postmodernism 3, 8–9 n.18, 13–14, 44, 140
Pound, Ezra 16–17
prayer 25–26, 27, 59–60, 77, 93, 94, 134, 150–151,
        194
    Donoghue's *Hood* 60–62, 77–80, 93
    Lavin's writing 60–62, 72, 74, 76, 93
        "A Happy Death" 73
        "The Living" 72–73
        "The Nun's Mother" 74–75
        "Sunday Brings Sunday" 75–76, 89–90
    McBride's *A Girl Is a Half-formed Thing*
        60–62, 80, 81–86, 87–93
    McCormack's *Solar Bones* 195

O'Brien's writing (Kate) 62–63, 93
   The Land of Spices 60–62, 64–71, 76
   Woolf's "An Unwritten Novel" 73
Price, K. Arnold 29–30
Proust, Marcel 16–17, 38–39, 101–103
   in Burns's *Milkman* 187
   Contre Sainte-Beuve 121
   In Search of Lost Time 149–150
   influence on Madden 109, 121
Pushkin, Alexander 38–39 n.24

Rains, Stephanie 107–108 n.29
Randall, Bryony 99–100
reading *see* close reading
Regan, Stephen 40
reverie *see* object reverie
Revivalism 5–7, 22, 34–35, 62, 135–136, 149–150
Rhys, Jean 56–57, 105–106, 145–146, 155–156
   "Mixing Cocktails" 94
Richardson, Dorothy 8, 33, 35, 145–146, 154–155
   Pilgrimage 8
Riddell, Charlotte 7–8
Robinson, Mary 45–46
Rooney, Sally 19–20, 201–202
   Beautiful World, Where Are You 1–4, 5, 11–12,
      15–16, 22, 51–52, 156–157, 181
   Conversations with Friends 51–52
   Joyce's influence 51–52, 168–169
   Normal People 15–16, 26, 165–172, 174,
      176–177, 178–186, 191–193
Rose, Jacqueline 91, 191
Rushdie, Salman 42–43
Ruskin, John, *Modern Painters* 8
Russian realism 38–40, 71, 179–180

Salkeld, Blanaid 5–6
Sanger, Margaret 44–45
Schofield, Anakana
   Malarky 51–52
   Martin John 3–4, 200–201
Seshagiri, Urmila 14–15
sexual abuse 24–25, 42–43, 82, 147, 148
   Burns's *Milkman* 173, 174–175, 178–179, 186
   Enright's *The Gathering* 95, 109, 110, 112,
      114–120
   Madden's *Molly Fox's Birthday* 25–26, 109
   McBride's writings 191
      A Girl Is a Half-formed Thing 60–61, 80–82,
         86, 87–89, 90–91
   Rooney's *Normal People* 186
Shakespeare, William 38–39 n.24
Shaw, George Bernard 13–14, 62
Smith, Elizabeth (L. T. Meade) 7–8

Smith, Terence 29
Smyth, Brendan 82
Sobieniowski, Floryan 141, 142–143
Somerville, Edith and Ross, Martin (Violet
      Florence Martin) 7–8
Spacks, Patricia Meyer 96 n.2
Sproull, Patrick 158–159
Stanton, Maura 38–39 n.24
Steele, Danielle 28
Stein, Gertrude 5, 16–17, 157, 171
   Bennett's *Pond* comparison 152
   Composition as Explanation 152
   influence on Ní Dhuibhne 144–145
   Tender Buttons 152
Stevens, Wallace 145–146
Stewart, Susan 125
Stinging Fly, The 16–17, 145
Stoker, Bram, *Dracula* 144
Stopes, Marie 44–45
stream of consciousness 3–4, 16–17, 26, 32–33,
      94–95
   Bennett's *Pond* 145–146
   Burns's *Milkman* 174
   Caldwell's "SOMAT" 54
   Enright's *The Gathering* 25–26, 95, 118–119,
      132
   Joyce 48–49
      Ulysses 30, 46, 95, 100–101
   Kelly's "Morning at My Window" 41
   Lavin's writing 71
   Madden's writing 48–49
      Molly Fox's Birthday 25–26, 95, 127–128,
         132
   McBride's *A Girl Is a Half-formed Thing* 80,
      87–89, 90–91
   McCormack's *Solar Bones* 26–27, 196–197
   O'Brien, Edna 48–49
      Night 30, 95, 102–103, 104–106, 132
   O'Brien, Kate, *The Land of Spices* 64–65,
      70–71
   Rooney's *Normal People* 170
   Woolf's *Mrs. Dalloway* 129–130
Stuart, Francis 13–14
Swift, Jonathan 62
Swift, Taylor 19–20
Synge, John Millington 13–14, 42, 62
   Riders to the Sea 92
   The Playboy of the Western World 96–97

Tanning, Dorothea 145–146
Taylor, Charles 64–65
Teresa of Avila 66
   The Interior Castle 70
Thoreau, Henry David, *Walden* 149–150

228   INDEX

Thurston, Katherine Cecil 7–8
Time's Up 19–20
Tolstoy, Leo 38, 38–39 n.24, 71
   Anna Karenina 38–39 n.24
Tramp Press 16–17, 200–201
Trotter, David 163
Troubles 12–13, 22, 24–25, 34
   Burns's *Milkman* 165, 172–177, 187–188
   Enright's *The Gathering* 109
   Madden's *Molly Fox's Birthday* 95, 109,
      127–132
   marriage plot 168
   Ní Dhuibhne's *The Dancers Dancing* 143–144
   O'Brien's *Night* (Edna) 101–102
Turgenev, Ivan 38–39, 71
Tynan, Katharine 5–6, 7–8

Vadde, Aarthi 58
Valente, Joseph 69
VIDA: Women in Literary Arts 19–20
Vogue 3–4

Waking the Feminists 19–20
Warner, Sylvia Townsend 121
Warren, Elizabeth 17–18
Webster, John, *The Duchess of Malfi* 126
Whelan, Bernadette 107–108 n.29
White, Clarence H. 147–148
Wilde, Oscar 13–14, 59–60, 62
   De Profundis 59–60
Williams, Linda 17 n.33
Winterson, Jeannette 158–159
Wolf, Naomi, *The Beauty Myth* 159–160
Woods, Thomas (Thersites) 29–30
Woolf, Virginia 5, 15–17, 29, 106, 121–122,
    154–155

Bennett's *Pond* comparison 145–146
Bowen comparison 35–37
influence
   on Madden 109
   on O'Brien (Kate) 62, 64–65
Lavin's studies 71
on Moore's *Esther Waters* 40
"Mr Bennett and Mrs Brown" 145–146
Mrs. Dalloway 129–130, 131–132
Murdoch's reading of 38–39 n.24
prayer 59–60, 66, 73
reverie 94, 124–125, 126–127, 129–130,
   131–132
"A Sketch of the Past" 189
"Solid Objects" 124–125, 126–127, 129–130,
   131–132
To the Lighthouse 66, 174–175
"An Unwritten Novel" 73
The Waves 71, 94
Wordsworth, William 166
Workman, Simon 42
Wurtz, James 104

Yeats, W. B. 5, 9–10, 13–14, 16–17
   "Among School Children" 140
   Cathleen ni Houlihan (with Gregory) 96–97
   death 12
   influence on Ní Dhuibhne 144–145
   "The Lake Isle of Innisfree" 96–97
   O'Brien, Kate on 62
   "A Prayer for My Daughter" 59–60
   reverie 96–97, 97–98 n.7
   "The Second Coming" 2–3
   "The Stolen Child" 92–93

Zumhagen-Yekplé, Karen 48

The manufacturer's authorised representative in the EU for product safety is
Oxford University Press España S.A. of el Parque Empresarial San Fernando de
Henares, Avenida de Castilla, 2 – 28830 Madrid (www.oup.es/en or product.
safety@oup.com). OUP España S.A. also acts as importer into Spain of products
made by the manufacturer.

www.ingramcontent.com/pod-product-compliance
Lightning Source LLC
Chambersburg PA
CBHW032123310525
27544CB00002B/7